Death of an Altar Boy

Death of an Altar Boy

The Unsolved Murder
of Danny Croteau and the Culture
of Abuse in the Catholic Church

E. J. FLEMING

Exposit

Jefferson, North Carolina

Library of Congress Cataloguing-in-Publication Data

Names: Fleming, E. J., 1954– author.
Title: Death of an altar boy : the unsolved murder of Danny Croteau
and the culture of abuse in the Catholic Church / E.J. Fleming.
Description: Jefferson, North Carolina : Exposit Books,
2018 | Includes bibliographical references and index.
Identifiers: LCCN 2018010179 | ISBN 9781476673455
(softcover : acid free paper) ∞
Subjects: LCSH: Croteau, Danny (Daniel Thomas),
1958–1972. | Murder—Massachusetts—Springfield—Case
studies. | Child sexual abuse by clergy—Massachusetts—Springfield—Case
studies. | Sexual misconduct by clergy—Massachusetts—Springfield—Case studies.
Classification: LCC HV6534.S5942 F55 2018 | DDC 364.152/3092—dc23
LC record available at https://lccn.loc.gov/2018010179

British Library Cataloguing data are available

ISBN (print) 978-1-4766-7345-5
ISBN (ebook) 978-1-4766-3203-2

Front cover image of Danny Croteau (courtesy Joseph Croteau);
background cemetery cross © 2018 OlafSpeier/iStock

Printed in the United States of America

Exposit is an imprint of McFarland & Company, Inc., Publishers
Jefferson, North Carolina

Exposit
Box 611, Jefferson, North Carolina 28640
www.expositbooks.com

Table of Contents

Acknowledgments

Without the many people who spoke to me, this would not have been possible. I cannot adequately express my gratitude to all those who talked about their most painful memories, events that can't be forgotten, no matter how much they wish they could. Special thanks to those who did so on the condition of anonymity. I apologize to anyone I failed to mention. Carl and Bunny Croteau graciously answered difficult questions and encouraged me to tell Danny's story from the time we first spoke in 2004. Danny's brother Joe took every one of my hundreds of calls and was generous with advice, stories, photos, and often-painful remembrances of Danny and Richard Lavigne. Thanks also to his other brother, Carl Jr. The book would have been impossible without their input and help.

R.C. Stevens provided invaluable information and background. He unearthed more about Danny's life and death in ten years than four sets of investigators in 35. Bill Zajac courageously penned hundreds of newspaper stories critical of a powerful Church—stories nobody wanted to write, accounts that eventually took down a bishop. Bill offered enthusiastic assistance, and invaluable files, since the first call the day I decided to tell the story. Warren Mason, whose anger forced the Springfield diocese to face its criminal past, provided direction and important recollections. My friend Darby O'Brien offered invaluable counsel for my Phoebe Prince book and did so again here, as did Luke Gelinas, another Phoebe colleague.

A special thanks to several people in the middle of Danny's story, from the beginning. Drew Nicastro courageously discussed events I'm sure he would rather have kept to himself. Sandra Tessier's details of Richard Lavigne's relationship with her and her family were critical to unmasking a suspect never investigated. Jack Downing offered stories that helped define the role of a bishop in all this. Carol Mazzarino, daughter of a central character in Danny's story, provided invaluable help. I am grateful also to John Stobierski, who fought legal battles for more than 75 cleric abuse victims; longtime Croteau family lawyer F. Michael Joseph; Mike Rezendes and Alan Wirzbicki of the *Boston Globe* "Spotlight" team, instrumental in exposing the Church's clergy abuse problem, for their assistance; and Sgt. Mark St. Germaine of the Rensselaer (NY) Sheriff's Department for trying to find records of an obscure 1971 arrest.

Joe Fitzgerald's remembrances of a long-ago high school classmate were central to the story, and Brian Fitzgerald offered invaluable advice and stories of life in his childhood neighborhood. To our old and dear friends, Bill and Linda Campbell, again, thanks. Once more, Linda offered invaluable assistance deciphering the psychological aspects behind people and accounts, and Bill provided dozens of Red Sox tickets over the years and took my mind off the dreadful stories by dragging me from my keyboard to play golf. Our family priest, Father Hugh Crean, suffered through hundreds of morning Masses with my brother and I as his altar boys when I was Danny's age. He showed me a very different Church and later offered insight into its often-bizarre workings. Rest in peace, Father. A special word of thanks to Robert M. Kelly for his book-length treatise on the history of the crisis in the Springfield diocese that can be found at www. springfielddiocese.blogspot.com/ 2009/04.

My mother used to cross herself and plead, "Oh, please, E.J., please don't write that book," but instilled in me a dose of Boston Irish Catholic Bad Attitude Syndrome that still makes me question everything and seek the truth. I miss her. My father, despite lifelong friendships with all of the principals involved in Danny's stories from the 1970s until today, encouraged me to write this book. Love and thanks to you both.

As always, none of this would be possible without Barb's support. Forty-five years later, she still lets me pretend I'm a writer.

Prologue

July 2004. I was on the porch of my father's place looking out over Buzzard's Bay at Cuttyhunk Island in the distance when a Sunday *Boston Globe* headline returned me to my last year of high school in small-town Massachusetts. "CROTEAU FILES TO BE OPENED." Underneath "Altar Boy's '72 Slaying," was a school picture like every one of mine and those of my brothers and sisters. The boy looked 13 or 14, junior high-ish. His was the unmistakable look of Catholic school kid, a particular veneer recognized only by those experienced in that particular confinement. He appeared impish, nose dotted with freckles, red hair askew. I didn't know Danny Croteau. I was a senior in high school when he was killed, likely entangled in some insignificant crisis to pay much heed. I only vaguely remembered a Springfield kid found dead in the river.

East Longmeadow, our leafy New England home, was ten minutes away but worlds apart from Danny's Sixteen Acres neighborhood in the gritty factory city of Springfield. His was a blue-collar, working-man's suburb of a city dominated by the mob and the Catholic Church. My crowd was certainly not as tough as his, nor were we allowed to run the streets at night like he did. Though I was 17 to his 14, Danny lived older than me. Our teen lives were poles apart. Mine revolved around a woodsy subdivision, a mother who cleaned, shopped and cooked, and a father who worked in an office. Danny's weary mother corralled seven kids— five of them teenage boys—while his father worked two and three jobs.

My days were full of sports and exploring the woods with a series of English Setters named Freckles, nights spent ignoring homework to watch television. Danny's days included the same neighborhood sports, but his nights included hitchhiking around Springfield and hanging with a gang of local troublemakers and thieves who drank, smoked, and did drugs.

3

The only thing Danny and I had in common was the Catholic Church. I did recall he was an altar boy and my parents' best friends Don and Ann Ryan were in his parish and knew the Croteaus and Danny's priest. They thought he was a little off, strange. Don's brother, Springfield's mayor Charlie Ryan was also a friend since grammar school. Their cousin, District Attorney Matty Ryan was another neighborhood pal. They all discussed Danny over the years. Dad's friends were altar boys, and every one of my uncles and a slew of cousins served. I served with my brother for years, as did most of our buddies. At the time, we didn't know we were lucky. The musty old chapel at St. Michael's, our little white clapboard church that dated to the mid–1800s, was a claustrophobic 150-seat mishmash of stained glass, creaky pews and frightening statuary. It was always deathly quiet, cloaked in the overpowering smell of burning candles and another age.

Everyone at St. Mike's was straight out of Central Casting. Father Wolohan, the crotchety dictator who ran the parish for 30-plus years, forever grumbled impatiently at us and roughly pushed us aside if we were too slow on the altar. His assistant Father Crean was in his early 30s, but even as dumb kids we recognized he was a special guy. He would earn a Doctorate in Belgium and serve at the Vatican, directly under the pope. A pleasant, chubby, older woman from Dublin—always wrapped in a dirty apron—ran the rectory. We never knew her name and she rarely spoke. She cleaned and cooked for the priests and a string of Father Wolohan's Scottish Terriers. They were at the door most mornings and fortunately did not share their master's disdain for altar boys. They were all pudgy and slow-moving like Fr. Wolohan because they shared meals with him and ate whatever he was served. As they died, they were buried under the pine trees behind the church. He always paused there for a second when he trudged from the rectory down the hill for morning Mass.

Every morning at 6:30—always without a word—the Irish lady handed us a big skeleton key to open the church and prepare the altar for the same 11 people who showed up every morning. This was decades before priests were ever called by their first names—to us, they were a reverent "Father"—or questioned about anything. They were revered, as infallible as the Pope. Danny and I were altar boys, but his church experience was far more difficult than mine. We were unaware until much later that we were blessed to have our bucolic little church. Danny was not as lucky. We wouldn't know for 30 years that he was among the tens of thousands of innocents ruined by abuse at the hands of a priest. The largest concentration of victims was in Massachusetts, a significant percentage of them around Springfield. As kids, we were not privy to the disquieting stories about Danny's priest our parents heard. We heard their whispers, but never details. While we raised our own children, the stories my parents heard became sickeningly public, and proven horribly true.

Danny Croteau was four months past his 13th birthday when he was brutally bludgeoned with a rock, strangled, and tossed into the muddy Chicopee River. Within months, he was forgotten by all but a few. For decades, he remained but a faint memory, recalled occasionally and quickly forgotten. But, amidst a mushrooming priest abuse scandal with its strike point not far from Danny's house, his story rose from the ether. But nowhere near all of it. Danny once threatened, "I'll tell!" This is his story.

1

Danny

Saturday, April 15, 1972, dawned a gorgeous spring day in Spring-field, Massachusetts, a factory town in the Connecticut River Valley, 90 miles west of Boston. That morning, the sun interrupted a week of rain. The ground was still wet from the previous day's downpour. It was Tax Day and opening day of fishing season. By sunrise, anglers stood along every western Massachusetts river, lake, and pond.

Springfield handyman Raphael Hererra wanted to fish the Chicopee River near the Governor Robinson Bridge.[1] The still-remote spot off East Main Street in Chicopee straddles the border with Springfield. Other than a cluster of drab houses half a mile away, the only sign of nearby life was a family-owned junkyard across the street. Hererra made his way down the quarter-mile gravel road from the street to the river, shaded by a canopy of overhanging trees, and parked under the bridge. Far from a picture-book fishing hole, if the wind came from the north, it carried the aromas of the Chicopee landfill two miles distant. The bridge was widened in the 1990s so the location is different than in 1972, but it remains more eerie than idyllic, more dank than welcoming. It has always been a scary place.

The dirt turnaround under the bridge was a popular lovers' lane. In those days, mornings found it strewn with beer cans, liquor bottles, and all manner of detritus. At 8 o'clock that morning, with throbbing traffic and the incessant rumbling of trucks on Interstate 291 above, Hererra pulled his tackle box and rod from the trunk of his car. He trudged the hundred feet to the water, and while attaching weighters and impal-ing some bait, glanced over and thought he saw a coat floating near the rocks just off the riverbank. He inched closer and realized it was a body surrounded by a blanket of muddy, reddish water. Then he noticed the ground all around him was thick with blood spatter. Terrified, he stumbled back to his car. Opening the door, he saw a large blood stain by his front tire he did not notice earlier. He sped back up the hill, flying gravel rattling off the car, found a phone at the junkyard, and called the police.

The Croteaus came from French Canadian immigrants who, with the Irish, made up the bulk of New England's working class through the 1800s. Springfield's large immigrant population was dominated by Irish and, to a lesser extent, the Quebecois. At the turn of the century, the third largest city in Massachusetts was already defined by its 19 neighborhoods. Each has historically been segregated politically and socio-economically. Though some populations shifted after the 1940s, many neighborhoods retain their original make-up to a surprising degree. Until the late 1900s, the South End of downtown was effectively closed to all but Italians. In the earlier years, neighborhoods southeast of downtown—Forest Park, McKnight, and Six Corners—represented upscale Springfield.

Immigrants crowded several shantytowns, working-class slums, like Holyoke's "Patch" and Springfield's "Hungry Hill." The close-in northeast Springfield neighborhoods—Hungry Hill, East Springfield, and Blunt Park—were crowded with working-class Irish, most from counties Kerry and Cork. The Irish shared "The Hill" with a smattering of Quebecois. The nickname has various derogatory origins. The Irish were said to be hungry from the famine that forced them there, or beat cops were always hungry because there were no neighborhood restaurants. Irish were initially considered backward, suited only for menial, grueling work like building canals, roads, and rail lines. Hungry Hill Irish worked the foundries and paper or textile mills lining the Connecticut River and made up most of the workforce at the huge Springfield Armory. The world's largest gun-maker was the birthplace of the famed Springfield Rifle.[2] Quebecois almost exclusively worked in Holyoke and Chicopee mills. The Hill horde got to work via a tangle of electric trolleys linking Springfield with nearby towns.

Several religious denominations appeared during Springfield's early history, but Catholic roots run deep, back to at least 1828, when Father James Fitton said Masses in private homes. The first Catholic church, St. Benedict's, was built in 1847. Through the 19th century, Springfield steadily became Catholic-dominated. By the late 1800s, there were 160 churches staffed by 325 priests, 30 church missions, three colleges, 60 parochial schools, a trade school, five orphanages, a home for infants housing thousands, five homes for the aged, and three for working girls.[3] The Springfield diocese, with offices in an Elliot Street brownstone, was laid out in 1870 and contained the five central and western Massachusetts counties. Huge political influence has been dispensed from the brownstone since. City officials at every level have always been Catholic, almost all Irish. The Church, therefore, has been tightly woven into Springfield's political and social fabric. An event without a Catholic official front and center is rarer still today.

Danny Croteau's grandfather, George Croteau, was born in Montpelier, Vermont, in 1905, the son of a Quebecois immigrant who toiled in the state's massive granite quarries. George left school after seventh grade to work with his father, and in 1925 at age 20, he married 17-year-old Helen Walsh, an Irish girl from New Hampshire. Arriving in Springfield, they rented a $12, second-floor apartment in a three-family home at 26 Allendale Street. It was just north of downtown in the heart of Hungry Hill. On January 27, 1931, their third son—Carl Elton Joseph—was born there. When he was two, they rented a house surrounded by farmland, ten miles away in East Longmeadow. Most of the hamlet's 3,000 inhabitants were Swedes and French Canadians. Since the early 1800s, they carved the giant red and brown sandstone blocks from the town's 50 quarries, used in the Smithsonian Institution, New York's Trinity Church, and schools like Yale and Princeton.[4]

By 1940, the brood included four boys and two girls, ages four to 13. George rode a trolley from East Longmeadow to the Armory while the children attended the only school, Center School, on a hilltop above the bustling town center. In 1945, George started a landscaping and paving business, moved everyone back to Springfield, and bought a two-family home at 140 Massasoit Street in the French-Canadian slice of Hungry Hill. They moved upstairs and rented the first floor.[5] Neighborhood houses were fronted by large porches and sat on postage stamp-sized lots surrounded by chain-link fences. Lives centered on the stoops and the Church.

Even with the four youngest at home, Helen worked the fountain at Kresge's store downtown.[6] Like most Hill boys, Carl left school after eighth grade and went to work. He was working for his grandfather when his mother rented the first-floor apartment to Springfield divorcée

The Croteau family home at 140 Massasoit Street in Springfield's Hungry Hill neighborhood, childhood home of Danny's father Carl and where he met Bernice "Bunny" Everett in 1949 when her divorced mother rented the first-floor apartment (author's collection).

Bernice Everett in 1949. She moved in with her eight-year-old son Richard and 12-year-old daughter, another Bernice.

The Everetts came from the same hard-working, immigrant roots as the Croteaus. Bernice's grandfather Robert was born in 1868 in England and arrived in the U.S. at 14. After marriage in 1897 to Irish-born Fannie, he worked in photography studios in Albany, New York, and Hartford, Connecticut. Their fourth child, Robert Jr., was born in 1907. They arrived in Springfield in 1918 and took a $25 apartment at 144 Monrovia Street in East Springfield/Blunt Park. The gritty wedge of Hungry Hill sat adjacent to hundreds of acres zigzagged by railroad tracks and dotted with grimy foundries and factories. The aptly-named Poor Brook framed the northern boundary. With the exception of Robert Jr., they all remained within a half-mile radius the rest of their lives.[7]

The girls left school after sixth grade. They took factory jobs. The boys spent two years at Springfield Trade High School training in the blue-collar trades before joining the girls in the factories. In 1924, Robert and Fannie bought the only home they ever owned, paying a then-princely sum of $6,500 for a new house at 30 Jenness Street. The three-bedroom, two-story was barely five blocks from Monrovia. Robert Sr. was an inspector at the huge Westinghouse Electric Company. Robert Jr., also a bishop in the Jehovah's Witness church, joined him there.[8] In 1930, Robert Jr. married Bernice Morgan, a local whose father was from New Hampshire and was a machinist at the Indian Motorcycle factory. Her mother was born in Springfield, the daughter of French-Canadian immigrants, and grew up blocks from the Jenness Street house.

The newlyweds moved onto Jenness and had a son and daughter there. When Robert Sr. died in 1933, Robert Jr. and Bernice moved into a rented bungalow at 100 Hood Street in a still rougher section of Blunt Park. A daughter, Bernice Beatrice, was born there in 1936. Over the

The Everett family home at 30 Jenness Street, childhood home of Bernice "Bunny" Everett. Several generations of Everetts lived within half a mile (author's collection).

next decade, they rented a series of bungalows but they never lived more than a mile from Jenness Street. In 1942, they were at 23 Atwood Place in the adjacent Six Corners neighborhood. The street was lined with tidy cottages, but Six Corners was mostly larger homes, including dozens of Gilded Age mansions. Around the corner was Mulberry Street, immortalized by Theodor Geisel. "Dr. Seuss" based his first book—*And to Think That I Saw It on Mulberry Street*—on his childhood there.[9]

Robert and Bernice divorced in 1944. She and the children stayed at Atwood five years, then rented the Croteaus' first-floor Massasoit apartment in early 1949. The younger Bernice, now called "Bunny," was a pretty 14-year-old. The day she moved in she met Carl, then a 17-year-old, chiseled from laboring in his grandfather's landscaping business.

Just a few months later, Carl enlisted in the Army. He left basic training at Fort Lewis, Washington, a heavy weapons infantryman, manning machine gun and mortar teams. He was a member of the 38th Regimental Combat Team, a 3,500-man fighting force in the 8th Army's vaunted 2nd Indianhead Division. A month later, June 25, 1950, North Korea and Russia invaded South Korea and pushed South Korean troops into the country's southeast corner. The 2nd was the first U.S. unit there, sent to drive the North Koreans from South Korea. The war would prove difficult, the steep, ubiquitous mountains hindering communication, and the severe climate making combat operations difficult. Falls were rainy, sub-freezing, and winters marked by daily snowstorms and sub-zero temperatures. The North Korean strategy of massive human wave assaults was furthermore daunting.[10]

Carl and the 38th arrived on August 20. The next morning, they were attacked by thousands of North Koreans near Andong, the start of a 16-day battle during which clerks, cooks, truck drivers, and even musicians were forced onto the front lines. The 38th engaged in 52 firefights in the first 60 days, losing 20 men daily, but by November, it pushed the North Koreans from South Korea while killing 7,000 and capturing 3,000. They fought to within 50 miles of Manchuria, on the Ch'ongch'on River, when China sent 1,500,000 battle-hardened troops against fewer than 500,000 allied fighters, most American. The 38th, and Carl, were in the center of the massive counterattack.[11]

For a month, the outgunned and outmanned 38th was tasked with holding the Chinese at bay so the remaining U.S. troops could escape south. To do so, they fought through "The Gauntlet," a six-mile pass with 40,000 Chinese enfilading machine gun and mortar fire from the ends and the sides. One artillery unit exhausted its stock of 3,206 shells in 20 minutes. The Gauntlet melee continued south into Kunu-ri, where Carl was seriously wounded on November 30. He was evacuated to a field hospital and when he returned on January 15, the 38th had gone from 3,500 to fewer than 600.[12] Carl, with commendations and a Purple Heart, returned stateside in May. He never once mentioned his experiences to anyone in the family.

Back in Springfield, he worked as a security guard at the American Bosch factory and earned a high school diploma via the GI Bill (and later an associate's degree from Holyoke Community College). On February 6, 1952, he and Bunny went to the downtown courthourse and were married before a justice of the peace and moved into her mother's Massasoit apartment. After their first child, Carl Jr., was born later that year, they bought a house at 106 Ferncliff Avenue in Sixteen Acres.[13] The suburb five miles northeast of downtown was a rural farming community before becoming a hub of Springfield's post-war building boom. By the early 1950s, area streets were lined with two- or three-bedroom, one-bath Capes and split-level ranches set on meticulously maintained eighth-acre lots. The town still retains that distinctly blue-collar feel.

The neighborhood was full of children, at least two or three in most houses. It was bordered on two sides by busy thoroughfares and was a five-minute walk to the Parker Street/Wilbraham Road intersection and its hodgepodge of grocery and drug stores, gas stations, and family restaurants on all four corners. Across Parker was woodsy Greenleaf Park, baseball fields, and the neighborhood church, St. Catherine of Siena. The house had a cellar, sun porch, and good-sized yard but quarters were close. Gregory was born in 1955, Joseph in 1956, and Michael in 1957. The boys slept in the basement. Carl worked two and sometimes three jobs at once, always at least 12 hours a day. He worked at a local Big Y Supermarket, Hershey Bag factory, American Bosch, any job to bring money home. He never complained and even went out of his way to drive a neighborhood mother without transportation to work every morning.

A fifth son, Daniel Thomas, was born November 12, 1958, so-named to honor actor Danny Thomas' lifelong devotion to St. Jude, one of the

Church's four patron saints of impossible causes.[14] Two sisters followed, Jacqueline in 1963 and Catherine in 1967. Danny's mop of dirty blonde hair, bright blue eyes, and a nose spotted with freckles gave him a permanent look of mischief. The chatterbox was a bright but a chronically-distracted day dreamer who rattled on constantly about things like becoming a scientist or going on safari.

Bunny said he was "a real boy" who reminded her of Huckleberry Finn. He was a relentless practical joker. Everyone was a target. He delighted in making his brothers laugh hard enough during family dinners that milk spurted from their noses and once traded Carl's pocket watch for a handful of baseball cards. One morning before school he yelled down to Bunny, in the basement, that the toilet was overflowing and flooding the hall. She charged up the stairs in a panic. Danny yelled, "April Fools!" and ran outside. During their annual Cape Cod vacation, 11-year-old Danny and his six-year-old sister Jackie were at the beach

The only home Carl and Bunny ever owned, 106 Ferncliff Avenue in Sixteen Acres. It has had the same look since the day the family moved there in 1953 (author's collection).

The Croteau family, ca. 1967. Top (left to right): Gregory, Michael, Carl Jr., and Joseph; bottom (left to right): Bunny, baby Catherine, Jacqueline, Carl Sr., and Danny (courtesy Brian Fitzgerald).

with a babysitter who gushed, "Your sister is such a pretty girl." Danny responded, "Girls are dumb. Watch this." He dipped a wet spoon in the sand and said, "Jackie, here. Have a snack." But he was a loving brother, joining her for backyard tea parties and often making his friends participate.[15]

He was friendly, some said overly so, and talked to anybody. Best friend Stephen Burnett described him as good natured, well liked, and a hard worker. By eight or nine, he fetched mail, raked leaves, and ran to the A&P or Acres Drugs for the elderly widow across the street. He never accepted her money. "She'd give him milk and cookies. That's all he wanted," Bunny recalled. He looked forward to snowstorms so he could earn a few dollars shoveling driveways and sidewalks, and he was a sensitive kid, once giving his grandmother a small ceramic owl because, he said, she was so wise.

With seven children under 14, the Croteau house was chaotic, the family rambunctious. Meals in particular were loud, full of laughter and shouting. Friday dinner was a favorite because everyone ate whatever they wanted, except meat, of course. Danny's choice was always Cheerios.[16]

The children, and most of the neighborhood, attended Our Lady of the Sacred Heart, a Catholic school for kindergarten through junior high, a couple of miles from the house. Marble mantels above separate entrances were etched "BOYS" and "GIRLS." Students wore uniforms, boys, shirts and ties, girls, light blue skirts and dress shirts. The Sisters of St. Joseph staffed the school and taught. Corporal punishment was the rule. The Sisters responded brutally to the slightest breach of decorum, forcing kids to kneel on pencils and brutally slapping or punching them for even minor transgressions. Students were beaten with anything within reach of the nuns, rulers, books,

Danny, ca. 1968, catching for his Little League team on the baseball field at Greenleaf Park (courtesy Brian Fitzgerald).

erasers, or their ever-present pointers. A favored punishment was to force a student back into a chair so his or her buttocks protruded from the backrest, where they were beaten with a belt. The Croteau boys were typical recalcitrant Catholic schoolers. Rare was the day one was not walloped. Joseph said there was never a week Carl or Bunny did not come to school to "bail one of us out of trouble."[17]

Their Catholic faith was important to Carl and Bunny, central to their lives. Today, 1960s attitudes toward the Church and priests seem archaic. At the time, 18,000 U.S. parishes housed 60,000 priests, by far the heaviest concentration in New England, home to the country's five most Catholic states. For more than two centuries, almost half of Massachusetts' population was Catholic. Springfield's percentage historically outpaced even those numbers. The Irish were 40 percent of the population, only reinforcing Church influence. It cannot be overstated that when Danny was growing up, the extent to which the Church and its

Our Lady of Sacred Heart School, attended by all the Croteau children (author's collection).

Irish controlled Springfield. A teeming mob presence centered in the Springfield's South End operated back to the 1920s, but Hungry Hill's "Irish Mafia" ran the city. They grew up together, went to school together, married sisters, brothers, cousins, friends, or neighbors, did everything together. They hired, appointed, or elected each other to every important board and commission. In 1972, Charles Ryan was the mayor. His sister was married to Jim Egan, whose prominent Egan, Flanagan, and Cohen law firm represented the diocese since the 1940s. Another Ryan, Matthew ("Matty"), was the district attorney. Church opinions were always heard and strongly considered.

The Church held sway over the largest paper, the *Springfield Republican* (then the *Union-News*).[18] In 1972, the Church was the paper's largest distributor. Tens of thousands of area Catholics bought their Sunday paper at churches after Mass. The editor in chief and the chief crime reporter were close friends of Bishop Christopher J. Weldon. They surreptitiously fed Weldon their stories and ran his. Coincidentally, the editor was a good friend of Danny's parish priest.

Weldon grew up in New York City, served at parishes across New York State, and was chaplain aboard the Navy aircraft carrier *Guadalcanal* during World War II. Appointed bishop of Springfield in 1950, he person-ified the gruff, obnoxious New Yorker and was wildly arrogant. He was often likened to J. Edgar Hoover, whom he emulated by keeping secret files on people and groups he considered threats. He was a micromanager who craved power and was unapologetically boastful while abusing it. A busi-nessman heading the building committee at an East Longmeadow parish talked to Weldon about selling a parcel of land to help finance a new church. He rejected the idea out of hand, huffing, "Absolutely not. That land belongs to *me*." He was furious when the man refused to kiss his ring after the meeting. He was not terribly popular with his priests, either, as most dis-liked the man they complained "acted like he walked on water."[19]

His power is difficult to exaggerate. It was applied sometimes subtly. In the 1970s, Daniel O'Connell's Sons was the oldest family-run con-

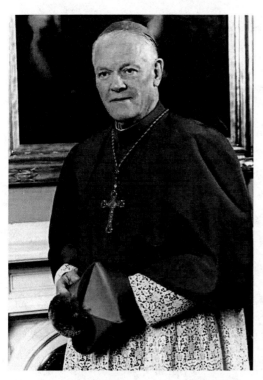

struction company in Amer-ica and for generations built every diocesan school and church. As the company's old-est shareholder neared death during Weldon's tenure, he made arrangements to leave his majority stake to a relative who happened to be divorced. He was warned that Weldon would be infuriated if that happened and the company would never again work for the diocese, so his will was changed and control given to a non-divorced relative. Weldon's edicts were fickle, though. When he learned a young man working for the diocese during the Vietnam war was a conscientious ob-jector, he ordered his immedi-ate firing, but when he learned the man was an O'Connell, he rescinded the order.[20]

Christopher J. Weldon, bishop of Springfield, a despotic ruler with connections to politi-cians, police, and newspapermen, exerted control over every aspect of city life (author's collection).

It is difficult to superimpose current attitudes toward clergy on those in the 1960s and 1970s. Priests existed on a pedestal, considered *alter Christus*—"another Christ"—and able to channel God's power to create a perfect society. Importantly, they controlled admittance into that society, during life and after death. The current custom of referring to a priest by his first name was unthinkable back then. The Croteau's priest was "Fr. Lavigne," never "Father Dickie." Priests received fanatical respect, utter reverence, and complete deference. Bishops and priests were thought of as infallable as popes. If a priest ordered something be done, it was done. Their edicts were never questioned and advice always taken on everything from psychological therapy and marriage counseling to parenting and financial questions. Priests were considered family members, called simply, "Father." For many children, they filled the role of surrogate parent, but with one with more authority. Children held them in even greater esteem, growing up, as they did, watching parents kneel reverently before their priest, confess sins, and fully submit.[21]

People's lives centered on the Church, as a Croteau friend confirmed: "All our lives were built around the Church. The priests were regular guests in our home." Having a personal relationship with your priest was a much-sought-after honor. An invitation to have dinner at the rectory or having a priest share a meal in your home was envied. Priestly attention was gratefully accepted without question or reservation. That sons served as altar boys was a source of great pride, so children were pressed to do so. Additional status was bestowed if children spent private time with priests. An altar boy dining with his priest, traveling with him, even sleeping over at the rectory, were notable events. An altar boy recalled, "My mother would say Father called and said he wanted company on his ride to a meeting and will take you to dinner. She would say, 'He doesn't have any friends. Be a good kid and be his friend.'"[22] That mindset meant priests' often extreme, sometimes obsessive, interest in families, particularly those with children, never raised question or concern.

The Croteaus' church, St. Catherine of Siena, was four blocks from Ferncliff. The 1,000-seat church replicated buildings in the saint's native Italy, with high, straight walls, a low-pitched roof, and a dominating bell tower. Father Thomas P. Griffin had been the pastor since the church's 1964 dedication, which the Croteaus attended. Parishioners were decidedly working class. The Croteaus attended 11 o'clock Sunday Mass as a group, weekly confessions for everyone, morning Mass most days for Carl and Bunny, and at least one novena a week. Carl regularly visited after work to pray a solitary Stations of the Cross. He and Bunny volunteered on innumerable parish groups, and the boys were altar boys.

The Croteaus' church, St. Catherine of Sienna, was just a few blocks from the family's house and central to their life (author's collection).

The trajectory of their lives was forever altered on May 6, 1967, when a new priest arrived.

On the surface, Danny was a typical pre-teen. Like his friends, he loved Boston teams and all sports. He participated in the daily football, kickball, or street hockey games on Lumae Street, used because it was wide and the houses had bigger lawns. He was smart but struggled in school, his priest describing him as "a young 13, about 10 mentally." Held back after 3rd grade, he was a year older than his classmates and at five feet, six inches, 135 pounds, was big for a 7th grader. He was "Hoss" to neighborhood kids, after the oversized Dan Blocker character on *Bonanza*. Danny comically underestimated his own strength—a friend said he was "strong as an ox"—and frequently gave friends accidental bumps and bruises playfully wrestling or participating in street sports.[23] A favorite stunt—sneaking up behind an unsuspecting friend and jumping on his back—often left shiners and scrapes. His aggressiveness was heightened because he hated losing at anything. Friends said he always had to be the winner at anything they did. That and his temper were sometimes a troublesome combination.

He was a talented wrestler and boxer. Thursdays, a University of Massachusetts student taught the seventh graders wrestling. Tuesdays, local college professor James Coleman gave them boxing lessons. He was a Renaissance man who lived in an orphanage until age ten. He fought in the Pacific during World War II, studied music at Juilliard, and designed guided missile warheads at Johns Hopkins Applied Physics Laboratory before becoming a tenured physics professor. He wrote five books and a syndicated science newspaper column, picked up by papers as far away as Japan. His upbringing shaped a lifelong commitment to children and community service. He was a volunteer youth counselor, served on YMCA Boards and even refereed weekend volleyball and basketball games. Coleman recalled Danny as a skillful boxer, "extroverted, well adjusted, open, and friendly." Strangely, the family priest warned Carl about "all this wrestling stuff," saying that he should "keep Danny away from Coleman." Carl said the cleric "didn't like him at all," but ignored the advice because Coleman "didn't strike me as the type." Danny rarely missed a session. He was an accomplished fighter.[24]

Danny's greatest love was the outdoors. He enjoyed the Boy Scouts for the camping trips and rarely missed Troop 118's Friday night meeting at Duggan Junior High. School janitors remembered the friendly Scout because, during every meeting, he made a 10- or 15-minute phone call he said was to his mother. From an early age, though, "what he loved the most was fishing." If he could not be found, Bunny assumed he was at a pond or stream, somewhere, with his inexpensive fishing rod.[25]

He had only a few close friends—his best pals were neighbors Steve Block and Steve Burnett—but all the kids liked him, according to Burnett. Strangely, none—even those two—ever went inside Danny's house. He was disciplined for the usual schoolyard infractions and was regularly banished to detention for fighting. Normally even tempered and slow to anger, he was not naturally aggressive and no one remembers him instigating a fight. His brother recalled, "Danny would never start a fight, but if you got him mad, watch out!" If he or the family were insulted, even slightly, he lashed out. The nuns called Carl and Bunny to OLSH at least once a month because of Danny's fights, most with multiple combatants, none of which he ever lost. His brothers' friends were older and bigger than Danny and had fearsome reputations for fighting. None would ever even nudge him in that direction. As tough and quick to fight as they were, they were physically afraid of him. Only one ever engaged Danny. He beat the older boy badly.[26]

Even so, nuns did not think him a problem student. In many ways, he was a typical 13-year-old who rode his bike everywhere and spent all his time outdoors with his friends. In other ways, he was not. Danny was a contradiction, equal parts cherubic altar boy and troubled kid trying to grow up too fast alongside a second crowd of unsavory friends of all classes and stripes, most of questionable character and worrisome reputation. He regularly socialized with older men. Danny could always get liquor, marijuana, "porno books," almost anything they wanted, from these anonymous friends.

He was very close to three men who worked at the neighborhood A&P. One, a grocery manager in his mid–20s, was reportedly paying Danny $10 to paint his bedroom. Once, during a football game after school, he ran across the street and jumped into a blue car driven by a man that looked almost 30. Danny claimed the man "brought him goodies." Friends recalled Danny sitting in another car, this one tan, looking at the driver's "dirty books." Both matched the description of his A&P friends.[27]

Danny spent time with a ragtag group of neighborhood trouble-makers known as "the Circle." The group got its start in 1965 and was made up of younger kids not included by the older boys with drivers' licenses who hung around with their cars in the library parking lot. That crowd was dubbed "the Motley Crew," "Motleys," or by some, "Razor-backs." The Circle moniker arose because the younger kids hung out in a small park behind the library, not far from Ferncliff, closer still to St. Catherine's. In 1967, four benches and five tall berms were arranged around a large oak tree. It was built for locals to read or relax, but it was rarely used for those purposes. The benches were not visible because the library had no windows on that side, so the bothersome younger teens appropriated them. The Circle and the Motleys were known by reputation to "run Sixteen Acres center." At the Circle, they played kids' games like "Jail," running over the mounds capturing players and putting them in "jail," but privacy allowed them to engage in more disruptive adult pastimes. They smoked cigarettes and marijuana, drank stolen beer and liquor, and raised significant hell.[28]

Anyone wanting to join the Circle was welcomed. Founding member Phil Chechile later said, "If you weren't cool, we made you cool."

The Circle, shortly after it was built in 1967 as a place for people to relax and read, was taken over by a group of local troublemakers that included three of Danny's older brothers (courtesy Brian Fitzgerald).

Interestingly, at a time of rampant racial bigotry, there were several black members. Not only were they accepted, they were fiercely protected. Anyone making derogatory comments about them was beaten. "If you said anything you weren't going to walk away under your own power," a member recalled.[29]

Not fully effecting the ominous aura of today's gangs, they still engaged in disturbing criminal mischief. Though only junior high schoolers, they drank—a lot—and most were serious drug abusers. Many later said their Circle years left them alcoholics and drug addicts. They tossed so many beer cans into a gully in the nearby woods it became known as "Bud Hill." They always needed money for their vices, so many habitually stole from their own families, from mothers' purses and fathers' wallets. One pocketed his sister's babysitting money, stole painkillers his father needed for injuries suffered in Korea, and even left his house unlocked during a family vacation so the gang could ransack the house for valuables.[30]

They were also notorious local thieves. They broke into cars and houses and stole money, stereos, liquor, cigarettes, anything they could use or convert into cash. They stole cars from Eastfield Mall parking lots and hid them in the woods behind Hillcrest Park Cemetery to be retrieved for joyrides. They taped wooden blocks to the pedals of one so a too-short Joseph Croteau could drive. He plowed into a tree. They stole guns, buried them beneath a headstone, and dug them up to shoot in the woods. They were despised at the nearby Parker Street/Wilbraham Road businesses. People said they never entered a store without stealing something or bothering customers. Outside, they smashed windows and vandalized buildings and parked cars, generally making themselves personae non gratae.[31]

The gang aspect was born out of contempt for common enemies, the pastor at a Protestant church vocally opposing a planned youth center and the Sixteen Acres police who chased them out of stores and rousted them from their park. Their most hated enemy—called "Mush" McCarthy—arbitrarily stopped and harassed them, took their liquor, and often roughed them up. The Circle responded with a prolonged guerrilla war. Tires on police cars were slashed and lights smashed. As two patrolmen had coffee inside Friendly's, the boys wrapped a chain around a tree and attached it to the rear axle of their patrol car. Another boy then sped through the parking lot in a stolen car, engine racing, smoke pouring from squealing tires, goading the officers to chase him. They sprinted to their car, and like in the movie *American Graffiti*, jumped in and accelerated. The rear axle was ripped off.[32]

There were a dozen similar gangs nearby in Ludlow, Indian Orchard, and Forest Park, some operating since the 1950s. The Circle maintained uneasy alliances with closer-in gangs, the Pine Point Gang, Boston Road Boys, Treetops, and the gigantic Clan, whose 150 members gathered near Western New England College and referred to the Circle boys as "Circle Jerks." They fought sometimes-violent battles with a few like the Bridle Path Gang, using rocks and clubs, and, sometimes, chains and bayonets. Combatants suffered everything from scratches and bruises to fractured skulls. Boxing coach Coleman was applauded for working with the Circle but was said to drive them to the donnybrooks.[33]

Members of the community were often the victims of their hijinks. When their hated pastor was on a week-long vacation, they ran a garden hose into a window well at his home. He returned to find his cellar filled to the ceiling, water pouring out windows. A member and his girlfriend ran away from home and hid in a small dugout cabin the boys had built into the side of a hill in the woods behind her house (a gathering place known as "The Gulley"). They furnished it with stolen chairs, a bed, and a small stove. During the five months before the couple was discovered, the boys delivered stolen food and household items to the hideaway.

Danny's brother Gregory was one of the co-founders. He later described life in the gang as "fighting, stealing cars, all the crazy things kids did in the 60s. I'm no stranger to violence. My nose has hit everything but the lottery." D.A. Ryan's son Marty was involved, as were his nephews Brian and Michael McMahon. Despite multiple arrests, the band rarely went to court because of those relationships. Once, a policeman approached two members after they stole several guns, saying only, "Tell Greg to be here tomorrow with everything they took."[34] He did as ordered. No one was arrested.

James Coleman was close to the Circle and, outwardly, tried to keep them out of trouble. He mentored, listened, and railed at them to "stick up for your rights! Don't let anyone push you around!" He even paid their bail. But he was a strict disciplinarian and demanded respect. Perhaps surprisingly, it was returned. He was tough, unafraid of confrontation, and relentlessly enforced his rules. Swearing and smoking were prohibited in his presence; "SMOKING STINKS" signs were affixed to his

Members of "the Circle Gang" were already drinking and using drugs at 12 or 13. Danny's brother Gregory, beer in hand, is at lower left in the black striped shirt (courtesy Brian Fitzgerald).

dashboard. To some, he was a parent figure. He was the only adult privy to their stories, and was, for all intents and purposes, a member.[35]

The Circle and Danny, four or five years younger than the members, were not an obvious pairing. Coleman said they liked him, that he was a "little brother" who could visit whenever he wished even though they understood Carl and Bunny did not want him involved. Coleman self-published *The Circle*, based on the gang, in 1970. He took liberties with some history. A member he said drowned in a local pond was actually killed by a shotgun blast during a camping trip, and he was accused of wrongly describing parents as disengaged, debaucherous, physically abusive drunkards. Even so, it is an enlightening view into the lives of the Croteau boys and their friends in the 1960s.[36]

Coleman blamed the boys' lot on grown-ups and parents, "stupid adults" whose indifference bred their defiance. His protagonists' unwavering disdain for adults was represented in a variety of stereotypes, like the curmudgeon spinster librarian called "Old Bitch Blandford," "stupid cops," and adults known collectively as "old codgers" or "hags." "Father Ravine," a priest in his 20s recently assigned to "St. Jude's," was a rare adult they admired. He rattled the stuffy place, brought in contemporary music, and let kids decorate the sanctuary with cartoon posters. Before he was ousted by the "codger" pastor, he hung out with them in the park, and they visited him at the rectory. "St. Jude's" was St. Catherine's. "Fr. Ravine" was Father Richard Lavigne, a new priest at the Croteaus' church.[37]

Coleman's book sold out in Springfield but was not universally praised or welcomed. Police wanted it banned, and readers were jolted by the revelations and language. Still more were outraged that the boys were portrayed as lawless, disrespectful thugs, their parents as uncaring and unmanageable as their children. Coleman received at least one death threat, and several parents wanted to sue him for slander until dissuaded by a lawyer. Coleman was already loathed by the book's most outspoken critic. He bailed the man's son out of jail after he stole a car when the father refused to do so. D.A. Ryan was particularly critical, slamming the book as inaccurate and criticizing Coleman for "using" the Circle to craft an unflattering story and "insulting" parents and authority figures. Some members were upset at their parents' portrayals, and within a few months, Coleman was effectively banished.[38]

Danny was a contradiction. The Boy Scout altar boy was actually more akin to members of the Circle than described over the years. A schoolmate recalled him as "much more hellion than altar boy." Behind the impish countenance, he had an edge, and he engaged in the same bad behavior as the gang. He smoked cigarettes, which, to be fair, was not unusual among his peers. Some began smoking at 10 and a few openly smoked at home at 14. He smoked marijuana and smuggled liquor into Scout meetings, teaching friends how to do so. He drank the ceremonial wine at church—"the most important part of the Mass for Danny," according to his best friend—and stole bags of Communion wafers to snack on. He once pulled a fire alarm at school. And, like other members of the Circle, he was a chronic shoplifter. He was caught stealing from the neighborhood A&P where his older friends worked, and he once pocketed a set of candle-making molds from Lechmere's department store. He used them to make candles with the nuns at school.[39]

Danny's turf was not limited to his neighborhood. Though his parents later said he never got "into a car unless he knew the operator," he hitchhiked everywhere.[40] His wanderings took him all over Springfield. He bummed rides to distant destinations like downtown, Eastfield Mall, or his grandfather's Chicopee neighborhood. He was picked up by OLSH teachers many times miles away from Ferncliff. Most of his escapades and running around took place at night. He was habitually out late, even during the week, disguising his actual plans by telling his parents he was at Scout meetings or school dances.

Perhaps the most startling contradiction between the image of Danny and the real Danny was the fact that a friend claimed he owned a Satanic bible and "would often play at having a black Mass." The boy said Danny claimed to have attended those masses and seances "in Chicopee on Friday nights … with boys and girls and cousins."[41]

Danny was by no means a seriously troubled or bad kid, but it is important to recognize that, although he may simply have been trying to grow up too fast, in the early spring of 1972, barely 13 years old, he was less saint than sinner, less altar boy than rogue.

2

Dickie

Three generations of Richard Lavigne's family spent their lives in Chicopee's Aldenville neighborhood, a magnet for French-Canadians since 1870, when Quebecois carpenter Marcellin Croteau built the first house there. Grandfather Adelard Lavigne was born in 1874 in Quebec's remote Notre-Dame-de-Ham. Home to barely 200 people, it was almost perfectly centered between Montreal and Toronto, just below the St. Lawrence River and Lake St. Pierre. After 3rd grade, he worked the family farm. In 1906, widowed and with a young son, he married Clerina St. Cyr. She was born in 1870 in the nearby settlement of St. Valère-de-Bulstrode. For 15 years, they bounced between Quebec and the Boston area before settling in Aldenville in 1920. Their six sons were all born back in Notre-Dame-de-Ham. When they tried to bring one into the U.S.—Edmund, born deaf and mute in 1912—he was "rejected as illiterate." Middle son Ovila Raoul was born in 1909.[1]

They were surprisingly well off. Clerina reentered the U.S. multiple times during the 1920s, always carrying at least $300 (several thousand, today). In the late 1920s, when the medium U.S. income was $1,300, the best suit cost $20 and a new Ford $400, Adelard paid $7,500 for a large house at 898 Granby Road in Aldenville. Money was plentiful because everyone worked except Clerina because of her chronic hip problems. Adelard was a painter at the Palmer Steel foundry along with son Wilfred. Alfred, Joseph, and Ovila worked in the carpentry shop at the Springfield Armory. Even the youngest, Girard, earned money doing odd jobs. When Clerina died in 1933, the Lavigne men scattered throughout Chicopee. In 1936, Ovila paid $3,500 for a house at 88 Edward Street, a 1,280-square-foot brick bungalow with a basement, two bedrooms, a bath, and a small front porch, built in 1919.[2] The houses in the neighborhood sat on large lots, most with backyard gardens that helped feed families.

In 1935, Ovila met Blanch Annette Cote (known as "Annette"), born and raised in Maine by Quebecois immigrants. Her father, Joseph Phidime Cote, emigrated from St. Fabien, Quebec, in 1896 at age 18. He worked in the bustling mill towns and fishing villages along the Atlantic Ocean near Cape Elizabeth, Maine. He ended up in Westbrook, with its mills and factories lining the Presumpscot River. On June 2, 1902, he married Albertine Auclair, a housekeeper who emigrated in 1885, and took an apartment on the river. He was a carpenter before joining the Westbrook Grocery Corporation, and by 1916 he was its president. In 1917, they bought a house across the river, three doors from the business at 720 Main Street.[3] The stately, three-story 1850 colonial was a quarter of a mile from their apartment, but much farther in circumstance, next to a genteel downtown with shops, parks, and large homes.

By 1920 Joseph and Albertine had seven children, three boys and four girls. She lost two others. The fifth, Blanch Annette, was born in 1915. Everyone was left in dire straits when Joseph died in 1927. Within three years, they were shoe-horned into a $21 apartment at 71 Belcher Street in downtown Chicopee. French was the language of choice in the austere Quebecois neighborhood—French was spoken at home—and locals worked in the factories two blocks away on the Chicopee River. Theirs were Spartan lodgings; they could not afford a radio. The older children worked as laborers. Annette and the younger siblings went to school. In 1937, she married Ovila Lavigne and moved to Edward Street. Into the 1940s, he was at the armory, and she was a secretary at a butter creamery. On February 18, 1941, she gave birth to a son, Richard Roger.[4] A daughter followed eight years later.

The devout Catholics attended St. Rose de Lima and the children attended Catholic schools. A teenage Richard—known as "Dickie"—wore his curly hair long, and was a talented artist and painter. That he was going to become a priest was never in doubt. "In those days, you just knew," said a childhood friend. "He was a smart boy from a very ethnic Catholic family. It would have been a big surprise if he wasn't a priest."[5]

His priestly ambitions did not lessen his strange childhood behavior, though. The neighborhood kids liked him, despite his laughable weirdness and strange behavior. Not frightening, just very odd. What friends found most peculiar was his bizarre relationship with his mother,

The longtime Lavigne family home at 88 Edward Street, Chicopee, bought by Ovila Lavigne in 1935, where Richard Lavigne lived on and off his whole life (author's collection).

who they said was extraordinarily sexually provocative in their presence. She titillated by wearing a very risqué wardrobe and walking around in skimpy bikinis. They laughed when Dickie touched her breasts and asked, "Are these real?" but they recognized the overly-affectionate, pseudo-amorous relationship was terrifically inappropriate. Once, his pals came upon the two on chaise lounge chairs, sunbathing, in the backyard. She was topless. His hand was on her breast.[6]

They also witnessed an even darker side to Dickie. He was obsessed with the occult and the paranormal and once left his younger sister in the basement of an unfinished house where she remained until found by searchers the next morning. And, though they all hunted small animals like squirrels, birds, and frogs, Dickie took unseemly pleasure in the actual killing. He enjoyed injecting them with bleach and watching their slow, painful deaths intently. He then placed the carcasses in small boxes and presided over elaborate backyard funerals. After a solemn march, he wound up a toy monkey organ grinder and offered a service including a eulogy as little cymbals clanged in the background.[7]

Some of Dickie's antics seemed comical on the surface. Just after high school, he brought a 14-year-old neighborhood boy home. The boy agreed to go only because he was infatuated with Lavigne's younger sister and was promised she was there. The elder Lavignes were not at home, nor was the sister. Instead, the boy said, Dickie tried "to hypnotize me to take my clothes off." Lavigne made light of the accusation, laughing, "I guess you can't be hypnotized." At the time, the boy laughed it off too.[8] That was just Dickie. He was strange.

He attended Assumption Preparatory School, an all-male Catholic boarding school 45 minutes east of Springfield that shared a campus with Assumption College. The schools were founded in 1904 by the Augustinians of the Assumption, a French order commanded by Father Emmanuel d'Alzon. He was born into French aristocracy, but his Assumptionists believed they were "trailblazers of Christ's kingdom," dedicated to Christianizing the world and restoring God to his rightful place over human affairs. The school motto was "Je Maintiendrai," "I shall uphold." They were the first order to use modern organizational strategies and media techniques, founded an early Catholic publishing house, and controlled the most influential newspaper in France. They believed people were imbued with innate good, that it should be sought in others, and that following God effected a better world. Interestingly, a core belief was that one should "embrace joy from well-being, success, and possessing what one desires." This is not meant to explain 175 years of Assumptionist philosophy; rather, it is an attempt to understand how those teachings affected a young Dickie Lavigne.[9]

The year before Lavigne arrived, a tornado destroyed the college, severely damaged the high school, and killed three nuns and a priest. The college was moved, but the high school and its 200 students retained prestige due to their affiliation. Most students were Franco-Americans from New England, but Catholic missions in locales like Kenya or Thailand sent a half a dozen annually. Franco-American culture, Catholic theology, and the French language were important. Everything was taught in French, classes were called "Eléments," and priests and a few nuns made up the faculty. Athletics were stressed, particularly basketball, and "the Greyhounds" teams were led by their mascot, "The Monk." Dickie was an indifferent student, a trait he never outgrew. He graduated in the dead middle of his 1958 class.

Dickie was involved in a disturbing incident just after graduation. He got a summer job as a recreation assistant, a camp counselor of sorts, at a small park in Chicopee. A month later, he was abruptly fired, labeled "an undesirable person to be around children."[10]

He went on to Assumption College. The 1,500 students were mostly French-Canadian and all male. Even female teachers were prohibited. As had been the case in high school, classes were in French. Aside from three classes, his curriculum centered on Catholic theology, philosophy, and French and Latin culture. He academic results remained unremarkable, with consistently middling results: Freshman, 2.83 (out of 4.00); Sophomore, 2.82; Junior, 2.87; and Senior, 2.90. He managed just two As during four years, and on June 6, 1962, he graduated with a bachelor of arts in philosophy and the Classics.[11]

With a recommendation from Springfield's diocesan chancellor, he entered the seminary at Our Lady of Angels near Albany, New York. It was founded in 1856 by the Vincentians, and in 1961 it was moved from

Our Lady of Angels Seminary, where Richard Lavigne prepared for the priesthood (author's collection).

Niagara Falls to a hilltop overlooking the Hudson River south of Albany. The small school offered a six-year path to ordination, referred to as "formation," for barely 175 seminarians. His schedule was laden with theology-intense courses like dogmatic theology, moral theology, ascetical theology, and pastoral theology along with sacred scripture, Church history, canon law, and liturgy and cathechetics.[12]

Academic apathy and mediocre results continued, his grades hovering barely above average. He earned just a single A in four years, in homiletics, and a D in cathechetics. In every other class, he scored in the low 70s–low 80s. Administrators never figured Dickie out. To the query on his second-year review "To what studies is he especially inclined?" his advisor replied, "Worked on paintings for the Seminary during summer." The next year's response was "good at painting."

At the end of his second year, Lavigne requested a loan from the diocese for expenses, which it provided. After the third year, he spent two months at the Nassau, Bahamas, mission of Haitian priest Father Guy Sansaricq, working with refugees escaping François "Papa Doc" Duvalier's brutal regime. Lavigne taught English and helped people find food, clothing, and work. He returned the following December.[13]

He graduated in 1962 with a masters in theology, ranked fifth among ten students, still blazingly average. Over four years, every grade but two was between 75 and 82. Overall, Our Lady believed Dickie was best suited for "general parish work … should be kept busy," and, interestingly, "never be allowed to teach." Lastly, they warned he needed "to be consoled in difficulties, and all his life will need the consolation of friends to aid him in his troubles."[14] Despite the tepid recommendation, he was ordained by Bishop Weldon at the downtown Cathedral of St. Michael the Archangel—"The Bishop's Church"—on May 14, 1966. The next day he celebrated Mass at St. Rose de Lima, after which everyone attended a luncheon at the Shaker Farms Country Club and then a reception at the church.[15]

The new priest became an immediate, and, ultimately, permanent thorn in Weldon's side. From the start, he pestered Weldon to teach at Cathedral High School with impassioned letters that he was "more than qualified and [had] an excellent rapport with children." He complained of having no supporter in the diocese, "no patron at court." He devotedly ignored the seminary loans and dozens of polite letters requesting the modest $17 monthly payment he agreed to make. The diocese even tried to pry the money using emotion, calling the loans a "moral obligation" that allowed other young men who, "like you, were in need of financial assistance." He still refused to pay.[16]

Lavigne began his career at two small churches. He described the postings as "not easy," but the disquiet was due to his own chronic petulance. He behaved like a spoiled child, feuding privately and publicly with the older priests and making himself the bête noire of both pastors. At Sacred Heart of Jesus in Easthampton, there was a curfew for the curates. When the pastor locked him out for being late, he broke a window with a rock to get in. He survived three months, but he did make some lifelong friends before he was transferred.

Mitchell and Blanche Tenerowicz were active parishioners and befriended Lavigne during his first days in Easthampton. Mitchell, known as "Doc T," or "Doctor Mitch," was a well known Hampshire County doctor. He was born in Springfield in 1923 and grew up in a small Ludlow apartment with six brothers and sisters. They were raised by their blue-collar Polish immigrant father after their mother's death in 1938. He flew with the Eighth Air Force in England, then earned two undergraduate degrees and a medical degree from Tufts University in 1953.[17]

In addition to running a thriving family medical practice, Mitchell served on the board of health as a public health physician, on the staff of Cooley Dickinson Hospital, and during the 1970s–1980s as associate medical examiner for Hampshire County and on the National Board of Medical Examiners.[18] He was school doctor for the public schools and church schools at Notre Dame–Immaculate Conception and Sacred Heart.

Mitchell married Blanche Dobbie during his undergraduate studies. She also traded working-class Ludlow roots for multiple post-graduate degrees, including a masters in nursing and a doctorate in human resources. Blanche was a nurse and managed her husband's practice while teaching at the parish school and serving on a diocesan education board. Mitchell and Blanche were socially prominent, belonged to the exclusive Country Club of Greenfield and were close to Lavigne for years. He was particularly friendly with Blanche; their relationship elicted whispers among the parishioners, particularly when he gifted her with antique-hunting finds like church pews, lamps, and an old pulpit.

The Tenerowiczes and their three children lived in a large five-bedroom house at 10 Park Street, a few blocks from the prestigious Williston Northampton prep school. They also owned a chalet at Jay Peak, Vermont, near Canada, and a lavish lake house on Lower Highland Lake in Goshen. Lavigne often weekended with Mitchell. Lavigne socialized with Mitchell and Blanche almost weekly, and he enjoyed free access to the chalet and lake house.

Mitchell apparently shared Lavigne's obsession with the occult, taking his children on a Halloween midnight trek with Lavigne and Joseph Croteau to a cemetery. Lavigne and Tenerowicz said they were going to make contact with ghosts living there. Lavigne also counseled Elizabeth (Beth) from age eight to 17, usually during private counseling sessions in his rectory quarters. Blanche usually drove Beth to those appointments.[19]

From Easthampton, Weldon sent Lavigne to Precious Blood in Holyoke. The pastor prohibited being seated for dinner after he gave the blessing. Lavigne arrived one evening just after the group said grace, and the housekeeper informed Lavigne he could not join the table. He huffed, "Well, if I can't eat, no one will" and dumped the entire dinner on the kitchen floor. Again, he lasted three months. He was sent to the Croteaus' church, St. Catherine of Siena, arriving there May 6, 1967. Weldon hoped Pastor Thomas Griffin, a wise and reasoned cleric, would curb Lavigne's juvenile ways. He could not. Lavigne increasingly delighted in his provocateur role. Through his career, he regaled priests and friends—often from the pulpit—with rousing tales of his insurgency, accounts of rebellion more colorful with each telling.[20]

He initially took St. Catherine's by storm, equal parts charismatic leader and polarizing upstart. Six feet tall and 165 pounds, with a strong jaw and prominent chin, he looked younger than his 26 years, even with a rapidly receding hairline, and "he would stare right through you" with piercing blue eyes. He maintained a weightlifter's physique from daily workouts, was a natty dresser, and drove a red 1964 Mustang. In his rectory quarters were a half-dozen easels holding his seascape, cloudy sky, and tall ship paintings. He "was the kind of person who won peoples' hearts," described variously as "an outstanding priest ... dynamic, exciting, fun to be around ... brilliant." He was most lauded for "the way he related to his altar boys."[21]

He replaced the conservative organ music with contemporary songs, guitars, and tambourines. The entire congregation was soon singing. He let kids decorate the sanctuary with their own artwork. *Peanuts* characters alternated with stained-glass windows. But his impassioned sermons, and overblown rhetoric, often confused parishoners, as did his habit of repeatedly asking, "Are there any questions?" at a time when people never, ever spoke out during Mass. He was likewise eccentric. People were taken aback by his obsession with the occult that ran counter to Catholic teachings. Remember the weird midnight trip with Joseph Croteau to a cemetery to chat with the spirits?[22]

Father Richard R. Lavigne, ca. 1967–68, when he was at the Croteaus' church, St. Catherine of Sienna (author's collection).

He remained a dedicated non-conformist, and, unusual for the time, never wore his clerical collar unless saying Mass. Street clothes made him relatable, human. He did don the collar at restaurants or hotels because they routinely offered priests discounts. Lavigne particularly savored his rebel persona and "60's-era radical" image; one parishioner said he "fancied himself the Bobby Kennedy of priests and loved to use the word 'disenfranchised.'" He gave intense sermons with a Marxist bent, saying the church belonged to its people for more than Masses. Most parishes had some kind of church hall, but other than a basement used for church suppers, club meetings, and the occasional movie, there was no such facility at St. Catherine's. He lobbied Griffin to turn the cellar into a teen recreation center. Griffin hated the idea, just one of many often heated disagreements between the two.[23]

Lavigne was among a small group of young priests who openly feuded with their older counterparts and caused Weldon considerable angst. He and a close friend, Father Gerald F. Spafford—known as "the Movie Star Priest"—were the acknowledged leaders of the agitators. Lavigne and Spafford ran with Springfield politicians and were out front at anti-war rallies or political events. At the time, leftist priests were social justice champions, like Carlos Mugica in Argentina and Daniel

Berrigan in the U.S. Lavigne and Spafford fancied themselves leaders of a crusade to force the Church into relevance for counterculture 1960s kids.

Despite the early accolades, many eventually became riled by Lavigne's revolutionary posturing. His sermons contained vitriolic anti–Vietnam War, anti-police brutality bombast. Audiences were left incredulous, full as they were with fervent supporters of the police and the military in a city with long, deep service traditions. Lavigne knew not to mention the topic to Carl. "He had his friends," a parishioner recalled, "but he really offended many of us with his talk of police brutality and a withdrawal from Vietnam." During one diatribe, the choir's lead tenor surprisingly yelled down from the loft, "Are you saying we should unilaterally withdraw from Vietnam?" Lavigne engaged him in a lengthy shouting match. The affable Griffin stepped in, asking the singer to avoid such confrontations. He replied, "I will if he will."[24]

Shortly after arriving, Lavigne was at the center of a public kerfuffle following the death of a priest. An older cleric's eulogy praised the cadre of older priests and dismissed the younger crop from seminaries with "country club atmospheres teaching false political and social theories." Lavigne was the only priest to speak publicly, strongly criticizing his older colleagues during several media interviews. Weldon was furious.[25]

He and Griffin were at serious odds from the start. Griffin bristled at the recalcitrant young priest and his conspicuous involvement with anti-government, anti-war coteries. He did not want the pulpit used to spread those views, he strongly opposed Lavigne's campaigns to open the church and relax the sanctity of the Mass, and he was troubled by Lavigne's forceful advocacy for children from outside the church. He wanted Lavigne to simply go about being a priest without the multiple distractions.[26] Battles with Griffin, bluster, and political views aside, to many parishioners—particularly those flattered by the attention he paid them—Lavigne was beloved. They liked that he brought new life to the church and passionately advocated for children. His interest in kids led to close relationships with scores of families, chief among them the Croteaus.

Lavigne went out of his way to socialize with families, announcing during his first sermon at every assignment that he "welcomed postcards inviting him for a beer." He often shared two, three, even four dinners a week with one family. He often showed up uninvited, sometimes walked out back and lit the grill before knocking. Most of his pastoral attention was directed at children, especially boys, who loved him because he ruffled feathers. He was one of them, a carefree big brother who spoke their language, understood their trials. He was the "cool guy," more playboy than priest, never serious away from church. He got them involved in church activities and swelled altar boy ranks. He rough-housed with them, wrestling and grabbing like a playmate. Interesting, Carl disliked that horseplay, and he asked Lavigne not to do so with his sons. Lavigne challenged them to footraces from the church to the neighborhood and was never once beaten. He got them out of school to serve Masses and funerals. He accompanied them into their changing room after Mass and helped them out of their cumbersome cassocks. He encouraged them to drink altar wine from the chalice, but only after morning Mass during the week, when the church was empty.[27]

He took them to movies and let them hang out in his rectory quarters and watch old films. He let them watch his favored movies, Alfred Hitchcock and gory horror or crime pictures they could not watch at home. He took them to Friendly's for ice cream, let them drive his car, let them peruse the *Playboy* magazines he kept under the front seat and beneath his mattress, and he joined in their neighborhood sports.[28]

He was unfailingly, exceedingly generous, and he always arrived bearing gifts, some small, like rosaries or crucifix sets, others large and expensive, like stereo equipment far beyond families' financial reach. On days off, he took them on day trips all over New England, some jaunts lasting a week. Vermont was a favored haunt, places like Santa's Winter Wonderland in Putney, and ski chalets owned by another priest and a wealthy doctor friend. He took them snowmobiling and scoured shops and barns for antiques, adventures he called "treasure hunting expeditions." Lavigne had excellent taste in art, aware which antiques were valuable, and which were not. He collected so much statuary, and boxes of church fixtures, he was known as "the Bishop's junkman." At one point, he was named diocesan coordinator of religious ornaments and statuary. He had the boys remove antiques and tools from remote barns he claimed were abandoned. Several times, they were chased off properties and through fields before speeding away down country roads. The kids found the dangerous episodes exhilarating.[29]

Lavigne's most frequent destination was a remote property in Ashfield, Massachusetts, where he was building an A-frame on land owned by his parents. The house sat on two forested acres at the end of a gravel driveway that disappeared into the trees off Tatro Road. On the open first floor was a living room with sliders opening onto a large deck looking back down the hill. A fireplace stood on one side, a kitchenette and bath at the back. A cathedral ceiling exposed the second-floor balcony fronting a smallish bedroom and tiny bath. The airy cottage was barely large enough for four or five guests. When he brought groups during summer, the younger boys slept outside on the deck. The inside was reserved for older boys. The getaway was completed in 1972, much of the work done by his altar boys. An exterior wall was dominated by a painting Lavigne had done of St. Luke, the Church's patron saint of artists. The getaway was invisible to neighbors and passing cars.[30]

Wherever he took them, he always paid, a fact not unnoticed by their usually cash-strapped families. The Croteaus often wondered how a priest with working-class roots had all that money all the time. He reached out to kids unaffiliated with St. Catherine's and visited the Circle in their hideout down the street. He easily ingratiated himself into the group that was shunned by most everyone else. A local said Lavigne seemed to be trying to straighten them out, and he was "making some inroads." He was "Father Ravine," after all.

Several Circle members were among his altar boys, including the D.A.'s nephews, Brian and Michael McMahon. There were several Ryans in the parish, including Matty's cousin Don, owner of a chain of drug stores and brother of Springfield's mayor Charlie. None of Don's nine sons became altar boys. His wife was put off by Lavigne's frequent, uninvited visits to the Ryan house, and she disliked the relentless recruiting of her sons.

There was strong divergence in opinion about Lavigne. He was an iconoclast, described as "sometimes positive, sometimes negative, but never neutral," and "people love him. People loath him. He stirred faith in some and fear in others." Some of his antics rubbed people—even the boys—the wrong way. He was exceedingly moody; one said, "You never knew from one minute to the next with him." Oddly, he was unreasonably demanding and obnoxious toward restaurant and bar servers, embarrassing the kids with irrational demands for food or service.[31]

And they witnessed an even darker side. Sometimes it appeared as eccentricity, like roaring at people arriving late for Mass, but more often it was frightening, like throwing a missal across the church at the parents of a crying infant. Inside, Lavigne possessed a fearsome temper that frequently erupted. And he relentlessly, mercilessly, cruelly teased. Worse, if he became enraged he became physical. He slapped kids across the face if he thought them disrespectful, once getting into a fistfight with Danny's brother Gregory at a Confirmation practice. Something unrecognized by the others made Gregory explode and punch Lavigne in the mouth. He returned a blow, and after some brawling, Gregory yelled, "Fuck you!" and stormed out. Another disturbing display occurred a year before Danny died. Lavigne took Joseph, Michael, Gregory, and Danny, along with Brian and Michael McMahon and two others, for an overnight at a remote Goshen cabin, half an hour northwest of Springfield. Danny, the youngest, became the target of what Michael McMahon described as "name-calling and mild ridicule," most from his brothers. Danny became increasingly upset when Lavigne joined in the insults and lashed out after Michael McMahon upended him during a Lavigne-orchestrated "tickle fight." Danny yelled at Lavigne to intervene. McMahon said Lavigne "struck me in the face so hard it knocked me down."[32]

Lavigne made his first recruiting trip to the Croteau house shortly after his arrival at St. Catherine's. To Carl and Bunny, a French-Canadian priest—from Chicopee, no less—was exciting. Neither had ever met a non–Irish priest. Bunny recalled, "He just popped up here all the sudden. We didn't invite him. He said he wanted to help us." Carl, working seven days a week, gratefully recalled, "Things were tough. We had seven kids. I was working two or three jobs to make ends meet. I'd get laid off sometimes." Lavigne became a de facto family member and confidant. He was exceedingly generous, regularly buying gifts and much-needed clothes and raiding the rectory freezer for large roasts and steaks, saying, "You need this more than we do." He took everyone to a shoe store where his father worked and bought shoes for everyone. He baby-sat the rowdy brood once for a week after Bunny was hospitalized for minor surgery. Carl said, "It was nice of him to do those things." Lavigne, he added, "was always at the house, coming over for coffee, for dinner, to play with the kids, to take them places."[33]

The older Croteaus were altar boys when Lavigne arrived. Danny signed on a few months later. Lavigne paid them to do odd jobs around the rectory, had them for dinner, and took them to restaurants, a rare treat. All spent nights at the rectory or Lavigne's family home in Chicopee. Carl and Bunny were, for the most part, unconcerned though Carl "never liked that sleeping over at the rectory stuff." He remained silent because "the kids never complained." They accompanied Lavigne on day trips and overnights all over New England. There were weekends at Ashfield, visits with his doctor and priest friends in Vermont, and visits to the doctor's lavish Goshen lake house. They camped at Boy Scout reservations and visited his favorite fishing holes, one a secluded spot near some abandoned paper mills on the Swift River in Palmer and another under a bridge over the Chicopee River, not far from his parents' house. He took Joseph and Danny to both multiple times. During one visit, Joseph was surprised when Lavigne's priest pals showed up.[34]

There were some odd signals, but they were dismissed or went unnoticed. When 14-year-old Joseph returned home drunk from an overnight at Lavigne's family home, Carl was told he got into a liquor cabinet. He reprimanded Joseph, despite Lavigne's reassurances that he was "a good kid. It was just a simple mistake. Don't be mad at him."[35] Lavigne called each boy at least once a week if he did not see him at church or around the neighborhood. Only Gregory never took to Lavigne. He never liked him.

After Danny became an altar boy, Lavigne spent less time with the brothers and more with Danny. Danny was soon around the church, and Lavigne, constantly. He was "always with Danny," a friend said. "Danny would get off the bus and run right over to the rectory, every day." They were together every Friday and Saturday night, and Danny served every Sunday Mass with Lavigne. Lavigne picked Danny up at school two or three times a month and saw him three times a week during vacations. The two were inseparable. Carl later said, "There were times we didn't know Danny was with Father Lavigne until Father would call us and tell us he was with him and wanted to keep him overnight."[36]

Lavigne's months at St. Catherine's were increasingly tumultuous. The number of parishioners replacing esteem with unease grew steadily, particularly among the older crowd, and, of course, Griffin. In less than a year, his personal dislike of Lavigne's demeanor and politics escalated to deep enmity. Griffin finally pushed Weldon to transfer Lavigne, and he was sent to St. Mary's, a larger parish on Page Boulevard a few miles distant. Most assumed the June 29, 1968, relocation was due to conflicts with Griffin, but rumors flew that the pastor was more concerned about Lavigne's interest in children, and there were rumblings he was gone because Griffin believed him to be gay.[37]

3

Death

The four years since Lavigne left St. Catherine's passed unremark-
ably for the Croteaus. Carl worked his multiple jobs, Bunny ran the
house, the kids were kids. By 1972 Carl Jr., was almost 20; Gregory, 17;
Joseph, 16; Michael, 15; and the girls, 9 and 10. Danny turned 13 the previous November. He still shoveled snow for cookies and a little cash,
played neighborhood sports with his friends, did the Scouts, and fished
when he wasn't with Lavigne, which was almost always. Late that winter,
he was awarded a religious medal at school. Bunny used an inexpensive
tape recorder to chronicle his excitement. He was going to give the prize
away. "Father Lavigne will love it," he said cheerfully.[1]

The only real upheaval during those years took place in 1971 when
the neighborhood was besieged by a brash Peeping Tom. All year,
women's underwear was stolen from or rearranged on clotheslines at
night, and people saw a tall, bald man looking through windows at them.
Carl Jr. happened to look out the bathroom window one night and saw
the prowler staring back at him from the shadows. Three times residents
chased but never caught the mystery intruder. He once outran two high
school track stars to escape into the night.[2]

Lavigne arrived at St. Mary's in June 1968, with his customary
aplomb, entering a welcome banquet clad in old-style clerical garb, complete with antiquated bib and oversized Roman collar. The ensemble
was robin's egg blue. He still shed his collar except during Mass and was
again quickly embraced for updating music, ministering to the children,
and growing altar boy rolls. One, who later became a priest, described
him as "an awesome priest ... way ahead of Vatican II changes. He was
intelligent, artistic, presented tremendous homilies. He had a great rapport with people." He again let kids decorate the sanctuary and designed
large banners sewn by parish volunteers that hung above the altar. He

became part of his altar boys' lives. One with an interest in art was taught to paint and gifted with brushes, oils, and canvas. Another with an ear for music was introduced to the Baroque era and brought to Edward Street to listen to classical albums.[3]

Once again, his brashness and "being too modern" alienated older parishioners. They were also put off by his volatile side. Entering the packed church for a Sunday Mass, he suddenly stopped the procession and screamed at the organist that he did not like the music. He rudely shouted the name of another hymn.[4] He was still ignoring the diocesan seminary loans. After three years of dunning letters and polite requests he pay $17 a month, the exasperated chancery threatened to withhold $50 from his weekly pay.

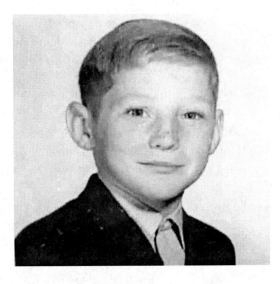

Danny, ca. 1967, during Lavigne's time at St. Catherine's (author's collection).

He still visited the Croteaus regularly, treated everyone to dinner, took the boys on day trips, and hosted overnights at the rectory. When he first moved, Danny and one of his brothers continued sleepovers, but by mid–1971, Danny was the only Croteau along for overnights, camping or fishing trips, or visits with Lavigne's Vermont pals.[5]

After school on Friday, April 7, Danny primped, dressing, according to Bunny, "better than he usually did [to go] going someplace with Father Lavigne." He donned a knit shirt, a tie, dress pants, and his favorite three-quarter-length, fur-collared herringbone jacket. The ensemble was usually reserved for Friday dances at Duggan. He called Lavigne a couple of times. Bunny did not "know if he contacted him, but he left." She heard nothing until midnight, when Lavigne called asking if Danny "could stay over" at his parents' house. As always, she agreed. When Danny returned the next morning at 9 o'clock, he did not explain how he got to and from Chicopee. Bunny assumed Lavigne and remembered Danny was listless and nauseous, "not saying too much. He just laid around for a while and complained about his stomach." During the day, he "vomited several times," but after dinner he said he was going to take the bus to the YMCA and left.[6]

The following week, Easter week in the Church, passed typically at Ferncliff. Danny was eager for the Saturday start of the fishing season. It rained all week, good for fishing. Thursday night and Friday morning, April 13–14, Springfield was deluged with more rain. Friday was an exciting day for Danny. The school week was ending, he said there was a Scout meeting to plan a Cape Cod trip and a Vermont trip everyone assumed was with Lavigne, and it was an "anything you want" dinner, but he was most excited about fishing. Carl said, "He bugged me all week about the opening of fishing season. He couldn't wait."[7]

An OLSH nun noticed Danny didn't take the bus home that Friday, hitchhiking instead. At 2:50, he was seen by David Richards a mile south of school at Breckwood Boulevard and Wilbraham Road, near Western New England College, headed in the direction of Ferncliff. At 3 o'clock, Liz Pacosa saw him half a mile closer to home being picked up by Joy Rochford, coincidently a fifth-grade OLSH teacher. Ten minutes later, she dropped him off at the end of his street. Carl was leaving for work, and at 3:15, he stopped and told Danny to head home and help Bunny with a rug he found for the back-porch sunroom. He said, "Sure, Dad" and bounded toward the house as Carl drove away.[8]

Danny helped with the rug and ran outside to join a kickball game. His mother, noticing his school uniform under his jacket, yelled for him to change into play clothes. He stuffed his tie in his coat pocket, changed into a tee shirt, dark corduroys and his high-tops, and then he ran back outside just after 4 o'clock. Bunny assumed he would head from there to the Scout meeting, but when he left the game, he said he was going to a party. Down the street, he ran into neighborhood paperboy Allan Moore and joined him on his rounds. About 4:30, they were seen walking down Kane Street, toward Parker Street and Greenleaf Park. Fifteen minutes later Mark Robitaille saw him in front of the barber shop next to Acre Drug "in a hurry to go somewhere." He was reportedly also seen outside Giovanni's Pizza.[9]

Most of what Danny did after 4:30 is a frustrating mystery, where he was and with whom. Neighborhood friend Tom Cote told Carl Jr. he saw him in the A&P at 7:30. If the memory is accurate, Cote was the last person to see Danny alive.[10]

Carl returned from work at 8:30. Danny had not returned from the Scout meeting Bunny thought he was attending and she began calling his friends. Worry grew as one after another said they had not seen him since he left the neighborhood. Perhaps because he talked all week about fishing early Saturday, Bunny's first thought was "water." She could not shake the thought he was somewhere in water. No fishing gear was missing, but Carl checked nearby ponds and streams anyway. Bunny kept making calls. Worry became concern. At 9 o'clock she called Danny's Scoutmaster, Edward F. Veroneau. She was surprised to learn there was no meeting that night. At 10:30, she called Lavigne at St. Mary's, said Danny "hadn't arrived home, and asked if he had heard or had seen him." He said he had not. Concern was now fear.[11]

Carl returned from a second fruitless search just after 11 o'clock, as Lavigne called asking if Danny turned up. When Carl answered, "No," there was prolonged silence. At 11:15, Carl and Bunny called Springfield police to report Danny missing, but they refused to take a report until he was missing 12 hours. Bunny yelled into the phone, "But he's only a kid!" Lavigne called around midnight, suggesting they call Chicopee police. The report was not filed until 2:11 a.m.[12] Carl and Bunny did not sleep. They spent the night mostly in silence, sitting in the kitchen and praying. They were still awake when Saturday dawned cloudless and sunny.

Still clinging to hope Danny stayed out all night to get an early start fishing, at 7:30, Carl made another search. By mid-morning, the neighborhood knew Danny was missing. Parents made calls, kids took to their bikes. Around 9 o'clock, Danny's brother Joseph gathered three pals to bike the six miles to the spot where he and Danny fished with Lavigne underneath the bridge. After the hour-long ride, they found the dirt road from East Main down to the river cluttered with fire trucks, ambulances, and a dozen police cars. They were turned away and headed back home.[13]

The riverbank was indeed chaotic, with over a dozen policemen, firefighters, and EMTs tramping around. Chicopee Police Department patrolman Burl Howard was the first to respond to Raphael Herrera's panicked call about a body in the river. Fellow patrolman John Ramos and lead detective Lt. Frank Stec arrived a few minutes later, along with detective Sgt. Paul F. Balthazar, Capt. Edward Rajowski, Lt. Edmund Radwanski, and Lt. Francis Saccavino, the department photographer. They were followed by medical examiner Dr. Edward Kraus. Following protocol, Chicopee called state police investigators assigned to D.A. Ryan's office. They were required by statute to examine any unattended death.

Police combed under the bridge and along the river while Kraus had the body removed from the water and performed an initial examination. The victim looked to be in his early teens, about five and a half feet tall, and he was wearing blue corduroy trousers, a wide brown leather belt, a white tee shirt, blue socks, and tan suede ankle boots with white soles. He also wore a short, zippered, tan suede jacket. An eight-inch by six-and-a-half-inch scrap around the left pocket was missing, evidently ripped off during a struggle. There was also a long, jagged tear on the left sleeve near the cuff. The boy's clothes were stained with blood.[14]

He had been badly beaten, covered with horrific head wounds. The right side of his head and face was a patchwork of grizzly gashes and indentations, and his jaw was broken below his mouth. Krause ordered the body taken to the Cerpiel Funeral Home, an old Chicopee mortuary a mile away. Some investigators thought the body was in the water for only a few hours, but most believed it was there all night. Inside a jacket pocket, police found a small wooden box containing a student dissecting kit, a blue necktie patterned with the initials "OLSH," and a crumpled yellow test paper. Carefully written on top was "Daniel Croteau, Grade 7, Our Lady of Sacred Heart School."[15] Principal Sister Helen Elizabeth confirmed he was a student who lived at 106 Fern-cliff Avenue in Sixteen Acres with his parents and six siblings. Ferncliff was five miles and three neighborhoods—Sixteen Acres, Pine Point, and Indian Orchard—from the bridge. They learned his parents filed a missing persons report that morning.

The Chicopee contingent, led by Stec and Radwanski, was joined by D.A. Ryan's detectives under Lt. James Fitzgibbon. "Fitzy" (or "Fitter") was the 48-year-old son of a policeman, respected for his tenacity and instincts. With him were Lt. Thomas Gilmartin and Det. James Mitchell. At that moment, the investigation became muddled by an unresolvable problem: an unyielding jurisdictional dispute between Chicopee and D.A. investigators. Locals were required to inform state police, but unless the crime involved a high-profile victim or unusual circumstances, authority was almost always ceded to local law enforce-

Long since overgrown by vegetation, when Danny was killed in 1972, a gravel road led a quarter of a mile from the street along the row of bridge pilings, ending just before the riverbank (author's collection).

ment. In this case, there should have been less interest because it was an unremarkable death and an early morning weekend call. The most experienced state investigators and sophisticated equipment were 90 miles away near Boston in Framingham. Adding to the tangle, the Springfield contingent was beholden to Ryan, not Framingham. He paid for their operation and provided office space and facilities inside his own. Investigations were poisoned because the D.A. agenda was often at odds with Framingham, and, most important, local departments.

Mutual mistrust further eroded the situation. Chicopee police bristled at presumptuous D.A. detectives poaching cases rightfully theirs, ignorant of local influences. D.A. police thought Chicopee isolated and unsophisticated, ill suited for tough cases. Chicopee and Springfield were both cosseted cultures. Like Springfield, Chicopee's working-class facade concealed a crooked reality. Chicopee was long known as one of the most corrupt cities in the state. Patronage ruled. No city job or contract was awarded without a clandestine meeting in a darkened restaurant or bar, during which a cash-stuffed envelope changed hands. There was a "fire department" café, a "police department" bar, a drop spot for every department where deals were closed. Every department had a "guy" who made the deals, took the envelopes,

Danny's killer parked to the right of the pilings, under the bridge, the site of the initial beating (author's collection).

even arranged for employees to take Civil Service exams for paying applicants. Such was the lens through which D.A. people viewed their Chicopee counterparts and vice versa.

Chicopee took umbrage when state police, no matter how infrequent, meddled in *their* investigations. The passive-aggressive squabbling arose that Saturday after Ryan's people unexpectedly took over the case. Everything eventually went off the rails, as the infighting led to petty feuds. The lack of cooperation resulted in little intelligence or forensic sharing. Information was retained, including leads, investigation and crime scene details, even potentially explosive evidence.[16] The impact was heightened because the crime scene work had to be completed quickly. It poured most of Thursday into Friday—an inch of rain—and more was expected later Saturday. If an April shower blew through Springfield, evidence would be lost. Egocentric behaviors on both sides, conflicting territorial ideologies, and the absence of clear crime scene command and control torpedoed the investigation almost as soon as it commenced.

Blood spatter in two locations showed that Danny, at least briefly, fought for his life.[17] The first, under the bridge 16 feet from one of two large support pilings, was marked by a 12-inch by 6-inch pool of blood surrounded by marks indicating a scuffle. Marks in the dirt indicated the body was then dragged, feet-first, 83 feet to the water's edge, where a second beating occured. Incapacitated at the original spot, Danny may have been near death before the second, more frenzied beating. The overkill pointed to a rage-driven assault.

The most gruesome injuries were inflicted at the river, judging by the substantial blood spray. There was a large pool of blood where the drag marks ended, and blood splashed over a 15-foot arc. Blood saturated the grass and dirt, and, near the body, blood was found on a 20-inch-long piece of rope with a frayed end and a crumpled plastic straw. A fist-sized rock, covered with blood and clumps of hair, lay six feet from the water. All the blood was spilled during the attack. Any blood that may have been there before the beatings was washed away by the rain. A few feet away from the pool of blood under the bridge, a set of fresh tire marks indicated someone parked under the bridge, backed out, and sped off. That scenario was supported by Roland Lacroix, a local who

Danny's battered body was found floating in the shallow water about five feet off the riverbank near the fallen trees visible in the background. The dirt and weeds were covered with blood spatter filling a 15-foot circle (author's collection).

saw a car "speed" down toward the river and turn off its headlights at 7:30 the night before.[18]

Horrible mishandling of the killer's tire prints was the first of many disastrous mistakes. When state police took over, Chicopee investigators were preparing half a dozen casts under the bridge. The process is done to exacting standards and varies only by medium, whether moist or dry soil, sand, mud, and so on. The impression is filled with a specified mix of water and plaster, left to harden for an hour, then dried in a lab for 48 hours. The first, most fundamental problem was that the castings were being produced by a Chicopee patrolman with little experience in the process, assisted by a police photographer with none. Most of their moldings were useless, "indistinct and partially obliterated," but one, a full tread near the blood pool, was perfectly detailed. After Chicopee ceded the case to state, the unusable impressions were removed, but the pristine imprint somehow was not. State police said a

The view from the killer's parking spot. Danny was dragged 83 feet from near the piling on the right to the riverbank just past the two tall tree trunks, where he was beaten further and thrown into the river (author's collection).

downpour Saturday evening ruined it, a claim that was later questioned. The substandard castings were only able to confirm the tread was a standard, with five ⅛-inch grooves three quarters of an inch apart, a common pattern used on every Ford. The unclear castings could never be used to match a specific car, much less a single Ford from thousands in western Massachusetts.[19]

Problems caused by jurisdictional issues were not limited to the crime scene. A trove of physical evidence was photographed, cataloged, and collected, including the bloody rope and straw, the torn jacket pocket, a Certs gum wrapper, a stained piece of paper, a stained newspaper, multiple stones, and, most critical, the bloody rock with hair.[20] Much of it, including the rock, was removed by state police and never seen again.

After obtaining Danny's information from Sister Helen, Chicopee police called the Croteaus at 10:30 and asked Bunny to call Carl and await the arrival of a patrol car. At 11:00, Lt. Keith Lemay and Det. Christopher Minnie arrived just as Carl returned home. Lemay said, "Danny's been in some trouble." Carl thought Danny had been picked up for doing something wrong. "No," Lemay quietly answered, "it's worse than that. Your son is dead. We found him murdered and floating in the Chicopee River." When the policemen and a shaken Carl entered the house, Bunny instantly knew Danny was dead. Knees buckling, she collapsed in Carl's arms, sobbing. Carl agreed to accompany the officers to police headquarters. The three bundled into the cruiser and left, passing Joseph and his pals as they returned from their trek to the river. Neighborhood friend David O'Keefe stopped Joseph down the street and breathlessly exclaimed, "Joe, your brother's dead!" He raced to the house, which was already filling with people.[21]

At Carl's request, they stopped at St. Mary's, which is barely half a mile from the bridge. Carl blurted out, "They found Danny murdered." Lavigne asked, "Do you want me to come along?" Carl was thankful for the company. At the station, detectives quizzed Carl, hoping for direction. Lavigne sat to the side, listening quietly, offering nothing. When Carl was asked to identify Danny's body, Lavigne interrupted, "No, no, no—let him stay here. I'll identify the body." Carl was even more grateful for his presence. Lavigne was taken to Cerpiel Funeral Home, where he confirmed the battered body was indeed Danny's. The autopsy then commenced.

Later that day, Lavigne solemnly advised Carl and Bunny to keep Danny's casket closed. They wanted it open, to see their son again, but he insisted, "You don't want to see Danny like that."[22]

Jurisdiction challenges also affected the autopsy. Small towns did not have their own medical examiner, so autopsies were performed by local doctors with little, if any, forensic training. The only appointed M.E.s were state medical examiners in Framingham, one of whom would have performed the autopsy if the murder occurred nearer Boston. Also, local autopsies were not undertaken in sterile laboratory environments. Danny's took place on a funeral home embalming table, certainly not an optimal location, with only basic tools and rudimentary measurement devices available. Dr. Kraus began at 1:30, assisted by Dr. George Katsas, a pathologist with the medical examiner's office in Boston. Fitzgibbon, Radwanski, and Saccavino attended, the latter photographing the proceedings.

The time of death could be established only as sometime between "last time the victim was seen alive 4:40 p.m. April 14 and 8:25 a.m. April 15." Privately, investigators believed the murder took place beween 8 and 8:30 Friday evening, a conclusion supported by Roland Lacroix's statement. The cause of death was summarized: "Daniel Croteau came to his death as the result of multiple blunt injuries of the head with fractures of the skull and laceration of the brain. Homicide."[23] He was brutally beaten to death, killed by multiple savage blows to the head. Murdered.

Both sides of the face above the mouth were a latticework of abrasions. There were multiple lacerations on the right side of the head; one cut was three inches behind his ear, two deep ones on the side of the eyebrow, one on the cheek an inch from his mouth, and another at the corner of the jaw. A massive skull fracture behind the ear drove pieces of splintered bone into the brain—by itself, a likely fatal blow. There were severe lacerations on the front, side, and back of the brain. Investigators decided the location of the wounds suggested a left-handed killer, attacking from the front. Danny's jaw was split in half, just to the right of the tip of the chin. Considerable force was required to inflict this injury. Fractures of this degree more often result from high-impact events like car accidents or plane crashes. There was blood in both ears, mouth, and nose, and blood had run down the throat into the lungs.

A secondary cause of death was mentioned, but, curiously, described in less detail, only as "blunt injury to the neck." There were ligature marks and multiple hemorrhages on the neck, most on the right side. Both eyelids, but particularly the right, were covered with petechial hemorrhages, pinpoint red marks that indicate asphyxia. Danny had been strangled. The concentration of petechiae on the right eyelid seemed to buttress the left-handed killer theory.

The combination of the brutality of the crime and the frenzied two-location attack, led investigator and profiler R.C. Stevens to describe a killer "seething with anger. The true murder weapon we see is blind rage ... uncontrollable rage and anger." Stevens believed the killer "lost control"; and that the crime may have been "impulsive."[24]

Danny's blood alcohol level was .18 percent, almost double the 1972 legal limit, over twice today's.[25] Those levels in a child his size indicated he was *very* drunk. And, oddly, in his stomach were multiple wads of chewed gum. Even so, investigators apparently did not look more closely at the Certs gum wrapper found near the body. Pubic hairs and red fibers were found on his underwear, the fibers all over his socks as well. Before he was killed, Danny was walking around shoeless.

Blood at the scene was Danny's type, O, but on the straw and rope, type B. Heavy rainfall cleaned the scene the day before, so that blood was also shed during the beating. Assailants commonly drip blood from injuries sustained during an attack of this severity, so the type B blood was likely the killer's.[26] One investigator theorized it may have come from a fisherman who cut himself, but the rainfall would have washed it away, if that was the case. Finding a suspect with type B blood would not make a case airtight. More than 12 percent of Caucasians have that blood type.

It is the unfortunate truth that the work at the scene was borderline shoddy in numerous respects. Overall, the available tools were less sophisticated than we have today. There were no dedicated evidence vans or specially-trained technicians or forensic specialists. Guidelines for collecting evidence and maintaining custodial integrity were much less clearly defined. But beyond that, though, blunders plagued every aspect of the work. The tire impressions were made by two men insufficiently experienced in the process. Investigators failed to consider that a piece of stonework from the concrete bridge piling may have been a weapon. One such remnant, mentioned in the original evidence inventory, was among several crucial items that were lost. Instantly settling on a left-handed killer was also a mistake.

The autopsy was also troublesome. Danny's strangulation injuries were described in much less detail than warranted. If his killer had a strong enough hold on his throat, he could have been rendered unconscious in as few as ten seconds. Better-described injuries would have made it easier to determine the killer's general body type. Absent accurate information, a re-creation, even a precise determination of the manner of death, were significantly more difficult.[27] Amidst the confusion, Danny's body was released to Ratliff Funeral Home in Indian Orchard.

Some of Danny's friends spent Saturday fishing, learning of his death when his picture appeared on the front page of the Sunday *Republican* under the headline "Boy, 13, Found Slain in Chicopee River." That morning, Mrs. Mary Bobek called Chicopee police. Her tidy bungalow at 675 Granby Road was five miles from Ferncliff, but barely one from the bridge. Until she saw Danny's picture, she paid little attention to an encounter the previous week. In 1992, she signed a statement outlining an event she first described during that 1972 call. Those records were, not surprisingly, lost. The investigation surely would have taken different directions if yet another mistake had been avoided.[28]

Bobek recalled the night of April 7 as bitterly cold and windy. At 10:30, she answered a knock on her front door to find a shivering boy she did not know. He "was very polite," she remembered, and said he was lost "and asked me if he could use the phone to call Father Lavigne." It is strange Danny claimed to be lost. His grandfather lived on Granby Street and Bobek's house was only half a mile from Lavigne's Edward Street house he visited many times. Danny called the St. Mary's rectory, then Edward Street. He asked, "Is Father Lavigne there?" but Bobek did not hear the rest of the brief conversation. She was leaving for work and offered Danny a ride, but he thanked her and waited outside because "Father would be right there." Just minutes later, a late model red Mustang pulled up, and Danny and the car drove off into the night. She identified Danny's herringbone jacket as the coat he was wearing.[29]

At 4:30 Sunday, Lt. Radwanski returned to the scene and happened upon Lavigne walking along the riverbank, staring into the water. Knowing his closeness to the Croteaus, Radwanski didn't make much of it. Perhaps he was "blessing the scene," he thought. Then he remembered

Friday night a week before his death, Danny showed up at Mary Bobek's front door, cold and shivering, asking if he could use her phone to call Lavigne (author's collection).

the Bobek call. He offhandedly asked if they could meet and Lavigne agreed to come to the station the next day.[30]

Lavigne's comments during the Monday morning chat raised immediate red flags for Radwanski. Lavigne claimed he first spoke with Danny earlier Friday, before a Scout meeting. Radwanski knew from Bunny and Veroneau no meeting was scheduled. Asked about Bobek's report, Lavigne said Danny called earlier that day asking to visit and discuss the Vermont trip. Lavigne said he instructed him not to come and claimed surprise when Danny later called. He made a point of saying Danny hitchhiked there, that he habitually did so all over Springfield. Then he said he picked Danny up at 7:30. Radwanski blinked. Bobek was certain it was 10:30. She left after the Mustang departed and was at work by 11 o'clock.

Lavigne said they went to Edward Street and he called Bunny to tell her Danny was spending the night. He said he went upstairs to bed, leaving Danny watching television in the basement. The next morning, the 8th, he fed Danny breakfast, drove him to the neighborhood, and left him at the corner. He claimed they did not speak at all the following week, that he next saw Danny when he identified his body at the funeral home. The claim that he took Danny to Edward St. concerned Radwanski. On Saturday, Lavigne said he was never alone with Danny, that they were only ever together "with his brothers or a gang of kids."[31] Radwanski became more suspicious.

Lavigne said he spent the night of the murder with his parents. They ate dinner between 5:30 and 6:15, then his father went to the Elks Club and he "did some errands" with his mother. She confirmed they purchased a bed at the Charlestown Antique Shop in Holyoke and mentioned a visit to another, unidentified store. Lavigne was strangely unsure about the time of either stop, but he was certain they returned by 8:30. He said Bunny called looking for Danny about 10 o'clock. That he was there to take the call seemed to support his timeline, but Radwanski remembered Bunny said she called Lavigne at the rectory. He said he was in bed by 10:30, awakened when his father returned from "the Elks Club about 3:00 a.m." Lavigne failed to mention his 11:30 call to the Croteaus, one Radwanski was aware of. Lavigne said he went to Holyoke the next morning at 7:30 to pick up the bed and he was home when police arrived with Carl at 11:30.[32]

Nothing was adding up to Radwanski, now with more questions than answers, and growing certainty Lavigne lied about his Friday travels. Statement Content Analysis (SCAN), a technique widely accepted as an accurate indicator of deception, supports his doubts. SCAN is the analysis of structure and content to detect whether information is truthful or intentionally incomplete, therefore deceptive.[33] Such an analysis indicates Lavigne was being deceptive about something. Not specifically that he killed Danny, but *something*. First, he offered specific times for dinner, when they sat down and when they finished, but he was unusually vague about the time of the shopping trips and the timing and number of his conversations with the Croteaus. Those types of vagaries display subconscious attempts to create or solidify an alibi, even when none is required. His arbitrary comment about his father's return from the Elks Club, offering too-specific information when none was required, is commonly accepted as indicating false alibi creation. Most revealing to Radwanski, though, was that the times and details about which Lavigne was most vague corresponded exactly to the time of the murder.

Still mulling over the inconsistencies, Radwanski was astonished when Lavigne asked, "In such a popular hangout with so many cars and footprints, how can the prints you have be of any help?" More dumbfounding, he then asked, "If a stone was used and thrown in the river, would the blood still be on it?" The detective had to hide his shock. Neither of those details had been divulged. When Lavigne then refused to offer a blood sample after learning some blood from the scene was type B—his own—Radwanski knew something was amiss.[34] Lavigne seemed oblivious that he had clumsily thrust himself into the investigation by his own statements. He did agree to take a polygraph test May 4.

Investigators were initially optimistic about a fast resolution. The victim was quickly identified. The murder weapon was retrieved, or should have been. Substantial blood and physical evidence was recovered. They had a tire impression from the killer's car, or, again, should have, and they had a strong suspect with ties to the victim and a questionable alibi. That confidence would fade quickly.

Danny was waked Monday. People began arriving at Ferncliff early, and by noon, the little house was packed. Bunny's sister Betty flew in from California and was met at the door by Lavigne. He took her aside and said it was important she convince Carl and Bunny to keep the casket closed. He said Bunny should not see his badly disfigured face. Betty did as she was instructed. The coffin was closed. Lavigne unexpectedly left shortly after.

Between 1 and 1:30, Carl Jr. answered the phone in the kitchen. He said, "Hello," and after a long, silent pause, said it again. A familiar voice said, "We're sorry for what happened to Danny. He saw something behind the Circle he shouldn't have seen. It was an accident." Carl Jr. stammered, "Who is this?" two or three times. The line went dead as his father approached. Seeing his son's distress, he rested a hand on his shoulder and asked, "Who is it?" The teen stuttered a summary of the conversation, to which Carl replied, "Take it easy. If another call comes in, just take it easy and keep them on the phone as long as you can." Carl, rattled by nerves and commotion, was certain he "recognized [the voice] but could not immediately associate it with a face."[35] He went downstairs to change clothes, wracking his brain trying to recall the familiar voice.

The Croteaus were surprised Lavigne left the house so quickly that morning, doubly so when he ducked the wake altogether. The only clergy there were Pastor Griffin and a sandal-clad friar in a brown robe. Oddly, he stood by the casket, weeping loudly. His distraught presence did not go unnoticed. Bunny recalled, "It was just so odd, because we didn't know this priest, and no one else seemed to know him." Carl added, "I remember Father Griffin being very heavy hearted during the wake and saying very little … [while a friar,] none of our family had

Danny's last school picture stood in a black frame on top of his closed casket (courtesy Joseph Croteau).

ever met, and who had no official function at either St. Catherine's or St. Mary's, cried a lot. This puzzled us because we didn't know him at all."[36] Det. Mitchell, monitoring the service, found "Father Barnabas" scrawled in shaky handwriting in the condolence book.

The next morning at 9 o'clock, about the time Danny's funeral Mass was just getting underway, led by Lavigne, Chicopee turned its evidence over to the state police. During the service, investigators checked tire treads against those from the scene. They noted the plate numbers of ten cars with similar patterns.[37] Danny was buried in Hillcrest Park Cemetery, barely a mile from home. The picturesque acreage is dotted with ponds and large, hundred-year-old trees. His plot was underneath a sprawling New England elm, not far from a pond Danny once fished. Lavigne joined the mourners back at Ferncliff, but stood off to the side for barely an hour before leaving. He did speak to Carl and Bunny. That was the last time they ever saw him.

Danny's murder had a chilling effect on the neighborhood. Chil-

Danny's marker at Hillcrest Park Cemetery. He is buried next to his brother Michael (author's collection).

dren were no longer allowed unfettered access outside. The loosely-observed "Home when streetlights come on" rule was now strictly enforced. Anyone driving by was studied. James Coleman offered a $100 reward for information. No one came forward.[38]

With few solid leads beyond Lavigne, investigators reached out to the public. That week, papers relayed appeals under headlines like "Police Appeal for Public Aid in Boy's Death" and "Public Asked for Help in Death of Boy."[39] Hundreds of leads were chased down, no matter how trivial or bizarre. An astrologer offered help. A woman said she resurrected murder images through hypnosis. Everyone had a Danny story. He was with a "hippie" in a Chicopee convenience store. A friend of Carl's said Danny "was picked up by a queer in a blue car about a week earlier." Bunny heard from her brother-in-law, who heard from a postal clerk, who heard from his son that he was with Danny at Western New England College at 5 o'clock Friday. The boy identified Danny's herringbone jacket, but police discounted the story.[40]

Anyone acquainted with Danny, even slightly, was interviewed—school, church and neighborhood friends, his teachers, even his boxing coach. A family friend was investigated after he appeared at the funeral with fresh scratches on his face. Scoutmaster Ed Veroneau, whom Carl described as "an oddball," and Veroneau's assistant, best friend, and business partner Richard ("Dick") Brown—who lived a block from Danny— were mentioned by the neighborhood kids. They said both were "very, very weird" and assumed to be child molesters. Veroneau was quickly cleared without anyone realizing he was already known to Springfield police and the Hamden County sheriff. Brown was not looked into at all.[41]

Edward Veroneau, Danny's Scoutmaster at Cathedral High School in 1964 (courtesy Brian Fitzgerald).

The boys were all interrogated as well, aggressively, for some reason. Joseph was called out of class at OLSH and taken to an empty classroom with all the desks pushed to the sides and a solitary chair in the middle of the room. He was grilled for more than an hour by three detectives.[42]

Investigators were discovering a different Danny than the innocent altar boy they thought they knew. The new Danny hitchhiked everywhere, smoked, drank, was a dedicated schoolyard fighter, close to the Circle, and a chronic shoplifter. He had suspicious friends. There was the man in the blue car with "goodies,"

Assistant Scoutmaster Richard (Dick) Brown at Springfield Technical High School in 1965. He was Veroneau's best friend and lived four houses from Danny (courtesy Brian Fitzgerald).

another in a tan car with porn, and an older friend at the A&P paying Danny to paint his bedroom. Danny got liquor and marijuana from these men. He was reportedly involved in a $400 drug deal, a huge amount for any Croteau to be handling, and he had a Satanic Bible and said he attended "Black Masses" with friends of both sexes including his cousins.[43]

A contrary vision of the family's devoted priest was likewise emerging. The day after the funeral, Fitzgibbon—already fixated on the murder—dropped by Ferncliff to offer his sympathies and chat. He first asked Carl and Bunny why they kept the casket closed. They relayed Betty's story of Lavigne's depiction of Danny's injuries. Fitzgibbon said nothing, but knew the worst wounds—on the side and back of his head—could have been concealed and the broken jaw was not outwardly visible. He then sat in a bedroom with each boy and was shocked to learn Lavigne abused them all, for years. Joseph was the first to tearfully admit to being a victim, followed by Carl Jr. and Gregory. When Fitzgibbon relayed this information to Carl and Bunny, they refused to believe him or their sons. The thought was so anathema, they could not speak to the boys about it. In fact, they never did. They did start reconsidering the thousands of little moments with Lavigne, though.[44]

Det. Mitchell discovered the mysterious "Father Barnabas" was Barnabas Keck, a Capuchin Franciscan friar and chapel assistant at St. Francis of Assisi Center and Chapel downtown. Born in Valley Stream, New York, in 1924, he attended St. Mary Seminary in Garrison, New York, entered the Capuchins in 1943, was ordained in 1951, and worked in Massachusetts, New York, and Connecticut.[45] Mitchell met the friar in his

Capuchin Franciscan Friar Barnabas Keck, a mysterious player in the Danny murder saga, came under suspicion due to his bizarre behavior during Danny's wake (author's collection).

tiny chapel office. The only thing on the walls was a cork bulletin board with a solitary item tacked on it, a newspaper story about the murder. Mitchell asked, "Why did you go to the wake, Father? Do you know the family?" The priest replied, "No," and the detective inquired, "Do you always go to the wakes of people you don't know?" Again, the priest said, "No," but added the murder so moved him, he wanted to pay his respects. The detective did not suspect Keck was involved, but he said to his partner, "Fitzy, there's something very peculiar over there."

Chicopee police visited Lavigne at Edward Street to discuss Father Barnabas' strange comments to Fitzgibbon. They saw two bath towels with large brown-orange stains that appeared to be blood. After a brief interview, they left with the towels.

Investigators were hearing more and more stories about Lavigne abusing boys. On April 30, a high schooler described multiple overnight stays at St. Mary's rectory. He said Lavigne gave him alcohol and fondled him. Most surprising, he said after one overnight, Lavigne forced him to go to confession and brought him to the St. Francis Chapel. Father Barnabas was Lavigne's confessor. Fitzgibbon understood priest-penitent confidentiality rules kept those conversations private, but still, it was an enormous coincidence.[46]

About the same time, Bunny answered the phone and heard a familiar voice. She was stunned when Lavigne said he "would not be contacting them any further in light of the circumstances." Neither she nor Carl recognized what those "circumstances" were, because they did not yet know Lavigne was a suspect. She remembered, "He just said we shouldn't talk again, and that was it. He never said he didn't do it. He was our friend, and that's all he had to say?"[47]

Perhaps realizing he was on police radar, Lavigne became increasingly erratic. Sandra and André Tessier, St. Mary's parishioners with whom he was friendly, witnessed several bewildering incidents. The day Danny died, Sandra's mother passed away in California. Four days later, she and André returned from the funeral, unaware of the murder. As they unpacked at 1 a.m., Lavigne knocked on their door. He blurted out, "Danny Croteau was murdered. I had to identify his body." They were saddened because they were close to Carl and Bunny, but speechless when Lavigne complained at length about everything *he* had to do after Danny died. "It was all about him," Sandra said, "like Danny being dead was not important."[48]

The second incident, a week later, was more bizarre. It began with a 3:30 a.m. call from Lavigne. He wanted to speak with Sandra right away and asked her to meet him at an International House of Pancakes on Boston Road. She was baffled by the request, but got dressed and drove to the restaurant. When she arrived shortly before 4 o'clock, he was ensconced in a back booth. He said to her, "I want to prove to you I didn't murder Danny Croteau." She stammered, "Father, why would I think that?" A large man in a blue windbreaker approached. She described him as "stocky, fleshy, way over six feet tall, who towered over us." The description is undoubtedly accurate. Her husband was a professional boxer. The man never introduced himself, but flashed a badge and said, "Fr. Lavigne had nothing to do with Danny's murder. A man driving a green truck killed Danny." Lavigne nervously interjected, "See, I told you I didn't do it." Still stunned, Tessier reassured him, "I never thought you *did*." The man and Lavigne "went on and on about the green truck, so I asked them, 'Did you tell the police about the truck?' The man said, 'I *am* the police. I'm a detective working on the case.'" He then abruptly left. Tessier was so rattled by the encounter she never thought to ask to see his badge, nor did she notice the car he drove. She and Lavigne left, he apparently confident she was convinced of his innocence, but she was having doubts: "as time went on, I kept thinking, he 'Doth protest too much.'"[49]

Lavigne's increasing instability was apparent to priests and friends he bombarded with calls, asking if they heard anything. One described a flurry during which "he was clearly looking for information about what was being said in Chicopee because we shared neighboring parishes." The friends "worried he was having a breakdown."[50]

A week later, police checked the tires on Lavigne's Mustang and his father's car. They said neither matched the tracks from the river, a claim later called into doubt. Bristling at the police attention, Lavigne stopped cooperating and hunkered down at Edward Street and St. Mary's rectory. When Fitzgibbon and another detective went to the latter to examine Lavigne's clothes from that weekend, "the priest who answered the door wouldn't let them in." They did not obtain a search warrant, a decision that would be regretted and questioned.[51]

Investigators were on a slippery slope dealing with the Church, but still extended surprisingly deferential treatment. It remains bewildering D.A. why Ryan never issued search warrants for Lavigne's home or rectory quarters. Mitchell later claimed there was insufficient evidence to obtain them, but Lavigne's contradictory statements, shaky alibi, odd questions, and abuse of the Croteau boys absolutely met any probable cause threshold. Detectives believed Ryan's refusal to obtain warrants was due to pressure from Weldon to move focus away from Lavigne.[52] In this instance, one of several, his curious decision gave the appearance of bowing to Church wishes.

On April 22, Fitzgibbon and a Chicopee detective visited the Croteaus to discuss the Circle phone call. They were speechless when Fitzgibbon asked if the mystery caller might have been Lavigne. At that instant Carl Jr., who had been unable to put a face to the voice, did so. Dumbfounded he had not realized it earlier, he said the voice was absolutely Lavigne's.

To that point, investigators had not divulged their suspicions about Lavigne, waiting for Carl and Bunny to recognize, on their own, what they believed. After Carl Jr.'s confirmation, Fitzgibbon said, "Father Lavigne did it. Carl, I'm telling you now, he's the one. I'm sure of it." Carl described the idea as "a knife in our heart." Bunny said, "It was very difficult to believe. He was like a member of the family." Carl later added, almost sadly, "The last thing you want to do is accuse somebody of murder. But you've got to listen to the people who investigate, and they were darn sure." Fitzgibbon reassured them, "Don't worry. We'll nail him." They went to Fitzgibbon's office and signed a murder complaint against Lavigne. A week later, Carl met his friend André Tessier at the Icelandic Club. Tessier described the two odd incidents with Lavigne, and Carl said he, and the police, thought Lavigne killed Danny. When Tessier asked him if he was sure, Carl said, "I have no doubt he killed Danny." Tessier went home and told his wife, "I don't want that man [Lavigne] to ever set foot in this house again."[53] Joseph would sign a sexual assault complaint in August. No one, outside of investigators and the Croteaus, was aware of the murder and sexual assault complaints.

On May 4, Lavigne entered a nondescript building on Boylston Street in Boston to take a polygraph exam. Unlike in television and movie depictions, the technology is about detecting basic deception versus confirming a specific lie. There are several methods, among them Voice Stress Analysis and the most frequently used test that monitors body functions like blood pressure, perspiration, breathing, heart rate, voice levels, and pulse. Responses to general questions with obvious truthful answers establish a baseline for each physiological function. Theoretically, a response to a specific question that prompts variations from those baselines, outside a predetermined range, indicates deception. The fluidity of those ranges is the first thorny issue with the science.[54]

The fundamental assumption that a body unconsciously betrays untruthfulness has been accepted for centuries, but never proven 100 percent accurate. For that reason, lie detector tests are almost never admitted as evidence in federal courts. First, measurements are impacted by environmental and physical factors like noise, embarrassment, anxiety, fear, even sexual excitement. Second, there are countermeasures that can be used to skew results, a fact borne out when CIA mole Aldrich Ames beat dozens of tests over decades. There are also problems with historically high false-positive results and significant error rates. In 2003, the National Academy of Sciences described evidence of polygraph accuracy as "scanty and scientifically weak." It is an inexact science that at best offers *indication* of deception at some level above simple chance, but nothing near confirmation. Certainty of a specific lie is simply not obtainable.[55]

Lavigne's test took about an hour. Witnesses included his attorney William C. Flanagan, two Chicopee policemen, and a Ryan investigator.[56] After answering baseline inquiries, Lavigne answered "No" to five questions:

- In April 1972, did you strike Danny Croteau's head to cause his death?
- Did you kill Danny Croteau?
- Were you present when Danny Croteau was killed?
- Did you dump Danny Croteau's body in the Chicopee River?
- Do you know who killed Danny Croteau?

The examiner concluded, "There were erratic and inconsistent responses" and he was therefore "unable to render a definite opinion as to the subject's truthfulness." Carl was later told the test somehow confirmed Lavigne "was a homosexual." The conclusion probably arose from responses in the pre-test interview or during baseline setting. Inconclusive results from a test administered by a police employee led Weldon to order Lavigne to sit for an independent examiner. Five days later, he sat for two sessions in the Chicago offices of John E. Reid and

Associates. Founded in 1947, it is perhaps the most respected interview science and interrogation company in the world. The "Reid Technique" and "Reid Technique of Interviewing and Interrogation" are the most widely used approaches to questioning in the world. The Reid examiner concluded, "There were no significant emotional disturbances indicative of deception on this subject's records on the [five] questions." His opinion was, "based on this subject's polygraph records, that he is telling the truth on the above listed questions."[57]

The Church was outwardly supportive of, and sympathetic to, the Croteaus. In June, St. Catherine's curate Father Leo E. O'Neil stopped by Ferncliff. He was a friend and frequent dinner guest who enjoyed in lengthy religious debates with Carl. That he was on the doorstep did not surprise. That he was "nervous and trembling [and] as white as a sheet" did. Carl said Lavigne molested his boys and others whose parents refused to come forward. Seeming nonplussed, O'Neil unexpectedly responded by asking Carl if he "thought Father Lavigne was capable of murder." Carl said, "Yes," and he described police suspicions Lavigne killed Danny. O'Neil "slumped in his chair." Carl became increasingly upset as the conversation continued. "At the time, it was all so unbelievable," he remembered. "We lost our son. One of our best friends is accused of his murder. It was just too much." Sensing Carl's impending breakdown, O'Neil proposed he "go out and get a couple of beers to calm down."[58]

A week later, O'Neil returned. Standing on the front steps, he stuffed a wad of cash into Carl's hand, more than $700 (perhaps $5,000, today). He said the Church was sending them to visit Bunny's sister in California. O'Neil said he and Pastor Griffin "thought it would be a good idea if they got away." Carl said, "We went to visit my wife's sister and went to Disneyland. Seven hundred dollars went a long way in 1972. I have no idea where they got the money."[59]

A month later, James Egan, senior partner in the diocese's law firm, knocked on the door. He asked Carl and Bunny, "What do you think of this? Is there anything you want?" Then he asked what "they wanted out of this." Carl, insulted, asked Egan, "What do you mean, what do we want?" After a few minutes of awkward silence, Egan said, "Well, if you decide you need something, let us know." He walked out. The Croteaus would not hear from the diocese ever again.[60]

Everything had become utterly bewildering. In the early days, Carl and Bunny could not grasp at all what happened to Danny or why. Neither could they initially accept the idea Lavigne was involved, even after learning he abused the boys, but during the following months, taking inventory of four years' worth of seemingly innocuous moments with Lavigne, the relationship came into specific relief, their original views upturned. Everything suddenly took a sinister pall. The attention. The financial help. The donated food. The clothes. The gifts. The interest in the boys. Especially that. All the time together. Rectory sleepovers. Overnight trips. The times they returned drunk or hungover. Then his advice to close the casket, absence from the wake, and quick exit after the funeral. Abruptly cutting off contact without ever "saying he didn't do it." The money from Father O'Neil and the odd visit from the Church lawyer seemed to confirm the grim realizations. It had all seemed innocent. Now, it was all disturbing. When Bunny finally accepted the reality, she obsessively tore through the house, "like a tornado," looking for photos that included Lavigne. She shredded the ones she found. She "didn't want any reminders of him."[61]

Carl came to believe Lavigne killed Danny because Danny "was going to squeal on him." Investigators listed the reasons for their belief in Lavigne's guilt in a later affidavit: "Unusual statements he made to investigators, the denial he and Danny were ever alone together, the telephone call to the Croteau home two days after the murder, the close relationship with Danny, the pattern of abuse similar to that of a Preferential Pedophile, familiarity with the crime scene, and the pattern of spending Friday nights together." Lavigne's guilt appeared evident, but the reality was there was no corroborating evidence, in part because people were surprisingly unforthcoming. The Church was clearly not.[62]

Neither were Danny's friends. For his part, Carl "had a gut feeling" the Circle had information about Danny's final hours they withheld. In 1976, neighborhood doctor Edwin T. Foster, known to all as "Doc," told Carl that one of Danny's closest friends knew something that was "eating him alive." Foster arranged for Carl and the boy to meet at his office, where he was asked if he knew anything. The boy "went ballistic" and screamed, "I'm not saying a thing! I'm not saying a thing! Leave me alone! I'm getting the hell out of here!" No one was talking.[63]

The case against Lavigne appeared to be, but was not, compelling. As a general rule, prosecutors need sufficient evidence to prove guilt beyond a reasonable doubt. What little remained that was mishandled left Ryan with a weak, entirely circumstantial case that never approached clearing that hurdle. Bizarre behavior and serial abuse do not prove guilt. Investigators complained, "There just wasn't enough evidence." In fact, there was none. They believed Lavigne and Danny were together that Friday, but they could never "put Danny with him." Lavigne could neither be placed at the scene, nor could he be tied to physical evidence recovered there. Even so, if Ryan was as convinced of Lavigne's guilt as he repeatedly claimed, he should have brought the evidence he *did* have before a grand jury. Short of that, he could have issued an indictment himself. It is hard to reconcile him doing *nothing*. Fitzgibbon suggested to Carl that if Lavigne were "an average guy who worked at the Bosch factory he would have been indicted and charged." That may have been true. It may not. It is important that Ryan recognized that no U.S. priest had ever been charged with murder.[64]

Ryan told the Associated Press he believed Lavigne was the killer, but there was no evidence to prove it. "I was upset about it," he said, "but I did what I had to do." Fitzgibbon promised Carl and Bunny he would "nail Lavigne," but the investigation fizzled out within six months. It was officially classified "inactive due to a lack of evidence" and a dozen boxes labeled "CROTEAU" were relegated to a musty evidence locker.[65] The murder, little known outside Springfield, faded from papers and memory. Quickly forgotten, it remained so for 20 years.

4

Contagion

By the early 1990s, the Church had become inundated by a priest sex abuse accusations. Since surfacing a decade earlier, the fallout had reached near-fatal proportions. Reams of bad press, more than 4,000 lawsuits, and thousands of settlements had already forced the sale of $250,000,000 of Church assets. But identifying a static "Ground Zero"—where and why the abuse began—is difficult. In 2002, the U.S. Conference of Catholic Bishops engaged John Jay College of Criminal Justice to analyze the nature and scope of the problem back to 1950. Results were updated in a second John Jay study begun in 2008. No attempt is made here to fully decipher thousands of data points or hundreds of pages of results from the studies (released in 2004 and 2010). Rather, a brief summary may explain the reason for the crisis and why it endured. The reports' conclusions are at once startling, disturbing, and illuminating.

The problem affected more than 95 percent of dioceses and approximately 60 percent of religious communities. From 1950 to 2002, almost 4,400 priests (4 percent of the total) were accused. Those numbers skyrocketed after 2002. The percentage of abusers among annual ordinations raised curious questions. Priests ordained in the 1940s–1950s made up 35 percent of abusers. Baby-boomer priests—ordained in the 1960s–1970s—made up almost 50 percent. Some blamed the 1960s sexual revolution. The most prolific Boston abuser said he abused because he was around children during "a time of sexual exploration." The 2010 update seemed to support the notion, suggesting 1960s–1970s increases were consistent with rises in other types of "deviant" behavior like drug use.[1]

Numbers were impossible to confirm. Victim estimates have run as high as 80,000–100,000, but the 2004 study identified only 10,667. Thirty-five percent of those came forward during the study's final months. A reasonable estimate is at least five times that. The incident totals, vastly under-reported historically, are equally impossible to quantify. Of the 10,667 incidents the study considered, 80.5 percent took place before 1985. A majority of those were reported in the two years just before the study was undertaken; only 810 were reported when they occurred. From the 1950s through the 1970s, a few dozen a year were reported. In the 1980s, hundreds were reported annually, and by the 1990s, thousands. Those numbers are also understated because tens—probably hundreds—of thousands of reports were passed on by clerics and buried in diocesan archives. The timing of the 4,400 reported incidents showed low numbers through the 1940s, a spike around 1950, steady increases through the 1960s–1970s, then another rise in the 1980s.

The number of serial abusers (accused of multiple incidents) was seriously skewed. Over half (56 percent) had a single allegation, but 25 percent of all accusations were against 149 priests who were responsible for 70 percent of the total.[2] Less than 8 percent of victims were threatened into abuse. Almost all abusers groomed and manipulated victims into compliance, using psychological exploitation and bribery. More than 40 percent used gifts, alcohol, or drugs.

Priests abused at a variety of locations. The majority—more than 40 percent—used rectories or their residences, 16 percent the church itself. Other popular settings were schools, cars, and vacation homes (10 percent each). Victims tended to be older. Through the 1980s, 4.5 percent were between one and seven; 20 percent between eight and ten; and 60 percent between 11 and 14. A small percentage were female. Girls made up about 50 percent of 1940s–1950s victims, but 30 percent by the 1960s, and well under 10 percent during the following decades. Perhaps counter-intuitive, abusers were not "dirty old men." They tended to be younger, more than 20 percent in their 20s, 23 percent in their 30s, and under 15 percent over 50.

The worst of the studies' notable flaws was that they were both funded by the U.S. Conference of Bishops. That influence bought some curious conclusions. For instance, the number of clergy classified pedophile was rendered meaningless by arbitrarily reducing the age of puberty from 14 to 10. Blame for a rise in abuse in the 1970s was laid on 1960s counterculture. The most jaundiced opinion, though, was the 2004 lead author's claim, "The abuse crisis is over." Most regrettable was the lack of consideration that the Church had any responsibility or that its indifference and secrecy played any part.[3]

For the Church, clerics abusing children is not a new problem. It has been an often-discussed issue for 1,600 years. A fourth-century Egyptian monk warned locals against bringing "young boys" to his abbey. Early saints Benedict and Basil, initiators of the monastic movement, forewarned the Church about liaisons between priests and "young men or boys." In his 1051 work *The Book of Gomorrah*, St. Peter Damian warned Pope Leo IX of the tide of "homosexual intercourse among clerics, and the abuse of boys." The first confirmed Church suppression occurred after a Piarist priest was accused in the 1630s. The order's founder Joseph Calasanctius commanded staff to "cover up this great shame in order that it not come to the notice of our superiors, otherwise our order ... would lose greatly." He became the church's patron saint of Christian schools.[4]

Secrecy and concealmennt remain official Vatican policy. The 1917 codified version of Church law decreed abuse criminal: "If clerics have committed an offense they shall be suspended, declared infamous, deprived of office, benefice, dignity, or position..." Even so, in 1922, the Vatican enacted the *Crimen Sollicititationis*—Latin for "Crime of Solicitation"—prohibiting even public *mention* of abuse. Accused priests were ordered immediately absolved and sent on a "pious pilgrimage" as penance, and the Crimen was ordered "diligently stored in the secret archives ... as strictly confidential." It was still in place when Pope John XXIII approved Alfredo Cardinal Ottaviani's 1962 update that was identical in content and replaced in 2001 by Pope John Paul II's *Sacramentorun Sanctitatis Tutela*. The *Tutela*, and several subsequent revisions, were basically unaltered versions of the original Crimen.[5]

The Vatican actually *required* local dioceses keep a clandestine repository for any allegations about priests "that might reflect poorly on legacy or memory," anything too scandalous for personnel files. Bishops must maintain actual, physical "Secret Archives" to which only they have access. Manchester, New Hampshire's were kept in a safe hidden in the bishop's office, and in Springfield, inside three locked cabinets in a vault buried in the regular archives. Secret archives contain files labeled "Unnatural Involvements" that run the gamut from alcoholism and drugs to pornography and pregnancies. Folders relating to sex abuse were headed "Unusual Patterns."[6] A Texas lawyer stumbled upon the damning—and detailed—reports in the mid–1990s. Since that time, the Church has settled virtually every suit.

Secret files are voluminous because priests are bound by canon law to a strictly enforced honor system. Any misdeed—even suspected or rumored, whether witnessed or overheard—must be passed up the chain. Father Thomas Doyle, a canon lawyer and secretary/canonist at the Vatican Embassy in Washington, D.C., studied thousands of abuse cases. He found that during the 1900s, virtually every instance witnessed or heard about by clerics was passed on. Those allegations never left the Church. In one extreme example from 1958, Davenport, Iowa, bishop Ralph L. Hayes forced his chancellor, Father Maurice Dingman, to swear on a Bible he would "maintain secrecy regarding all fact" concerning an accusation. Dingman was forced to sign a legal document confirming his promise.[7]

Strange dynamics drive the Church's 2,000-year obsession with protecting priests. First, bishops' most primary, defined directive is to "avoid scandal at all costs." Second, they are sworn to keep the "secrets of the Church." Third, the Church thinks itself a family that must be protected. When St. Catherine's pastor Griffin was asked if Lavigne would be punished, he was told no by Elliot Street, which said, "The family hasn't changed their position." A New Hampshire victim informed Manchester bishop Leo O'Neil a priest molested him and asked he be fired. O'Neil—who, as a curate, gave Carl $700 for a vacation a week after the murder—dismissively responded, "What do you want to do? Crucify this guy?" Bishops blindly adhere to Vatican posture rightly described as an addiction to a "narcotic of secrecy." Bishops reinforcing that culture essentially propelled the abuse problem.[8]

For the Church, above all is the mandate *"Outsiders, particularly police, must never be involved."* From 1940 to 2000, the Church involved police in less than 10 percent of incidents they confirmed. The adjusted number is less than 1 percent, because 95 percent of *that* 10 percent were reported after 1990. In 1963, after Fall River, Massachusetts bishop James Connolly received multiple reports about Father Edward O. Paquette, he penned a scathing letter ordering him to "vacate the rectory ... and leave the diocese" and warning "you are liable to prosecution." Rather than informing police, Connolly found Paquette a parish in Vermont.

There, after molesting two boys while giving them communion in their hospital beds in 1974, Paquette's pastor recommended Burlington bishop John A. Marshall—later Springfield's bishop—move "quickly, without fanfare and farewell parties and that it be publicly announced as a sick leave." Just four years later, after sending Paquette to a church treatment center, Marshall wrote the director, "Despite the demands of two sets of irate parents that 'something be done about this,' Father Paquette's pastor and I are determined to take the risk of leaving him in his present assignment. Our thinking is that, knowing the awareness of others, concerning his problem, Father Paquette will have reason for 'self-control.' Do you think that the danger of scandal is already too risky?"[9]

Even had Connolly involved police, legal repercussions were unlikely. In 1959, the Manchester, New Hampshire, police chief learned of allegations against Father Donald Osgood. He called Bishop Matthew F. Brady to assure him they would be buried. But the chief was concerned. He was about to retire, and "if a non–Catholic comes in as chief, the whole thing might blow sky high." Brady ordered Osgood "to leave Lancaster that day, if possible." In the rare case police pressed an issue, the Church responded by deliberately impeding the investigation. A particularly egregious example was a 1990 directive from Cleveland's auxiliary bishop A. James Quinn, a civil and canon lawyer. He advocated the diocese conceal misconduct by sending reports to the apostolic delegate in Washington. That office had immunity from prosecution.[10]

Church documents, hundreds of thousands back to the 1940s, describe cover-ups engineered at the highest levels and confirm rank and file priests recognized the problem and knew the identities of all their abuser brethren. Letters from the late 1940s–early 1950s from Philadelphia's Father Joseph P. Gausch to Father Charles L.G. Knapp—both dedicated abusers—are illustrative. Gausch openly described "escapades with young teenagers" and glibly described a seventh-grader as "the latest obstacle to my spiritual advancement." "The trick" to finding victims at high school football games was "to appear interested in the game and not the players." He assumed his friend "could see the set up"— his grooming process—and dreamed of a vacation home where he could host "handpicked overflow" for a week at a time. Of his commitment to the process, he boasted, "That, pal, is zeal," and he warned it was just a matter time before he "reached out and snatched [a child]. I've come THAT close so often."[11] The diocese received dozens of similar letters and hundreds of reports in Gausch's secret archive files. He was never once disciplined.

The first confirmed direct warning to a modern pope was made by Father Gerald Fitzgerald, who founded the Paraclete order and ran Via Coeli, a Jemez. New Mexico treatment center for priests. In 1962, he warned Pope Paul VI and his assistant, Cardinal Alfredo Ottaviani, there was a problem with pedophile priests and no "cure."[12] Most modern popes have covered for abusers. Rome's handling of Father Marcial Maciel Degollado was perhaps the most shameless. The Jesuit founder of the Legionaries of Christ was a hopeless morphine addict and uncontrolled womanizer. He secretly married two Mexican women and fathered three children with each, and he kept a mistress living in Switzerland with three more offspring. He visited monthly and sent them tens of millions of dollars. He was a pederast who raped his own children and sexually assaulted hundreds, perhaps thousands, of his seminarians who were prohibited from criticizing him or questioning his motives. For 50 years, from 1950 to 2006, the Vatican received hundreds of abuse complaints, many from Degollado's own priests. All were ignored due to his friendships with business tycoons, three popes, and the Vatican secretary of state. Most important, his $25,000,000,000 ecclesiastical empire, with its $65,000,000 annual budget, was a huge Vatican cash cow. Despite Degollado's history, Pope John Paul II lauded him as an "efficacious guide to youth" in 1994. In 2004, he named Degollado administrator of Jerusalem's Notre Dame Center.

Complaints about Degollado were the purview of German bishop Joseph Ratzinger, prefect of the Vatican's Congregation for the Doctrine of Faith. He was responsible for exposing priest abusers and turning them over to authorities. Instead, for years he stonewalled cases and refused to seriously discipline anyone. His abysmal handling of Degollado and Father Lawrence C. Murphy are disquieting examples of Ratzinger's moral bankruptcy. He ignored Degollado's deviancy for years, blocked the case in 1998, and did nothing until forced to respond. He ordered Degollado "lead a life of a recluse." He then arbitrarily added a ten-year statute of limitations in canon law that specifically prevented victims from pursuing cases against Degollado. Murphy ran St. John School for the Deaf, in suburban Milwaukee, Wisconsin, and abused at least 200 over two decades. During the 1990s, hundreds of victims came forward, and two successive Milwaukee bishops begged Ratzinger to offer the deaf community "a healing response from the Church" by ordering a canonical trial and defrocking Lawrence. Ratzinger ignored the requests and buried the case for years before he grudgingly approved a tribunal. Held in secret. Lawrence went unpunished because he said he "repented, was elderly, and [promised not to] do it again." Ratzinger based his 2001 Vatican procedures for investigating and prosecuting abusers on the Crimen that ordered claims be buried. In 2005, Ratzinger became Pope Benedict XVI.[13]

The absence of punishment was the greatest reason for the eventual scope of the crisis. Philadelphia "punished" Joseph Gausch for committing decades of abuse by advising if he needed "psychiatric consultation you should seek it." Another Philadelphia priest with "countless" accusations went unpunished because the diocese determined he was not "a pure pedophile" because he also abused women. The most severe penalty a priest could expect was a vacation at a Church-run addiction facility. Of all the repugnant Church strategies, though, the most appalling was its transfer policy. The directive was clear: "Because of the scandal which already has taken place and because of the possible future scandal, we will transfer."[14]

If a priest was accused, he was simply moved. Where he was sent depended on the allegations. First offenders were moved among parishes within the diocese. As distasteful as it sounds, the worse the crime or the greater the number of complaints, the farther, in miles, the banishment. Transfers—what the Church called "bishops helping bishops"—were done quickly and secretly. Dioceses used specific distant parishes as dumping grounds for repeat abusers. Springfield sent its worst to the same churches in White Plains, New York, and Woodbridge, Virginia. Most disconcerting, new parishes were never directly warned about their new curates. Most pastors assumed abuse was behind the delivery of a new priest, but everyone else pretended nothing was suspect. In one atrocious example from Boston, when Father Paul Shanley—an admitted child rapist and public advocate of sex between men and boys—was transferred to California, Cardinal Bernard Francis Law wrote, "Father Shanley has no problem that would be of concern to your diocese."[15]

Church detachment has always been deplorable. Before Manchester, New Hampshire, bishop Ernest J. Primeau transferred unrepentant abuser Father Donald Osgood, he sought recommendations so Osgood would not "shop around on his own." Primeau recommended they "avoid a rural diocese … he might be better off in a more populated area with plenty to occupy himself," and casually added, "Possibilities: Denver, Spokane, Portland, Oregon, Oakland." Osgood served a three-year banishment to Via Coeli, after which Primeau installed him in an Albuquerque parish, telling the new pastor Osgood "has worked hard and has done well. His recommendations are very good."[16]

Historically, the Vatican mandated the policy. For decades, it sent European abusers to countries with little policing of abuse and, in fact, little police presence at all. Hundreds of rogue priests ended up in Africa and South America. Rome still believes abusers are someone else's responsibility. As recently as 2014, the Vatican posited at the United Nations' Convention Against Torture in Geneva that priests are "under the jurisdiction of the authorities of that country."[17]

Church responses to the issue have always been sadly comical. A ten-year study spawned the February 2, 1961, Papal encyclical *Instruction on the Careful Selection and Training of Candidates for the States of Perfection and Sacred Orders*, new rules to address abuse. Among the directives was that those "afflicted with evil tendencies to homosexuality or pederasty" be barred from priesthood. In 1964, an outside expert hired by Manchester, New Hampshire, convinced the diocese there were two types of homosexuality, "congenital and conditioned … that may be likened to an allergy. [Congenital] exists from birth and cannot be changed … the person can control their sexual expression the same as a normal person.… [Conditioned] comes into being in a normal person but changes early in life due to psychic trauma." The expert was the town chiropractor.[18]

The Church compounded its ignorance by treating sexual abuse as a moral failing versus psychological or psychiatric disorder. An unsettling 1957 letter from the Paraclete's Father Fitzgerald to Manchester's bishop Brady offered insight into the bizarre belief system. Fitzgerald deemed *any* cleric abuser schizophrenic and "duly warn[ed]" seminarians the consequences of being exposed "would be deterrent to these vicious habits." Not until the early 1990s did the Church finally agree that abuse was not "moral fault, but psychological and/or social disorder." Abuse, it decided, "may be a crime which needed confinement."[19]

The Church was able to keep its secrets in part because, until the 1980s, virtually no victims reported incidents. To anyone. Silence was, in large measure, due to cultural attitudes toward priests. Clerics were revered, presumed pure of thought, and assumed infallible. An altar boy, in particular, faced uncertain prospects accusing a priest; he was more likely to face reprimand himself. Discussing 1960s abuse by his parish priest, a victim said his family was "extremely proud" he was an altar boy, and if he made an accusation, they "would think he was [making it up to] start trouble." Further, victims almost universally believed the abuse was *their* fault, not the priest's. "I did not recognize until later, after years of therapy, that I really believed the abuse was my fault," one Lavigne victim said. Parents were also loath to demand a priest be punished. In the early 1980s, a group of Louisiana parents suspected their priest was molesting their children. They approached him during a church picnic and asked, almost apologetically, "if he was involved with any children." He admitted he was and asked them to find him a psychiatrist. Amazingly, a victim's mother made the appointment. The parents made the appointments and paid for the sessions. They did not report him.[20]

There are countless other atrocious examples of priests receiving undeserved benefit of the doubt. In 1976, Father Joseph F. Maguire— later bishop of Springfield—was informed by a father that his son was molested by a priest Maguire knew was an abuser. Maguire responded, "I'm sure it was just horseplay." In the late 1980s, Philadelphia's secretary of clergy consoled a priest who admitted abusing an 11-year-old by proposing the boy "seduced *him*." In 1994, a victim describing an assault when he was 12 was told he "misinterpreted" his priest reaching into his pants and grabbing his genitals.[21] Church diminishment was perhaps best encapsulated by Philadelphia bishop Anthony Bevilacqua's response after the scandal erupted there. He boasted that, in the previous 50 years, his diocese identified only 35 priests credibly accused of sexual abuse. *Only 35.*

———————————

The first rumblings of the modern-day scandal arose in Newfoundland in the mid–1970s when a group of priests from the Christian Brothers of Ireland order were charged with decades of sex crimes. They were spirited out of the province, and the head of the order convinced the largest newspaper to kill the story. Another brother was convicted of child molestation in 1982. There was, again, little public reaction because he was sentenced by a church-influenced court to just 12 days in jail. People only learned of the two outrages because an anonymous call to a television talk show in 1989 ignited a media firestorm and a government investigation. The inquiry resulted in the convictions of 11 brothers, $70,000,000 in settlements, and the shuttering of the order's vast network of schools from Newfoundland to Vancouver.[22] The case provided U.S. Catholics an inkling of what was to come, but few noticed.

The first stories of U.S. abuse dribbled into papers in 1981. There was no outcry until May 1985, when the *National Catholic Reporter* reprinted an exposé that originally ran in rural Louisiana's *The Times of Acadiana*. Jason Berry's story about homosexual priest Gilbert J. Gauthé was the first confirmation the Church systematically buried horrific crimes. Berry followed "Gil" from his indictment a year earlier on 33 counts of child sex crimes. He and his Boy Scout leader brother, Richard, molested scores, starting before Gauthé entered the seminary in 1968.[23] Ordained in 1972, he blatantly abused at every assignment, once casually admitting his victims numbered "35, 36, 37, something like that." Investigators believed the number was more than 75; some believed it was more than 100.

The entire diocese recognized it. Rumors and accusations flew at every assignment as Gauthé started Boy Scout troops, took his charges on camping trips to his bayou hunting cabin, and hosted overnights in his rectory quarters. A half-dozen nuns, working with the desperately poor sugar cane workers in his parishes, complained to pastors. Nuns at four churches forbade children to *approach* the rectory if Gauthé was inside. One later said, "God forgive me for what I thought when [an abused boy] returned to class, and I saw the expression on his face." The Lafayette diocese transferred Gauthé ten times. Police were aware. In March 1980, Richard's wife reported him after she caught him molesting her sons. She claimed he and Gil abused kids "for years." She was not believed.[24] Three weeks later, on April 5, 1980, a group calling itself "Concerned Parishioners of St. John's Parish" sent Bishop Gerard Frey a letter warning him about Gauthé. Frey decided the complaints were superficial and declined to investigate. He never spoke to Gauthé, who continued abusing.

In May 1983, Frey's assistant stunned a victim's parent when he said, "We've known Father Gauthé had a problem for some time but we thought it was resolved." He opposed punishment, pleading, "We're talking about a man's career here." On June 27, the parent's lawyer approached Frey directly. The next morning, the housekeeper entered Gauthé's rectory quarters and found him and his belongings gone. Frey stonewalled, claiming Gauthé suffered a nervous breakdown. He actually hid Gauthé at the House of Affirmation in Whitinsville, Massachusetts, a Church treatment center (later closed after allegations of rampant abuse *at* the facility). Frey offered to pay for counseling, but first ordered that victims come to church and confess their sins. The diocese's insurance companies secretly paid $4,000,000 to the first nine victims in October 1984, but only after Berry reported the payment did the public learn of the Church shenanigans. Gauthé was indicted, and a front-page *New Orleans Times-Picayune* story began "Catholic Church officials knew for almost seven years about Gauthé's sexual activities with boys." Overnight, a small priest scandal became a huge Church scandal.[25]

In 1985, Gauthé pled guilty to abusing 11 boys and was sentenced to 20 years in prison. The floodgates were opened. Joseph Ratzinger's pal Father Lawrence C. Murphy admitted to molesting the 200 deaf students at his school in Wisconsin. Father John Ritter, founder of New York's Covenant House and honored as one of President George H.W. Bush's "Thousand Points of Light," plundered his own treasury and abused a dozen. In Dallas, Father Rudolph ("Rudy") Kos' 1966 marriage was annulled after his wife said he refused sex because he preferred boys. He entered the seminary, where he seduced half a dozen fellow students, and after his 1981 ordination, he molested hundreds of boys.

The numbers were astonishing. More than 40 of 88 Phoenix, Arizona, parishes staffed abusers, and bishops and priests "passed boys around like party favors." In El Paso, Texas, a fraternity of pedophile priests operated for 40 years and met with larger groups in three states. Davenport, Iowa, had a similar network associated with a faction from Chicago, Illinois.[26] Despite systemic, widespread damage, little outrage materialized. Even the muted public response, for the most part, dissipated quickly.

The first Massachusetts stories arose in the late 1980s. The scope of Boston-area abuse—hundreds of priests, thousands of victims—

marks it as the most appalling regional scandal. The first name to emerge was Father James R. Porter of Fall River, an hour south of Boston. In the late 1950s, after molesting dozens at a Church camp, he entered St. Mary's Seminary in Baltimore. The place was so notorious for unbridled abuse and homosexual activity it was called the "Pink Palace." He abused hundreds, perhaps thousands, during his career. At his first assignment in North Attleboro, the chain-smoking, charismatic Porter organized the Little League, coached CYO basketball, took charge of altar boys, even won the Knights of Columbus bowling title. He molested his first victim within a week of arriving, under his pastor's knowing gaze.[27]

Stories of Porter's abuse are truly horrifying. He abused one girl in a hospital bed. She had just survived a horrific automobile accident that killed her uncle; her parents asked Porter to break the terrible news to her. He possessed a ravenous sexual appetite and was a brazen, compulsive abuser. A girl he raped at ten said, "He did it everywhere. At the kids' homes. At the church. In the rectory. He fondled people openly everywhere. At church dances. In the halls. In the pool." He abused on the altar, in the confessional, even beneath a Virgin Mary statue behind the rectory. He molested kids on roller coasters and fondled them as they stood in line at baseball practice. He molested one boy in his bedroom as his parents sat in the next room, another under the table during dinner with the family. Porter took a ten-year-old boy to a baseball game and then to his family's beach house in Rhode Island. He gave the boy a piece of mincemeat pie laced with sedatives, then raped him after he passed out. He molested groups, forcing the boys to wrestle naked while he masturbated. After being exiled to Minnesota, he took nine of his new altar boys to a Minnesota Twins baseball game, after which he molested every one.[28]

His fellow priests knew all about Porter. At his first parish, Assistant Pastor Father Armando A. Annunziato walked in on Porter raping a boy, "shut the door and walked out." Interrupting another assault, Annunziato looked the victim "in the eye, turned around, and walked back upstairs." Complaints inundated Fall River beginning in 1962, and by 1964, the diocese confirmed he had molested at least 40 children. After he was picked up in New Hampshire for molesting a boy—Bishop James L. Connolly was relieved the victim was "non–Catholic"—he was sent to a Church hospital for electroshock therapy. The day after his release, he molested two boys. He was then sent to the Paraclete center in New

Mexico but was allowed to work in Albuquerque parishes where he molested dozens more. In 1969, he was pronounced cured, his "problems under control," and transferred to Bemidji, Minnesota. His first year, he molested at least two dozen. In late 1973, he was finally reported directly to Pope Paul VI, who, rather than punishing Porter, allowed him to quietly leave the priesthood.[29]

In 1990, Porter's name came up in Massachusetts when Frank Fitzgerald, a private investigator who was one of Porter's Attleboro victims, approached the diocese searching for him. Boston refused to cooperate, even claiming not to know his birth date or Social Security number. Porter's friend Annunziato advised Fitzgerald, "I think it best to leave this in the hands of God." Instead, Fitzgerald went to the state police, the FBI, and the media. He found Porter in Minnesota, and, amazingly, recorded him admitting to molesting between 50 and 100 children while "hiding behind the cloth." The *Boston Globe* picked up the story, to the chagrin of Boston's cardinal Bernard Francis Law. Incensed, he blamed the paper for the hubbub. He said, "By all means we call down God's power on the media, particularly the *Globe*."[30]

Massachusetts was about to awaken to a scandal.

5

Exposed

As the Porter saga unfolded in Boston, a familiar name arose in Springfield. In late September 1991, a family from Shelburne Falls, a tiny village of 1,700 in central Massachusetts eight miles from the Vermont border, accused their priest of abusing two of their sons. He was the pastor at St. Joseph's Church. His name was Richard R. Lavigne.

Shelburne Falls is rural to the point of remote, surrounded by hundreds of square miles of mountains, rivers, and forest. It is actually two hamlets—Buckland and Shelburne—squatting on opposite sides of the Deerfield River. The Mohawk Trail, a scenic 90-mile highway meandering the length of the state, passes through the middle of town. Shelburne Falls is known for glacial potholes lining the riverbed, its trolley museum, and for having the second oldest bowling alley in the country. It is small-town New England, the setting for Kate Winslet's 2013 film *Labor Day* and Robert Downey, Jr., and Robert Duvall's 2014 movie *The Judge*. Downtown is a grid of narrow, tree-lined streets, dotted in 1991 with art galleries and businesses like Davenport's Service Station and the Foxtowne Coffee Shoppe.

After St. Catherine's, Lavigne worked at two Springfield churches before his transfer to Shelburne Falls. St. Joseph's parish was a collection of three country churches: St. Joseph's in Shelburne Falls, St. John the Baptist Mission in Colrain, and St. Christopher's Mission in Charlemont. There were about 600 parishioners among them. The churches were hoping for a strong priest. The previous pastor habitually said Mass drunk. Lavigne was still the rebel priest, roaring into his August 1977 welcome picnic on a motorcycle. He moved into Spartan third-floor rectory quarters, an eight-by-10-foot room, just big enough for a bed, a couch, and two chairs, with a stall shower behind wooden sliders. As always, he was initially well received. One parishioner said, "He was truly a Renaissance man [who] elevated and raised the consciousness of the entire Church." Another later added, "I love the man. Father Lavigne [was] good to our family and [did] wonders for our Church." He immediately began pestering Springfield for funds to renovate the three old chapels, supervised the projects, and filled the sanctuaries with statues he found on his antiquing trips.[1]

He overhauled the altar boy program and was devoted to the children, still the hip young cleric who spoke their language and understood their problems. He took them for ice cream and to movies. He invited them for rectory overnights, and took them for weekends throughout New England and on trips across the U.S. and Canada. He took them camping, most often to Ashfield and a cabin at the Church's Camp Holy Cross in Goshen, and a lake house he said belonged to a wealthy female artist friend.[2] Just two months after Lavigne's posting, Weldon retired. Father Joseph F. Maguire came from Boston as his replacement.

Lavigne was still vocally anti-government. He was still divisive. Parishioners described him as a "charismatic … wonderful priest," but "someone who elicited strong feelings, positive and negative." He was more volatile. A young couple at the normally-relaxed Saturday afternoon service with their 18-month-old son was shocked when Lavigne approached just before Mass and loudly berated them. He yelled, "If your child makes any more noise, you'll all have to leave the church!" He roared at another couple with an infant in tow, "If your children make any more noise, you'll have to go outside!" The embarrassed couples fled.[3] He was appointed pastor March 6, 1982.

Lavigne regularly visited another nearby Catholic community, though they were not his responsibility. The Holy Trinity Lay Community was 15 families who lived on a 200-acre farm on remote Number Nine Road in tiny Heath, population 700. The ultra-conservative Catholic sect was not only unrecognized by the Church, it was also formally ostracized. It was an offshoot of the Apostolate Formation Center, a small group founded in 1968 by J. Roy Legere, a bizarre preacher who believed he was Jesus' twin brother. Three priests ministered to 500 people from 100 families in the rural northern Connecticut town of Somers. The group was outwardly devoted only to daily prayer and Bible study. A year after Legere died in 1978, Charles Shattuck, a devoutly Catholic, decorated Vietnam War veteran, joined. In 1983, he learned Legere and the early membership conducted homosexual rituals with children. Legere's "Divine Intimacy of the Holy Seed" promised an "infusion of Christ." Shattuck approached Bishop Daniel P. Reilly, who admitted two members had warned him of the sex ritual some years earlier. With a promise of secrecy, Reilly allowed Shattuck to reorganize as the Holy Trinity Lay Community, but after a 1985 newspaper story exposed Legere, Reilly banished Holy Trinity even though no current members were affiliated with the group when the acts took place. Worse, he refused to exonerate Shattuck, a perverse insult a local priest called "a Peter-like betrayal." But Shattuck's standing was damaged in 1987 when he and Trinity were sued by the state for mishandling $30,000 in donations. He quietly moved the dozen remaining families to Heath.[4]

Locals disliked and distrusted them, piqued by their refusal to participate in civic affairs. The tense relationship led to feuds. Residents of Heath worried about being "taken over by a cult" and fretted about suffering the fate of Antelope, Oregon, a rural town overrun by the Rajneeshee sect in the mid–1980s. The local rallying cry became "Remember Antelope!" Shattuck was described as "a kook, a religious fanatic, a cult leader, another Jim Jones," though all Trinity did was gather in Shattuck's basement for nightly prayer and rosary devotions and eke out a living farming their rocky fields.[5]

When Lavigne first reached out, Trinity had built nine houses and was constructing a small chapel. After years of being shunned by the Church, it literally "thanked God" for the attention. For three years, Lavigne visited frequently and ministered to the members, who began attending St. Joseph's services. He was considered a trusted friend and group member. He brought food and helped Shattuck find work. When Shattuck's seven-year-old son was hit by a truck and killed, Lavigne arranged the funeral, performed the service, and was by the family's side for weeks. He also took an interest in the dozen remaining Shattuck children. He paid them for work around the rectory, took them fishing, had them for overnights, and even took them on vacations to California, New York City, and Canada. Such luxuries were well out of Shattuck's reach, the tiny congregation his only source of income. Lavigne lobbied Elliot Street on Trinity's behalf, writing Maguire of their "great devotion to the mother of God and who … have suffered a great deal from ostracization…. Like all of us when we are hurt, they are in need of compassion and healing…. I know what it means to be maligned without just cause."[6]

In late 1990, Lavigne and Shattuck had an abrupt and acrimonious falling out. Contact ceased and Trinity members left St. Joseph's en masse. No one discerned the reason for the fracture. Locals blamed it on Lavigne not being "Catholic enough for them." For his part, Lavigne blamed Trinity: "God knows I tried to give them a fair hearing and wound up being used when I realized they were only in the parish for what they could get from us." Lavigne turned against Shattuck and sent Elliot Street monthly reports on Trinity activities, writing in April 1991, "I think it's only a matter of time before things blow up in some way."[7] Blow up, they did.

On October 19, 1991, Greenfield police issued an arrest warrant for Lavigne based on statements from three boys—then 9, 18, and 20—describing incidents between 1988 and 1991. At 4:20 the next afternoon, Chicopee detectives staked out his parents' apartment at 30 Colonial Circle and arrested him. He was the first priest in western Massachusetts history charged with child sexual assault. He was taken in handcuffs to the state police barracks in Shelburne Falls, informed the charges were two counts of rape of a child under 16 and one count of indecent assault and battery on a child under 14. When given the accusers' names, he said, "That's absurd," and said their father fabricated everything, that he was not credible because he was "a chauvinist and a bigot." He said he never touched "any kid" inappropriately. At the barracks, it appeared Lavigne wanted to confess something, asking a detective, "Can I be honest with you? Can I trust you?" but after being reminded of the Miranda warning he received, he suddenly went silent and asked for a lawyer. He was booked, fingerprinted, photographed and placed in a cell. The next morning, he left Greenfield district court on $10,000 bail, but returned for his arraignment the following Monday, October 21. Standing with lawyer John M. Callahan and surrounded by half a dozen Church officials, he pled not guilty and was released. Lavigne hired Callahan for the arraignment. Curiously, he was not assigned a diocesan attorney.[8]

St. Joseph's reacted with shock and disbelief. Just two months earlier, 300 parishioners celebrated the 25th anniversary of Lavigne's ordination with a Mass and dinner at the local community center. The fire department turned away another 300. Interim pastor Father Robert M. Thrasher said everyone was supporting Lavigne, offering "love and support. I can tell you that." Supporters fought back tears as they spoke to reporters. One woman said the arrest "almost killed me. He is the most beautiful man." A father said his nine-year-old son cried for an hour after hearing the news, saying, "It just couldn't happen. It's not fair, Daddy." Recounting the story, the man turned away and sobbed. Altar boys sprung to Lavigne's defense, one saying, "He' been a mentor to me. He taught me many things about life. I just can't believe any of this that's going on. I just can't fathom anything like this happening." The sentiment was echoed by another who said, "This totally blows my mind."[9]

Perhaps most stunned was police chief Mark DeJackome, parish council president. Fellow Council member Thomas Campbell described the charges as a "disaster," and yet another said, "There is a tremendous amount of deep and loyal support for Father Lavigne by an awful lot of people." Several women panned the process, one offering, "He's been condemned already. He hasn't had a chance. And he's being treated like a serial killer." Another intimated something darker: "there might be a conspiracy to destroy him."[10]

Republican reporter Tom Shea went looking for Carl and Bunny and found them at St. Catherine's. Bunny was selling raffle tickets and settling in for Bingo. Carl was in the sanctuary doing a solitary Stations of the Cross. Watching Carl on his knees, alone in the dark, Shea said, "I've heard thousands of sermons on faith. But I have never witnessed one so humble. So vividly powerful."[11]

The diocese stood lockstep with Lavigne, saying he was "on leave from pastoral duties … by mutual agreement. We will give him a great deal of moral support. He's expected to be innocent until proven guilty … a brother priest." Lavigne was widely liked by fellow priests. Father Hugh Crean, as vicar, responsible for the diocese's 250 priests, added, "We are truly a brotherhood, and what hurts one of us, hurts all of us. This is difficult on all."[12]

On October 27, parishioners packed St. Joseph's for a prayer service. Replacement pastor Father Kenneth J. Tatro read a statement from Bishop Maguire addressing the "pain and anguish" the allegations caused. Of Lavigne, he said, "As a member of our spiritual family, he is entitled to our prayers, our consideration and compassion." He mentioned "alleged victims" and concluded, "We are not in a position to determine the facts of the case. We do know under our system of government and under our Constitution, the presumption of innocence prevails until guilt is proven."[13]

Lavigne went into hiding, first a month at Ashfield, then the Institute of Living in Hartford, Connecticut. The IOL was founded in 1822, one of the nation's first two psychiatric hospitals. He was incommunicado, but a priest friend said he was "apprehensive and insists on his innocence." Another described him as "wounded and confused by the charges, the accusations, the speculations, the television reports and newspaper headlines." A month later, he wrote St. Joseph's that the Lord was by his side maintaining his innocence and bemoaning the personal attacks in the press. Everyone became doubly loyal after rumors surfaced that his accusers were members of the Trinity group they so deeply disliked.[14]

After two decades, Danny was catapulted back onto front pages by two bombshells in a *Republican* story about Lavigne's troubles. First, Lavigne was described as the only suspect in the murder, a disclosure attributed to Carl and a retired Chicopee detective. Second, Carl criticized Ryan's uninspired pursuit of Lavigne, claiming that he begged him to indict "but nothing came about. God only knows why they didn't go through with it." He and Bunny appealed to D.A. William M. Bennett to reopen the investigation. Publicly, Bennett replied cryptically, "There is no statute of limitations on murder. A murder case can always be prosecuted." Privately, he told the Croteaus he would reopen the case.[15]

Carl's unflattering censure hinted at something behind Ryan's inaction. That something was Weldon. His relationship with Ryan surely leant itself to deal making. They were close friends, and Ryan staunchly Catholic, a consummate politician. He was famous locally for his John Wayne–like backstory: teenage boxing champion, college baseball hero and star quarterback, World War II fighter pilot in the Army Air Corps in the Pacific who worked his way through Georgetown Law. In his first political campaign, he soundly beat eight Democrats and a Republican for the D.A. seat. The shrewd and well-connected Ryan ran local operations for John F. Kennedy's presidential campaign in 1960 and advised D.A.s throughout New England. When Danny died, he was in his 14th year in office.[16]

Ryan was a polarizing figure. One writer said, "Whether hated or loved, there were more than enough to fill both camps." He was tempestuous, belligerent, and had an explosive temper. One of his lawyers said, "If you did something wrong … he would yell until the windows buckled.... It was one of the scariest things I've ever been through." He was street smart and unafraid to tackle unpopular cases, but dogged about his close relationships with mob bosses beginning with Sam "Big Nose" Cufari in the 1970s. Springfield might seem an unlikely mafia hub, but all five New York families operated there. Since Prohibition, it was rife with mob activity, money, and murder. For years, Ryan unapologetically played weekly racquetball with Cufari's successors Frank "Skiball" Scibelli and Adolfo "Big Al" Bruno. Ryan's allegiance to Bruno allegedly went back to 1979, when "Big Al" dispatched a married underling having an affair with—and beating—a close relative of Ryan's. Informants claimed Bruno bragged about killing the man to cozy up to the D.A. Bruno reportedly had another married boyfriend of the same relative beaten and escorted out of Massachusetts in the trunk of a car (Weldon threatened to excommunicate the man's mother). When Bruno was jailed in 1987 under Ryan, he was housed in a private room inside the local jail and was allowed to leave daily before breakfast and return after dinner. Even so, in private conversation, Ryan referred to Italians derisively as "wops" or "Guineas."[17]

Carl said Ryan thought indicting Lavigne in 1972 was a fool's errand. "Where," Ryan asked, "am I going to get 12 jurors to convict a priest?" But for years police and insiders felt the real reason for his reticence was a request from Weldon. Such a deal was first suggested under an October 24, 1991, headline: "DIOCESE DENIES COVER-UP-BISHOP KNEW PRIEST WAS A SUSPECT IN '72." The story detailed Church intransigence during the investigation and confirmed rumors Weldon pressured Ryan away from Lavigne. The supposed deal was discussed all over Springfield. The diocese denied everything, Vicar Crean saying, "To my knowledge there was no cover-up at all. I can't imagine there would be. Bishop Weldon ... was not the kind of man who would say, 'Just forget that now and be a good boy.'"[18] Church denials were universally questioned, the story largely accepted as true. Even Crean's use of the phrase "To my knowledge" was taken as tacit admission.

Over the years, Ryan's dedication to aggressively pursuing Lavigne grew suspect to investigation insiders, as did certainty he was pressured by Weldon. If true, it explains Ryan's curious decision to take control of a seemingly minor Chicopee murder case in the first place. Clearly, Weldon learned of Danny's death and Lavigne's connections almost immediately. Weldon was probably informed as soon as Ryan became involved early Saturday and Danny confirmed a young Catholic victim. The absolute latest he learned of potential Lavigne involvement was Monday, after he incriminated himself. The Weldon-Ryan relationship demanded both facts be relayed promptly. We know Chicopee told him.

Republican reporter Dick Garvey covered the police beat for 30 years and had extensive contacts in all area departments. A Chicopee investigator apprised Garvey about Lavigne on Sunday, and Garvey immediately contacted Weldon's closest friend and advisor, Father David Power. During a clandestine meeting in a secluded corner of the paper's parking lot, Garvey updated Powers, assuming Powers directly informed Weldon. Powers would later opine Weldon made no deal, that he ordered Elliot Street cooperate, in part, because he had long soured on Lavigne. Garvey kept Weldon informed as the investigation continued.[19]

It is logical to assume that, whenever Weldon was notified, he presumed Lavigne was involved. He was surely familiar with Danny's name, knowing for years his troublesome priest was an abuser. His secret archive contained reports with very specific dates and events and victims' names, so he knew Danny was a victim of Lavigne's. Knowing that, it is reasonable Weldon assumed Lavigne might have killed Danny. It is equally reasonable he would manipulate Ryan. Weldon had influence over every aspect of Springfield's operation, and it could have been brought to bear from multiple directions.

The idea of Weldon protecting a murderer might seem farfetched. For decades, though, he was indifferent to thousands of dreadful crimes and hundreds of abuser priests. The Jack Downing case is representative of the Weldon mindset. Downing was a devout Catholic who founded Western Massachusetts' first drug treatment program. A patient told him a well-known priest was having sexual relationships with a married woman and her teenage daughter. The priest took them to a lake cottage and had relations with the mother in the daughter's presence. He then undressed the young girl, covered her breasts with baby powder, and masturbated on her. The priest's pastor told Downing, "I know about it, but I can't do anything about it. These younger priests won't listen." Downing friend and Weldon staffer Father Dan Doyle arranged a meeting at a Chicopee hotel. Sitting poolside at the Shine Inn, Weldon warned Downing, "You can't tell anyone about this. Great harm would come to the Church, and to [the priest]. We'll make sure it doesn't happen again." When Downing angrily pressed Weldon to respond more forcefully, Weldon ordered his security detail to forcibly remove Downing. Weldon sent the priest to a New York church treatment center, but then appointed him guidance counselor at Holyoke Catholic High School.[20] Downing approached Weldon about abusers half a dozen times. He responded once. Weldon was undoubtedly as dedicated to protecting his Church from the scandal of a single murder as he was to hiding thousands of abuse cases. Given the man and his history, a different response is hard to imagine.

The Weldon-Ryan deal has long been assumed as fact. It has even been claimed Weldon's carrot was a promise Ryan would remain D.A. for life if he sidestepped Lavigne. In that narrative, Weldon promised Ryan no one would ever run against him in Catholic-dominated Springfield. That particular quid pro quo might not have been necessary. Weldon's control extended to local police departments and he was rumored to already be manipulating Chicopee P.D. A city run by a complex bribery system certainly lent itself to following directives from Weldon.

The diocese was under siege. Maguire was infuriated by what he deemed biased reporting and complained about having to repeatedly "respond openly and courteously to the countless questions."[21] Crean added, "All these little innuendoes seem … in some respects to assume guilt even before the judicial process has taken place." Two days later, on October 25, Maguire imposed a news blackout, ordering "diocesan personnel make no further comment."[22]

In the following days, more damning Lavigne stories surfaced. On October 27, the *Republican* reported his firing in 1958 by the Chicopee Parks and Recreation Department. A now-36-year-old victim came forward with an incident report hidden for 35 years by CPR. On May 13, 1958, 17-year-old Lavigne was hired as a $30-a-week assistant recreation leader at Garrity Grove Park. The six-acre facility, in a remote, wooded area, had a playground, a playing field, a tennis court, and two scruffy baseball fields. Today it straddles the Massachusetts Turnpike, but then it had a small pond concealed by trees. Lavigne was basically a camp counselor-babysitter. He supervised games and played with kids, baseball and kickball outside, checkers and board games inside.[23]

After visiting the park on July 30 with his mother and sister, the six-year-old told his grandmother he was taken to the secluded pond hidden by overgrown brush by "Dickie," who tickled him, then opened his own pants and requested the boy touch his genitals. He then opened the boy's pants and fondled him. He recalled, "I was little, but I must have known it was wrong. I told my parents." His grandmother called the parks and recreation department, and that night, the commissioner and an assistant visited. Lavigne was immediately fired for being an "undesirable person to be around children." A sign of the times, the firing was "as far as it went. Police were not contacted. My parents weren't looking for anything beyond [the firing]." CPR refused to turn over Lavigne's employment records to the *Republican*.[24]

Amidst the swirling stories, Lavigne's defenders convinced themselves the Trinity group set him up and sent blistering letters to the *Republican* accusing it of bias. A woman from upscale Longmeadow excoriated the paper: "Your extensive, persistent and repetitive coverage of the Rev. Richard Lavigne's case alarms me ... featuring, in ragsheet manner, hearsay evidence, maudlin details and misleading evidence. The is anti–Catholicism. A newsworthy story should not be a platform for slander." Another woman described coverage as "anti–Catholic, but more it's 'anti-human.' He has been tried and lynched by the media." Yet another critic, a South Hadley man, wrote "I'm getting damn fed up with what you're doing to the priests. Is this the kind of garbage you want to put up with?"[25]

Carl and Bunny were deluged by reporters and television news crews from across the U.S. People called from all over offering support and prayers. They also had many prank callers. It was so overwhelming, a friend gave them an answering machine, the first they ever used. They were relieved Danny was, as Bunny said, "not forgotten. I just want this resolved so I can get some sleep." Carl added, "We pray for the truth to come out. We live with it each and every day of our lives." They absolved the Church, saying, "We have no fight with the Catholic Church, the diocese, our parish, St. Catherine's, our pastor, or Father [Charles F.] Gonet." Their commitment wavered at times. By the late 1970s, they had drifted from the Church, and for a time there were fewer morning Masses and confessions, even missed Sunday Masses. St. Catherine's curate Leo O'Neil nudged them back by advising, "Don't let anyone come between you and God."[26]

They never mentioned abuse but Carl and Bunny did admit they believed Lavigne was involved in Danny's murder. Their opinion was not widely admired. Scathing letters and irate callers derided them for criticizing the Church. "How could you accuse a priest of something like that?" they were asked. The venom was unexpected. Stories of abusive priests were commonplace by then, but the faithful continued to ignore the gathering storm.

The media firestorm continued as the Shelburne Falls investigation widened. Hampshire County D.A. investigators catalogued dozens of allegations from multiple victims. In just a few months, 18 boys accused Lavigne, including altar boys from St. Joseph churches and one from St. Mary's, molested during a Canadian vacation. A Chicopee boy living next door to Lavigne's aunt and uncle came forward, as did Lavigne's own cousin, the 10-year-old son of his father's cousin. Another father claimed his three sons were victims. Other victims contacted investigators, but refused to come forward, fearing Church reprisal. Letters arrived at the state police barracks in Northampton describing similar allegations, among them an October 25 missive that hid another bombshell. A man, then 20, claimed he and his brother—both Lavigne victims—informed Father Leo O'Neil, then Weldon's auxiliary bishop, about the abuse. O'Neil promised them Lavigne would be kept away from children, closely supervised, and forced into counseling, but he did nothing.[27]

In October and again in November, state police detective Harrington contacted O'Neil, then bishop of Manchester, New Hampshire, for decades another abuse cesspool. O'Neil stonewalled, first claiming to be busy, then simply refusing to meet. He suggested they talk to Elliot Street and said it was "Springfield's problem." He was similarly taciturn the rest of his life. When contacted in 1993, he claimed not to remember a single question asked in 1991. O'Neil always knew about Lavigne. He discussed him repeatedly with other St. Catherine's priests and Carl. And, of course, there was the Disneyland money.[28]

In November, Lavigne retained Boston attorney Max D. Stern, a shrewd legal strategist voted one of "the Best Lawyers in America." He did not come cheap. The bill would exceed $200,000. In December, a Stern representative said Lavigne was "set up" by Holy Trinity. A few weeks later, the 1972 allegation that Lavigne's first polygraph test indicated he was homosexual surfaced in the *Republican*, leaked by an unnamed "police official." William C. Flanagan, a partner in the firm that represented the diocese for 60 years, and who represented Lavigne in

1972, denied the claim. "That issue never came up," he said, "I was witness to the test, and Father Lavigne passed. That's why the investigation was stopped. He wasn't the man." On December 28, his client Maguire shocked 325,000 local Catholics when he resigned. Most believed he stepped down due to the Lavigne uproar, though he denied it.[29]

Lavigne supporters, particularly at St. Joseph's—who showed their support with blue lights in their front windows—remained resolute. To raise money for lawyers, they held tag sales, car washes, and bake sales. Just after New Year's, 1992, "Friends of Richard Lavigne" mailed 400 donation requests. The letter read, "Our good friend, Father Richard Lavigne, is presently suffering the most painful experience of his life. Criminal accusations have left him crushed and deeply hurt. To defend his name and his life, he has retained the services of a prominent Boston attorney…. A priest's salary is hardly sufficient to defray these costs. In order to help our friend, whose 25 years as a priest have touched our lives in many beautiful ways, a defense fund has been established." Money was sent to a small post office near the home of Lavigne's sister.[30]

Lavigne had quietly returned from the Institute of Living to Ashfield and remained out of sight. Once or twice a week, though, he visited his Shelburne Falls loyalists. He resembled the hunted man he had become, hiding under large hats or hoods, wearing wigs and fake beards. He sat facing front windows "nervously watching cars driving down the rural roads, and hid in the bathroom if visitors showed up." He complained of boredom, that the experience was "gut wrenching." He was most frightened of the jail time he assumed was his fate, but he said, "The people who have leveled charges against me know them to be untrue" and just wanted to go back to St. Joseph's, "where I belong." During a visit with one of his victims, who had not yet come forward, he offered a hint of worried self-awareness when he uneasily said, "[You'll] probably make a mistake and say something to really get me in trouble."[31]

6

Trials

Through fall 1991 and into early 1992, a parade of victims—from 4th grade to college—filed before a Franklin County grand jury talking about Lavigne. On February 14, Valentine's Day, he was indicted on charges involving five victims, raping and molesting two and fondling three. The victims were identified only as "J.S.," "J.P.S.," "C.P.," "M.B.," and "A.D."[1] The J.S. indictment included three counts: assault on a child under 16 with intent to have sexual intercourse or unnatural sexual intercourse with a child, indecent assault on a child under 14, and indecent assault on a child over 14. J.P.S., assault on a child over 16 with intent to have sexual intercourse and three counts of indecent assault on a child under 14. C.P., two counts of indecent assault on a child under age 14. M.B.; two: indecent assault on a child under 14 and indecent assault on a child over 14. A.D., one count of indecent assault on a child under 14.[2]

The incidents took place between February 1982 and April 1991. Lavigne faced harsh sentences. The rape charges carried life. Each assault and battery on a child under 14 carried ten years and assault and battery on a child over 14, five years. It was surprising there were no federal charges for transporting a child across state lines, since assaults occurred during trips throughout New England and on vacations to far-away states.[3]

Three days later, February 18, John A. Marshall was installed the sixth bishop of the Springfield diocese. He spent 20 years over Vermont's 145,000 Catholics. He was old-school, deeply opposed to modernization, and openly criticized Vermont legislators for funding Planned Parenthood.[4]

At his February 25 arraignment in Greenfield District Court, Lavigne pled not guilty before telling reporters the allegations were untrue

97

and he expected vindication. It was confirmed J.S. and J.P.S. were indeed Charles Shattuck's sons. Stern angrily claimed the case arose after a Shattuck lawyer advised against suing the Church. Only then, he said, "the witch hunt began and charges ensued." He said one boy—supposedly J.S.—was directly pressured by investigators, that he had "as recently as December, told us categorically nothing had ever happened between himself and Father Lavigne." Stern reminded reporters of the "Divine Intimacy of the Holy Seed" homosexual rite, even though no Trinity members were involved. His comments hinted the case was far from iron-clad.[5]

Details of Lavigne's relationship with the Shattucks were eerily reminiscent of those of his relationship with the Croteaus, his process playing the same progression. As soon as Trinity arrived from Connecticut in the summer of 1986, J.P. said Lavigne acted "in a very friendly, big brotherly, way towards me and my brothers."[6] Everyone liked him. He cracked jokes during shared dinners and was less "grave and serious" than with families without altar boys. The small church only had eight, between 7 and 18. He quickly recruited three Shattucks. Shortly after J.S. signed on, Lavigne began paying him for rectory lawn work, small carpentry jobs, even running errands. He picked him up at school and had him at the rectory for dinner.

Gradually, J.S. spent less time working and more time visiting privately in Lavigne's third-floor quarters. Lavigne took him for ice cream and movies in Greenfield, the nearest "city." As always, he wore street clothes, sans collar. Though young, J.S. recognized Lavigne giving him wine and his "locker room sense of humor and dirty jokes," almost all about penises, were inappropriate. In spring 1987, Lavigne invited him on a two-week Arizona vacation. His parents agreed, and Lavigne took him on a shopping trip that left J.S. unsettled. He insisted on joining the boy in dressing rooms and purchased clearly too-tight underwear and unusual items like jock straps, matching bathing suits, and weird clothes J.S. would never normally wear.

Charles Shattuck began to have misgivings and reassured J.S. when he left for the airport, "If anything goes wrong, I'll find a way to get you home." In Phoenix, Lavigne and J.S. stayed with Lavigne's friends Bob and Helen McCarthy, who left on their own vacation the next day, leaving Lavigne and J.S. at their home. During the week, Lavigne gave J.S. wine and let him drive his rental car, though he was barely 14. Lavigne, in the only bedroom with air conditioning, said J.S. could join him. J.S. agreed, weary after two sweltering nights. Their first night together, he endured an awkward bout of back tickling before falling asleep only to awaken to Lavigne holding his penis. Lavigne said he was worried J.S., who had a bed-wetting problem as a child, might soil the bed. He said, "If you started to go, I was going to squeeze it." Lavigne manipulated J.S. into sexual situations day and night. Once, Lavigne noticed minor chafe marks from J.S.'s ill-fitting swim suit. He said he needed to apply ointment to a rash only he saw on J.S.'s penis. He said, "I am responsible for anything that happens to you while we are on vacation." J.S. was forced to lie, legs spread, on the bed while Lavigne applied the salve.[7]

Lavigne took J.S. camping in the Grand Canyon, where he zipped two sleeping bags together to force tandem sleeping. During the night, J.S. awoke to find "his pants pulled down" and Lavigne fondling him. Despite the repeated humiliations, J.S. was too terrified by violent outbursts by Lavigne to call home. Lavigne was infuriated when an invitation to go skinny dipping was refused, shrieking, "You're no fun! Friendship is based on trust, and if you don't trust me, what are you doing here?" During the tantrum, he shook J.S. violently by the shoulders. When J.S. rebuffed a suggestion he sleep nude, Lavigne screamed, "Don't come to me if you feel chafed tomorrow!" He was particularly incensed when J.S. asked him the reason for all the sexual advances. Lavigne warned J.S. daily not to tell anyone, that they would both get in trouble. He threatened, "If you tell anyone what happened, I will just have to tell your parents about your drinking and illegal driving."[8]

When they returned to Shelburne Falls, Lavigne took J.S. to the rectory rather than home. Lavigne assaulted J.S. first when instructing him how to properly wipe himself after using the toilet, then in the shower, and lastly in bed. After that night, Lavigne hid J.S.'s presence from the other priests, even carrying him upstairs piggyback to hide the sound of a second set of footsteps. J.S. tried to avoid Lavigne, but manipulation and abuse continued into 1988. Lavigne paid for orthodontia the Shattucks could not afford and drove J.S. to appointments. He bought him gifts, gave him money, made music tapes for him, and promised him a car. There were week-long trips to New York City, Pennsylvania Dutch country, Canada, and day trips to Ashfield and around New England.[9]

When J.S. gradually limited encounters to once a month, Lavigne realized he was pulling away and complained about the "wall between us." He was increasingly concerned but J.S. worried about his prospects if he tried to end it. His concern was justified. Lavigne was simultaneously molesting J.S.'s younger brother J.P.S. and had already threatened the younger boy with a butcher knife, saying he and his parents would be hurt if he spoke to anyone. Fear prompted then-high school sophomore J.S. to accept an invitation for a California vacation that July. After repeated sexual episodes during the trip, J.S. made it clear he wanted out. Lavigne, furious, abruptly ceased paying for his orthodontia and said, "I am reminding you, I had long ago said, if the relationship ever stopped it would be your fault." He even demanded J.S. return all the gifts but still called repeatedly asking J.S. to reconsider the breakup.[10]

In the months following, Lavigne sent cards, which J.S. tore up and threw away. A graduation card in spring 1991 came with cash and an odd inscription: "I thought you would like to know [fellow altar boy] David Hanham committed suicide." J.S. took it as a warning not to reveal the relationship or his younger brother's abuse. In July, J.S. apprehensively told his older sister, emotional and shaking as he recalled the events. She was already fretting that Lavigne was molesting J.P.S., so she went against J.S.'s wishes and informed their parents. They went to the police that day.[11]

The appalling details of Lavigne's abuse did not dissuade St. Joseph's supporters. In April 1992, more than 500 signed a petition urging the court give Lavigne five separate trials rather than a combined proceeding. Parishioners Michael Slowinski, Bea Cevasco, Peter Dolan, and Margaret J. Carlson spearheaded the effort. They wrote, "We don't believe the average jury can perform the mental gymnastics to separate a mountain of evidence in five separate cases and separate it into five separate, neat piles and not let one pile spill over into the others." Signees included choir and church council members, altar boys, CCD teachers, even the director of religious education. They were pastors and curates from area parishes and the pastor and ex-pastor at Charlemont Federated Church. They were selectmen, members of the planning board, the school committee, the public works, and the board of zoning appeals, even the dump. They were retirees, artists, housewives, cafeteria workers, truck drivers, and teachers.[12]

The petition was signed by the owner of the local funeral home and the "Grocery & Meat Store," an Air Force pilot, even the town Avon representative. Others signed simply as "Concerned Citizen" "Lavigne's Neighbor," or just "Personal Friend." There were some interesting names like "Nancy Clark, Assist. to Exec. Director, International TV & Radio Society, New York City" and "Lawrence Broschart, Supervisor, Yankee Atomic Electric Company."[13] The group hired a lawyer, though with no legal standing, and the court was not bound to consider the unusual document. In the end, it made no difference. On April 30, the charges were separated into five trials to be held away from Shelburne Falls to avoid pre-trial publicity issues. The first was set for June.

Through spring 1992, investigators continued unearthing allegations. A 33-year-old Chicopee patrolman claimed he witnessed Lavigne molest a friend at St. Mary's. "It's been going on a long time," the cop said. Two of Lavigne's cousins also came forward.[14] At the same time, Bennett's investigation continued, but he was clearly treading water.

The first trial would be held 125 miles east of Shelburne Falls in superior court in Newburyport, an upscale, picturesque seaport village an hour north of Boston near New Hampshire. It dates to the early 1600s and 200-year-old buildings line cobblestone streets next to a vibrant waterfront. The 1809 brick courthouse is the oldest active superior court in the country. There were not enough potential jurors in Newburyport, so the jury was impaneled on June 22 in the Boston suburb of Lawrence, known as the "the City of Workers," a blue-collar town which was the poorest in the state.[15]

The trial was based on late 1983–early 1984 incidents alleged by M.B., including that Lavigne "placed his hands on the [12-year-old's] buttocks" at Ashfield. M.B., his mother, father, and brother were scheduled to testify. Lavigne's witnesses included the boy's father, himself, and two other men. Presiding was Judge Vieri Volterra, "Guy" to friends. Lavigne confidently introduced himself to the 40 potential jurors, alongside lawyers Stern and Patricia Garin. During the voir dire process, Lavigne sat ramrod straight, nodding whenever his lawyers spoke. Seven potential jurors were eliminated by the prosecution, six by the defense. Whenever Stern got one removed, a tight-lipped grin crossed Lavigne's face.[16] After three days, an eight-woman, seven-man jury with three alternates was impaneled and sequestered in a Newburyport hotel. The trial would begin the next morning.

Shelburne Falls awoke June 26 to pelting rain. A Lavigne supporter described the accompanying thunderclaps as "God knocking."[17] Thirty-three parishioners, young and old, all in their Sunday best, made the two-hour trek to Newburyport. A dozen Springfield supporters, including priests Timothy J. Campoli and John A. Roach, joined them in the second-floor courtroom, all expecting an exoneration and quick return to St. Joseph's. After Mass at Immaculate Conception Church next door, Lavigne arrived with his sister's family. His supporters greeted him with smiles, tears, and long hugs. As he slowly worked his way through the group, he, too, began to cry. Tucked into a corner on long wooden pews were about a dozen M.B. supporters, most in work clothes. Disgusted, they watched Lavigne greet his friends.

The courtroom froze when Volterra said, "I understand there has been a change in plea?" A church member with "a bad right ear" thought he misheard Volterra. Sandwiched by his lawyers, Lavigne rose. When Volterra asked him how he pled to molesting a child under 14, and a child over 14, he wearily replied, "Guilty." His supporters were thunderstruck, many again in tears. Volterra summarized the agreement, then M.B. spoke. Now 20, he said, startlingly, "Sometimes it is very difficult to forgive, but being a Christian I do with all my heart forgive you, and I will continue to pray for you always." The prosecutor read a less sanguine statement from a victim not present: "Father Richard Lavigne totally violated my image and trust in the clergy. A man of the cloth is someone you can always depend on. When I was little, I thought it was my fault and I did something to make him do what he did.... Not only did he choose to do what he did, he chose to hide it. I have lost all interest in the Catholic Church."

There was no sentencing agreement. Volterra would decide. He had expressed agreement with prosecutors' request for six months in jail, an 18-month sentence with 12 months suspended. Stern requested probation and psychiatric treatment, saying, "Richard Lavigne is a good man ... there is no evil in this man's heart. What he did on these two occasions does not take away from the good works he has done and from the fundamental goodness and worth of this man." He said the parishioners were "lost" without him and cited the crowd that came "all the way from Western Massachusetts to stand up for Father Lavigne ... how this man has inspired them spiritually, how he rejuvenated the faith of the older members of the church, and how he inspired the younger people to get involved...." The night before, Lavigne had called a few to warn them of the plea.[18]

Lavigne slowly rose and said, "I am sorry for the harm I have caused, and I ask for their forgiveness. As far as the other people who have accused me, if I have harmed them in any way by anything I have done, even if unintentionally, I ask for their forgiveness as well." He sat down, then Volterra shocked everyone with a rambling defense of Lavigne and the Church.

Lavigne during the trial (author's collection).

He bemoaned that Lavigne's "exemplary" career was "destroyed" and championed his "outstanding" ministry. He downplayed the sex crimes as minor, "at the low end of the spectrum" since all he did was touch "the buttocks of the two young men." After all, he reasoned, prosecutors only asked for a six-month sentence. He then excoriated the media for overblown coverage of a case that "did not merit the attention received." It deserved, he said, no more than "one column in the back pages of a regional newspaper, and perhaps a 30-second slot on Springfield TV." It should not have become a "cause célèbre," he chided, then he further lambasted the press for "relying on sensationalism and sexual pandering." Then he defended the Church, quoting a debunked *New York Times* claim that only 1.4 percent of priests committed sexual misconduct. The number, he preached, "must compare favorably as against the number of sexual offenders in the population."[19]

Volterra was further apologetic to Lavigne in sentencing. He barely criticized him for abusing "his power as an authority figure" and said he supported "short" incarceration versus a "draconian" sentence demanded for "public consumption by a less scrupulous prosecutor." Then, rather than the jail time he disingenuously supported during negotiations, he sentenced Lavigne on two concurrent, ten-year probation terms. Instead of jail, Volterra sent Lavigne to St. Luke Institute, a $500-a-day Church-affiliated facility near Washington, D.C., for seven to ten months. He could not live in a home, work, or have unsupervised contact with children under 16, and he could never again serve as a parish priest. Lastly,

Volterra ordered him to pay a victim witness fee of $50, the equanimity of which is impossible to distinguish. If he violated any terms, he could serve ten years.[20]

A smug Volterra exited the stunned courtroom as Lavigne's supporters, most still crying, descended en masse for more long embraces. For his part, Stern said, "I think this is a very sad day in a man's life, a life he's known for 25 years, his undying love for a parish, that life is over."[21] The plea deal, he said, "enables him to walk away with some dignity and start a new page in his life." Outside, a mob scene erupted. Lavigne and his entourage were engulfed by a surging crush of reporters and camera crews that chased them, running, down the sidewalk. Stern shouted at the media posse that they were a bunch of "vultures" as the Lavigne group ran a two-block gauntlet and disappeared into the parking lot behind Immaculate Conception Church where he had taken Mass that morning.

Even after Lavigne admitted guilt, the St. Joseph's crowd remained befuddled. One said, "At first I was surprised, but in retrospect, I shouldn't have been. I don't believe for one minute Father Lavigne is guilty of anything." A parishioner's son plaintively asked his father, "Why did Father Lavigne say he was guilty when he wasn't guilty?" The man could only reply, "I'll explain it to you on the ride home." The small group supporting the victim, unsurprisingly, took an opposing view. "If he wasn't a priest," one woman bitterly spat, "he'd be going to jail, not some country club."[22] The lack of jail time angered many, especially the Shattucks. They only agreed to drop the more serious charges because Lavigne would serve six months in jail. He not only skirted jail time, but also sidestepped two child rape charges and eight molestation counts. Those more serious charges carried much longer sentences than the lesser counts to which he pled guilty. Heads shook again when Volterra later said he did not order jail because he did not view the crimes as serious. He claimed worry that a trial would tax an already financially strapped state, and he predicted Lavigne would win an appeal based on the state legislatively extending the statute of limitations.

Carl and Bunny were horrified. Carl said, "It's an outrage, a slap in the face. An L.A. verdict," comparing it to the Rodney King beating trial that resulted in shocking innocent verdicts for four policemen. Bunny sighed, "The decision wasn't as great as I'd like. At least he admitted some guilt."[23]

People outside the family were also angered by the outcome. A week later, someone torched a car parked in the driveway of Lavigne's sister, with whom he had been living. The day before, a reporter had informed unknowing neighbors of Lavigne's presence. Surprisingly, two days after his plea, Lavigne gave an interview to an Amherst radio station saying he was writing a book to explain how he was "paying the price" for his lifelong rebel status: "Very few people know who I am. They know me from working with me, or my sermons, or the jokes I tell. But very few people know and understand me. I've got a lot to say. It's hard for me not to be able to tell my side of the story. But for now, I have to stay quiet. I'm a very, very trusting person, and I know if I go to the press with my story at this point, I could create problems for my defense. Being too trusting has always been one of my problems."[24]

The diocese footed Lavigne's $250,000 legal bill. A fellow priest said he was pleased the chancery was helping his friend, saying, "It's the Christian thing to do." Bishop Marshall's response was muted: "This series of events has truly been a tragedy for all concerned. I ask your continued prayers for the victims and their families, for Father Lavigne and his family, St. Joseph Parish, and for all who have been troubled by this matter." Marshall and the Church faced more pressing issues. Father Julian Pagacz of Northampton was charged with raping one girl and molesting another. Father Gary LaMontague of Springfield was charged with raping and fondling a woman. The day Lavigne pled, jurors heard final arguments in the Hingham rape trial of Father John Hanlon and James Porter pled guilty to charges based on his 30 years of child rape. One attorney, Jeffrey Anderson, was handling 200 active abuse cases in 27 states. A Springfield priest correctly foresaw an even deeper underlying problem. He warned Marshall the diocese using donations to defend accused abuser priests was not sitting well with the flock.[25]

On June 29, Lavigne entered St. Luke's manicured 43-acre campus outside Washington, D.C. The 32-bed treatment center was tucked behind an old girls' high school. Patient 12596 was driven past "Private Property" signs lining the driveway that wound alongside lush lawns below the low-slung brick building that looked more college dorm than medical facility. St. Luke was not Church-owned but affiliated with the Daughters of Charity Health System. Every incoming dollar, though, came from Church coffers. Priests, as well as a few nuns, were treated for sexual disorders, depression, anxiety, or drug and alcohol addictions. For Lavigne, it was as stress-free as prison was worrying. St. Luke went to great lengths to avoid any similarity to a penitentiary. A staffer said, "We do not have locked cells; we are not a prison." The only features even barely suggestive of one were the locked front door and an intercom in the glassed-in reception area. Patients ordered there by courts faced restrictions no tighter than those visiting via Church placement. The director claimed, "This is not summer camp," but for all intents and purposes, it was. Patients enjoyed single rooms with television, phone, private bathrooms, and daily maid service. Meals were prepared by a professional chef, served by waiters in a tastefully decorated dining room overlooking the grounds. The treatment regimen was equally relaxed, consisting of medical monitoring, individual and group therapy, pastoral discussion, and dietary counseling.[26]

Daily exercise classes were available, as was a twice-weekly program at a nearby luxury spa. On weekends, patients were unrestricted. There were group outings around D.C., movie and theater trips, and weekly parties celebrating birthdays and special occasions. The post-release schedules were even less demanding. For the first two of a five-year aftercare program, residents returned twice a year for a week-long follow-up, then once every other year. The only other requirement was to join a 12-step program of some type. It was illuminating when a Lavigne caregiver was asked about St. Luke's success rate for curing sex offenders and he replied, "like alcoholism, no one is cured."[27]

While at St. Luke, Lavigne kept in regular contact with his Shelburne Falls devotees. Many were victims still silent. He wrote scores of letters, made hundreds of calls. His remained devoid of self-awareness. He continued abusing Dana Cayo even after his indictment and frequently called from St. Luke's wondering if he "missed him." He disregarded Cayo's repeated "no" responses and proposed a "camping trip to Mt. Washington (New Hampshire)" after his release. Letters to other victims and their families evidenced a mind tortured by insecurity and a deepening persecution complex. His thoughts were suffused with strange logic. "I, for one, have given up on trying to convince anyone of my own situation," he wrote a parent. "People will believe what they will, one way or another. I have suffered, yes, but Gethsemane is at the heart of the ministry. Jesus wasn't killed because He was popular. He was killed because He spoiled the party for some people."[28]

To a pair of victim brothers, he was more upbeat, thanking them for their fundraising efforts and writing "Few priests can boast of having such great kids in their cheering section. I miss you all very much." He said St. Luke was like "summer school," and complained only about the weather.[29] His letters were decorated with whimsical sketches of flowers, boats, animals, and religious icons.

As Lavigne enjoyed St. Luke through the fall, Elliot Street received several dozen, mostly anonymous, letters from additional victims. It could no longer ignore the Lavigne problem after dozens of incidents were detailed in a lawsuit filed by ex-altar boys Paul Babeu, James Hernandez, and Lawrence Opitz. On September 16, Vicar General Father Thomas L. Dupré, a canon lawyer, penned an internal memorandum confirming the diocese had "'probable cause,' or indeed 'moral certainty' Lavigne is a pedophile and represents a danger to children." He said he did not believe Lavigne "should be trusted with any children under age sixteen." The fairly straightforward logic was years late in coming.[30]

As 1992 came to a close, the diocese remained strangely unresponsive to the avalanche of allegations. On December 14, Marshall held a bizarre press conference to announce the formation of a Diocesan Misconduct Commission to investigate improper conduct of diocesan personnel and address "exaggerated media coverage." He was as intransigent and defensive as his predecessor Maguire and angrily said, "The thing is magnified beyond all perception."[31] Marshall tried to avoid mentioning the press and ignored reporters' questions until he proposed that biased media coverage was actually a "left-handed compliment" of the Church's role in society. He failed miserably in claiming the diocese handled misconduct cases "to the best of our ability. You get the impression people think we are coddling these priests because we don't … chop their heads off. There are human beings who need help."

The nine-member commission included a retired judge, a nun, a psychologist, and a retired insurance agent. A hotline was set up for abuse complaints. If deemed "legitimate and serious," they would be investigated and recommendations for corrective action given to Marshall. He clumsily showed his true intentions when he warned prospective callers that his commission would have to "report lawbreaking activities to civil authorities [and] attract media attention." Despite the obvious scare tactic, the first call came in 20 seconds after the line opened.

Bennett's murder investigation was still paddling in circles. It was effectively closed, but it was collecting ever more abuse allegations against Lavigne. The 1972 investigators assumed there were more victims than the Croteau boys, but they were certain none would come forward. And, of course, investigators did not know to look for those victims in the first place. Robert Meffen headed the Crime Prevention Bureau in Springfield from 1966 to 1980 and said cleric abuse was rarely mentioned, Lavigne, never: "I don't recall him at all. Not a word."[32] It must be remembered the diocese was aware about everything, in real time. By the time of Lavigne's trial, Bennett had statements from 19 victims, incidents as old as 30 years and as recent as 10 months. As they learned more about his anger, brutality, and increasing threat levels, investigators became certain Lavigne was capable of murder. The new information added little to the case for Danny's murder other than confirming a propensity for violence and an abuse pattern that included Danny. The stories were creating a picture of a psychopathic pedophile who preyed on children his entire life.

Most surprising through 1993 was that so little outrage developed as the mountain of evidence confirmed priest abuse was not limited to a few rogue priests like Lavigne and the four in Western Massachusetts charged in the days around his trial. The problem was obviously systemic but people directed their anger at victims. The *Republican* received far more letters supporting than criticizing clergy. When 11 new victims announced lawsuits, victim condemnation intensified. One writer chastised the paper for "bias against everything Catholic" and accused "'so-called claimants [of being] frauds and phonies [who] rather than getting on with their lives [let lawyers] 'heal' them with cash. Someone else always will be the reason for their troubles, but never them ... [they] will never, never look into a mirror for the cause of their problems."[33]

Boston's Porter was back in the news, too. He had escaped to Oakdale, Minnesota, married and fathered four children, but he was then convicted and jailed for molesting a babysitter. More than 200 victims had come forward from Massachusetts and Minnesota to New Mexico, and he was extradited to Massachusetts to face charges. The state was able to prosecute because the statute of limitations froze when he bolted in 1967. In October 1993, he pled guilty to 41 of 43 counts and was sentenced to 18 to 20 years.[34]

The rising number of Springfield cases, Porter's catalog of abuse, and 20 Boston priests accused by that fall left no doubt Massachusetts had a problem, but the Church continued dismissing everything, and the majority of Catholics apparently did not care. Patrick J. Schlitz, a lawyer defending priests, claimed the Porter publicity "had 'skewed' the public's perspective on clergy sexual abuse and … churches have overreacted to the problem." He even said Church transfer policy wrongly "imputed upon the Church this evil intent." Boston's Cardinal Law bemoaned "the tragedy of a priest betraying the sacred trust of priestly service" and said priest abuse was a "rare exception." He cared only about "the unfortunate manner in which allegations against a former priest are made public."[35]

The lack of outrage was more surprising because, by the end of 1993, the Church had been sued in all 50 states and settlements passed half a billion dollars. It had also been confirmed that Church officials at every level knew of—and kept detailed records—of abuse, did not disclose anything to police, and systematically covered it up. The faithful's mystifying silence endured through the decade. By the mid–1990s, there seemed little interest in abusive priests, Lavigne, or Danny.

7

Resurrection

Within a month of Weldon's October 1977 retirement, Dupré—then diocesan co-chancellor—convened a meeting with a dozen priests at St. Bartholomew Church in Bondsville, Massachusetts. The remote hamlet was a curious location for the meeting, deep in the woods 30 winding country road miles from Springfield. Dozens of better-equipped churches with logistically friendlier locations could have more easily hosted the meeting. The only thing Bondsville *was* well suited for was Dupré's most pressing requisite: secrecy. During the meeting, Dupré ordered the destruction of all mention of abuse in the secret archives. A 17-year-old waiter eavesdropped on the weighty conversation and remembered, "I could tell this was really big." When the decision was made, he said, "The whole tenor of the meeting changed. I could tell the other priests were relieved." He was "relieved for [the priests], figuring this was an evil bishop who had all this info on these good guys."[1]

Dupré understood Weldon wanted the records to vanish, so he ordered secret archive files for every priest in the diocese destroyed. Five years later, Dupré boasted about the scheme during a meeting of the presbyteral council, the bishop's priest advisors, and he said Weldon ordered the housecleaning. According to witness accounts and court filings, Dupré laughingly told the assembled, "Fortunately for the Church, upon his [Weldon's] retirement, he destroyed many personal and personnel files ... [the diocese] was lucky." A priest who overheard the remark said Dupré had "glee in his voice and glee in his eye, almost gloating about it." Dupré later tried, unsuccessfully, to walk back on his comments, claiming he "vaguely recall[ed] saying something about this in an off-hand manner in passing, perhaps in answer to a question at a meeting."[2]

The cleansing was thorough. When victim lawyers later accessed the secret archives, there was not a single mention of abuse between 1970 and 1986. After the scrubbing, Dupré put Father Richard F. Meehan in charge of the archives. He had just returned from a Church sex treatment clinic, where he had been exiled for abuse.[3]

Weldon's successor, Maguire, repeatedly denied knowledge of abuse, but in July 1987, a Shelburne Falls woman wrote him a warning about Lavigne. She said he was "acting in an imprudent way" with Trinity boys. "We loved Father Lavigne," she said, and "did not want to hurt him [but were concerned he showed] great interest and spends a great deal of time with the boys, picking them up at school, etc." She worried "people are beginning to talk ... about going to the newspapers." Neither Maguire nor his then-assistant Dupré responded.

Bishop Thomas Ludger Dupré was directly involved in much of the clandestine Church behavior surrounding Danny's death and aftermath (author's collection).

Dupré forwarded the letter to Lavigne, writing, "As far as I am concerned that ends the matter."[4] The next bishop, Marshall, lied during a deposition when he said the diocese was unaware until the 1990s. Lavigne was at St. Joseph's during the years about which Marshall claimed ignorance.

Lavigne was quietly released from St. Luke on January 27, 1993. He returned to Ashfield, welcomed as a conquering hero. Other than saying his status was being reviewed the diocese was mum. Unaware of Lavigne's release, the next day, 11 victims came forward. Four held a press conference and described incidents in a Canadian motel, a remote Massachusetts cabin, an Arizona house, Lavigne's family home, St. Catherine's and St. Joseph's rectories, even churches. The victims were scattered across the country: Little Rock, Arkansas; Biloxi, Mississippi; western Massachusetts; Los Angeles. They were insurance agents, members of the Air Force, factory workers, and civil servants.

One was a movie director and one was a distant cousin of Lavigne. Two were nephews of Weldon close confidante Maurice E. DeMontigny. Another two, Brian and Michael McMahon, were ex–Circle, St. Catherine's altar boys, and D.A. Ryan's nephews. Michael was the boy slapped to the ground by Lavigne for teasing Danny during the Goshen camping trip. The group's lawyer, Michael Wiggins, was negotiating a settlement with Elliot Street.[5]

Bunny happened to see the press conference because a television was on as she cleaned the house. She was shocked, hearing Danny's name. "My body went numb," she said, "For 21 years I've lived every day hoping for some break in Danny's case. I'll probably go to my grave wondering." Carl said the 11 were "just the tip of the iceberg. We've been hearing things for years. Now we have faces with the whispers."[6]

On March 21, Marshall announced, "There are no circumstances under which I will permit Father Lavigne to serve as a priest in Springfield or any other diocese." Lavigne's plea deal prohibited such work anyway. Marshall was conciliatory, offering victims "a sincere apology and whatever assistance the diocese will extend to repair the harm."[7] Lavigne was still technically a priest, but a man without country. He settled in at Ashfield with a $1,030 monthly diocesan pension and an $8,000-a-year medical plan. Stern was then defending Lavigne in nine different Massachusetts courts.

On March 23, Danny's brothers Joseph and Gregory came forward. Joseph detailed incidents at Lavigne's family home, rectories, and Ashfield. Gregory described an attempt in a Vermont motel after Lavigne gave him a container of orange juice laced with vodka. Worse for the diocese, the brothers said they informed Father Leo O'Neil in 1988. O'Neil responded, "It was the first I've heard of it," and he promised "Lavigne would never harm another child." Not long after, O'Neil was named bishop of Manchester, New Hampshire. Barely two weeks after the Croteaus came forward, two more victims—from Springfield and Franklin County—also did. That brought the number of Lavigne accusers to 13. One of the original 11, Raymond Gouin, echoed Carl's "tip of the iceberg" sentiment, saying, "This is only the beginning. Believe me."[8]

Bennett's investigation remained basically inert through summer 1993, everyone involved still convinced of Lavigne's guilt but with nothing to prove it. The 1972 investigative files were reanalyzed, witness accounts reviewed, and witnesses re-interviewed. Unfortunately, the probe produced more setbacks than new clues. The dreadful handling of evidence and the problems with the forensics became clear, as did the crippling loss of key evidence, including the rock caked in blood and hair, other rocks and pieces of the bridge, the tire impression, and a bath towel retrieved from Lavigne's house. All vanished. A Chicopee detective somehow thought the bloody rock was "the only [missing item] that was significant." There was even confusion about evidence they still had. Original lists included two towels—one blue, one salmon—but current versions listed one and did not describe color. Fitzgibbon admitted the failings to Carl: "A lot of mistakes were made." Ryan recognized the magnitude of the forensic blunders. A staffer said, "Throughout the years, Matty used the case as a reference point for the need for better forensics."[9]

Bennett was simultaneously fighting several complicated court battles over evidence. First, the *Republican* sued for the release of the original investigative files, firing in October the first salvo in what would become a decades-long legal brawl. The court did order the release of a small portion in November, but the only document with new information was the 28-page affidavit in support of a request for a search warrant. Second, Bennett was fighting Lavigne over blood. Bennett believed DNA tests on the type B blood would place Lavigne at the river. A few months earlier, he sent the blood-stained straw to Dr. Edward Blake's lab in Richmond, California. Blake was perhaps the world's foremost DNA expert, a pioneer in the field. He did the DNA analysis for O.J. Simpson's defense team and freed an Illinois man from death row. By 1993, DNA results had freed a dozen men from prisons. Blake had a hand in eight of those cases. Biologic samples from blood, semen, hair, saliva, fingernails, skin, and so on could be easily compared. Every person, with the exception of identical twins, has unique genetic coding. Blake's test—polymerase chain reaction (PCR)—required only 1/1,000th of a drop of blood and was well suited for the type of evidence Bennett had: tiny, aged, degraded samples. His preliminary DNA tests for Bennett were inconclusive, though.[10]

Investigators believed the blood the most critical piece of evidence. Well, the evidence they had not misplaced, anyway. On September 2, a judge authorized taking Lavigne's blood, and the next day, two state troopers and Fitzgibbon took Lavigne from Ashfield to Baystate Medical Center in Springfield. Three vials of blood were drawn and placed in storage. Bennett had the blood, but it was useless without court approval. Carl questioned Lavigne's unwillingness to provide the sample, saying, "If he's got nothing to hide, why is he hiding? If I knew a blood test would clear me of a murder, I would bring a gallon of it in."[11]

A few days later, Lavigne was indicted by a Franklin County grand jury on child rape charges for an incident in Shelburne Falls in 1984 or 1985. More than a dozen Shelburne Falls regulars attended, along with Pastor John Roach of St. Brigid's Parish in Amherst. The statute of limitations had long since passed, making indictment largely symbolic. The charge, as expected, was dropped. The next morning, Lavigne was charged with three counts of assault and battery and child rape, based upon the allegations of Joseph Croteau, who had filed a civil suit. His memories had been repressed until Lavigne's 1991 arrest, but there were provisions in state law allowing extentions to the statute of limitations under such circumstances. The court held to the 1970s deadline and the charges were dropped. The civil suit was permitted to move forward.[12]

Bennett was farther from charging Lavigne in 1993 than Ryan was in 1972. His prospects were evaporating due to the now-confirmed evidentiary blunders. Nothing new was uncovered except the immense scope of Lavigne's sex crimes. He had been accused by dozens, most by then around 30 or older, but one as young as nine. Almost all were altar boys representing every assignment Lavigne had received, including Precious Blood (1967), St. Catherine's (1967–1968), St. Mary's (1968–1976), St. Francis' (North Adams, 1976–1977), and St. Joseph's (1977–1991). Lavigne's methods and madness are detailed in Chapter 9. Suffice it to say, his dedication to abusing children was extraordinary.

In early January 1994, the diocese confirmed settlement payments to 17 victims, totaling between $1,300,000 and $1,400,000. Elliot Street remained detached. In February, Marshall met with eight victims, who, to a man, complained about his lack of compassion. "This was business," said one, while another said, "I expected warmth and all I got was his stone face. I give up." Maurice DeMontigny, there supporting his two abused nephews, had a surprisingly opposite take, saying Marshall "conveyed a true sense of concern."[13]

More priests warned Marshall that parishioners were grousing about the financial cost of the abuse. The diocese was increasingly concerned that donation baskets were lighter. A letter was sent, to be read at every Mass, saying, "Please know this financial settlement will in no way be derived from your gifts to this parish or to the forthcoming annual Stewardship Appeal." Church leaders might stubbornly refuse to admit knowing anything, but above all, the money flow must be protected. A few months later, the diocese paid between $20,000 and $50,000 to a victim of Father Edward M. Kennedy, their fourth lawsuit-confirmed abuser.

Time remained an interminable slog for Carl and Bunny. That fall he said, "It seems like I've spent my life waiting. I'm sick of it. I'd like some answers." Bunny said she woke up every day hoping "maybe today. The waiting doesn't get any easier. It's torture, pure torture."[14] It continued.

Just before Thanksgiving, the Massachusetts Supreme Judicial Court ruled police violated Lavigne's rights when they took him from Ashfield to Springfield and forced him to provide blood. The court ruled the trip illegal because Lavigne had not been charged with anything. The blood was ordered returned. An appellate judge summarized Bennett's real problem: "It appears the Commonwealth does not have probable cause to arrest or to indict him." The blood was all Bennett had left. Without it, he confirmed, he had nothing with which to "charge anyone in this investigation."[15] He, and his investigation, were dead in the water. Again.

Lavigne lawyer Stern claimed victory and hoped the decision brought "an end to this investigation in very short order." Then, a few days later, he surprised everyone when he announced Lavigne's permission for the testing, because Lavigne had "nothing to fear." Many wondered why Stern, who said his client did not "think he should [remain] a suspect, because he didn't do it," fought the testing if Lavigne was innocent. It was because Bennett doggedly refused to drop the investigation into Lavigne even if DNA tests cleared him.[16]

As Christmas 1994 approached, Lavigne fled Ashfield to the anonymity of Boston. The city's most popular tourist spot, visited by 18,000,000 annually, is Faneuil Hall Marketplace, four warehouses dating from 1742 set around a cobblestone promenade with the deserved nickname "the Cradle of Liberty." In 1764, colonists protested England's Sugar Act there and birthed the cry "No taxation without representation!" George Washington toasted the new nation there. Samuel Adams and Susan B. Anthony led rallies there. Each building houses a collection of shops. The largest is Quincy Market. During the 1994 holiday season, its large rotunda was decorated with ten 20-foot banners strung from the dome below crossed gold staffs topped by angels. A man calling himself "Roger Coty" represented Parabel, the company that produced the hangings. Workers said Coty was the spitting image of Lavigne. Parabel's post office box was the same used by Lavigne to receive pension checks.[17]

That summer, Father Timothy J. Campoli, pastor at Blessed Sacrament in Greenfield, tapped Lavigne to design and manage the conversion of a crying room into an adoration chapel. The "bishop's junkman" acquired lanterns and fixtures from a razed church to hang above the altar. Only a few tradesmen realized that general contractor "Dick" was the disgraced priest from newspapers and television. Only a few church members realized, and those that did refused to talk to reporters. Lavigne, still contrarian, wanted to paint a large crucifix turquoise.[18]

Meanwhile, the fight over Lavigne's blood was lurching toward a conclusion. After a year in a Baystate Medical Center freezer, the three vials were sent, with the stained rope, to Blake. He clarified Bennett's conundrum: Even if the DNA matched Lavigne's, it did not conclusively link him to the murder. "DNA can only eliminate a suspect," Blake cautioned. Likewise, the absence of a match did not exonerate Lavigne, only confirming his blood was not on any evidence. It was all very confusing. Even the best possible result—Lavigne not excluded from leaving the blood—was a pyrrhic victory for Bennett. The DNA on the straw was "moderately common," present in more than 10 percent of males. Lastly, there were conflicting reports about the amount of blood on the rope available to test. Carl was told there was not enough. An assistant D.A. said there was "lots."[19]

In mid–June, the *Republican* hinted that Blake's results could not exonerate Lavigne. Stern refuted the notion, saying the tip was "not accurate."[20] Everyone was on edge for their own reasons. Carl and Bunny religiously watched television police dramas about forensic technology like *CSI*, and for the first time felt they understood what was happening and thought they might find answers. Stern was confident the results would once and for all clear Lavigne. Bennett was equally certain they would convict him. The diocese simply prayed the Lavigne fiasco would go away.

People on both sides were surprised, for their own reasons, when Blake determined the blood on the straw was not Lavigne's, and the results, at best, confirmed Lavigne was among 10 percent of the population with similar characteristics. The blood evidence could never convict Lavigne. Blake cemented the fact when he concluded, "If this is their only evidence, then forget it." Worse, the tests reportedly exhausted the blood on the straw, potentially preventing further testing. Even so, Bennett initially argued for more. As expected, Stern and Lavigne fought the notion.[21]

The vague results neither exonerated nor convicted Lavigne. They did confirm Bennett's last, best investigative hope was lost. Like Ryan before him, Bennett had nothing directly implicating Lavigne. He was at a dead end, so on October 26, he closed the re-investigation. He felt for the Croteaus, "It's certainly frustrating for the family that's had to live with this uncertainty for 23 years. I feel we've kept faith with the family," but he rightly concluded, "There's nothing more we can do." Stern proclaimed victory: "There has never been any doubt in our minds that Father Lavigne is totally innocent of this crime. As a result of the cloud of suspicion that has been maintained about his head for so long— fueled by constant inflammatory media coverage—he has been hounded from one end of the Commonwealth to the other and his health has been destroyed." For the third time, an investigation into Danny's murder whimpered to a close. Bennett had come to believe the murder was not solvable. Carl resigned himself to celestial justice, saying Lavigne "might have beaten man's law but he hasn't beaten God's law."[22]

On March 14, 1995, Thomas Ludger Dupré, the former chancellor who spearheaded the 1978 secret archive scrubbing and had for more than a decade ignored warnings about Lavigne, was appointed Springfield's seventh bishop. Short, bald, and bespectacled, Dupré was notoriously uncomfortable around people, even close associates, and he was said to appear "ill at ease even in a staged photo." His predecessor Marshall created the ineffectual Misconduct Commission but was, at least publicly, a hard-liner who refused to allow abuser priests back on the altar. Dupré, on the other hand, wanted to create a reentry system for them.[23]

Heading into 1996, the *Republican* was in its third year battling with the Church and Lavigne for the impounded records. Bennett emerged as a surprising Church-Lavigne ally, claiming release might jeopardize some future investigation by somehow discouraging witnesses from coming forward. On March 27, the appeals court unbound some files, including a portion of the autopsy report, the Chicopee P.D. investigative summary, and Trooper Thomas J. Daly's lengthy affidavit in support of the search warrant. The extensively redacted documents offered no new information, but they did confirm Lavigne was the "prime [and only] suspect." Daly's 28 pages outlined the case against Lavigne, but his personal theories and conclusions, particularly that Lavigne killed Danny, were censored.[24] The release did little more than reinforce the bleakness of any case against Lavigne.

The documents painted a picture of a suspect who certainly appeared guilty. Described were his awkward presence at the crime scene, curious questions about bloody rocks and tire tracks, and refusal to provide blood after learning blood at the scene matched his type.[25] His odd behavior with the Croteaus—badgering for a closed casket, missing the wake, and cutting off contact, among them—added to a portrait of guilt, and his many lies—denying being alone with Danny, their contact that week, and so on—exposed the true nature of his relationship with Danny.

On September 17, as a jury was being impaneled for Joseph Croteau's suit, Lavigne agreed to a settlement that prevented a trial during which he could be compelled to testify. That was never a certainty, though. Two months earlier, he went into hiding to duck subpoenas. He moved into his parents' Chicopee bungalow at 86 Haven Street, remaining there with his mother after his father Ovila died in late 2000. His funeral was at the same St. Rose de Lima Church where he and his children were baptized.[26]

Lavigne had changed little physically since his arrest. By then 56, he was the spitting image of another reputed murderer, Claus von Bulow, piercing blue eyes no less dead-looking, carrying himself with the same arrogant swagger. The diocese banned him from working with children in 1993, and he was just halfway through a ten-year probation ordering no unsupervised contact. Neither constraint deterred him from trying, though. For years, he regularly visited his friend Father John Roach at St. Brigid's in Amherst. Pastor Bruce N. Teague, himself victimized as a child, was fiercely protective of the church his grandfather helped found in 1929. He detested Lavigne's frequent presence, and he was alarmed Lavigne volunteered to join Roach hearing children's confessions.[27]

Teague warned the diocese, but he was repeatedly ignored. Since he had no power to bar Lavigne, he called Amherst police. They issued a trespass order prohibiting Lavigne from setting foot on the property under threat of arrest. Dupré responded by formally reprimanding Teague for "going outside the Church" and then harassed him about minor parish matters, while refusing repeated parishioner requests to meet. Dupré even penalized Teague for taking trips to Boston to help care for his terminally ill father and forced Teague out by not reappointing him pastor. One spoke for many when he said, "Father Teague was driven out of here because he protected children and dared to challenge to diocese about Lavigne while other priests were still socializing with Lavigne, and yet the diocese continues to coddle a convicted pedophile. It's an absolute disgrace." For his part, Teague said, "They were unhappy with me. I was a whistle-blower, and people got mad at me. I thought I was doing the right thing, to protect the children."[28]

Even with Danny off the front pages once again, people reached out to Carl and Bunny. In 1997, an elderly man called and gave Bunny a name and detail he thought might help the investigation. It turned out to be a lead that investigators had already followed, but the fact the man remembered Danny gave Bunny hope. The number of people wondering about the murder, even remembering at all, was dwindling by the late 1990s. Hope was in short supply. In 1997, after an event at St. Catherine's on the 25th anniversary of Danny's death, Bunny said, "All we're looking for is justice to be served, a chance for some closure. We still pray— every day—someone will come forward that knows something. Twenty-five years is a long time, but not long enough to forget what happened to Danny."[29]

In early 2002, Dupré touted the misconduct commission's success, boasting, "Thanks to that initiative, we are in a relatively good position." He was opaque about Church responsibility, proposing "in a pastoral context, it does not matter who was legally responsible." Despite the boast, diocesan strategies and commission processes were under withering attack. Dupré and his lawyers employed every imaginable tactic to discourage accusers, blunt suits, and stall trails. During their half-century relationship with the Egan law firm, the diocese developed and obeyed "a well-defined playbook of strategies for dealing with allegations." As described by writer Robert M. Kelly, the strategies were (1) to maintain position (we're broke, we're special, it's someone else's fault);

(2) to avoid decisions (make decisions by not making decisions, stall, litigate), (3) to avoid responsibility (hide power, create layers to diffuse accountability), and (4) to withhold information (never admit guilt, never give up defenses, maintain secrecy).[30]

Elliot Street followed the approach to the letter. They strung along one victim, whose allegation was made in 1988, long enough that the statute of limitations expired. They did not pay his claim for 16 years. The commission engaged in protracted foot-dragging, blaming delays on a lack of trained investigators. Four brothers met with the panel and Dupré, then waited over more than a year before the commission said the priest would "face our accusations." Stonewalling only increased. The commission waited another seven months to request yet more information, most of which it already had. They told another victim he should simply "should forgive the priest, pray for him, and move on." Amidst all his machinations, Dupré did not appreciate or simply ignored ominous trends. In the nine months after his paradoxical "relatively good" comment, the commission received 35 complaints. During the previous three years, they handled exactly four.[31]

Three nuns also faced accusations. One, Sisters of St. Joseph's Mary Jane Vidnansky, allegedly became pregnant during a two-year sexual relationship with a teen in the mid–1970s. She told him she underwent an abortion. The newer complaints contained even more abhorrent accusations. Worst, multiple statements hinted groups of priests and associates operated in organized rings. The first whiff of such a network arose in 2002 in suits that described group abuse by five Springfield priests—Thomas J. O'Connor, Francis P. Lavelle, Edward Kennedy, J. Roy Jenness, and Ronald E. Wamsher—and Greenfield Scoutmaster Bruce A. Mooney. Jenness hosted the secret 1978 Bondsville conclave, attended by Lavelle, Kennedy, and Wamsher, where Dupré ordered the secret archives cleansing. Records of the five were among those destroyed.[32]

The public was not accepting or even seriously considering how vast the Church's problem was. Little backlash was heard when it first arose in the late 1980s, then again in the early 1990s, and yet again in the mid to later 1990s. Even as numbers skyrocketed into the 2000s, there was mostly silence. Finally, in late 2003, a year during which 30 priests were accused in Springfield alone, long-sleeping Catholics were forced to recognize their ugly reality. The volume of accusations, the number of abuser priests, and the payoffs climbing past a quarter billion dollars were finally impossible to ignore. A 2004 *Washington Post* story reminded everyone that "the scandal exploded in 2002. The problem obviously simmered for over a decade before priest sexual abuse was finally accepted as scandal." The story succinctly confirmed "the moral dilemma should have been acknowledged decades earlier."[33]

By then, the plague was international in scope. A 2003 *New York Times* study detailed the thousands of accused priests around the world and the dozens of bishops forced to resign everywhere from Argentina, Germany, Ireland, and Poland to Scotland, Canada, Switzerland, and Austria. In the U.S. alone, 1,500 priests had been accused and five bishops forced to resign. The fallen included Boston's cardinal Bernard F. Law and Fall River bishop Sean Patrick O'Malley. Boston became the U.S. flashpoint, partly due to the numbers, mostly because of Law. He was once the most powerful member of the U.S. Conference of Catholic Bishops and Vatican spokesman on weighty matters like foreign policy and abortion. He was the first bishop accused of hands-on management of organized cover-up operations. Law was a serial excuser. He gave Father George C. Berthold, dean at two Boston seminaries, a glowing recommendation for a college teaching position in North Carolina less than two years after he fired Berthold for recurrent abuse. He paid tens of millions in hush money to families to shield more than 70 priests. After he paid off five families to protect Father Ronald H. Paquin, he reinstated Paguin and assigned him to another church. He described Father John J. Geoghan's 150 rapes as "isolated incidents," while transferring him a dozen times over ten years. Geoghan's (still-rising) cost to Boston exceeds $125,000,000. He was stomped to death by a cellmate in 2003.[34]

After Law himself was outed as a repeat abuser in 2002, and two hours away from a grand aury subpoena and multiple indictments, Pope John Paul II accepted his quiet resignation the minute it was tendered, a radical departure from Vatican protocol; it typically took months, sometimes more than a year, to finalize resignations and replacements. Then, in scenes worthy of a spy thriller, John Paul snuck Law out of his residence—with media trucks camped outside—in the middle of the night. He was trundled onto a private jet and whisked to safety behind Vatican walls, where U.S. law enforcement was powerless to intervene.[35]

Things were little different at Elliot Street, still clinging to the claim it never knew anything and hoping the crisis would pass. The local hypocrisy was as mind-boggling as the national and international hypocrisy. Angry parish priests still offered fiery semons denying the calamity. Pastor Gary Dailey of St. Mary Mother in Lee, Massachusetts, often angrily rebuked people critical of the Church. One Sunday he blamed their beliefs on Satan's desire "to plant anger, judgment, condemnation, and disunity amongst his parish," adding with flair, "Satan will not scatter [our] flock." A year earlier, his curate Father Paul Laflamme impregnated the rectory housekeeper. Dailey was accused of ordering her to "get rid of the problem" and fired her when she refused an abortion.[36]

Dupré maintained his determined defense of Lavigne despite a growing avalanche of criticism and worsening press. Held during a particularly heated period of public debate, Dupré's annual Catholic appeal fell more than 10 percent short of its $2,900,000 goal. It was the first time in 30 years the fundraiser had failed.[37] Dupré's response in September 2002 to a letter from prominent businessman who chided him for not punishing Lavigne offered a clear view of his utter disdain for critics and contrary facts. At times defiant, at others deluded, his response exemplified ingrained Church denial.

First accusing the writer of not being an "informed Catholic," Dupré warned of a rush to judgment that "we are in a country that believes … the innocence of any accused person until proven guilty." He cited death row vindications to support the possibility Lavigne could eventually be "found innocent," somehow forgetting his previous guilty plea. His most puzzling notions described the Church's supremely flawed familial structure; he believed priests deserved special consideration because they were part of a "family," in a relationship with the Church similar to "husband and wife" or the "adoption of a stranger." Abusers, he suggested, were like family members: "if a brother or nephew committed a crime, families would not disown the guilty party." To the contrary, Dupré preferred to "extend a helping hand." Regarding Lavigne, he mentioned only the most recent accusation, as if his earlier crimes had never occurred. Most telling was his response to the proposition that a priest was "just a man." Dupré believed, "Yes, he is a man. But he is a priest forever. Whether a priest ends up in heaven or hell, he will always be a priest."[38]

Lavigne completed his probation that June and was still technically a priest. Said to be suffering from heart issues, he was still receiving his diocesan pension and health benefits, and still had supporters. Linda Poirier grew up with him and claimed not to have seen any of the bizarre childhood behavior others on the street witnessed. She thought, "He's being unfairly targeted."[39] Classified by the state sex offender registry board as a Level 3 Offender, with the highest likelihood of reoffending, he nonetheless went to court to avoid registering.

In late 2002, more impounded documents were released, including several dozen new victim accounts and details of the Arizona vacation with the Shattuck boy. By Christmas Lavigne was named in 15 suits. In the following months, he was sued three more times. For the first time, Dupré was named as a defendant.[40]

8

Downfalls

Unknown to Dupré, the previous April saw the onset of a storm. Chance events, coincidences, and unrelated incidents coalesced to end Lavigne's quiet retirement and bring Dupré down. Irish-born nun Sister Mary McGeer was a feisty, 44-year member of the Sisters of St. Joseph and assistant to the pastor at St. Michael's Church in East Longmeadow. The upper-middle-class enclave is among only a few Springfield suburbs to historically flourish. The picturesque town center boasts the most dangerous traffic rotary in the world, where locals perilously navigate the convergence of seven busy streets at a nightmarish maze of yield and stop signs. St. Michael's was the only Catholic church in town and among the most prosperous in the diocese.

One April morning, Sister Mary noticed a crumpled fax in the trash that she had not seen before. She retrieved it, smoothed it out, and read a letter from ex-parishioner Warren Mason, one among thousands of newly-lapsed Catholics upset with the Church. He was particularly angry that only one clergyman spoke out against Lavigne in the decade since his arrest. St. Michael's pastor, a month from retirement, had thrown Mason's letter away. Sister Mary put it in her desk, planning to give to incoming pastor, James J. Scahill. Like McGeer, Irish and feisty, he grew up in Hungry Hill and was a no-nonsense priest whose first assignment in 1988 was, coincidentally, St. Catherine's. He later served 14 years at another Lavigne posting, St. Mary's. He heard stories at both.

The day Scahill arrived, Sister Mary gave him the letter and convinced him to meet with Mason, saying, "Maybe you could convince him to at least return to the Church." By the time they met, Mason had become more incensed after Chicago's archbishop Francis George suggested, during an NPR interview, that sex between a priest and a minor girl was excusable, even understandable, if the priest was drunk, but he was still most infuriated by the lax punishment of Lavigne and the fact that he remained on the payroll. Mason said, "As long as Richard Lavigne and his kind are being financially supported by this diocese I'll never give another dime!"[1]

Every parish gave the diocese 6 percent of weekly collections for cash needs. Mason recommended Scahill hold back that money until Dupré stopped supporting Lavigne. To gauge parishioner opinion, Scahill mentioned it during the next day's Sunday sermon. The entire congregation rose, as one, in a prolonged standing ovation. Scahill then approached Dupré at a Presbyteral Council meeting and asked him about the "lucky diocese" comment he overheard at the previous gathering. Dupré dismissively said he knew nothing about destroyed records. The next day, Scahill pressed Dupré at Elliot Street and broached the subject of holding back the 6 percent until Dupré ceased paying Lavigne and initiated the laicization process. An incredulous Dupré, red-faced and livid, could only scream, "What?" He threatened to suspend Scahill and remove him from St. Michael's, howling, "You cannot do that. There will be no conversation relative to this matter. You absolutely cannot do that."[2]

Dupré's response left Scahill with but a single thought, that "no doubt Lavigne has something on the Bishop or his friends."[3] Dupré initially convinced Scahill to postpone any action and keep quiet until after a bishop's conference two months hence, but Mason persuaded Scahill otherwise. When he announced the holdback to his congregation the next day, he was met with another ovation. He began withholding the money. Mason contacted *Republican* reporter Bill Zajac, who had aggressively covered the scandal for years. Their "6% Solution" became a media sensation, dominating national television and front pages.

An epic battle was underway between what the public perceived as forces for good—Scahill, et al.—and evil—the Church and Lavigne. The players and their roles were obviously stereotypical. Scahill was the crusader priest standing up to the Church, with Mason as Sancho Panza to Scahill's Don Quixote. Zajac was the small-town reporter, champion of the moral good. Lavigne was the evil predator he was in real life, Dupré, the face of an obstinate Church. A victim lawyer said, "When this is all over, Scahill will probably be considered for sainthood." Stories about the standoff filled the front pages of newspapers everywhere, *Los Angeles Times*, *The Washington Post*, *The New York Times*, even *The Wall Street Journal* and London's *The Times*.[4]

Publicly, Dupré responded in measured tones. He expressed his "disappointment" and said Scahill was a "compassionate and good pastor" whose decision was "regrettable."[5] Privately, he was blinded by rage, and he threatened to oust Scahill from the diocese, but he had been masterfully backed into a corner. He still did nothing about Lavigne. Dupré's prospects worsened over the summer. Zajac was involved in the *Republican's* court battle to release files relating to Lavigne and the accusations of abuse made against him, and documents released in the fall contained more bad news. Multiple statements described more abuse by Lavigne, included details of Vermont trips, and, worse, the sharing of victims. Disgusted readers had only heard half the story.

The Dupré-Scahill confrontation intensified through 2003, neither budging. Dupré was furious when he learned attendance at St. Michael's spiked 30% after Scahill took his stand. Dupré blinked in January 2004, initiating the lengthy, convoluted laicization process to defrock Lavigne, but he continued to pay Lavigne's pension and cover his medical plan. Dupré seethed behind closed doors, but could do nothing to punish Scahill. Scahill was already paying a hefty personal and professional price. Dupré vilified him inside the church and no fellow priest offered even halfhearted support. In fact, he was openly shunned. Priests turned their backs to him, ignored him, and refused to speak to him publicly or privately. "They thought I was trying to destroy the Church," he said, "but should we not stand up when the Church does the wrong thing?"[6] Church solidarity during a crisis and avoiding scandal are prime directives. Scahill was, after all, causing disunity and perpetuating scandal.

Scahill imagined he might receive pushback, but he was unprepared for the vitriol. "I knew damn well what I was stepping into, that this would create a lot of anger and resentment," he explained, "but frankly, I had no way of knowing just how deep this went." Sister Mary witnessed the abysmal treatment, saying, "There's a very strong silence that goes on. As a result, priests are not breaking that silence." Scahill's trials mirrored those of Father Bruce Teague, shunned and eventually forced from his parish for involving police to keep Lavigne away from children. Both incidents evidenced a shameful dynamic. "It's almost like the type of stuff you see in cult behavior," Teague said. "Someone on the outside would say, 'That's crazy.' But when you're on the inside, you say, 'It's perfectly right, because everything is divinely inspired.'" A Dupré priest even approached Zajac requesting he pen a story smearing Scahill. He told Zajac that Scahill was mentally unbalanced and had suffered a nervous breakdown. He had—30 years earlier. Zajac refused to write the hatchet piece. Despite Dupré's initiation of the defrocking process, Scahill refused to resume the diocesan tithe until Lavigne's financial benefits ceased. Dupré fumed.[7]

At the same time, Lavigne's legal woes continued. In March, another wave of victims came forward, pushing the total past 30. Among them were two women, Elizabeth A. Germond and Susan F. Morris. Beth Germond was the daughter of Lavigne's closest friends Mitchell and Blanche Tenerowicz, with whom he socialized almost weekly—often bringing victims along—for years. Lavigne enjoyed free access to their Vermont chalet and Massachusetts lake house. Lavigne abused Beth from age eight to 17, usually during private counseling sessions. Blanche drove Beth to those appointments.[8]

Then, Bennett announced he was again reopening the investigation into Danny's death. Carl and Bunny pleaded with him to "go the last mile" and Bennett agreed to do so. Bennett clung to the hope Blake's newer testing methods might yield results from the rope, able as investigators now were to match DNA using as little as a single skin cell. In March, Bennett asked Lavigne for more blood but he refused, setting off another court battle that would drag on for two years.

Over the years, Bennett's investigators followed dozens of leads that initially seemed promising. Among them were four witnesses (in 1991, 1993, 2000, and 2004) who claimed to have seen Lavigne "either with Danny that day or near the site by the river." Each account was flawed, though. The 1991 sighting could not be corroborated. The 1993 witness' claim he saw Lavigne fleeing "at a high rate of speed" was undermined by a further assertion he heard what he "thought was an 'animal' moaning." No such noises would have carried to the street. Danny was making no sounds, moaning or otherwise, when his killer drove away. He was dead. The 2000 witness described a car thundering down to the river and disposal of a body. That claim was knotty because Danny was not killed elsewhere, then dumped. The 2004 witness claimed to have watched the murder, but that was improbable due to the terrain.[9]

Bennett's latest inquiry was saddled with the same core issues as the others. Like Ryan, he appeared not averse to pursuing Lavigne, but judicial deference to the Church continued. Hampshire County D.A. Judd Carhart and his assistant David Angier refused multiple requests to subpoena Manchester, New Hampshire, bishop Leo O'Neil, who was at St. Catherine's in 1972. Their incomprehensible reason was that doing so "would be ill-perceived by the Grand Jury members and/or the public."[10] Bennett's major complication, though, was personal. He was known as outwardly arrogant, bitingly condescending, and for unfailingly rejecting opinions contrary to his. Worse, he was obsessed that no other department, or investigator, solve *his* cases. Bennett's treatment of R.C. Stevens is an example.

The *Republican* retained Stevens to investigate the murder, Lavigne, and Danny. The former state police investigator was among the most respected private detectives in New England, consulting on dozens of high-profile cases. Stevens gathered boxes full of information and scores of leads missed by Ryan and Bennett, including Lavigne's childhood and seminary history, relationships with other abusers, and abuse history. He delved deeper into Danny's life and relationships then either Ryan or Bennett had, and he identified suspects not previously considered. Stevens offered to share his files, but while Bennett and his lead investigator Peter Higgins publicly welcomed the assistance, they habitually rebuffed Stevens and ignored his data. Bennett agreed to share information only to delay delivery and to eventually refuse to provide it. He only grudgingly allowed Stevens to review the initial case files, but forbade him from making notes or copying anything, even ordering a hulking state policeman stand over him during the process.[11]

Stevens arranged for Dr. Henry Lee to analyze the blood evidence. Dr. Lee was the world's most renowned forensic scientist and had consulted on the most famous cases in U.S. history, including the JonBenét Ramsey, O.J. Simpson, Laci Peterson and Vince Foster cases as well as the reinvestigation of the assassination of President John F. Kennedy. Bennett publicly welcomed Lee's assistance, but ignored multiple information requests from Lee. Bennett and Higgins pointed fingers at Lee, claiming they called him several times but received no response. Lee said he never received a single call from either.

A further example of Bennett's intransigence was his stubborn legal battle with the *Republican* even as his positions were repeatedly and soundly bludgeoned by courts. He clung to the illogical excuse that the case was still technically open and the pretext that release of information would scare witnesses away, but each release confirmed Bennett's missteps and people he should have at least *considered* a suspect. Personal connections and investigative avenues were likewise ignored or unrecognized.[12] Despite fighting the paper tooth and nail over everything, Bennett had the chutzpah to ask it to share the $10,000 cost of Lee's work. Bennett chose to ignore Lee's offer to help, anyway. No one else was going to solve Danny's murder, or so it seemed.

Bennett's was not the only department taking wrongheaded positions. On April 1, Lavigne finally registered with Chicopee P.D. as a Level 3 Offender. CPD inexplicably refused to post neighborhood notifications, even though state law required it. CPD claimed it was "unnecessary because of all the publicity he had received." Bunny said, "I wanted to put up signs all around his block warning everybody."[13]

In June, Scahill, still withholding his 6 percent, met with Dupré. During the contentious meeting, Dupré threatened him with suspension and accused him of breaking his oath as a pastor and costing the diocese "thousands and thousands and thousands of dollars." Scahill's campaign was also hurting the yearly stewardship appeal underway at the time. By the fall, Dupré was in scramble mode. In two years, 50 complaints were filed against his priests, nuns, deacons, even lay employees. The diocese was a defendant in more than 20 suits alleging Elliot Street cover-ups. They so clogged the courts, a judge combined them into one action Dupré was furiously trying to settle. Even as his lawyers tried to have another half-dozen suits quashed, Dupré continued to minimize. He assured reporters, "I think when this all is made public the problem is going to be seen more in perspective." Asked about the lengthy settlement negotiations, he dismissively said, "You don't hand out money to people just because they ask for it."[14]

In September, five more victims squared off with the diocese. For more than a year, Dupré and his lawyers used every conceivable strategy to delay, stonewall, and obfuscate. The previous June, the diocese argued the First Amendment protected the "'intrinsically religious' relationship between a bishop, diocese and priest," so civil courts had no authority over the two dozen suits in play. The court disagreed, so the diocese then argued state charitable immunity laws somehow safeguarded churches from suits. Every frivolous iteration prolonged victim agony.[15]

130 Death of an Altar Boy

Dupré's enmity toward Scahill had worsened and things came to an embarrassing, public head that fall. Trying to discredit Scahill, Dupré invited the media to attend their depositions regarding the Weldon-Dupré purge. On September 25–26, the sides squared off before the press in the offices of diocesan law firm Doherty, Wallace, Pillsbury, and Murphy. Dupré's strategy backfired monumentally. His press liaison Mark Dupont earlier claimed Dupré "absolutely [denied] saying anything" about file destruction, that Scahill made a grievous "oversimplification of a complicated conversation." He accused Scahill of being prone to "wild speculation" and "exaggerated facts."[16] Dupré's circus proved Dupont's claims baseless.

Under oath, Dupré denied diocesan knowledge of abuse during Weldon's tenure. Scahill roundly debunked the statement, providing a list of priests—like O'Neil and Griffin—who discussed it multiple times. Dupré fared just as poorly denying secret archive destruction. He claimed to have "no knowledge any Church records were destroyed," doubling down by again denying the "lucky diocese" comment. He said he "never would have said Bishop Weldon would have destroyed papers. I do not have knowledge that Church documents were destroyed by anyone." He implied Scahill misunderstood him, that he may have been describing the culling of Weldon's papers by his assistant after he died. Scahill refuted this by naming the other priests who heard Dupré's comments. Dupré had no believable response to a single Scahill rebuttal. Worse, Dupré appeared duplicitous when he refused Scahill's demand he release the 18 priests at the meeting from their privacy oath so they might weigh in, under oath, about who was telling the truth. Dupré's deposition debacle was just the latest black eye for the diocese.[17]

Just a few days later, Dupré and Scahill crossed paths at a gathering of priests in Ogunquit, Maine. A red-faced Dupré dressed Scahill down before the group for being disobedient, disloyal, and costing the diocese money. Scahill's measured response, which infuriated Dupré, was simply "I am not disobedient. There is no virtue to obedience that requires the surrender of virtue. There is no virtue to obedience that requires one to go myopically blind, like the soldiers of Hitler." Back in Springfield, Scahill demanded a meeting with Dupré, during which he stridently criticized Dupré's personal attack and bogus money agenda. He further enraged Dupré by noting the obvious contradiction between the claim Scahill was costing Dupré money and Dupré paying millions to Lavigne victims. When Scahill—now not simply asking, but demanding—Dupré end financial support of Lavigne, Dupré became unhinged and bellowed, "Don't tell me what to do!" When he again threatened to suspend Scahill, Scahill yelled at Dupré, "Don't threaten *me!*"[18] He walked out, leaving Dupré screeching in the background.

A month later, on November 12, Dupré further seethed when Scahill was among six priests honored by the Survivors Network of Those Abused by Priests (SNAP). Scahill called out the Church and its bishops. "It is regrettable that you should have to establish an award to give to a priest for integrity," he said. "Integrity is something that should be expected from us. Yet, inexplicably, the vast majority of clergy has been silent. In their complicit silence, they have betrayed truth and turned their backs on children and minors. By and large, the clerics have been myopic company puppets instead of being men." On November 20, the Vatican informed Dupré it was defrocking Lavigne. Dupré ignored the dispatch.

In the two years since Scahill's crusade began, local displeasure with Dupré mounted, as did ever-louder calls for his ouster. Nationally, the news remained all bad. Settlements skyrocketed into the hundreds of millions. In Boston alone, more than $95,000,000 was paid to 550 victims, and in Springfield, more than $7,500,000 to less than a few dozen. An expected U.S. Conference of Catholic Bishops report, anticipated to confirm a century of Church cover-up, further inflamed. To the Church's dismay, into the fall, the Dupré-Scahill standoff remained on front pages. The *Boston Globe* described the Church as "laden like a boil that needs to be lanced."[19] As 2003 ground toward 2004, every article increased Dupré's loathing of Scahill, but he still refused to announce Lavigne's defrocking. His true motivation was far more damning than a rogue priest.

Like most bellwether events in the Danny Croteau saga, Dupré's ruin evolved from happenstance. By that December, Bill Zajac had written hundreds of articles about the diocese, Danny, and cleric abuse. A week before Christmas, he answered the phone at his desk, and an anonymous voice said, "Check out Dupré being an abuser." Zajac did, and he discovered Dupré abused Holyoke natives Thomas Deshaies and his best friend Tuan Tran, then in their 40s, as teens. Zajac was acquainted with Deshaies' mother, Helen. She was the secretary at his children's Holyoke school, Precious Blood, Lavigne's first parish. She was stunned when Zajac asked her about Dupré and abuse. She called her son at his University of Connecticut office and he confirmed he'd been abused, but adamantly refused to discuss it with anyone, including her.[20] Furious, she wrote Dupré. He ignored her letter.

By chance, that same week, Tran emailed Dupré. The next morning, Dupré made the surprising announcement he was considering early retirement for "health reasons." It was odd because he was known for his vigor and never taking a day off. A week later, Helen Deshaies heard him on television, announcing a fund to support priests accused of abuse. She was so angry she "was yelling at the television and swearing. I couldn't believe what I was hearing." She sent Dupré another, more heated letter. When he again ignored her, she called Zajac. She said Thomas was introduced to Dupré at age 12 by Tran, then 15, whose family attended Dupré's West Springfield church. The Vietnamese immigrant Trans were, like most of the parish, new to the country. The church sponsored them because their father was not allowed to emigrate. Their first months were spent in a diocesan convent. For the Deshaies, Dupré was a frequent houseguest and family advisor. He counseled Thomas after his firefighter father died during a blaze and appeared a generous, caring benefactor to both boys. When Tran developed an alcohol problem, Dupré paid for rehab. Dupré invited their families to his 1995 installation as bishop. All those years, he was abusing both boys.[21]

The *Republican* decided against running the story, technically because it was unsubstantiated, but in point of fact because it seemed almost too fantastical. Dupré was, after all, a sitting bishop. For months, Helen Deshaies tried to coax her son out of his silence while a frustrated Zajac kept mum. Meanwhile, Dupré was condemning Zajac for supporting Scahill and bashed him in the press and inside the diocese. So Zajac called Scahill. He said only, "If Dupré tries to come after you, mention this name." He said "Deshaies" and hung up. Dupré received an anonymous email at the same time. It touched on abuse, Deshaies, and Tran.[22]

Meanwhile, the Bennett-*Republican* tiff raged on, the files still sealed based on a 1996 appeals court ruling, but in October, superior court judge Peter A. Velis ordered everything released as long as witness names and addresses were redacted. The trove included initial police investigative files, autopsy reports, and documents pertaining to the Lavigne blood fight. Velis was reversed in November by a state appeals court judge on appeal by Lavigne and Bennett, still pressing the scared witness fantasy. Even Massachusetts supervisor of records Alan N. Cote asked the court to order release, and in December, the *Republican* appealed to the Massachusetts supreme judicial court. Carl joined the *Boston Herald* in an affidavit supporting release.[23] It appeared a final decision was on the horizon.

The diocese continued attacking any dissenters, in or out of the ranks. Comments from Elliot Street loyalists devolved into unseemly ad hominem attacks on anyone the least bit critical. On December 8, a small group of protesters—mostly made up of victims' parents—outside Dupré's offices carried signs demanding his resignation. Most passersby on the quiet street ignored them, but a stream of staff entering the building laughed, insulted, and mocked the group. Even two elderly nuns in full habits "loudly jeered" as they entered the building.[24]

News for Lavigne continued to disappoint. By the end of 2003, he had been accused by almost 40 people. Then, on January 20, 2004, Dupré announced his defrocking, the first laicization in Springfield history. Dupré was roundly criticized for delaying the announcement he was ordered to make in November. He first claimed not to have received the news until January 9. Then he had Vicar General Father Richard Sniezyk offer a patently fabricated excuse, that the decree "had to be translated from Latin." Lavigne, according to Dupré, vigorously fought the process and was "disappointed." He would be removed from the payroll May 31 unless "he is 'truly indigent.'"[25]

Of Lavigne, Dupré said his priesthood "had unfortunate and tragic consequences," but, he insisted, "along the way, much good was achieved." He added, prophetically, "The enormous harm that occurred, and continues today, cannot or should not be forgotten." He was again forced to deny 1960s–1970s diocesan knowledge of Lavigne and resurrected the increasingly dubious claim he only learned of Lavigne and abuse during a Maguire meeting in 1986. The diocese tried to distance Dupré from the Lavigne-Danny problem, claiming, "Even after being named Chancellor of the diocese in 1977, there was no instance in which any particulars of the Croteau case came under his review." Unfortunately, Father O'Neil's suspicious $700 gift to the Croteaus was outlined in the latest document release. The clear appearance of bribery cast further doubt on Dupré reliability. The diocese apparently even recruited O'Neil's family to suggest the gift was in keeping with his habit of "giving away his money to help, to comfort," except it was unlikely the money was his. Either way, the public was having none of it.[26]

Lavigne's defrocking was universally praised. Victim Peter Bessone wept when given the news, saying he "prayed to God, every day 'Don't take me until I see this man defrocked.'" His cousin David, a fellow Lavigne victim, killed himself in 1985. Peter, battling cancer, visited the cemetery the next day to "tell David the news. David can rest in peace. I'm finally going to be able to die in peace." Carl said, "It was welcome but long overdue. At least there's some justice." Some of the flock disagreed, donating more than $100,000 to Dupré's fund for accused abusers. To placate critics, Dupré said any money paid Lavigne would not come from the diocese but from the fund Scahill dubbed a "felons' fund."[27] Every single donor demanded anonymity.

Dupré's stubborn refusal to discipline Lavigne baffled insiders. The reason became clear just weeks after the defrocking announcement. Thomas Deshaies refused his mother's repeated urgings to come forward, refusing to even discuss it. He did take her advice he see a therapist, who recommended he convey his anger directly to Dupré. At the same time, Dupré sensed something ominous in the wind after the anonymous email and reached out to Deshaies and Tran. In early October, Deshaies and Dupré met at the Publick House in Sturbridge, Massachusetts, an hour east of Springfield. It was probably among the more fascinating conversations to have taken place there since its 1771 opening. After Deshaies told Dupré he never wanted any sexual relationship, Dupré accused him of authoring the email (he did not). Dupré then unemotionally said he "was sorry and did not realize you did not want a sexual relationship" and hoped they could "remain friends the rest of their lives."[28] The conversation ended abruptly when two women approached the table to greet Dupré.

In early November, Helen Deshaies, following Scahill's standoff with Dupré and unaware of the Publick House meeting, called Scahill. He was shocked to recognize her name as the one Zajac mentioned using against Dupré. She described Dupré's abuse of Thomas and Tuan. When she described her unanswered letters to Dupré, his then-surprising retirement musing suddenly came into relief. Scahill met with her through the fall. Zajac and the *Republican* still held the story, waiting for one of the two to file a lawsuit that would support the public telling.[29]

In the interim months, Dupré made half a dozen impassioned speeches urging Catholics to support a constitutional amendment banning gay marriage and that included extremely critical attacks on the homosexual lifestyle described as "vitriolic and overly aggressive." Tran, living in California after coming out as gay in 1989, heard the comments and was infuriated enough by Dupré's hypocrisy to travel across country to sit with Scahill. Thomas Deshaies was still refusing to go public, but he agreed to attend the meeting.[30]

A few weeks later, in November, they met with Scahill and described their relationships with Dupré and provided details of the abuse. Their experiences were eerily reminiscent of Lavigne's relationships with the Croteaus and Shattucks. Dupré deftly groomed the families, first offering assistance; for Deshaies, it was helping him through his father's death, and for Tran, teaching him English to help his acclimation. Dupré encouraged them to become altar boys, plied them with gifts, introduced them to museums and opera, and took them camping and on day trips around New England. He even took Deshaies to Canada for a week. Dupré introduced them to homosexual sex by forcing them to read homosexual pornography he kept in a locked briefcase. Before assaulting them, he got them drunk on wine and cognac and made them read his magazines.[31]

When Deshaies complained, Dupré warned the "alternative was a promiscuous gay lifestyle at bathhouses" where he would surely contract AIDS. Dupré railed about the disease, showed them "pictures of men dying with AIDS so they wouldn't have sex" with anyone else and warned, "This is what could happen to you. Therefore, you come to me." They were terrified by the frightening stories and awful images. Like Lavigne and many cleric abusers, Dupré was quick with God excuses. "[Our] relationship was a logical expression of love, and God teaches love," he said, adding, "I'm God. You are sleeping with God." Deshaies' ordeal lasted into his college years, Trans' when he began dating girls in high school. After the abuse ceased, Dupré kept in contact through calls and holiday and birthday cards that frequently included cash. In 1990, he called to say he could not accept his earlier appointment as auxiliary bishop unless they promised never to discuss the abuse. They agreed.[32]

Scahill urged them to come forward, perhaps too intensely, because his entreaties scared them off and they retreated into silence. He wanted to alert the Church but was uneasy about calling Elliot Street. With Sister Mary and her partner Sister Betty Broghan present, on November 14, Scahill called Boston and left a message with Bishop Sean P. O'Malley's private secretary, saying that he needed to discuss "dire" matters.[33] O'Malley ignored the call, so Scahill contacted Massachusetts attorney general Thomas F. Reilly. Reilly called back ten minutes later and within two hours was at the rectory 90 miles from his Boston office. Reilly listened to Scahill but said he could do nothing unless the men came forward. O'Malley later denied receiving any call from Scahill and scolded him instead: "An unsolicited phone call of such an ambiguous nature is not the way you handle serious matters such as this." Scahill produced telephone records proving O'Malley a liar.

At the end of January, hundreds of Carl and Bunny's friends gathered at an Enfield, Connecticut, hotel to celebrate the Croteaus' 50th wedding anniversary. During the party, Dupré walked in, invited by a relative. Carl and Bunny were furious.

Scahill called Zajac to discuss the Deshaies-Tran meeting. Zajac wanted to run the story that had been shelved for more than a year. He was sure some paper, somewhere would stumble onto the bombshell. Warren Mason had warned if the *Boston Globe*—investigating Dupré— scooped the *Republican*, the "the biggest story in Church, maybe Springfield, history" would be lost. On Monday morning, February 9, Zajac called Deshaies at the University of Connecticut, urging him to talk. He refused, so Zajac drove the hour-plus to Storrs, arriving unannounced at 2 o'clock. Deshaies angrily threw him out, yelling, "How can you ask me these questions?" Driving back to Springfield, Zajac was more determined to release the story, even without the victims' assistance. His editors finally agreed, requiring he first contact Dupré. He called Elliot Street to request an interview, saying only he needed to speak to Dupré about a past relationship with two men. As expected, he heard nothing.[34] That night, diocesan press liaison Mark Dupont worked late. At 1 a.m., lights were on in Dupré's private quarters.

The next day, Tuesday, February 10, was a big day in Massachusetts. In Boston, the state legislature was taking historic votes on gay marriage.

In Springfield, it would be bigger. Dupré's day began typically, saying Mass in his private chapel. His schedule was crowded, first on the docket an early morning funeral. Dupont called Zajac back at 9:30 and asked him to fax a list of detailed questions. At 9:45, Dupont received the summary of the Deshaies-Tran allegations, and without reading it, sealed it in an envelope marked "CONFIDENTIAL" and had it hand-delivered to Dupré. He evidently read it. After lunch, during a 2 o'clock meeting with a Peruvian bishop, he was distracted and agitated. After barely 20 minutes, he abruptly ending the meeting—expected to last two hours—and hurried to his office. He shut the door and called the papal nuncio, the Vatican's U.S. representative, in New York.[35]

Half an hour later, Dupré called his inner circle together and told them he was retiring. He ordered the announcement be put off until the next morning, mentioning nothing about the fax. The brief meeting tumbled Elliot Street into chaos. The bishop was leaving, and no one knew why. Dupont, the main press contact, learned when he was handed a typed statement at 4 o'clock. Sniezyk learned at 7 o'clock when Dupré called and asked him to return to Springfield from a Florida vacation. Dupré offered nothing beyond pleasantries, betraying no concern about anything. Shortly after, he secretly fled Elliot Street for St. Luke.[36]

In the morning, the diocese remained in a frenzy. At 6 o'clock, the Vatican announced Dupré's retirement, said to be for health reasons. An hour later, the diocese issued a confirming press release and scheduled a 2 o'clock press conference, during which Sniezyk discussed the stunning announcement. He said the "last two years were very trying [and] took a toll on his health" so Dupré checked into an unnamed hospital for treatment of "heart and back issues." Sniezyk lauded Dupré's dedication to his work, saying he stayed "up until midnight or one in the morning to answer ever letter he received," and praised his "personal sense of fairness, always trying to be fair to everyone."[37]

Zajac watched bemusedly, recognizing that Dupré's flight confirmed his story and realizing not a soul there knew the real reason. Zajac asked Dupont if Dupré read his fax or left any responses. Dupont claimed the fax was destroyed and asked for a copy. Zajac liked Sniezyk and understood his story would make him look duplicitous, so Zajac took Sniezyk aside and filled him in. The cleric was flummoxed, "shocked beyond words." Poor Sniezyk, just then entering the loop, had to immediately organize damage control. He hastily arranged another press conference for 4:30, during which he acknowledged the abuse allegations against Dupré and claimed the diocese knew nothing. At 5 o'clock the *Republican* released the story on its website, then gave it to the local ABC television affiliate. The Dupré bombshell exploded during the evening news. Aftershocks rattled throughout Springfield.[38]

Dupré's cowardly flight left the diocese near collapse. Within hours of the second press conference, he was safely behind St. Luke locked front door. The diocese had suggested heart issues forced the retirement. Among medical issues St. Luke specifically did *not* treat was heart ailments. Dupré joined John Geoghan and Richard Lavigne as the Institute's other Massachusetts alumni.[39]

The Vatican claimed the resignation unremarkable, that Dupré's chat with the papal nuncio was routine. Dupré probably called the nuncio to inform him of the accusations and suggest the urgency of a quick exit. Sniezyk, temporary head of the diocese, publicly toed the party line. Privately, he was incensed. A few days later, Zajac said to him, "You must be pissed." The normally unflappable Sniezyk angrily replied, "You have no idea. Wait until I see him. I'm going to give him a piece of my mind for leaving me and the diocese in this position." His fellow priests agreed. Dupré was now "bishop emeritus" but priests refused to utter his name during daily group prayers for those retirees. A smattering of Dupré's friends remained oblivious. Pastor Father George McFarland of Sacred Heart—a Lavigne assignment—spoke to reporters, ashen-faced and weeping, saying, "He is as honest as you can get."[40]

As a young priest, Sniezyk recognized "cliques of priests" abused children and were protected by the Church and its lawyers. He told Zajac the diocese needed to "come clean about the 'old-boy network'" that for so long perpetrated abuse. "I wonder," he asked, "what it would be like to feel good about my Church for ten minutes?" His tenor inexplicably changed a few days later, when he spoke to the *Boston Globe* about abuse in less measured, more curious terms. He said the crisis had more to do with the culture of a bygone time than with priests. He described 1960s–1980s clerics as simply believing sex with young boys was acceptable, and that when he heard the stories then, he "didn't think much about it." Priests, he said, "did good ministry, they were kind, compassionate," but did not recognize the damage they were inflicting because "it was that era of the '60s, and the whole atmosphere out there was, it was O.K., it was O.K. to do."[41]

When Scahill was asked about Sniezyk's comments, he was incredulous, saying, "he's saying priests were that lame in the brain not to know this was wrong? Any sensible person would know this is evil." Scahill's reaction to Dupré's stunning fall was more deliberate. There was a palpable air of suspense among the 900 at Sunday Mass, everyone awaiting his response. He never mentioned Dupré by name, saying only "I take no pleasure in these sad days." He said he never meant disrespect, just wanted attention focused on victims. He did, though, answer to the nagging question about Dupré's foot-dragging, saying the resignation indicated "where some of the resistance [to punishing Lavigne] was coming from."[42]

On February 10, after watching his story reported globally, Tran hired high-profile Boston lawyer Eric MacLiesh, Jr. Deshaies then agreed to join a suit. The next morning, Bennett agreed to investigate the allegations and Boston's O'Malley rushed to Rome to stress the urgency of an immediate replacement to head the crumbling diocese. MacLeish released a statement February 19 describing Dupré's abuse history, briefcase full of gay pornography, and sex trips to Canada. The diocesan death spiral seemed irreversible. On February 24, Bennett traveled to Boston and met with Deshaies and Tran. On March 5, he confirmed a grand jury would hear "credible and consistent" allegations and an investigation into diocesan handling of abuse claims would be launched. Bennett obtained a search warrant for Dupré's chancery quarters and office, and he demanded the personnel files of every priest. More than 10,000 pages were confiscated. For the first time in history, the diocese was not handled with kid gloves.[43]

A third Dupré victim came forward while Tran and Deshaies were providing Bennett with a trove of confirming documents, including boxes of photographs, credit card receipts, phone records, Dupré's letters and cards, and so on. Dupré faced more than a dozen serious abuse-related charges and the diocese potentially faced charges relating to the reporting of the sexual assaults, but Bennett realized the statute of limitations made anything he did basically symbolic.[44]

Dupré was not the first bishop taken down by abuse accusations. By then, eight U.S. prelates admitted to allegations. Six resigned or retired. Internationally, eight more suffered similar fates, including a

German bishop charged with sexually abusing a woman during an exorcism. The diocese maddeningly downplayed everything. In February, it released the results of an audit of abusive priests and claimed over 50 years just 1.6 percent of 1,003 priests faced credible accusations. The results were positive, it implied, because the numbers were below Fall River's 2.4 percent and the national average of 4 percent. The diocese vastly under-reported the numbers. A lawyer representing multiple Springfield victims said the report did not "represent a fraction of [the priests] accused."[45] Bennett also discounted it, noting Dupré's dismantling of the secret archives and abuser Richard Meehan being in charge of the records for the previous decade.

On March 10, Father Timothy A. McDonnell, a New York state auxiliary bishop, was named the eighth bishop of Springfield. As comfortable with people as Dupré was awkward, McDonnell was a "what you see is what you get" priest known for his sense of humor. The quick replacement was a nod to Vatican acknowledgment of the crisis. His new posting was under siege. The day of the appointment, the Scahill-Dupré saga was on *USA Today*'s front page. "One Church Topples a Bishop: Quiet Rebels Take a Stand Against Abuse" was a stinging rebuke of the Church and Elliot Street with an unflattering theme, that Scahill and his "rebel [parish] toppled the bishop" using the only thing the Church cared about: money. Dupré's insulting vilification of Scahill was described, as was Church stonewalling and Mason's critique of the priesthood: "Where are their voices now?" Also detailed was Boston's O'Malley ignoring Scahill's call and castigating the priest for not making "more than a single phone call." The Church could have looked no worse, something that angered McDonnell. Then, even more bad news. The next day lawyer MacLeish announced a Deshaies-Tran suit against Dupré and the diocese, which did nothing to diminish church hubris. When O'Malley was ordered deposed, his spokesman said there was no need because he was "a man of his word."[46]

McDonnell's first order of his business was to attack Scahill. During their first face-to-face at a Presbyteral Council gathering, he angrily said to Scahill, "You attacked me personally. You basically called me a coward and said I was a 'lackey' for the Vatican." Scahill infuriated McDonnell when he dismissively replied, "I didn't use the word lackey."

McDonnell screamed at Scahill, "You've done as much damage to the diocese as Lavigne!" Nose to nose, the two shouted at each other for several minutes before McDonnell summarily kicked Scahill off the council.[47]

Meanwhile, Bennett's attempt to build a case against Lavigne was proving a Sisyphean struggle. Earlier, on April 6, his investigators raided the Chicopee house Lavigne shared with his mother on a leafy street not far from Elms College. Lavigne told another priest of a letter he allegedly received, supposedly claiming, "I know what you did." He sent it to Stern, suggesting the writer "was the real killer." Bennett, certain Lavigne wrote it himself as a smokescreen, was looking for the correspondence. Stern faxed it to him, but two days later investigators were back, looking for possible digital remnants on Lavigne's computer. Annoyed by the gaggle of reporters, Lavigne took pictures and when asked if he had anything to say, snapped, "I wouldn't talk to you if my life depended upon it."[48] Nothing was found linking Lavigne to the letter. Like so many once-seemingly promising leads, it turned out to be nothing.

On May 28, the diocese finally caved to Scahill and its critics and severed its financial relationship with Lavigne. A simple one-sentence press release confirmed support would cease at month's end. Scahill sent McDonnell his $60,000.[49]

In early August, the diocese settled with all but one of 46 victims. The lone holdout—Francis Babeu—went solo because he wanted the diocese to admit to mishandling complaints. Elliot Street promised $6,800,000, along with proceeds from the sale of two land parcels expected to fetch $585,000. Each victim was to receive a minimum of $80,000, with payoffs averaging about $150,000. Amounts would be determined by an arbiter based on type and length of abuse. The diocese also agreed to pay for lifetime counseling and appoint a victim to the Misconduct Commission. To pay a tab expected to eventually exceed $10,000,000, the diocese began dumping properties all over western Massachusetts.[50]

On September 27, a grand jury indicted Dupré on two counts of child rape. He was the first bishop in U.S. history charged with sex crimes, but the case was symbolic, as the statute of limitations was long expired.

The Croteaus were re-evaluating every Lavigne-related moment since 1972. Over time, they realized hundreds of seemingly innocent moments were, in fact, warning signs missed. The exhausting examinations deflated Carl and Bunny. He sadly said, "Why I didn't grasp it at the time, I don't know." But it was not surprising a consummate manipulator's fastidious grooming process went unrecognized. Even all the negative chatter when Lavigne left St. Catherine's was lost on them.[51] Everything now appeared in a different light.

There was Lavigne's physical play and roughhousing, chalked up to his interest in physical fitness. The time 14-year-old Joseph returned drunk from an overnight, they believed Lavigne's story about a raided liquor cabinet. "Like a fool, I chastised Joe," Carl said. Then the morning Danny returned sick from an overnight, and spent a listless Saturday vomiting. Again they believed Lavigne, that Danny, too, stole some liquor. A dispassionate look at Lavigne in the days around the murder was particularly disquieting. They kept Danny's casket closed on his recommendation, only to realize Lavigne probably "couldn't bear to look at Danny's face." Then Lavigne spent barely an hour with them before the wake and was a no-show at the funeral home. Then his inexplicably short post-funeral visit. And, of course, his breaking off contact, which led Carl to wonder, "He just called and said we shouldn't talk again, and that was it. He never said he didn't do it. We knew him well for five years, and that's all he had to say? If someone named me as a suspect in a murder, I'd go to his family and say, 'I didn't do it.' That's what most people would do, right?"[52]

The actions of Lavigne's fellow clerics were now suspect, too. Father O'Neil's $700 appeared more bribe than gift and intimated the Church knew something about Lavigne and the murder. That O'Neil only casually asked if Carl thought Lavigne capable of murder added to that appearance. And, of course, the mystery monk, Father Barnabas, who never met the family but grieved so bitterly, likely "heard Father's confession right after the murder."[53]

Most troublesome were recollections of Lavigne's time with the boys, Danny in particular. Lavigne spoke to each at least once a week and saw them at church and around the neighborhood. In a typical week, he and Danny were together four or five times. Lavigne was such a frequent presence at the neighborhood games, sitting in his car down the block, Danny told non–Church friends Lavigne was his "uncle." Best friend Steve Burnett recalled the times Danny was "having a good time and all the sudden I would see Danny crying and I would ... see Father Lavigne parked in the big four-door car. Danny would say 'I have to go' and would run to the car crying." Burnett's memory paints a gloomy picture of a frightened boy sadly resigned to his fate.[54] The only bitter solace for Carl and Bunny was the confirmation Lavigne was indeed a monster.

That summer saw the end of the *Republican*'s ten-year battle for the 1972 files. In late July, the Massachusetts supreme judicial court ordered the release of most of the remaining files. Included in the 19-page inventory of 2,038 pages were Trooper Daly's 28-page 1993 search warrant affidavit, Chicopee's 1972 investigation reports, witness statements including various Croteau interviews, Lavigne's initial statements, polygraph results, photographs of the straw and rope, full autopsy records, and statements relating to the 1991 charges. Beyond providing detail, the cache did not buttress a case against Lavigne.

To the chagrin of the diocese, that August, the Weldon-Dupré file sanitization went public when a "John Doe" suit detailed the 1977 Bondsville meeting and Dupré's discussion of the cleansing. The plaintiff was the teen waiter who listened to the entire conversation. It was the first confirmation of a Weldon-Dupré-diocese cover-up. Elliot Street lumbered into 2005 engulfed in a morass of suits, settlement negotiations, more accusations, and bad press. That summer, the diocese reported the latest tally: 117 victims and 42 clergy facing accusations—33 priests, eight order priests, and a deacon.

Carl and Bunny rarely heard from Bennett. "Unfortunately," Carl said, "we're always the last to know." The problem was there was nothing new to know. When they did hear from Bennett, it was the worst possible news. Bennett had Dr. Blake test the last piece of evidence, the blood-stained rope, and Blake determined the blood was not Lavigne's. Since 1972, every investigator, two D.A.s, the diocese, and most of Springfield was certain Lavigne killed Danny. It appeared everyone was wrong. The results left Bennett no choice but to quietly close yet another inquiry into Danny's murder. The whimper of an ending confirmed the subsequent investigations were as flawed as the original. Bennett found previously unmentioned evidence on Danny's body and clothes, including red fibers, human and animal hair, and unidentified biologics. Apparently, no further testing was done on any of it. It is difficult to square that no attempt was made to match the fibers to those from the Croteau and Lavigne houses, or anywhere, really.

Danny had again been dragged from the shadows by new suits and the Dupré saga. Lavigne was proved a monster to scientific certainty, but, once again, not a murderer. So three dozen boxes were again relegated to their darkened closet to be forgotten for a fourth time, the story still untold.

9

Predator

For the damage he caused the Church, Lavigne was described as a "one-man Chernobyl"; "no other priest was even close." By 2008, he faced accusations from 50 victims with scores more probably remaining in the shadows. He was responsible for most of the $20,000,000 paid by Elliot Street by then. He once told a victim, "The problem with the priesthood is that you can't be yourself. I like vacations because then I can be myself again for a while." The "problem" was he enjoyed abusing children, his "vacations" were with young boys, and being "myself" meant being a serial child abuser. A predator.[1]

That Lavigne would become a lifelong serial abuser did not surprise those who knew him. Signs were impossible to miss. People at every stage—childhood neighbors and friends, relatives, teachers, classmates, fellow priests, parishioners, police, seemingly everyone—recognized the many scary facets of Dickie. Psychopath. Sociopath. Abuser. All were steeped in narcissism. His entire life was a torrent of narcissistic behaviors too lengthy to effectively summarize. Narcissistic personality disorder is characterized by a pattern of grandiosity (fantasy or behavior), an overwhelming need for admiration, and a lack of empathy. Narcissists have an overblown sense of self-importance and believe they are intrinsically special or unique. They crave attention, are often arrogant, have an undeserved sense of entitlement, and are unapologetically exploitive. For a narcissist, *everything* is about them, about their own importance. Lavigne examples abound. A clinical psychologist described his behavior during the Tessier visit after the murder as a "textbook narcissist making the situation all about them" and his late-night diner encounter with Sandra Tessier "a classic narcissistic attempt to sway opinion before it originated."[2]

His early years were marked by deep depravity on many levels. It is no surprise he developed into what investigators described as a thrill-seeking psychopath. Childhood events paint a disturbing picture of a distinctly antisocial boy confused about his sexuality. He was always peculiar. Childhood friends and neighbors recalled the many strange behaviors, taking particular note of the bizarre seemingly sexual relationship with his mother. Young friends recognized that her flaunting sexuality and his behavior with her was aberrant. If they did have a sexual relationship, Dickie was a victim of childhood sexual abuse.[3]

There are confirmed connections between childhood sexual abuse and "Peeping Tom" behavior that often leads to becoming an abuser. The creepy "tall, bald man" that prowled the Croteau neighborhood in the 1970s could easily have been Lavigne. He matched the description exactly. The peeper outran younger, athletic pursuers in the manner Lavigne habitually beat his altar boys in races from the church. Also recall the man Carl Jr. saw peering into the bathroom one night. It is improbable a voyeur would ignore unobstructed windows and choose to struggle through dense bushes surrounding that particular window unless he knew it was a bathroom. The choice indicates the Peeping Tom was familiar with the house, as Lavigne was. Lastly, it is certainly coincidental the incidents took place throughout 1971, ceased during 1972 after Danny's murder, and resumed in 1973.[4]

By 11 or 12, Lavigne was an experienced animal abuser, catching frogs and other small animals, torturing, and killing them. Studies dating to 1806 confirm causal links between childhood animal abuse and other, unrelated childhood trauma. An odd relationship with his mother would undoubtedly exacerbate other problematic tendencies. Studies confirm unmistakable connections between childhood animal abuse and increasingly violent behavior in teens as well as aggression toward others, sexual and otherwise, in adults. The resulting adult behavior manifests itself in all manner of psychoses and antisocial personality disorders.[5]

Animal cruelty does not simply indicate a trivial personality flaw. It confirms severe mental disturbance. Research suggests people who commit acts of animal cruelty almost never stop there. Virtually all progress to hurting humans, often in the extreme. Men who abused animals as children are five times more likely to be arrested for violent crimes. In a 2001–2004 Chicago police department study, 65 percent of those arrested for animal crimes were arrested for battery against people.

The connection is particularly astounding in domestic violence cases. A six-year study found that partners of 80 percent of women entering domestic violence shelters abused or killed family pets. In families where physical child abuse has occurred, animal abuse was present in 88 percent of the cases.[6]

Robert K. Ressler, who developed the basis for the FBI's serial killer profiling unit, said, "Murderers ... very often start out by killing and torturing animals as kids." Virtually every serial killer in American history abused animals. Albert DeSalvo, the "Boston Strangler," trapped dogs and cats in boxes and shot arrows into them at ten. Jeffrey Dahmer impaled frogs and the heads of cats and dogs on sharpened sticks. "BTK" murderer Dennis Rader detailed in journals hanging dogs and cats as a child. Washington, D.C., sniper Lee Boyd Malvo killed dozens of cats with marbles from a slingshot at 14. Almost every modern-day school shooter was a childhood animal abuser. Oregon's Kip Kinkel and Mississippi shooter Luke Woodham tortured animals. The most famous school killers—Columbine murderers Eric Harris and Dylan Klebold—bragged about mutilating animals.[7]

Interesting as pertains to Lavigne, studies confirm links between childhood animal abuse and sex crimes as adults. A 1988 study found 50 percent of convicted rapists and 40 percent of child molesters abused animals as children. An Australian study determined "100 percent of sexual homicide offenders had a history of animal cruelty." In addition to being an animal abuser, Lavigne tortured humans. According to a neighbor, he once led his younger sister down the street and convinced her to climb down a ladder into the unfinished foundation of a house under construction. He then removed the ladder and walked away, leaving the six-year-old alone in the dark. A group of neighborhood searchers found her there the next morning.[8]

How and why he became a pedophile are complicated questions with no easy answers. The first question asked by a clinical psychologist reviewing Lavigne's history was "Who raped him?" A staggering percentage of abusers were abused as children. The sexual component of Lavigne's development into abuser arose from various events. First, of course, is the reported quasi-sexual relationship with his mother. Second, he may have been an abuse victim himself at Assumption Prep. The school was riddled with abuse by Assumptionist faculty members. Two, later charged, taught multiple classes attended by Lavigne.[9] Being victimized, whether at the hands of a teacher or a mother, is a huge violation that forever skews a child's definition of trust. In Lavigne's case, it would intensify antisocial components of his personality and produce a spectrum of borderline personality disorder issues. At its base, his personal standard for normal was permanently altered, perhaps irretrievably.

Lavigne was confirmed a pedophile at 17 when he was fired from a camp counselor job for molesting a six-year-old. He was already an experienced abuser. Recall the 14-year-old he enticed into his house and tried to hypnotize into removing his clothes. Lavigne also took him to a remote Granby swimming hole, and while letting him drive, asked if he could masturbate him. At the time, the boy saw the episodes as weird, not the overt sexual inducements they were.

The strongest influence on Lavigne's pedophilia likely came from the seminary as it most directed how he lived. The experience reinforced a supremely flawed psychopathy. The model for seminary life has changed little over 1,000 years, still based on French models of early Sulpician and Vincentian orders. It is a theological training forum based on Christ as priest and, crucial here, victim. Preparing men for priestly "burdens" seems a contradictory tenet but has remained central. The calling has less to do with servitude than blind devotion to a closed society. Historian John Tracy believed seminary ideals "far more benefitted the monk and friar than the parish priest." The cloister aspect results in chronic, severe under-development—psychological and sexual—that created thousands of abusers in the mid–1900s.[10]

The Church has always taken a closed approach to priest education and training, refusing outside input. The secretive process is still considered an in-house affair, private Church business. Seminaries are fully closed societies, controlled incubators where everything is completely structured, leaving virtually no time for non-religious pursuits. Strict rules govern every minute and apply to every facet of life, particularly personal. The system replicates military indoctrination, browbeating recruits to think institutionally, never individually. One seminarian described it as "brainwashing," one teacher saying, "We own you! We own your body, we own your soul!" Seminarians are even discouraged from forming connections with fellow students. First and foremost, unbreakable bonds of full compliance must be forged with God and Church, the divine. Second, and equally obligatory, is obedience earthly Church hierarchy. Under an umbrella of solemn vows of obedience to the bishop, each echelon is completely subservient to the level just above. An abuser priest described the progression: "The pastor told me, 'When I was a curate I was shit on. Now it's my turn to shit on you, and when you get up there, you can shit on everybody else." The extreme micromanagement is a near-fatal structural weakness that exacerbates every problem faced by the Church.[11]

More than half of seminarians drop out or are invited to leave once it is determined they cannot fall in line. Blindly accepting orders and forfeiting will and decision input leaves priests woefully unprepared. Studies dating to the 1940s confirm that not only does seminary life *not* prepare seminarians, it badly stunts their development. A 1948 William Bier study found seminarians typically answered personality test queries as a woman would. A 1952 Charles A. Weisberger study found their responses mirrored those of psychopaths. The 1968 Coville-D'Ary-McCarthy-Rooney study concluded that more than 70 percent of seminarians were "psychosexually immature, exhibiting traits of heterosexual retardation, confusion concerning sexual role, fear of sexuality, effeminacy and potentially homosexual dispositions." Almost 10 percent were considered "clinically sexually deviant."[12]

A 1972 Eugene Kennedy study perhaps most clearly made the connection when it reported that seminaries produce "undeveloped persons whose level of personal growth is not equal to that which is expected at their age." Not a surprising outcome, since it is considered a sin for seminarians to speak of sex in any context. A Boston priest who abused hundreds described himself after the seminary: "I had the sexuality of a thirteen-year-old boy. I was stuck as a thirteen-year-old. Whenever I felt pressure, I would hang around with the thirteen-year-old kids." The results are unsurprising. For years, seminaries modeled Father André Guindon's book *The Sexual Language*, which proposed "studies disprove lasting harm results from pedophilic contact. Rather, the trauma comes from the familial panic which is the usual response to the incident."[13]

At best, if a seminarian had no existing problems when he enrolled, he did when he finished. The training exacerbates existent issues. Because of this, seminaries created a mob of priests in the mid to late 1900s with serious moral, ethical, and psychological failings. It is a truism that seminaries produce men "who have done nothing but will be treated like princes." Lavigne's was a typical seminary outcome. His existing issues were reinforced, refined. He was Kennedy's "undeveloped" adult male. He exhibited the psychosexual immaturity and the confusion over sexual roles and sexuality described by Coville-D'Arcy et al. He fit Bier's mold of seminarians who respond like women and Weisberger's comparison to psychopath responses, and he clearly exhibited the sexual deviancy found in 8 percent of seminarians.[14]

Another consequence of the seminary system is further development of sexual preference. Lavigne's was clearly heightened at Our Lady, where seminarians honed sexual trades through classic group processes. An ex-seminarian summarized the progression as individuals over time naturally drifting together into one of three distinct cliques: heterosexuals, homosexuals, or pedophiles. Men with common "interests" studied, ate, and socialized together, almost never with anyone linked to another group. Group norms and groupthink naturally evolved. They learned from and taught each other how to execute each group's individual processes. That information transfer is evidenced by the manner abusers from the same orders employed identical, specific grooming and abuse techniques; for instance, offering chewing gum to hide the smell of alcohol, using sacramental wine to weaken defenses, and using hygiene instructions to initiate physical contact (for example, instructing boys how to clean and wipe themselves and pushing toilet paper into the rectum). When seminarians graduate, they are classically-trained abusers.[15]

Lavigne's personality problems were as obvious as his sexual issues and pedophilia. Our Lady identified concerns the first month and four years later was no less flummoxed by him. The incongruities and his demeanor, behavior, and attitude troubled superiors more than his mediocre academic record. He was seen as "fundamentally humble and charming," but there was worry over his temperament. He tried to hide low self-confidence with arrogance, was distinctly aloof, and totally disengaged. After the first year, he himself told Rector William J. Gormley the experience was "somewhat of a disappointment." Our Lady never got a handle on Lavigne. His sermons were "among the best they ever heard," but he could not "communicate them very well." His admired artistic temperament made it impossible for him to be subservient to anyone with less. Perhaps most prescient, he was thought an "excellent young man with very high ideals" but with disturbing personality traits, and Our Lady fretted "his emotional stability is not the best, barely falling within the general ambit of being safe."[16] Disquieting concerns, all.

Annual faculty-staff evaluations reinforced Our Lady's apprehension. The assessment was described as a "Psychological Profile" but was more opinion than science. Students were rated 1–5 on 45 personal and psychological attributes, disparate descriptors from "outgoing" and "good mixer" to "keeps quarters in order" and "good posture." Half a dozen faculty opinions were averaged for each element. Lavigne was as unremarkable psychologically as academically. In 150 appraisals over four years, he received not a single 5, only a dozen 4s or 4.5s, and averaged barely 3. Interestingly, his best scores were for attributes not personality-driven, like "does work on time" and "clean and neat." He received consistently disappointing scores for anything in the personality spectrum, like "good tempered" (2.8), "outgoing" (2.4), and "polite" (2.5). A clinician who reviewed the assessments suggested Lavigne's results mirror exactly the model for antisocial personality disorder. The highest compliment anyone could muster about Lavigne was that he was a talented painter.[17]

In the beginning, Gormley worried Lavigne was not a viable seminarian at all, that he was "one those young men for whom the seminary will be more than an average trial. Time alone will tell where God's will is." At the end, Gormley was equally concerned about Lavigne's basic suitability as a priest: "No doubt there are good grounds for general disappointment."[18] Our Lady recognized he was leaving very confused, psychologically and sexually. They sent him on to the priesthood anyway.

As opposed to the more common "situational" abusers who do not prefer children and abuse simply because the opportunity presents itself, Lavigne was described as a "preferential, risk taking" abuser—preferential because he targeted children, risk-taking because he gathered victims "slowly … with elaborate ritual seductions undertaken even when they are counter-productive to getting away with it." He was blatantly outwardly unconcerned about exposure, emboldened by each incident. He abused his rectory guests with other priests there. He abused at least four sets of brothers. His outings were public—movies, dinners, and so on—and he shared hotel rooms with young boys in his care. A clinical psychologist concluded it was not about sex for Lavigne. Rather, it was the hunt. He was more obsessed with and received more gratification from grooming, coercion, and manipulation than sex. Sex was secondary.[19]

Many factors contributed to his enormous success. First, the era was rife with relaxed cultural norms and preferential attitudes toward priests. Second, Catholics as a group kept things "in the family" and never discussed private matters publicly. Importantly, Lavigne carefully targeted vulnerable, financially-beleaguered families like the cash-strapped Croteaus. They tended to be less educated, less inclined to recognize, let alone question, ulterior motives. Most victims struggled with life tumult, like the Circle, and were less capable emotionally and academically. Disgraced Philadelphia priest Joseph Gausch described the type as "not stupid, does not study, wretched home conditions."[20]

Parents were unintentionally complicit in the abuse their children suffered. Boys were encouraged to spend time alone with priests, actually *forced* into abuse by parents. Recall the mother coaxing her son to visit their priest, to "be a good kid and be his friend." One victim sobbed as his mother dropped him off for an overnight with Lavigne. She ordered him to stop crying and get out of the car. When she picked him up the next morning, he described discomfort at seeing Lavigne nude. She thought nothing of it. Virtually every Lavigne victim was dropped off by a parent, often with snacks and a change of clothes. Victims were even allowed to stay with Lavigne on school nights. He simply drove them to school the next morning. He took many away from church for day trips, weekends, even lengthy vacations. Parents felt gratitude, never unease.[21]

Antiquated attitudes allowed priests free reign to slowly groom and then abuse. Gausch described the "same pattern, where I got to know one of the children ... they would come over to the house a few times, and there would be just some wrestling or tickling or something like that, and there'd be some molesting, and from that point on we'd go into the sexual activity." Carl described Lavigne as "a cute operator, sharp as a tack. He knew how to maneuver himself into a family." Bunny added, "He was very, very good at making friends." He targeted boys, and occasionally girls, under ten, and he was a talented, methodical groomer who made victims "feel like something special." For some, it was the first time in their lives they had felt this way. A victim described elation at "being chosen."[22]

His targeting was not random. Initial contact occurred when children or families were particularly susceptible. The first visit, Lavigne immediately removed his collar, loosened his shirt, and usually took off his shoes. He was, first and foremost, just a friend. He commiserated with parents and became a trusted advisor, listening to complaints, giving advice and support, and he always offered gifts straightaway. It might be as small as a favor, as substantial as money, but he always had *something*. He bought food, helped find jobs, and flooded everyone with often expensive gifts. He brought food to the Croteaus regularly and purchased clothes and shoes for the entire brood. Danny was an easier target because, though he was a popular kid, he had few close friends. Steve Burnett believed Danny "latched onto Father Lavigne because he didn't have many friends."[23]

Through it all, Lavigne manipulated. He told Carl that Danny's boxing coach was a homosexual preying on boys. Carl later said, "He had no kind words for Coleman … he planted the bad seed in people's minds, and he was the real molester." Most clever, Lavigne aligned himself with the children instead of—and, usually, versus—parents. He subtly pitted parents against children by letting the kids do exhilarating things that were prohibited at home. They idolized him. Victim Raymond Gouin "thought he could walk on water. He was like a combination big brother and another father. He was dynamic, powerful, interesting, nothing like any priest I had ever met." The kids thought he was one of them. He understood their problems with everyone—parents, teachers, girlfriends, pals. He treated them as peers, equals, "like adults." He told scary stories "twelve-year-olds loved [about] voodoo dolls, hands that reached out and grabbed you in the dark, and walls that bled blood." He also shared locker room humor he never shared with adults, including sexually-charged jokes meant for older audiences and "college jokes" about men and erections. He laughed when he spoke about the size and prowess of his own penis, which he often did, and he let them read *Playboy* magazines stashed beneath his rectory mattress and under the front seat of the Mustang.[24]

He joked with them after Mass and changed out of his ceremonial robes in their presence. He followed them into their changing room and helped them out of their cumbersome cassocks. One boy recalled that, even at ten, he thought it strange Lavigne helped them disrobe. Priests never did that, but he was always "with us when we changed … while he watched."[25]

He shared their interests and showered them with attention. He conferred special nicknames; for instance, he called Gouin "Ray-Ray." He hung out, watched television, played board games, and joined in neighborhood sports. He painted with a ten-year-old interested in art and listened to classical music with another who liked music. He bought them baseball gloves, hockey sticks, and expensive radios and stereo equipment. He took them to nice restaurants. The gifts all came with promises of even more extravagant presents. He took them on day trips in his convertible, to Friendly's for ice cream, to Vermont looking for antiques, and to New Hampshire, Connecticut, and Rhode Island beaches. He took them for weekends all over New England, camping, fishing, snowmobiling, sometimes just exploring. He took them on expensive vacations to exciting destinations like Florida, California, New York City, and Canada. These gifts, too, came with promises of more exotic trips to places like the Bahamas.[26]

He let them help build the Ashfield house. They hung sheetrock and plywood, climbed ladders, and used power tools, exciting work for young boys. In fact, a significant amount of construction was done by Lavigne's pre-teen work crews. They reveled in the work, and they laughed when he exposed himself, urinated in their presence, and invited them to do likewise. He got them out of school, sometimes for funerals and weddings where they received $10 or $20 tips, but often just to hang out at the rectory. He convinced them to skip school on their own to visit. He even did their homework, writing so many papers for one that the boy was punished for submitting work teachers were certain was not his. Most important, Lavigne made it easy. He never challenged. Conversations were invariably small talk, never about deep subjects. The relationships were stress-free.[27]

He took them skinny-dipping, let them stay up all night, and eat anything they wanted. With him, they were renegades, impressed he "didn't worry about the law" he regularly encouraged them to break. They broke into barns and stole, sometimes chased off by enraged farmers. He let them, at 12 or 13, drive his cars. He allowed one to tool around the church parking lots after first getting him drunk. Alcohol was an integral part of Lavigne's process. Though a teetotaler himself, he urged them to imbibe, even letting them drink ceremonial wine in the sacristy from his personal chalice. It was normally empty after Mass, and Lavigne would refill it for his boys. After Masses, Danny and shared a full chalice, but only during the week, because nobody else was in the church. Never on crowded Sundays. He gave them three or four glasses during his rectory spaghetti dinners and beer when they worked at Ashfield, and he always had a supply of gum so no one smelled liquor on their breath.[28]

He also gave them hard liquor. He chugged glasses of water he claimed were full of vodka and dared them to do the same. That amount of alcohol consumed so quickly often rendered them unconscious. One, who had never tasted spirits, took the dare and downed a glass of vodka from the bar in Lavigne's basement, dropped the glass, and passed out cold. Lavigne duped boys into drinking, once giving Joseph Croteau orange juice spiked with vodka. Another boy asked for a glass of water and got sick after chugging what was actually a potent martini.[29]

The gifts, attention, everything, was clever manipulation that ingratiated Lavigne deeply into victims' lives. He was an unquestioned, trusted friend, and an authority figure who could do no wrong. One victim said, "He was someone we confided in about almost anything and someone I trusted unconditionally." He became jealous and spiteful, and he got "very upset" if they showed interest in the opposite sex and he discouraged girlfriends. He scolded, "I know why you want a girlfriend. To have sex with her."[30]

Getting to physical acts was an equally meticulous, cautious process. He first asked targets to see a movie, go for a ride, or maybe work at Ashfield, unthreatening "dates," of sorts. Subtle, never overt, advances were made during those outings, the first steps of a dance orchestrated to end in physical abuse. He might innocently put his arm around them during a movie. They might be told they seemed tense, needed to relax, to "loosen up," problems solved with seemingly innocent foot or back massages. When the date was over, there were innocent hugs, perhaps harmless kisses on the cheek, excused because "God wants everyone to get along, and care for one another, and some people express this differently. You can express how you feel by touching and embracing, even men." He reassured them he enjoyed their company, and, importantly, that they were "the only one who knows how I truly feel."[31]

After a few benign outings, an invitation for an evening at the rectory was offered. They were rarely refused. "It was an honor," after all, to spend time alone with him. He sometimes used subterfuge to get boys there. He arranged for a clock-making kit, ordered for one boy, to be delivered to the rectory, forcing the boy to come there to work on it. When it was completed, Lavigne kept it so the boy had to visit to see it. Evenings began with dinner, prepared by Lavigne, and served with two, three, or more glasses of wine. After the second or third dinner, an invitation to stay overnight was extended. The boy was made to call home for permission, excuses offered like watching television, listening to music, or they needed an early start for something the next morning. Lavigne then got on the phone to reassure parents that it was "perfectly all right." After a couple of overnights, he sometimes did not bother to inform parents of the sleepover. Remarkably, none complained.[32]

Before retiring, Lavigne offered more wine "to help them sleep." His quarters contained just a single bed, so his guests either slept on the floor or with him. He cajoled them into the latter, in the winter because he was cold or "the room was cold and we can keep each other warm." And there were always reasons for them to remove their clothes. They were used to such requests. If it was even barely hot when they worked at Ashfield, he ordered them to "take off your shirts now." He said they should never sleep in clothes because "they might get wrinkled." Rather than pajamas, he supplied Victorian-style nightshirts that hung below the knees. He wore the same, making everyone appear as characters in a Dickens novel. He harangued them to remove their underwear, saying that it was "unsanitary" to wear the undergarments to bed. He also badgered them to sleep nude. During summer, the room was hot or the air conditioner broken. He specifically requested motel rooms without air conditioning.[33]

Lavigne made no overt physical passes for three, four, sometimes five overnights. The final step in the seduction, introducing obvious physical acts, was as ritualistically planned as the rest of the process. Harmless hugs and kisses on the cheek became playful wrestling matches and "tickle fights" during which he tickled the boys all over while deftly maneuvering himself on top of them. The contact gradually included genitals and buttocks, Lavigne making the initial contact appear accidental. If he encountered any resistance, he stopped and "acted like nothing happened." Tickling progressed to more expansive back rubs and massages, a "French thing so it was OK to touch them. It was just a touch of affection." He first massaged them, then directed, "Now it's your turn."[34]

After gradually increasing the amount of nudity, Lavigne would simply get in bed naked. Eventually, the boys would as well. Lavigne used a small pen flashlight to confirm they were not awake. Victims described waking to Lavigne rubbing their upper thighs and genitals. If caught during the act, or if he sensed unease, he was quick with excuses. He sometimes blamed a chemical imbalance that made him black out and become "all over the place and restless." He told victim John Shattuck he was squeezing his penis to prevent bed-wetting. Some never awoke. One victim was only aware he had been molested because his shirt was stuck to his stomach in the morning.[35]

If not immediately rebuffed, Lavigne asked the boys to touch him. He said learning sex would gain them friends with whom they could "play." The manipulation became more creative as the sex level increased. He encouraged them to masturbate, claiming that doing so made their penises larger, "like mine." His justifications also became more imaginative. He said he must put medication on their penises, and they on his, because of chafing from wet bathing suits or tight pants. He said anal sex was good for them because it helped "relax inside muscles."[36]

The bathroom was central to Lavigne's process. Victims always needed showers. They were filthy and sweaty from working at Ashfield. They smelled of campfires or from fishing. If activities did not get them dirty, Lavigne would craft one "so he could clean them." He insisted he "help" them in the bathroom, hand-washing them or brushing their teeth. He would say, "I'll do it myself because there is a right way and a wrong way to clean" or "Don't forget to wash under your armpits and under your sack." They might be told they "dried off wrong" and then he would dry them himself, rubbing them with a towel, front and back, up and down, repeatedly.[37]

He often used hygiene as an entré, sometimes laughingly saying, "Always remember and never forget: No matter how you dance, no matter how you prance, the last few drops go down your pants." He harangued them about properly cleaning their genitals and rectum after using the toilet and cleaned their genitals for them because they "did not know how to clean themselves." He inserted toilet paper and his finger into their rectums so they learned "how to wipe themselves." He lingered in the bathroom, watching them, always with a harmless excuse for being there, like needing to brush his teeth or getting something from the vanity.[38]

Lavigne never forced the process. If he encountered resistance, or sensed hesitance, he backed off for "a couple of days" or visits before renewing his efforts. He used passive-aggressive behaviors to respond to pushback, questioning friendship or trust, and he became bitterly petulant whenever his advances were rejected. After a deflection by John Shattuck, Lavigne threatened to move away and never see him again. When another boy rebuffed him during the first day of a planned three-day weekend in Vermont, Lavigne abruptly ordered the boy into the car and drove the two hours back to Springfield in silence. Once when he was spurned in the rectory, he refused to take another boy home, turning his back and saying, "Tell your parents I can't take you home."[39] If a boy resolutely refused to participate or appeared frightened, he disengaged and thereafter shunned the boy and his family.

Sex often took place away from the rectory. Lavigne visited motels all over New England. There was Ashfield, a cabin at the Church camp, the Tenerowiczs' Goshen lake house and Vermont chalet, and his friend Father George A. Paulin's chalet in remote northern Vermont. Weekend trips became extended vacations, first a week, then two. He took his victims all over the U.S., to California, Florida, Pennsylvania, and Arizona, and he took them to Montreal and Nova Scotia, Canada.[40]

All the while, he reassured them what they were doing was not wrong. In fact, it was acceptable, even recommended, by God. "It's OK to touch," he said. "It was something God wanted to happen" or "We're all God's children. We express love in different ways. This is my way, this is how I express it, there is nothing wrong with it." At the same time, they were told it was ultimately their shortcoming if they thought sex was immoral. Victim Paul Babeu believed "it was my fault and I did something to make him do what he did." Whenever one victim rejected Lavigne, the boy "would beg forgiveness and act like I did something wrong." Many of Lavigne's victims spent years in therapy to learn they were not to blame for what had happened.[41]

Lavigne's was a very risky, brazen venture undertaken with contradictory methodologies. Outwardly, he was unconcerned about exposure and oblivious to timing or circumstance. After undergoing his first polygraph examination, he returned to St. Catherine's and molested Steve Block in the rectory. Even getting caught did not deter him. His friend Father Robert Thrasher walked in on him at least twice, once in a rectory kitchen where he found Lavigne with his penis exposed, his hand jammed into a 12-year-old's underwear. Thrasher turned and walked away. Neither startled nor concerned, Lavigne warned the boy to say nothing, and resumed the act. Pastor Griffin walked in on another kitchen assault. Like Thrasher, he did an about-face and walked out.[42]

Lavigne abused everywhere, frequently in venues with others present, where he could be caught—in rectories, church sanctuaries, motels, cars, tents, homes of his parents and friends, the boys' homes. On one overnight at Ashfield, Lavigne assaulted one in bed with the rest lay scattered on the floor. He abused numerous sets of brothers, even relatives that included cousins. While on the one hand indifferent to discovery, on the other, he went to extreme lengths to avoid detection. He drove multiple cars, including his Mustang, church vehicles, and cars belonging to his parents, friends, even his cousins. During one weekend excursion to the Tenerowicz cottage in northern Vermont, he disappeared for an hour and returned with a different car.[43]

He exposed himself to an 11-year-old girl through the confessional grate while grilling her about her "impure thoughts" and then forced her to fellate him there. Later, as she knelt before him receiving communion in the sacristy, he lifted up his robe and rubbed his penis in her face. He forced an eight-year-old girl to fellate him in the church, the day after visiting her home for her birthday party.[44]

In public, he treated his victims indifferently and displayed little affection, deceptions they recognized were intended to "hide any relationship." He secreted them around, picking them up and dropping them off down the street, away from their homes. He never picked a Croteau boy up at the house. Victims were hidden from motel clerks, forced to wait down the street or in the woods while he checked in. He signaled them to make their way inside by flashing the room lights. One boy clambered two stories up an outside wall, using bricks that randomly protruded from the face, before tumbling through a window into the room. The covert exercises were necessary, he said, because he could not afford to pay for an extra person. "Priests didn't make much money," a believing victim said.[45]

He was especially secretive shuffling them in and out of rectories. He usually brought them in when the other priests were either away or already in bed. His friend Thrasher, who witnessed Lavigne abusing, claimed no knowledge of boys sleeping over because he retired early. He dead-bolted the door and closed the blinds when they were in his quarters. If parishioners unexpectedly arrived when boys were there, they were hidden, ordered to make no sound. If they accidently did so, and people or Lavigne heard, they were physically or sexually punished.[46]

Lavigne was masochistic, physically and psychologically. He screamed at a teen organist in front of the congregation for playing a hymn he did not like. When the boy cried after Mass, he was told cruelly, "You're the one crying. That's your problem. You deal with it." A victim recalled, "Every time I was with Father, he did something to make me feel uncomfortable: sexual abuse, violence, or humiliation."[47]

His psychological abuse was usually couched in a practical joke, like dumping buckets of ice-cold water into showers. He insulted and relentlessly, excessively teased. One boy said he "always turned everything into a cruel joke" and another said he "would always tell me how [intellectually] slow I was." And remember the Goshen overnight trip, when Lavigne encouraged the boys to ridicule and insult Danny, who only lashed out after Lavigne enthusiastically joined in the taunting? Shawn Dobbert was told "no one would like me because I was fat and he was the only one who loved me. I'd have no friends until I lost weight." Lavigne said if he lost weight he "would share him with friends as his reward." Until then, Lavigne said, he was "not good enough to share."[48]

His abuse was overt. After forcing one boy to kneel before him and masturbate him to climax, Lavigne berated him, screaming, for allowing a quick climax. Humiliated, the boy begged for forgiveness. If a victim pleaded for an end to whatever corporeal punishment was occurring, Lavigne increased the torture. "I would say, 'That's enough,'" one said, "but he would not give up, instead, would hold me down and let out a groan-like laugh and keep doing it to me."[49]

Lavigne was a particularly sadistic physical abuser, and he enjoyed inflicting pain. Indifferent to suffering, he took pleasure in discomfort and tears, his appetite for inflicting suffering prodigious. Seeing a ten-year-old examining the ceremonial chalices and communion wafers in the sacristy safe, Lavigne said he must be punished for sinning in church. He pulled his pants down, viciously slapped his buttocks, then ejaculated on him. Lavigne routinely smacked boys' testicles with the back of his hand and laughed, "Oh, come on. That doesn't hurt." He gave them painful "wedgies," lifting them off the ground by yanking their underwear up from behind. He left large bruises he called "cow bites" by forcefully squeezing their thighs. Sometimes, after forcing victims to perform fellatio while kneeling in front of him, he viciously beat them. They must feel pain as Jesus did, he said. When Steve Block complained, Lavigne said, "Jesus suffered on the cross, and so you could suffer a little."[50]

Lavigne became increasingly uneasy about the prospects of keeping such a large number, perhaps hundreds, of victims silent. He was rightfully obsessed the secret be kept. For some, the abuse lasted from early grammar school into high school. With so many victims over such a long time, Lavigne must have been anxious about the prospect of being discovered. He relentlessly, regularly entreated his victims, "You're not going to tell anyone, are you?" or warned them, "If anyone knew I was doing this to you, I would get fired and you won't be an altar boy." He also said they could be taken from their families and people would think they were "strange." Theirs was a state of perpetual confusion, never knowing what to expect, made to decipher impossible contradictions. After sleepovers, he served the boys breakfast and then forced them to go to confession because "we should be ashamed of ourselves." What they were doing was acceptable in God's eyes, but a sin that must be admitted. At an evening pool party, Lavigne, naked, swam up to two boys and demanded their confessions. After one assault, he took his victim by the arm and without comment dragged him to a small closet and ordered him inside. He turned out the lights and locked the door. The conflict swirling inside the boys is easy to imagine.[51]

They feared daunting outcomes if they came forward. A victim described the quandary: "Father Lavigne was a prominent man…. If an eleven-year-old came forward, he did not have a voice. Who would believe me?" Another recognized, "There was no one I could talk to about it. I felt dirty, used, and ashamed." Yet another added, "For years I thought I was the only one abused by him. Because I was ashamed, I kept it to myself." When Raymond Gouin's parents asked him if Lavigne was molesting him, he "denied it. I didn't want anyone to know." One McMahon brother denied it to the other, also a victim. None of the four brothers who later sued a group of priests were aware any of the others were being molested. One African American victim remained silent because "nobody would believe a 'colored' boy."[52]

Parents were more problem than help. When a victim told his mother about an assault, she scoffed and said Lavigne "was a priest and a priest wouldn't do that." The few parents who did broach the subject did so only barely. They were stymied by the same shame, more afraid than their children to accuse priests of inappropriate behavior. When a New Bedford policeman tried persuading parents of a dozen victims to support charging their priest, one couple said, "They were involved in the church, and if they made the accusations, they might as well pack their bags and move out of town." When the policeman detailed abuse for a mother, she asked, "Do you know how lonely the life of a priest is?"[53]

Coming forward to another priest was pointless. A boy abused from age 8 to 17 by Father Donald A. Desilets told Desilets' pastor, Richard O. Matte. Matte ordered the boy to take off his clothes. When Father Bruce Teague was nine, he was molested at his Boston-area parish. The priest angrily blamed Teague for being transferred and vilified him for breaking his vow of secrecy.[54]

Complaints from Lavigne victims were more improbable because, beyond abuse, he scared them to death, petrified them. Kevin Sousa, who later became a priest, said, "I was terrified of this man." First, he was imposing, an athletic six-footer. Second, victims said they were more afraid of his temper than the abuse. He became "violently mad" if displeased in any way. He violently slapped their faces if he was even slightly aggravated. Angered by a boy fishing with him, Lavigne launched a rock at his head. Upset with a Circle boy, Lavigne squeezed his thigh so hard it left a cluster of dark, bloody bruises. Another was so frightened of Lavigne, he carried a jack knife. John Shattuck's father promised to get him home if anything happened during the Arizona trip. He suffered through a week of dreadful abuse without calling home because "I was too scared."[55]

For myriad reasons, all remained silent. Abuse was not discussed, particularly among friends. James Coleman was close to a dozen Circle victims. He never once heard a whisper. His daughter said had he "heard anything, he would have gone right to police." Another reason for silence was that Lavigne's manipulation was so regularly punctuated with menace—some implied, some explicit, all terrifying. He appealed to the boys' fear of their parents. He gave them alcohol but threatened to tell their parents they drank. He let them drive his car but threatened to tell their parents they drove illegally. He even threatened eternal damnation, that the boys "were God's workers and if I ever told anyone, God would send me to hell."[56]

His veiled threats were equally effective, the inferences unmistakable. Recall the graduation card inscribed with a reference to another victim's suicide? After molesting a boy and dropping him off at a secluded spot along narrow, winding Route 2, Lavigne lurched his car directly at the younger, who jumped onto the grass. Lavigne backed up, rolled down the window, and dryly said, "You have to be careful. Accidents happen." Driving another boy past Danny's murder site, Lavigne blithely said, "That's the spot where Danny Croteau was murdered." He warned Steve Block not to mention abuse to anyone "or else." After molesting Danny's pal Tommy Martin, Lavigne warned him not to tell anyone while wrenching his arm so forcefully Martin fell to the ground in excruciating pain. He repeated the threat almost every time he abused Martin.[57]

Lavigne leveled even more portentous threats. As he cut carrots for soup in the rectory kitchen, he waved a knife at a nine-year-old Shattuck boy and snarled, "If you tell anybody, I'm going to hurt you." Before going back to the carrots, Lavigne stuck the knife in the boy's face and added, "Or your parents." He promised death to Paul Babeu if he said anything. When another victim tried to put an end to abuse that lasted from age 9 to 19, Lavigne threatened to "take the air out of [his] lungs." More ominous, he added, "I did it before, and I can do it again."[58] By the time Danny died, Lavigne was nearly obsessed someone might talk. Danny was clearly edging closer to doing so, but there may have been a reason he was even *more* a threat, more a target.

10

Murderer?

Richard Lavigne has been proven an awful person. He molested scores, maybe hundreds, a magnitude and depth of detestable behavior difficult to chronicle. He ruined countless lives without an iota of concern or remorse, but is he a murderer? Forty-five years later, most remain convinced he is. Investigators, D.A.s, the public, Carl and Bunny, everyone, it seems. Even the diocese. In 2004, Sandra Tessier was discussing her son's abuse with Vicar General Richard Sniezyk and asked hypothetically, "Why didn't my son just stab Lavigne?" Sniezyk calmly replied, "Because if he did, Lavigne would have murdered him, too."[1]

Carl was certain until the day he died, once musing, "It would be another tragedy to face God after I die and hear Him say, 'Guess what? He didn't do it.'" How reasonable is that? Back to 1972, investigators have said evidence against Lavigne was compelling, even ironclad. His lawyers remained equally adamant it was not. Max Stern never wavered in his belief Lavigne was "no murderer. Not even close."[2]

The fact remains that multiple blunders impacted four inquiries, with leads missed or ignored, evidence mishandled or lost, decision-making dreadfully poor. All were caused by galling outside factors. Few early investigators were equipped for the technical aspects of the investigation. The jurisdictional tug-of-war between the Chicopee police department and Ryan's people led to bungled crime scene processing and fumbling of evidence. The same issue poisoned Bennett's later investigations, which could never rise above his ego problems. Whether Ryan may have obtained an indictment, let alone a conviction, can be forcefully argued from both directions. The reality was, he was presented with a fatally weak case.

It has been convincingly argued Ryan was never going to bring Lavigne into a courtroom, regardless of the evidence. Many believe he

164

purposefully hindered investigators due to pressure from Weldon. The investigation's lack of depth regarding Lavigne and his associates supports that insistence. To what extent Ryan acquiesced to Church pressure is a question with no conclusive answer. His disinterest in charging Lavigne is offered as proof of collusion, but contrary to what many imagine from police reality shows or courtroom television, the law is quite specific about what is required to presume guilt. A common abridgment is the triad "means, motive, and opportunity." Means: Did Lavigne have the ability to commit the crime? Motive: Was there compelling reason for Lavigne to commit the crime? Opportunity: Did Lavigne have a reasonable chance to commit the crime? Additionally, can it be proven Lavigne took the opportunity to commit the crime? The conclusive presence of the first three, applicable *specifically* to Lavigne killing Danny, must be confirmed with certainty to presume a guilty verdict. Given all the issues, the latter became a moot point.

Within 24 hours, through his own devices, Lavigne became a suspect. His unusual behavior and incriminating comments definitely made him *look* like a suspect, so investigators became laser focused on proving he *was* the killer. Investigators believed he was the "prime, if not only, suspect" because of "the close relationship that had existed between he and Daniel, his presence at the crime scene the day after the body was discovered, the unusual questions he asked of investigators and his admission he was alone with Daniel on April 7."[3] To measure the potency of the case against Lavigne, a dispassionate review of the evidence must be undertaken, and connections investigators failed to recognize studied. His consciousness of guilt must be defined. The evaluation offers mixed results.

Lavigne had the means, evidenced by a lifetime of serious psychological issues and a history of manipulative antisocial behavior with roots in an alleged pseudo-sexual relationship with his mother. During his early teens, he was a chronic animal abuser who once abandoned his own sister in the basement of an unfinished house. His emotional instability so worried seminary administrators, they questioned his basic suitability for priesthood. He was a committed masochist, evidenced by particularly tortuous childhood animal abuse and adult habits of beating his victims after molesting them, slapping their testicles, and teasing and taunting his victims. He was an insatiable, predatory abuser and compulsive child molester, a risk-taking pedophile who abused in every possible manner and venue. Even after exposure, a very public trial and public vilification, he targeted children at Father Bruce Teague's church.[4]

Lavigne exaggerated and embellished personal stories and was a habitual liar. For decades, he lied to pastors, priests, the diocese, friends, parishioners and children. He lied to investigators. Then, there was the suspicious result of the first polygraph examination, his responses called "erratic and inconsistent."[5] But abuse and lies do not make Lavigne a murderer. They make him a sex offender and liar.

Whether Danny's death was a premeditated killing for a specific reason or an unforeseen crime of passion will never be known without a confession. It may have been a spur-of-the-moment crime. Danny and his killer (or killers) apparently believed he was returning home that night, at least initially. After all, why give him gum to hide the smell of alcohol if the plan was to kill him? Something infuriated his killer sufficiently to brutally beat and strangle him in a frenzy of overkill. Most blows were delivered after death. There was blind rage. The attack's intermittent and frantic nature speaks to that, but about what is unknown. Lavigne was unpredictable, with a hair-trigger temper that could be ignited by anything, and he was no stranger to hurting children. He was especially volatile, and more violent, when angered. He was clearly capable of ferocious rage evidenced by Danny's injuries. Most important, the serial threat-maker and intimidator bragged about killing before.

Lavigne was also left-handed. Almost every investigator who looked into this case believed the killer was left-handed due to the placement of the major wounds on the right side of Danny's head. So, yes, Lavigne had the means to kill Danny. The problem is, not a single supporting fact or shred of evidence confirms he did.

Did Lavigne have motive to kill Danny? Yes, he had plenty. First, he was increasingly concerned about being exposed, with scores of victims in his wake who might talk. The diocese, rectory employees, and fellow priests knew. Several of the latter witnessed assaults. Lavigne could no longer laugh off the threat as he had, crowing, "They can't do anything to me."[6] There were just too many victims.

Perhaps Lavigne was worried that Danny, specifically, might be his downfall. Danny's life was perforated with conflict. At his core, he was a boy entering teen years that are unpredictable by nature. He was having sexual relations with multiple older men. It was a role he accepted but increasingly hated. He loved Lavigne on some level but simultaneously detested him for the abuse, and that antipathy—about Lavigne and the others—was deepening. The feelings visible to friends were seen by Lavigne, who must have been increasingly worried Danny would turn against him. At 13, Danny was not as malleable as his younger victims, not as vulnerable to manipulation. Danny was street-wise and savvier than his age would suggest, a tough kid running the streets with a questionable crowd. He stole, drank, and used drugs, but he was still a child, after all. A child who in the months before his murder was becoming increasingly withdrawn and more vocal about being abused. His hate for his abusers was becoming all-consuming.[7]

He certainly appeared close to talking. To friends, his hints about abuse by Lavigne had become only thinly-veiled. Tommy Martin "knew exactly what that meant" when Danny said Lavigne "hurt him." Martin said Danny, surprisingly, did not care who knew. His comments also led Michael McMahon to "figure out Lavigne molested Danny."[8] More concerning, Lavigne worried about Danny for a long time. His "I'll tell!" threat at the Goshen cabin indicates Danny was not above using silence to leverage Lavigne a full two years before he died.[9]

But Danny may have occasionally taken advantage. As distasteful as the relationship had become, accounts suggest he may sometimes have been a willing participant. Bill Zajac was told Danny cruised downtown Springfield's well-defined gay neighborhoods trading sex for money, often at a small service road behind the *Republican* known as the setting for such transactions. Friends said Danny "always had money," so those reports cannot be completely discounted.[10] If true, there are any number of additional suspects with equal, maybe greater, motive.

Lavigne may have been further concerned because Danny's open discontent and unguarded comments indicated he lost control over him. Lavigne resembles that composite killer profiled as someone "who needs to be in control all the time [whose only response] was blind rage." Carl believed Danny was killed because he was about to come forward, that "Danny was about to tell me everything. I think Danny was going to squeal on him." Investigators agreed, one saying, "I thought Danny Croteau was … going to blow the whistle on him … and he decided to shut the kid up."[11] But "him" could also have been any of a dozen other abusers.

There remains another chilling possibility, one giving the killer even stronger motive to silence Danny. Investigators and Danny's friends believed Danny was blackmailing someone and that was why he "always had money." Blackmail was surely in the purview of Danny's confused life, not uncharacteristic for a tough street kid who knew the ropes. If he were doing so, that could easily have propelled someone to sufficient rage to brutally kill him, but there is no certainty Lavigne was the one or even the only extortion target.

Lavigne surely had motive, but again, every fact supporting that conclusion is unconfirmable and entirely circumstantial. Everything is based on what witnesses "believed" or "thought." Nothing they actually "*knew.*"

Lastly, there is little doubt Lavigne had opportunity to kill Danny. They were together the previous weekend and apparently had multiple contacts the next week. Investigators were certain Danny not only spoke to Lavigne on the phone that Friday, but had also spent part of the night at Lavigne's quarters at St. Mary's, where he spent most Fridays.[12] Both are possible. The last sightings of a hitchhiking Danny began near OLSH school and led, in a straight line, to within a mile of St. Mary's.

Lavigne was familiar with the crime scene from fishing there, and it was only a short distance from the Eton Street home of former seminary pal Donald Charland, where he took part in regular poker games with friends. Lavigne's rectory was barely a half-mile hike, another straight line, through the East Woods from the bridge.[13]

In terms of alibi, Lavigne's was weak, confirmed only by his parents, and he had trouble remembering exact dinner times and when and where he and his mother traveled and when he spoke to the Croteaus. Neither did St. Mary's priests confirm Lavigne's presence. It seems they were never asked.

Danny went to the river with someone he was comfortable with. Chronic hitchhiking aside, Joseph Croteau is certain "Danny would never go somewhere like that with anyone he didn't know well." The autopsy showed tantalizing similarities to Lavigne's methods. Danny was drunk and his stomach full of chewed gum. Lavigne fed victims alcohol and gave them gum to hide the smell.[14]

Then there was his manipulation of Carl and Bunny to close the casket, that inferred desire to avoid seeing Danny's face. The Circle phone call Carl Jr. insisted was made by Lavigne and Lavigne's absence from the wake, his curiously brief post-funeral visit and his abrupt cessation of contact all add to the suspicion.

As for Lavigne's consciousness of guilt, his behavior in the immediate aftermath was unquestionably incriminating. First, his questions to investigators about the bloody stone and tire impressions were odd. There may have been more to the tire question. According to a retired Chicopee detective, in the week after the murder, Lavigne had the tires on his Mustang replaced.[15]

But what appears to be convincing evidence confirming opportunity, in fact, is not persuasive. All the propositions are flawed in some way. It cannot be proven Lavigne was with Danny that week. Familiarity with the scene proves nothing, nor does a weak alibi. Thousands of priests gave their victims liquor before and gum after abusing them. Peculiar questions and odd behavior are just that, as is an unconfirmable voice identification. In toto, everything is perplexing, and nothing *proves* anything.

Did Lavigne have means, motive, and opportunity to kill Danny? Yes. Kind of. The equally-reasonable case for Lavigne's innocence was summarized by his lawyer, Stern: the usable tire impressions did not match any car to which Lavigne had access; the blood at the scene—the killer's—was scientifically proven not to be Lavigne's; Lavigne passed a polygraph test (Stern was silent regarding the inconclusive results of the first); Lavigne had an alibi, such as it was; Carl Jr.'s voice identification is unreliable, since he initially claimed not to recognize the caller; Michael McMahon's recollection of the "I'll tell!" incident was likewise frail—he did not mention it when first recounting the altercation; and alternative suspects—according to Stern a "very large number … and many more not named in the indictment"—were not investigated.[16]

Anecdotal or circumstantial evidence rarely a successful murder case make, no matter the volume. The physical evidence was equally problematic, mishandled as it was. Nothing that remained was conclusively tied to Lavigne. Lastly, it appears only one other person was even remotely considered a suspect. Bennett's DNA expert Blake tested a sample from Ed Veroneau's sister. The blood at the scene was not his, either.

No physical evidence was tied to Lavigne. The best tire impression was lost. The most important piece of physical evidence, the rock caked in blood and hair, disappeared, as did the stained towel from Lavigne's house, along with half a dozen other items. Nobody tried to connect the fibers on Danny's socks to locations tied to Lavigne or to anyone else, but the handling of pubic hairs found on Danny's clothing perhaps best encapsulates the comically-bungled investigations. In 2002, state police chemist Edward Bernstein performed trace analysis on three pubic hairs found on Danny's socks and underwear. When they were subsequently retested at the Agawam state police lab, an extra pubic hair of unknown origin was discovered. It belonged to Bernstein.

Even though Lavigne was never linked to a single piece of evidence, Ryan was beseeched on all sides to indict based on the circumstantial evidence. The fact remains that doing so would have been problematic. People believe a grand jury indictment means guilt, but nothing is further from the truth. In his book *The Bonfire of the Vanities*, Tom Wolfe famously quoted New York appellate judge Sol Wachtler's unfortunately-accurate cliché: "A grand jury would indict a ham sandwich if that's what prosecutors wanted."[17] In half the country, the decision to indict is made by a grand jury composed of 12 community members (the rest utilize the more adversarial preliminary hearing process).[18]

Grand juries meet secretly, judges and lawyers barred except a prosecutor presenting evidence. The jury can request and be shown almost anything, even something that might be inadmissible at trial. It is fundamentally easy to obtain an indictment. In the infrequent case a grand jury refuses to bring charges, a D.A. can skirt the process entirely by issuing one himself or simply scheduling a trial. Investigators were confident there was enough evidence and probable cause for Ryan to obtain an indictment, issue one himself, or at the very least, try the case.

Investigator cajoling aside, Ryan was bound by thousands of pages of American Bar Association guidelines defining every facet of his obligation. Above all, it was his "singular responsibility" to make the decision. Further, he was ethically bound to seek justice, not merely a conviction, no matter the outside political, religious, or public pressure. He was not bound to bring charges if evidence *might* support doing so, and he was actually discouraged from doing so if he had personal reasonable doubt. The ABA specifically directed no indictment or trial should be initiated—and a trial be stopped, if ongoing—if Ryan personally believed there was insufficient probable cause or evidence to gain a conviction.[19]

But Ryan's gravest concern was evidentiary. Nothing tied Lavigne to the murder. That it not to say such evidence never existed. Police lost it. Neither could Lavigne be placed at the scene or with Danny, whose whereabouts are an utter mystery after 4:30 Friday. Investigators conceded the glaring gaps, one admitting, "All we needed was a little bit of evidence but we didn't have it. We tried our darndest to pin the murder on Lavigne, but we just couldn't do it."[20] The truth remains there was as much inference supporting Lavigne's innocence as proving guilt. Hence, Ryan's dilemma—at least his public one.

Already limited by investigative issues and ABA mandates, Ryan was coerced from every quarter. He was bombarded with opinions and demands from police, his investigators and prosecutors, Weldon, prominent Catholics, private citizens, and friends and neighbors. During dozens of meetings in the 1970s, Carl and Bunny pleaded with him to indict. He said he could not, that his "hands were tied" because he had no "reasonable chance of obtaining a conviction." As the runaround Carl and Bunny felt they were enduring increased as the years passed, conversations between Carl and Ryan grew more contentious. In 1975, Ryan asked Carl, "Where am I going to get 12 jurors to convict a priest?" Carl said he "went wild," so much so an assistant D.A. warned him, "Cool it. You can't talk to Matty that way. Nobody talks to Matty that way."[21]

Ryan complained to associates he could never get "twelve people in Springfield to convict a priest of murder in 1972."[22] He was probably right. He also faced equally heavy external pressure. In 1972, it was rare to see a priest charged with *any* crime; murder was unheard of. Ex-priest Dr. Fred Berlin, director of a Johns Hopkins University treatment center for priests with sexual disorders, said charging a priest with something as serious as murder shocks people into disbelief because "it's just so much the antithesis of what you expect of a priest." Ryan was as susceptible to that internal predisposition as any Catholic in the 1970s. A reporter friend said, "A priest killing a kid simply was not part of his reality. Such a thing would not ever cross his mind." Denials from the diocese aside, he faced direct or indirect coercion from Weldon, who did not want a priest charged with murder in any case, whether or not Elliot Street believed Lavigne was guilty. Friends argued Ryan was never swayed by Weldon, insisting he "had no interest in protecting the Church from the embarrassment of having one of its priests accused as a murderer." Multiple investigators told Carl and Bunny and many others that Ryan and the diocese conspired to protect the Church.[23] Proving that contention is difficult.

Irrespective possible deals and pressure, Ryan's was a no-win situation. He believed Lavigne was a murderer, telling many, "I know it's him." A friend said, "He was really frustrated he couldn't go for an indictment but in good conscience, the evidence just wasn't there." His vexing reality was anything that remotely linked Lavigne to Danny's murder was utterly circumstantial. There was simply more conjecture than fact. Common sense and ABA guidelines prohibited him from prosecuting a case he believed unwinnable. If he took the scrawny case before a Catholic jury in a Catholic town, conviction was unattainable. With apologies to Wachtler, it may be easy to obtain an indictment, but given how little prosecutorial latitude there was, for Ryan to do so would have been unethical, possibly illegal.[24]

One Ryan decision remains questionable and evidences a Weldon deal. His refusal of multiple Croteau requests to indict Lavigne for molesting Carl Jr.—who had sworn out a formal complaint—is indefensible. His questionable excuse was that doing so "hindered the murder case." There was simply no legitimate reason, other than Church pressure, for not bringing that case.

As public dissatisfaction with Ryan and the Church grew over the years, the whole affair began to smell. In 2008, a lawyer representing a group of victims summarized why: "The state support of the Diocese in concealing the facts has historic implications. All of Western Massachusetts has known the situation stinks—the murder of Danny Croteau and failure to prosecute the murder."[25] Weldon-Ryan or Weldon-Chicopee arrangements explain the convenient loss of so much critical evidence and multiple flagrant, indefensible crime scene errors. Anecdotal evidence supports the allegation. According to a D.A. from a neighboring Massachusetts jurisdiction, the "loss" of the tire tread was directed by the Weldon-Ryan cabal. Two state troopers claimed it was known early on that the impressions matched the tires on Lavigne's Mustang. They claimed the pristine impression was destroyed by state police, on Ryan's orders, to protect Weldon. The troopers further said the casting was not damaged by rain, but was actually disposed of later. A lead Chicopee detective told intimates it was done on specific Weldon order. Both comments, though unconfirmed, paint the investigation in different tones.[26] It does seem improbable so much critical evidence was lost unless someone desired that outcome. A retired investigator quipped, "That bloody rock probably ended up as a doorstop in the evidence room." But anecdotal evidence—even in great volume—of a Weldon-Ryan deal is unconfirmable. It has been categorically denied by Ryan associates and Weldon underlings since first mentioned publicly in 1991, but the question remains.

Even without confirmation of Weldon involvement, that Ryan and Bennett investigations were bungled is undeniable. In November 2004, Bennett summarized the obvious: "The lack of physical evidence has always been a stumbling block." But he was consistently less than diligent about pursuing any. Why two D.A.s would torpedo four investigations is a mystery. An argument can be made that Ryan's failure was caused by loyalty to Weldon, but Bennett's resulted from the simplest of reasons: ego. Similar issues clouded the initial inquiry, but worsened during Bennett's, fraught as they were with error and omission. Arrogance and his determination that only his group would solve his cases led him to disregard important information from R.C. Stevens and reject Dr. Henry Lee's expertise. He also did not utilize agencies that could have provided assistance, including the FBI's Violent Criminal Apprehension Program (ViCAP), cold case and behavioral science units.[27]

Bennett did not coordinate efforts with Chicopee, didn't even establish a case database. State police CPAC reports identified more than 15 pieces of unidentified physical evidence from the scene. None wound up on evidence logs or was tested. Bennett's lack of custodial evidentiary integrity prevented utilization of newer forensic techniques that may have provided resolution. No further testing was done on the mysterious red fibers stuck to Danny's socks and coat, or additional biologic materials on his clothes discovered in 2003. Stevens confirmed the fibers were not from the Croteau house, but Bennett refused requests they be tested for links to other locations. Accompanied by Bill Zajac, Stevens visited Lavigne's old Edward Street house. The woman living there was unaware of her home's history. She left Stevens in the basement, where Lavigne entertained countless victims, to go upstairs and answer the phone. He used a pocket knife to lift up a corner of the carpet. Underneath were the remnants of the previous floor covering: red shag carpet.[28]

Bennett's lead investigator Peter Higgins was as obstructionist as his boss. In 2008, a judge excoriated him for offering a "list of statements

... riddled with errors."[29] Ryan seemingly wanted the investigation directed away from the Church. The Bennett-Higgins endgame appeared to have morphed from solving the case to making sure no one questioned why it was never solved. The whys of a shadowy Weldon-Ryan deal and Bennett's seeming indifference to solving the case cannot be explained. The bottom line is, it appears Lavigne did not kill Danny, at least not by himself. Who did? Who helped?

11

Killer

One of the early investigators said they tried to "pin the murder on Lavigne, but we just couldn't do it." Trying so hard to "pin" it on Lavigne meant no one else was investigated in any real depth. Within days of the murder, Carl was told, "We know who it is," and assured, "We'll nail him."[1] But the Lavigne fixation meant alternative suspects were only lightly considered. Tunnel vision, beyond lost or mishandled evidence and lack of investigative curiosity, doomed every investigation. Investigators were so enthusiastic about Lavigne, they tightly grasped anything that seemed to even *remotely* link him to the murder. Facts were stretched and manipulated to fit preconceived assumptions and narrative. In doing so, any number of potential suspects were unidentified or ignored outright. More critical, no alternative scenarios were seriously explored. It is perhaps unsurprising Ryan did not, but it is completely mystifying Bennett seemingly never considered that Lavigne did *not* kill Danny, at least not by himself. This, even after it was confirmed Lavigne's blood was not at the scene. It was someone's, after all.

Without question, the most troublesome investigative obsession was that the wounds clustered on the right side of Danny's head had to mean the killer was left-handed. It dovetailed nicely with the notion Lavigne was the killer because he was a southpaw, but the murder simply did not play out that way. The supposition is easily refuted. It verges on impossible that Danny was subdued by one person, attacking from the front. Remember, Danny was a big boy, "strong as an ox," a not-so-gentle giant? He was not inherently aggressive, but a hair-trigger temper made him mercury-quick to fight over the slightest affronts. Carl and Bunny were called to school at least once a month because he was fighting. Most of those battles were against not one, but two or even three boys. He was never known to have lost a single schoolyard bout, unsurprising since he was a ferocious fighter, talented wrestler and hard-hitting boxer. Even the older, rough and tumble Circle—who engaged in vicious, often bloody, street fights—were afraid of him and would never "get him going [or] get Danny mad."[2]

It is improbable Danny was face to face with a single attacker, overpowered and rendered immediately defenseless by a first punch—at least, one he saw coming. He retaliated violently over minor insults and surely would have responded wildly to any frontal assault. He was evidently able to counter that night. Signs of a struggle at the site of the initial confrontation evidenced a scuffle, brief as it may have been. Even after receiving one or more grievous blows, he still fought for his life. His heavy jacket was torn near the wrist, and a square of fabric surrounding a pocket was shredded. Since he was unconscious within minutes, it stands to reason the first blow or blows came from behind. Strikes delivered with a right hand.

It is possible Danny was with one person, but it is more reasonable that there were two. Facts support the two-attacker scenario. It is reasonable to assume Danny was brought to the river for sexual activity or on that pretext. Given Lavigne's familiarity with the site, Danny was there before, probably for that purpose. He was not unfamiliar with multiple abusers acting in cohort. Assuming he was with men he knew and trusted, to whatever degree, he would likely be less concerned about someone behind him. It would be easy for an attacker to get in that position while his attention was drawn to his front. Overpowered, and unconscious after a few blows from the rock, he was dragged to the water, viciously beaten again and strangled, then tossed in the river.

It is reasonable to assume Lavigne was one of two men with Danny. He had a violent temper and a history of beating victims, regularly threatened violence and death, and was concerned he was going to be exposed. He had cause to silence Danny. But he was incapable of overpowering Danny alone, especially from the front. He could not best Gregory in a fistfight. Danny was much tougher and stronger than his brother. If Lavigne attacked from behind, the head wounds would have been on the left side, since Lavigne was a lefty. Since Lavigne was probably at the river, he must have been with someone. Someone right-handed. But who?

Any number of men could have been there, but Ryan and Bennett stumbled across few possibilities. In the two days police took to limit their focus on Lavigne, as many as two dozen reasonable suspects with close ties to Lavigne and Danny were summarily eliminated or not considered at all. All had questionable histories, unconfirmed or nonexistent alibis, and motive at least equal to Lavigne's. They were easily identified and located, their identities were known, they were directly connected to Lavigne and Danny (many, to both). Every one was part of a distinct group that overlapped with other distinct groups, yet none were investigated beyond cursory consideration.

It is inconceivable how Ryan's and Bennett's people missed—or ignored—a potential Boy Scout connection to the murder. Ryan's misstep borders on investigative neglect. Bennett had an even sharper view, and his misstep is simply unpardonable. The very first person that Ryan's people spoke to (after the Croteaus) was Danny's Scoutmaster, Ed Veroneau. Bunny told them she called him because Danny claimed to have had a meeting that Friday. Had they looked into Veroneau, the investigation would likely have had a different outcome.

Danny particularly enjoyed the Scout campouts at Camp Woronoco, an hour northwest in the Berkshires, near Russell, Massachusetts. It was on the site of Strathmore Paper founder Horace A. Moses' 1919 estate, 1,900 woodland acres with a private 90-acre lake and spectacular views that included Moses' first mill, nestled in the Westfield River gorge.[3] Moses was among the first Boy Scouts of America (BSA) benefactors. When another camp was destroyed by a hurricane in 1944, he donated 1,200 acres for the Horace A. Moses Reservation. Western Massachusetts troops had open access to the site, as did the Church. Lavigne was apparently a regular visitor.

The 1991 *Washington Times* exposé "Scouts Honor" described the BSA as "a magnet for men who want to have sexual relations with children. Pedophiles join the Scouts for a simple reason: it's where the boys are." The BSA was founded in 1910. From that moment, abuse was as rampant in the BSA as grotesquely as it was in the Church. Within ten years, the BSA was maintaining a secret "Ineligible Volunteer" list of people banished for abuse, boxes full of index cards stored in a vault at headquarters. By 1935, 2,919 names and thousands of incidents had been carefully cataloged. Similarities to the Secret Archives are unavoidable. When courts unsealed BSA abuse records in 2012, more than 14,000 pages came to light. Like the Church, the BSA hierarchy hid crimes and orchestrated cover-ups. Police departments, prosecutors, and even pastors assisted in BSA cover-ups. The accused were given two months to quietly resign, offering reasons like business demands, chronic brain dysfunction, even duties at a Shakespeare festival. The BSA treated victims as poorly as the Church did and their abusers received similar deference. In 1987, officials in Washington State refused to oust an accused Scoutmaster "because he is a nice guy."[4]

It is difficult to understand how Ryan avoided Veroneau. He had been on Springfield P.D.'s radar since 1966. Born in Springfield in 1945, the son of a plumber's helper, Veroneau grew up at 279 Stapleton Road, near Cathedral High School. Most of the class of 1964 recognized him as an "odd duck" who never attended a single social event in four years. Just one friend socialized with him. His sole extracurricular pursuit was as an equipment manager and trainer, taping athletes and cleaning locker rooms. That job, and an obsession with police and EMTs, earned him the nickname "Doc." Outside school, he was a volunteer EMT and Red Cross first aid instructor. He was enthralled with electronics, volunteering with the Hampden County Sheriff's Department Auxiliary maintaining communication equipment.[5] Classmates thought he was gay, though he gave no outward indication.[6]

He was a habitual self-aggrandizer, later claiming to have been a lieutenant in the Sheriff's Department and a prison guard. He boasted of a degree from the National Law Enforcement Academy in Florida. It was a mail-order diploma mill. He also claimed to be a trustee of the Police Hall of Fame, another scam run by the same man who ran the "Academy." He boasted about "saving lives" during unspecified EMT emergencies. He bragged about his "great rapport with youth."

He had a run-in with Springfield police in 1966, reportedly accused of inappropriate behavior with a child. The case was not prosecuted and the 21-year-old fled Springfield for Loudonville, New York, near Albany. He enrolled at Sienna College, a Catholic liberal arts school, planning on a sociology degree, then the priesthood. His junior year, spring 1968, he worked on a sociology professor's survey of the crime-plagued Martin Luther King projects in nearby Troy. The experience inspired him to create the Counselor Streetworker Program, under the auspices of the Troy Urban League and Council of Churches. His stated goal was to help young blacks from the projects—more than 500 were eventually involved—by working with police, parents, churches, and aid agencies. He converted a donated basement at the Westminster Church into a neighborhood workshop and resource center. Kids gathered to paint, listen to records, read, watch movies, or tinker with electronics. He claimed to use his own salary when fundraising efforts failed to produce the money needed for the program's operation, and, indeed, the first summer he slept in donated quarters at Grace Methodist Church.[7]

Veroneau offered the children private counseling sessions—"emotional first aid"—and recruited Sienna students to tutor in reading, math, and art. The kids performed community service projects, most of which involved repairing damage caused by their peers' vandalism. They washed store windows, swept sidewalks, even installed burglar alarms in stores. Veroneau and his charges also installed a two-way radio and public-address system in a Troy P.D. patrol car. He took small groups on weekend camping trips. The program was inarguably successful. Neighborhood delinquency complaints dropped 85 percent and Veroneau spoke before community groups and was featured in newspaper articles. He continued his exaggerating, telling a reporter he stopped gang "rumbles fought with chains and switchblades." After his graduation from Sienna in 1969, he moved into a two-family house at 455 3rd Street in Troy. The first major item he bought was a used police car at a local department auction. He owned similar cars the rest of his life.[8]

In late 1970, then 25, he was hired by the Rensselaer County Sheriff's Office, but he was dismissed within a few weeks after it received a Springfield P.D. report detailing his 1966 issues. Local police were concerned enough to quietly keep tabs on him. Just a week later, on February 2, 1971, he was arrested after buying a .38 caliber pistol at a sporting goods store using his revoked sheriff's badge and ID. He was charged with impersonating a police officer and weapons possession. Surprisingly, a grand jury declined to return indictment. A month later, he returned to Springfield and immediately volunteered with the Scouts. Despite his record, he was appointed Scoutmaster of Troop 118 which met Fridays at Duggan Junior High. He and pal Dick Brown also ran the troop's Explorer Post, training older boys in advanced first aid, camping, and survival skills. Veroneau and Brown took them on training and camping weekends to Woronoco, and during summers, Veroneau ran the camp health "lodge" providing medical services to campers. When Danny died, Veroneau also worked as an EMT and ran a home security business, giving him access to scores of homes.[9]

Ryan's investigators talked to Veroneau within days of the murder. It defies reason he was not even *considered* a serious suspect. One would think a prior arrest in 1966, for allegedly abusing a young boy, would have piqued someone's interest. That assumes, of course, that investigators checked into Veroneau at all. It appears they did not, because if they did, they would have uncovered his New York arrest a year earlier. It is impossible to conceive how that was ignored as well.

Dick Brown lived at 32 Burns Avenue, just four houses around the corner from the Croteaus. Danny's final walk out the neighborhood took him past Brown's house. Like Veroneau, during high school Brown had few friends and and an early obsession with police. Over four years, his only extra-curricular activities were "Student Patrol," "Corridor Patrol," and "Lunch Room Patrol." Also like Veroneau, Brown drove a series of used police vehicles, dark colored Dodge Polara and Ford sedans bought at auctions. The cars retained police accouterments like large antennas and floodlights and appeared to be authentic patrol cars. Veroneau and Brown installed police scanners, according to the neighborhood kids. They all assumed the two men were auxiliary policemen because they carried badges and tactical gear. All of this might have piqued investigator interest, had anyone looked.

Neighborhood parents were concerned about Brown and Veroneau because they were "strange and really weird" and repeatedly invited boys into their homes. Their concern was justified. According to several neighborhood kids, Veroneau was molesting some of them in his basement at Stapleton, a bizarre tableau that evoked a horror movie set. The musty cellar was a labyrinth of half a dozen small rooms with flimsy plywood walls, each full of dusty workbenches and unfinished electronics projects. The largest room was dominated by a security command center with an entire wall covered with rows of electronics and television monitors. One boy visiting the creepy space stood "between him [Veroneau] and the stairs in case I had to run. The guy looked like some kind of serial killer. He reminded me of the Son of Sam guy, David Berkowitz." The boy fled when Veroneau put a gay porn tape into the VCR.[10]

In an earlier attempt to seduce the boy, Veroneau admired male passersby and added, "Girls, guys—it's all the same, right?" Another boy Veroneau hired for his security business accompanied him to New York and awoke in the middle of the night to Veroneau trying to perform oral sex on him. He ignored the assault because he was "afraid the guy would kill him."[11]

Veroneau and Brown even scared the older Circle. The kids knew the men as aggressive, with hair-trigger tempers, both physically imposing. Veroneau was six feet tall and 250 pounds, and Brown almost six feet, five inches and "scary, massive." Veroneau, for one, was constantly overly physical with kids, instigating aggressive roughhousing and wrestling and grabbing them violently by the neck or shoulders. Like abuser priests, Veroneau encouraged them to break the law. He kept a large gun collection and took kids to Woronoco to blast machine guns in the woods, urged them to drink, and reportedly had them steal for him.[12]

It is outrageous that Ryan did not somehow stumble across Veroneau, Brown, or both. At that time of his investigation into Danny's murder, Ryan was prosecuting their close friend Roger Norton. Thirty-three when Danny died, Norton had a master's degree from Springfield College and had worked for the BSA since 1963. He earned a salary of $10,080 and was a program director at Woronoco and the camp ranger, responsible for maintaining the property. He lived on-site in a small trailer and drove around in a Korean War–vintage Jeep. Veroneau and Brown visited Norton often, often in the company of kids taken there for Scout—and non–Scout—outings. He was friends with Lavigne and other priests who brought kids there. Among them were members of the Circle and Danny. How many were abused there is unknown, but incidents shed light on the nature of the relationship between the boys, Veroneau, Brown, and Norton. David Skipton—who lived next to Brown—enlisted Joseph Croteau and two Circle friends to act as lookouts while he broke into the camp store. He was quickly caught, but surprisingly went unpunished except for having to return the stolen stock. Sometime later, Skipton was unloading equipment at the store and threw a brand-new sled into the lake. When he was warned, "You'll get in trouble," Skipton laughed: "Don't worry. They won't do anything to me." Another boy took Norton's snowmobile from outside his camper and rolled it into the lake. The other boys assumed neither was punished because they "had something big on Brown, Veroneau, and Norton."[13]

Barely three months after Danny's murder, with Ryan in the middle of the initial investigation, Norton was indicted on 55 counts of sexual misconduct, unnatural acts, indecent assault, sodomy, and rape. Thou-

sands of sexually-themed photographs of young boys were found in
Norton's trailer. In the pre–Internet era, the collection took years to
assemble. Norton's assaults began two months before Danny was killed.
In 1972, such cases were rare and garnered a lot of interest. Still, Ryan
or his investigators did not look for a connection. A local BSA executive
claimed that half a dozen fathers preferred frontier justice to waiting
for courts. A week after Norton's arrest, the fathers dragged him from
his camper and hauled him deep into the Woronoco woods. He was
stripped, his underwear jammed down his throat, and he was water-
boarded in the lake. He was then tied to a tree, horsewhipped, and
warned, "Don't ever come back here again or we'll kill you." Norton pled
guilty and was sentenced to two years.

　　The files Ryan had on Norton confirmed a BSA connection to
abuse, facts similarly detailed in the file Ryan had on Danny. Both files
were at the top of Ryan's pile, but he and his investigators never questioned a connection to Veroneau despite his 1966 Springfield problem
and 1970 New York arrest, and a possible Norton-Veroneau-Brown connection was missed. Veroneau and Brown were also close friends with
a "curly-haired hippie type" mentioned in statements as a friend of
Danny's. He drove kids to and from Duggan in a VW van and was never
found. Ryan's missed connections are a remarkable error, but Bennett
also overlooking the BSA is even more astonishing. He missed more,
and clearer, links than had Ryan. When Bennett first investigated
Danny's murder in 1991, the BSA scandal was in newspapers across the
county, but it appears Bennett never delved deeply into BSA associations
with Danny. Though Veroneau was dead by then, having committed
suicide in 1984, he was only briefly considered. Bennett went no further
than DNA testing.[14]

　　Why Bennett did not look deeper is bizarre. He must have known
about Veroneau's 1966 run-in with Springfield and his 1970 New York
arrest. More startling, Veroneau was arrested on July 20, 1977, for assault
and battery, rape, and abuse of a child under 16. In Springfield. Veroneau
met the victim at a Cathedral High School career day event representing
an ambulance service where he was a dispatcher. He enticed the boy
to the Stapleton house and raped him in the basement. The boy ran
out and flagged down a passing police cruiser on Bradley Road. In
1979, Veroneau was convicted and sentenced to three and a half years
in jail in the Hampshire County Jail and House of Correction. It seems

inconceivable Bennett dig not dig deeper into Veroneau's connections to Danny.[15]

Like Ryan, Bennett also ignored the "hippie" in the VW, further distancing himself from the Veroneau-Brown-Norton connection. In addition to their visits to Woronoco with their Duggan troop, Veroneau spent summers there as an on-site medic. One boy recalled visiting Veroneau's quarters for an allergic reaction and Veroneau insisting he needed a shot in the buttocks. Hard to believe, but Bennett whiffed on Roger Norton specifically. Twice. When the 1991 investigation commenced, Norton's 1972 conviction was on record, and, incredibly, Bennett knew of Norton's 1989 indictment on multiple sexual assault and child rape charges involving two boys, cousins. When police went to his camper, Norton escaped into the woods. He was found three years later in Goodyear, Arizona, living under an assumed name. He was extradited, convicted, and sentenced to 16 to 20 years, just as Bennett's investigation was getting underway. A year later, while Bennett was actively investigating, Norton pled guilty to yet another sexual abuse charge, molesting a five-year-old. The trail of Bennett's missed BSA connections went even farther incredibly. By the time of the second investigation, Bruce Mooney—yet another BSA official—was accused of involvement in Springfield cleric abuse. He was tied directly to Lavigne and acquainted with Veroneau, Brown, and Norton.[16]

Had Bennett looked further into Veroneau and potential BSA links to Danny, he might have learned that Lavigne took boys to Woronoco and knew Veroneau, Brown, Norton, and Mooney. Perhaps Bennett's most egregious error was missing an even more suspicious, easily identified possible BSA connection. In 1991, Bennett had files concerning Sandra Tessier's early-morning meeting with Lavigne and a supposed policeman a week after the murder. If pressed even slightly, Tessier would have told investigators that Lavigne's faux cop was "big, way over six feet tall [and] stocky" and closely resembled Brown. Brown was six feet, five inches tall, athletically built, and barrel-chested. Tessier was never asked by anyone to describe Lavigne's friend.[17]

Another unvetted BSA volunteer, Clifford Phelps, was familiar with Veroneau, Brown, Norton, and Mooney. Phelps was removed from Pack 132 in Chicopee for unknown reasons, and when Danny died, Phelps was living in Sixteen Acres.[18] It is an absolute mystery why Bennett neglected to investigate or missed the many serpentine connections between the BSA, Lavigne, and Danny. Any among the BSA contingent should reasonably have been suspected of involvement in Danny's murder. Some of the boys from the neighborhood remain convinced Veroneau and Brown were involved.

Danny's older local acquaintances should have been more seriously considered. He was close to three A&P employees. One, produce manager Robert Fox, was living in Florida during the later investigations. Danny often assisted Fox with his duties, left the store with him multiple times, and was reportedly painting Fox's bedroom for $10. His shift that Friday ended at 4:30 or 5 o'clock, the time Danny was last seen near the store, but Fox's alibi was never confirmed. Thirty years later, he told R.C. Stevens he knew nothing about Danny or the murder, but he was never fully investigated.

Investigators never identified the older friend who took Danny for rides and gave him "goodies." Just a week before the murder, Danny abruptly exited a street hockey game and jumped into the front seat of a blue Ford Galaxie driven by a round-faced man with black hair. The description matched all three A&P employees, and the car matched the 1972 statement describing one driven by a "queer" trying to pick up boys near Duggan. The man in the "tan car" who showed Danny "dirty books" was never identified, and no one found the "curly-haired hippie type" who took the kids to and from Duggan in a VW van and was close to Veroneau and Brown. Danny was reportedly seen in Chicopee with a "curly-haired hippie" the day of the murder.[19]

It appears police did not dig deeply into James Coleman, either. Despite his efforts to help the Circle, allegations of interest in young boys—specifically, that he performed oral sex on Circle boys—were never settled. An early statement appeared to refer to him: "kids around 16 Acres said a queer operating [redacted] would pick up kids and try to make them, around Duggan Junior High School." The statement further mentioned that Danny was at that specific man's "home on Tuesdays to practice wrestling."[20] Danny, of course, attended Tuesday boxing lessons at Coleman's house.

Some neighborhood characters with ties to Danny also escaped investigators' attention. Earl Hollister and his sons, Clark and Gary, lived at 61 Sunrise Terrace, just down the block from the Croteaus. The Hollisters reportedly had a disquieting family history of incest and sex abuse, and, curiously, the grandfather of the boys was murdered in Chicopee, killed by blunt force trauma to the head. His killer was never identified but Clark claimed his own father beat the man to death because the older man was molesting younger family members. Clark was a Lavigne victim who allegedly sexually assaulted his brother Gary. Gary claimed Clark murdered Danny. The Hollisters somehow escaped in-depth investigation.

Priests as a class and their associates with ties to Lavigne and Danny were evidently not seriously considered. Bennett knew abuser priests used gum to hide the smell of liquor yet seemingly did not make a connection between the Certs gum wrapper and the gum in Danny's stomach. Also, surprising, apparently no further testing was done on the wrapper, especially DNA testing, nor were cleric connections thoroughly investigated.

Take the mysterious monk, Father Barnabas Keck. His odd attachment to Danny was presumed to be the result of hearing Lavigne's confessions, but his own contradictory statements should have raised eyebrows on their own. In 2003, he told the *Boston Globe* that Lavigne—or any priest—never confessed to the crime, curiously side-stepping priest-penitent confidentiality. Stranger still, he absurdly claimed he would not have recognized Lavigne anyway. Lavigne was well known among Springfield clerics due to his activism, and Keck heard his confession multiple times, must have remembered him bringing multiple boys to confession with him. The reason for Keck's deception is unclear.

When Lavigne began working parishes in the late 1960s, an organized network of abuser priests was already in place. The "old guard" that preceded him had long operated together, though perhaps on a smaller scale than later groups. Senior member Father Timothy J. Leary was born in Worcester, graduated from Holy Cross and then the infamous Pink Palace, St. Mary's, and was ordained in 1936. He was headmaster and athletic director at St. Jerome's School in Holyoke, then rector at St. Michael's. Just after his installation in 1950, Weldon tapped Leary to oversee his signature project, the largest Catholic high school in New England, a $5,000,000 campus on 30 acres in East Forest Park. Cathedral

High School opened in 1959 offering 3,000 students 100 cutting-edge classrooms, a chapel, a library, a 1,400-seat auditorium, the biggest gym in the state, and a dozen athletic fields. A Sisters of St. Joseph convent was built on 14 donated acres across the street.[21]

Leary, named a prelate of honor by Pope Paul VI in 1963, was energetic, dynamic, and beloved by students, so it was a surprise when Weldon moved him to St. Michael's, likely because Leary was a persistent abuser, offering Cathedral admissions and scholarships in exchange for sex. He passed boys off to Father Frannie Lavelle, a younger priest who repeated the promises. Of course, no enrollments or scholarships materialized. A Leary victim ended the abuse after realizing "they weren't going to help get me the education I wanted so badly." Leary assaulted another boy inside St. Michael's Cathedral and in cemeteries after funerals. He made regular $25 payments to ensure his silence, as did Lavelle after he took over Leary's boys.[22]

Father F. Karl Huller was another member of the Cathedral abuser clan. Born in Holyoke, he enlisted in the Army after his 1942 graduation. He earned medals and commendations during frontline action with George S. Patton's Third Army from Normandy into the Ardennes and then served as an aide to Bavaria's military governor.[23] After the war, he graduated from Holy Cross and the Pink Palace and was ordained in 1954. He spent five years at St. Mary's, where Lavigne later served, then during the 1960s was a teacher, guidance counselor, and athletic director at Cathedral. Huller abused dozens there, often during private office counseling sessions. Scores were victimized by Leary, Huller, and Lavelle during their overlapping tenures at Cathedral.

Father David P. Welch was very close to Weldon and for 36 years was editor of the diocesan newspaper. He faced multiple accusations from the early 1950s through the 1970s. He targeted altar boys, one recalling that Welch pulled up "in a black car, honking his horn, and three or four of us would ride around with him." He obsessively talked about sex and took groups to a lake where he insisted they swim naked while he masturbated, dressed in his "black clerical suit and collar."[24] He was also chaplain at Camp Holy Cross in Goshen, for four decades a favored haunt of abuser priests.

Father Leo P. Landry was born in Concord, New Hampshire, in 1929, spent a year on a football scholarship at New England College, and then entered the Stigmatine seminary in Waltham. He was ordained in 1958. Stigmatine rolls were laden with abusers who victimized hundreds at the order's Boston-area facilities. Elm Bank Minor Seminary was on a lavish estate on the Charles River in upscale Wellesley. The centerpiece was a century-old, 40-room brick mansion housing 30 teen pre-seminarians. From the 1940s through the 1970s, it was the site of near-constant abuse. A half-dozen Stigmatine teachers were later sued, impressive because there was never more than ten there. Those victims were abused by multiple priests. Victim John Vellante said, "We went there thinking it was a holy institution but it turned out it was a hunting lodge, and we were the captured prey." When prefect Father Joseph Henchey passed two accusations on to Boston, he was removed and transferred.[25]

Landry abused at every assignment. He was a talented groomer, plying his victims with favors, plum assignments, liquor, meals, and Boston Bruins hockey games. He stole collections to take victims to dinner and abused at the rectory, Church camps, and a Boy Scout camp where he kept a trailer. He fondled one victim while driving along a country road in New England, and on another occasion, he gathered a group of boys in a field and forced them to masturbate. He abused one boy in his own home while the boy's single mother was at work. With the confessional at its center, Landry's diabolical scheme—"a great source for him, a pedophile's dream"—ensured a steady stream of victims. Pastors, housekeepers, and school nuns were all aware of his process. He took small groups of boys to the auditorium, ordered them to disrobe, and said, "Their bodies were about to change and they were going to get urges, and they might be inclined to masturbate. He cautioned that they sinned if they did, and must confess, to him." After manipulating an admission to the school, he ordered private counseling and absolution that had to take place away from the church. They were led to his rectory quarters, ordered to again disrobe, then he manipulated their penises to "teach" them masturbation. They were then forced to confess.[26]

Landry abused hundreds and was transferred a dozen times from the 1950s through the 1960s. He also abused with priests in eastern and western Massachusetts and in New Hampshire. In the early 1960s, he bounced between Pittsfield, Agawam, West Springfield, and even Ontario, Canada. In the late 1960s, he was sent to the abuse hotspot

Manchester, New Hampshire. After receiving a complaint in the first month of Landry's assignment, Bishop Ernest Primeau suggested Landry write an apology instead of forcing him to attend mandatory counseling. Landry mirrored Lavigne. They both used forced confessions to confuse victims. Both sometimes abused girls, and were physically, verbally, and psychologically sadistic. Landry began innocently, telling girls, "Let's rub rear ends" or "You know you want my body." He progressed to rubbing his penis against their backs, and, eventually, he became aggressive. Girls were refused bathroom passes, were kicked, had their buttocks slapped, were "hip-checked" into lockers, grabbed violently by the neck, and publicly insulted. He yelled at one, "You are stupid ... and an annoying little shit," and asked her how much her parents paid "to send you here so they don't have to look at you?"[27]

Weldon's old guard abused together, à la Leary and Lavelle. By the early 1970s, it was easy because priests united into larger networks that operated in organized fashions. It seems outlandish, but back to the early 1950s, abuse rings operated from New England down the Eastern seaboard. The individual rings were in contact with neighboring groups that together formed an extensive web. Documents dating to 1958 confirm Church knowledge of multiple rings in Boston, Worcester and Greenfield, Massachusetts, Vermont, and New Hampshire. Rings in Greenfield and in Springfield worked more or less in tandem, both laden with Stigmatines acquainted with Lavigne.[28]

The Springfield-Greenfield ring included priests, non-clergy friends, and Boy Scout officials, again all with ties to Lavigne. The priests shared assignments, socialized together, and had regular contact with non-priests, BSA officials and the old guard. The roster changed as priests dropped out or were transferred, but there were between 12 and 20 core members. Some had been abusing together for a decade before Lavigne arrived. Their activities, including overlap with rings in New Hampshire, New York, Boston, and Worcester, were chronicled in multiple civil suits.

The first inkling of a formal Springfield ring arose when four brothers in 2003 filed a suit naming priests Ronald Wamsher, Frannie Lavelle, J. Roy Jenness, Thomas O'Connor, Edward Kennedy, and Greenfield Scoutmaster Bruce Mooney. The latter was not charged with abuse per se, but "actively aiding" abuse by providing victims drugs and alcohol and conspiring to keep the abuse secret. The "Greenfield 6" shared victims at churches, rectories, private homes, and BSA camps. Jenness shared with Lavelle, Kennedy, Wamsher, and O'Connor. O'Connor and Jenness abused together with Mooney's assistance. Some victims were shared and abused by all five priests. Lavigne was close to everyone. He took boys to a cabin in Huntington owned by Jenness and BSA camps connected to Mooney.[29]

Lavigne casualty Paul Babeu said, "I was passed along to another priest who abused me in Vermont ... passed off as if I was an object." In 1987, he wrote Vermont's then-bishop John Marshall—later Springfield's bishop—describing tandem abuse by Lavigne and his close friend George Paulin. Marshall later lied, claiming he never heard "any rumor, innuendo or complaint, directly or indirectly, Lavigne possessed pedophilic tendencies."[30]

This menagerie and its Springfield counterpart—the "Holy 13"—comprises the largest group of potential suspects in Danny's murder. It is bewildering that Bennett did not look more deeply into any of them. When Bennett began his second inquiry, 60 area priests had been confirmed as abusers, as were two of four BSA members tied to the clerics. All had close connections with Lavigne, and Bennett knew of Babeu's story.

Ring members met at churches, rectories, private residences, state parks, and Church or BSA camps. They gathered—with their boys—at private residences in Springfield, Easthampton, Westfield, the Chicopee home of a Lavigne friend, and as far away as Sturbridge. They used half a dozen vacation homes in Vermont and Massachusetts. A favored lair was the Church-run Camp Holy Cross in Goshen. Members also used BSA reservations, including a Chesterton facility and Woronoco, the latter frequented by Lavigne, Veroneau, and their abuser friends.[31]

The 1970s incarnation, described as a "victim swapping nest of homosexuals," met regularly and abused together, often with non-priest associates. They met in pairs and in larger groups to share and trade boys, bacchanalias one victim called "pass-around-a-little-boy parties." Greenfield lawyer John Stobierski, who represented more than 50 victims, described the events: "Boys were shared by priests ... a family of brothers."[32] Members passed them on as they aged out of one abuser's preferences to others with older tastes. Lavigne preferred younger boys, and reportedly handed his victims off when they reached 11 or so. He remained in contact and still occasionally abused the boys, but he was no longer their primary abuser. Danny was abused by men other than Lavigne, and it is believed Lavigne passed him on to a priest friend in the year before his death. That handoff may have led to murder.

R.C. Stevens described the well-organized operation: "These priests formed their own Internet before any Internet existed. It allowed them to exchange information and strategies, share children, and rid themselves of them."[33] Many relationships between ring priests originated at seminaries and deepened during parish assignments. Half a dozen learned the trade at the Pink Palace that spawned old guarders Leary and Huller. Several, like Landry, were Stigmatines who began abusing at the order's notorious Waltham sites. The associations are so intertwined, they are difficult to effectively chart. The "Holy 13" included Lavigne, Alfred C. Graves, George Paulin, Wamsher, Lavelle, Jenness, O'Connor, Kennedy, John A. Koonz, Donald Desilets, Gerald Spafford, Richard J. Ahern, Donald V. Dube and Joseph E. Flood.

Alfred Graves was Lavigne's closest priest friend and a frequent roommate. When Danny died, Graves was at OLSH, where students recognized him as an abuser. According to a victim's lawyer's investigator, Graves grew up in a dysfunctional family with a history of sexual abuse. He may have been abused by relatives himself, and he was alleged to have fathered a child with his niece. After his 1967 ordination he worked at St. Mary's Church in Orange before his transfer to OLSH in August 1970. He was a serial abuser, but unlike Lavigne, he had tastes for older boys. His grooming processes mirrored Lavigne's. As Recounted by Andrew Nicastro, Graves began by giving his altar boys "the best assignments like weddings and funerals where we could make some money." Lightly-sexual sleepovers were followed by increasingly sexually charged evenings. Some were unsuccessful. One night, Nicastro was in bed when, for the first time, Graves approached naked. Nicastro ran into the bathroom and locked the door. In the morning, Graves ordered him out and never spoke to him again. Graves and Lavigne socialized frequently and took trips together with their boys, including Danny. They attended Donald Charland's regular card games at his house near the river. It was rumored that Lavigne handed Danny off to Graves as he approached 13. Graves was never investigated.

George Paulin, another longtime friend of Lavigne, spent most of his career in Vermont's isolated "Northeast Kingdom." After his ordination in 1970, Paulin worked at St. Mary Star of the Sea in Newport, a village so rural parishioners who went fishing before Mass sat in back on folding chairs if they smelled like fish. As had happened with Lavigne, flamboyance initially drew people to Paulin, but then he lost favor by "ruffling a feather or two." He surrounded himself with children, usually after appointing himself youth pastor. "He was always with kids. He was the kids' priest," a victim recalled. He groomed families to get to sons, targeted boys he was counseling, and abused victims in their own homes. Lavigne brought boys to Paulin's ski house in Vermont, sometimes joining but often leaving them with Paulin to go antique hunting. After being dropped off by Lavine, Paul Babeu rebuffed Paulin's advances, and the priest laughed: "Apparently, Father Lavigne hasn't broken you in yet."[34]

Frannie Lavelle was a Holyoke native, a commanding presence who drove new Volvos and looked like Cary Grant. Weldon ordained him in 1970 and appointed him master of ceremonies in 1974. He later served as private secretary to Weldon and Maguire, while being shuttled between parishes in Greenfield, Westfield, Adams, Springfield, and Northampton. A former parishioner said most church members recognized him as a homosexual. Another, astonishingly, offered, "I never considered him to be a predator. He preferred older teens. I think he just got careless with whom he was having relations."[35] He traded boys with old guarder Timothy Leary and was a Greenfield 6-er.

J. Roy Jenness, another Greenfield 6-er, was born in Fitchburg, Massachusetts, in 1923. He enlisted in the Marines after graduating high school in 1943 and was a frontline radioman during bloody World War II battles in the Pacific at Saipan, Tinian, Kwajelein, the Marshall Islands, and Iwo Jima, where he was awarded a Purple Heart. After the war, he attended St. Anselm College in Manchester, New Hampshire, the Benedictine Novitiate in Latrobe, Pennsylvania, and Grandé Seminary de Montréal.

Jenness was bright and spoke seven languages. He was a skilled groomer, plying with marijuana, pornography, and his preferred Cutty Sark whiskey. He abused even before his 1956 ordination, along with his closest friend, Fr. Donald Osgood. Osgood was a copious abuser whose first accusation was made within days of arriving at his first assignment at St. Patrick's Orphanage. The diocese and local police buried the case. Jenness, Osgood, and fellow priests, abused hundreds at St. Anselm's. They met at Osgood's quarters and the Sacred Heart Hospital chapel, where he was chaplain. Jenness abused with Osgood, and hosted regular masturbation parties attended by a larger group of priests and their friends.[36]

Through the 1960's–1970's, Jenness was transferred across Western Massachusetts, in and out of Sheffield, Springfield, Huntington, Adams, Holyoke, Greenfield, Pittsfield, and Amherst (St. Brigid's, later home to Lavigne whistleblower Fr. Bruce Teague). He was part of the Greenfield 6 clique. Victim Paul Herrick described the group's "pass-around-little-boy parties" in Sturbridge and said Jenness and his compatriots molested him 250 times over five years. His worst tormenter was Jenness but his friend Father Edward Kennedy participated in the sex parties.[37]

Edward Kennedy was variously described as "weird, strange, and an awful, pretentious man." He wore a poorly-fitted, obvious red toupee and considered himself a *bon vivant*. While championing Springfield's poor, he took expensive extended vacations, once spending more than a month in Ireland. He was an accomplished groomer, like Lavigne, targeting families devoted to the Church. He also initially impressed his victims and their families with "swagger and style" and personal attention. A victim recalled Kennedy "doted on me in a way I was not accustomed to, [with] liquor [and] fine dining." He took victims on vacations to Hawaii and New York City, entertaining so extravagantly, one said he was "wined and dined to the point it seemed Kennedy knew every good restaurant between Vermont and Connecticut."[38] He was at St. Brigid's in Amherst in the late 1960s and St. Patrick's in Monson until the late 1960s. He then ran the large Spanish Apostulate, serving Springfield's Puerto Rican and Mexican communities, from where he poached scores of victims. He handed them off to the Greenfield 6 and others, but his most frequent beneficiary was his closest friend, John Koonz.

John Koonz was born in 1937 into a prominent Cornwall, New York, family that moved to North Adams, Massachusetts, when he was an infant. His brother became a well-known lawyer who won one of the first and largest settlements in asbestos litigation. Koonz was introduced to group abuse at St. Anselm's, and after he graduated in 1959, he attended the Pink Palace. Ordained in Springfield in 1963, he worked in Ludlow, Millers Falls, Dalton, and Springfield's historic Holy Name parish. He also held prominent diocesan positions, elected secretary of the priests' senate, and named Franklin County deanery director. He drove a series of new Mercedes sedans, wore expensive clothes, and, like Kennedy, was gratingly pompous. The two were close to Lavigne and frequently exchanged boys. Kennedy dropped carloads of Spanish Apostolate kids at Koonz's country property near Greenfield, where they did odd jobs, mowed fields, did landscaping, and were abused. As pastor at St. Agnes in Dalton in 1979, Koonz first abused Paul E. Manship during counseling sessions following his father's death. When Manship enrolled at the University of Massachusetts in Amherst, Koonz handed him off to Kennedy, then at a nearby parish.[39]

Thomas O'Connor, another Greenfield 6-er, was at St. Patrick's in Monson from the 1950s through the 1960s, leaving just before Kennedy arrived. Fellow 6-er Ronald Wamsher was a Philadelphia native who was transferred among a dozen western Massachusetts parishes during his career. Donald Desilets was ordained in 1952 and was repeatedly transferred after complaints in Chicopee, Springfield, West Springfield, and Holyoke (Precious Blood, where Lavigne worked before St. Catherine's).[40]

Gerald Spafford was born in Springfield in 1940 and attended the Pink Palace with close friend John Koonz. After his ordination, he was assigned to Springfield and quickly earned the nickname "the Movie Star Priest." He was handsome, polished, effortlessly social, and tightly connected with Springfield's Irish Mafia. He drove a string of black Porsches and bought $500 cashmere topcoats (perhaps $2,000 today) and $450 hand-tailored suits from the exclusive A.O. White men's store. A manager described Spafford as "one of our best customers." He was close to Kennedy and Koonz, frequented Spanish Apostolate functions, and was among Lavigne's close friends dating to their days as young activist priests.[41]

Richard Ahern was born in Quincy, Massachusetts, in 1927 and entered the abuser-strewn Stigmatine order in 1954. His career was a litany of transfers up and down the Eastern seaboard. He was accused at almost every assignment back to Our Lady of Angels in Woodbridge, Virginia, in the late 1950s, through Mount Carmel in Pittsfield in the 1960s.[42] He was a director of the Stigmatine retreat house in Waltham and in the middle of the order's Elm Bank minor seminary abuse trail. He was forced from there to St. Ann's in West Springfield, then to far-flung parishes in White Plains, New York, and Richmond, Virginia, and then to Pittsfield, Lynn, Agawam, and Boston. He was prolific, abusing one boy while counseling him after his father's death and assaulting another after ordering two older boys to hold him down. He also abused with priest friends during weekend getaways. Many complaints against Ahern included his best friend and fellow Stigmatine Joseph Flood. They allegedly shared victims, often during New Hampshire getaways.

Flood was born in 1916 in Revere, Massachusetts, and ordained in 1949. Like Ahern's, his career was a string of complaints and transfers. After his first assignment in Lynn, Flood followed Ahern to New York and Virginia, and then returned to Agawam. After a complaint just weeks later, Flood "volunteered" for missionary work in Thailand, coincidently the worldwide epicenter of the child sex trade. He remained there nine years. When he returned in 1962, he was named director of the Stigmatine retreat house in Waltham, where he remained the rest of his career.[43]

In addition to its core members, Lavigne's ring included priests who were involved occasionally or who "dropped out" after periods of participation. Donald Dube was born in Chicopee Falls in 1935, and he graduated from the Séminaire de Saint-Hyacinthe in Quebec in 1955, the Seminary of Philosophy in Montreal in 1957, and the Grand Séminary in Montreal in 1961. His ordination by Weldon was followed by an almost unparalleled record of transfers, working in Fairview, Northampton, West Springfield, North Adams, Ludlow, Springfield (twice), and Chicopee (three times, including Lavigne's family parish, St. Rose de Lima). Dube was close to Lavigne and to Lavigne's parents at St. Rose. When Dube was there, Lavigne was at St. Catherine's.

Michael H. Devlin worked in parishes around Greenfield for most of his career. Several assignments in western Massachusetts in the 1970s brought him into contact with Springfield ring priests, though he was closest to Lavigne and Graves. At St. Thomas in West Springfield, he was accused of abusing boys brought to him for counseling by their parents. Weldon transferred Devlin numerous times and finally locked him away from kids as Baystate Medical Center chaplain. He was allowed to say weekend Masses at All Souls in Springfield. He abused numerous boys there.

David Farland was a Springfield native who graduated from Cathedral High School and was ordained in 1974. He taught religion at his alma mater, and during two decades of transfers, he served as Springfield Fire

Department chaplain. He was a frequent presence at fire stations, counseled firefighters, and was often among first responders at fires. He participated in invocations, wakes and funerals, and fallen firefighter
ceremonies. Farland also served as diocesan co-vicar and head of the
Office of Psychological Counseling, similar to an employee assistance
and counseling program for priests. Among his assignments, he was a
longtime pastor at St. Joseph's in Pittsfield.

Clarence W. Forand was transferred among half a dozen western
Massachusetts parishes during his career. A masterful manipulator and
groomer, he abused one altar boy 1,000 times over ten years. He took
his victim to New York City for Broadway shows, to Maine for lobsters,
and to Boston for steamers. Forand had a curious response to the allegations: "We were very good friends until I left St. Anne's. It must have
been a misunderstanding ... our relationship was like a 'father and son
or big brother and little brother.' Gary was a good honest soul. I don't
understand how he would have thought I hurt him. I think he maybe
missed me when I left." The Church punished Forand by placing him
under "prayer and penance" conditions.[44]

How involved Lavigne's card-playing friend Donald Charland was
in the ring activities is not known. Charland befriended Lavigne in the
seminary and lived barely a half mile from river. Lavigne—with his
boys—reportedly visited Charland's Eton Street house regularly.

It must be considered that Danny may have been killed by a
stranger. In addition to being abused by priests, he may have been trading sex for money, as reported to *Republican* writer Bill Zajac. That, of
course, introduces the possibility he was killed during a random
encounter. The murder location makes that likelihood remote. It is
doubtful Danny would bring someone he just met or barely knew to the
secluded location. He and the person or people he was with were obviously familiar with the site. Which brings us back to Lavigne and his
friends.

It is reasonable to assume, and, frankly, most probable, Danny's
killer was among Lavigne's ring. Every member was in frequent contact
with the others, Lavigne, and dozens of victims, including Danny.[45]

Their motivation to remove him from the equation intensified as his dislike of the abuse increased.

By the time he died, Danny was making more frequent and increasingly clearer inferences to friends that he was being abused and was sick of it. Almost two years earlier at the Goshen cabin, he directly threatened Lavigne, "I'll tell!" Several times in the months before the murder, he was seen in tears getting into Lavigne's car to be driven off, likely, to be abused. From all appearances, he was inching closer to exposing his abuser, as his father believed. Danny was an obvious threat to Lavigne and to his friends.

Regarding Danny's "I'll tell!" threat, Michael McMahon theorized that "if Danny had been threatening Lavigne with exposure [two years earlier], who knows how serious these threats became by the time he was murdered in 1972." One can guess how often and more directly Danny warned, "I'll tell!" during those two years. If, as some believe, he was extorting abusers using the threat of exposure, their specific motivation only increased. It certainly remains difficult to square Danny's friends' stories about him always having money. Since he had no legitimate source, it stands to reason he was either charging for acts or blackmailing abusers. Either situation provided Lavigne and multiple people connected to him motive to kill Danny.

Dispassionate analysis and physical evidence support the conclusion Danny was at the river with two men. The most probable pairing is Lavigne and an associate from his ring. Strong arguments can be made for each of the half dozen most likely prospects, but a number are more plausibly murderers. If Danny was at his tipping point, the men on the short list were most motivated to silence him.

Alfred Graves, Lavigne's closest priest friend, is a strong candidate. Graves and Lavigne shared quarters at the time of the murder, and it is rumored Lavigne handed Danny off to Graves a year earlier. Andrew Nicastro recalled that Graves was mostly even-keeled, but had a rarely-seen hair-trigger temper. When Nicastro fiddled with the rectory thermostat against Graves' admonitions, the priest wrenched his arm painfully behind his back, dragged him through the house by the neck, and threw him out the door onto the sidewalk below the front steps. He bounced at the feet of a group of parishioners approaching the rectory.[46]

Lastly, the BSA contingent must be seriously considered, specifically Ed Veroneau and Dick Brown. It is not known if either was abusing

Danny, but it is not out of the realm of possibility. Veroneau was a confirmed abuser, Brown rumored to have been. Both were allied with Lavigne and BSA abuser Roger Norton and were closely associated with Danny. Brown appears to have been the policeman with Lavigne at the meeting at the diner with Sandra Tessier. Both terrified neighborhood kids because of violent tendencies, particularly Veroneau. After a string of legal and professional setbacks, he committed suicide in 1984.

All these men had motive to kill Danny. None were deeply investigated. The frustrating reality remains that, even if a new investigation was undertaken, crafting a convincing case seems impossible. Ryan's 1972 evidence disasters and ego issues imbuing Bennett's office are too high a hill to climb. Suspect 40-year-old recollections further muddy the waters. Many witnesses, potential suspects, and people tied to the players have died. And most of their records have likely been long-since reduced to dust.

Of course, the possibility remains, though faint, that new information could arise. Some in the Circle had ties to the ring and the Holy 13 through Lavigne. Three of Danny's brothers and half a dozen Circle boys were abused by Lavigne and others. It is a virtual certainty that some of those boys, now men, know more about the murder than they divulged, something Carl long believed. After all these years, the final hope for conceivably making a case rests on a confession or trace evidence being tied directly to someone, but neither seems terribly likely.

12

Legacies

Ignoring for the moment hundreds of PTSD-related victim suicides, priests have killed. Boston's Father Ronald Paquin engaged in
decades of "rampant and unbridled pedophilia" and was shown in the
2015 film *Spotlight* casually telling a *Boston Globe* reporter, "I fooled
around. But I never raped anyone and I never felt gratified." In November 1981, driving under the influence after a weekend of drunken sex
games with four altar boys at a friend's cabin in New Hampshire, Paquin
passed out behind the wheel. For the second time. Sixteen-year-old
Jimmy Francis tried unsuccessfully to grab the wheel and take control
of the careening car. It rolled, he was ejected, and the car crashed down
on top of him. Francis' death was thought to be the first death directly
caused by a priest. Boston paid Paquin a nearly $80,000 severance pack-
age when he was finally dismissed. Priests have done worse. In 2002,
Wisconsin priest Ryan Erickson shot and killed a local funeral director
and his college intern after the man confronted Erickson about abuse.
More was made of the fact Erickson was a priest than he was a murderer.[1]

The Vatican has learned little, even as its survival has been threatened, and its troubles are far from over. For decades, the Church in Australia was unresponsive to shocking levels of abuse (by 7 percent of its
priests), even as abuse-related suicides became epidemic. Most responsible for the culture was Cardinal George Pell, Archbishop of Melbourne
and later Sydney. The country's highest-ranking Catholic was under constant scrutiny for 20 years when, in late 2016, he was moved to the Vatican
and appointed chief financial advisor to Pope Francis. In June 2017, Pell
was charged with multiple sex crimes dating back to the 1970s. Fortunately for him, Australia has no extradition treaty with the Vatican.[2]

Just two days after the charges were filed, Francis was forced to remove German cardinal Gerhard Mueller as head of the Congregation of the Doctrine of Faith, the Vatican's abuse police, after he was ordered back to his native country to face multiple abuse allegations. Mueller's legacy after his failed five-year tenure was a backlog of 2,000 cases. At the same time, he presented himself as an immovable hard-liner, clashing with Francis about allowing divorced Catholics to receive the sacraments. Rome wasn't done. The next day, Vatican police broke up a "drug-fueled gay orgy" at the home of the secretary to Cardinal Francesco Cocco-palmerio, perhaps Francis' most key advisor. The apartment was owned by the Doctrine of Faith. Coccopalmerio once recommended his secretary for a promotion to bishop.[3]

For decades, the Vatican broke its every promise by inadequate action and repugnant behavior. Never acknowledging a problem, the Vatican instead pathologically diminished it. By 2014, Rome claimed there were 3,973 abuser priests. The identities of almost half (43 percent) were kept secret. In 2002, three years before he became Pope Benedict XVI and then responsible for punishing abusers, Joseph Ratzinger complained, "In the United States, there is constant news on this topic, but less than 1% of priests are guilty of acts." He undoubtedly realized "1%" was a lie by a factor of five. In the two decades before he was named pope, he authored the Vatican's most offensive opinions regarding sexuality. Among them, he proposed homosexuality is "an intrinsic disorder" and victims of anti-gay violence bring it upon themselves by defending behavior "to which no one has any conceivable right."[4]

In 2014, Pope Francis created the Pontifical Commission for the Protection of Minors, a group of outside experts to develop "best practices" for fighting abuse, ousting abusers, and ending policies that "rewarded clerics who keep a tight lid on child sex crimes and cover-ups." It was a debacle. The two members who were abuse survivors resigned almost immediately. The commission's ham-fisted 2016 guidelines offered not a single instruction for dealing with victims. It didn't offer strategies for identifying or treating abusers. In fact, the report offered no advice on how to prevent abuse at all, and Francis vetoed the signature proposal—a tribunal to prosecute bishops that hid abuse—after Vatican underlings complained. The commission is most notable for excusing the Church from involving police, that in countries "where reporting is obligatory, it is not the bishops' duty to report suspects." Responsibility, he said, lay with victims' families, because "the vast majority of sexual assaults against children are committed within family [and by] friends and neighbours."[5] French monsignor Tony Anatrella, credited with authoring the report, is a psychotherapist who believes homosexuality is caused by psychological issues. He also champions gender theory and believes acceptance of homosexuality hurts children "exposed to radical notions." In 2016, he was accused of sexually assaulting multiple patients.

Francis next appointed a Chilean bishop notorious for covering up for his country's most infamous abuser. The bishop was caught on tape calling Catholics opposing the selection "leftists" and "stupid." Francis suffers from the same "allergy to criticism" that has historically badly tainted Rome. Critical Catholics were pilloried for "savaging the Pope's reputation" while the Vatican likened its station to the agony "Christ suffered on the cross or by Jews during the Holocaust." *Boston Globe* columnist Kevin Cullen rightly explained that the Vatican cannot possibly solve its embedded problems until it confronts the reality that "its managers, its bishops, enabled thousands and thousands of kids to be raped and abused by predatory priests. The enablers were never disciplined, never held accountable, never made to pay … for the pain they inflicted on so many innocent lives." Rome's misguided attitudes have led to virtual ruination. Between 2007 and 2014, more than three million members fled the Church in the U.S. alone, 10 percent of the roll and more than was gained from worldwide conversions. There is a more telling statistic—more than a third of American adults were raised Catholic, but 41 percent no longer identify with the faith.[6]

Beyond intransigence and obstinacy, the Vatican is obnoxiously duplicitous. Pope John Paul II's handling of Boston's disgraced Cardinal Law is but one appalling example. Hours before Law was to be indicted on multiple abuse charges, with news trucks and reporters surrounding his chancery, John Paul arranged for Law to escape in the dead of night and be flown by private jet to the Vatican. Once the legally immune Law arrived, John Paul awarded him the plum position of archpriest of the Basilica di Santa Maria Maggiore. In 2012, Law was reported to be "the person in Rome most forcefully supporting" Baltimore archbishop William E. Lori's unseemly plan to investigate—and silence—the Leadership Conference of Women Religious, a group of anti-abuse American nuns.

The U.S. Church is no less ruined. By 2014, more than three billion dollars had been paid to settle thousands of suits. Boston paid

$150,000,000, Los Angeles, $750,000,000, and by 2017, there were 450 cases still to be settled. In New York, the Church was forced to borrow $100,000,000 to fund settlements, and cases bankrupted dioceses in Spokane, Davenport, San Diego, Tucson, and elsewhere. The loss hit the Church's lighter pocketbooks hardest. Belleville, Illinois, paid four million dollars, an immense sum for a small diocese. Settlements and plunging donations left thousands of other dioceses in financial collapse, forced to sell valuable real estate holdings, slash service programs, and even borrow money just for day-to-day obligations. Considering the cost, the faithful's belated response is surprising. By the late 1980s, the crisis in the Church was broadly acknowledged. There was no measurable reaction. The crisis blew up twice more during the 1990s. Still nothing. Catholic uproar of any consequence did not occur until 2002. By then, 700 priests had been removed—350 in 2002 alone—and 10,677 victims had accused 4,392 clerics. By 2012 that tally was 17,249 victims and 6,427 priests, a staggering 5.9 percent of all priests ordained between 1950 and 2002.[7]

The U.S. hierarchy was as consistently deceitful as its masters in Rome. In 1986, the crisis was first publicized when Gil Gauthé was exposed in Louisiana and accused of sexually abusing dozens of young boys. The church asked the Institute of Living in Hartford, Connecticut, to launch an inpatient program for impaired professionals, particularly priests, sent there under the guise of treatment for substance abuse, depression or problems with authority. Only after years of treating priests did the Institute recognize the majority were abusers dumped there by the Church to avoid arrest and scandal. Springfield sent half a dozen. In 1995, IOL director L.M. Lothstien demanded the Church send priests with their complete files and admit the real reasons for placement. The Church never sent another priest to the IOL.[8]

Not all dioceses are as intractable as their Church. Chicago, for one, has remained consistently forthright since the 1980s. Its pastors were among the first in the nation to offer apologies from the pulpit. In 1991, Cardinal Joseph F. Bernadin appointed an independent three-person lay board to address the issue, and a year later, he proposed banning accused abusers altogether. As of this writing, the diocesan website has dozens of pages of information on abuse and lists the names of all 60 priests who have been accused of abuse.

It remains to be seen if the Church will awaken to its global reality.

SNAP director David Clohessy was convinced it could not; he believed change was impossible because "the hierarchy is an entitled, rigid, secretive, all-male monarchy. No new protocols or policies or procedures will radically undo a centuries-old self-serving structure that rewards clerics who keep a tight lid on child sex crimes and cover-ups." In the meantime, donations and Church membership continue their freefall.

Elliot Street evolved no more than the Vatican. From 1972, when priests stopped police from searching Lavigne's quarters, into the 2010s, when even bishops became openly uncooperative, the diocese continued to show bad judgment. Over time, intransigence turned to outright truculence. Weldon lied endlessly about his knowledge of abuse. Maguire, annoyed he was forced to answer questions about Danny at all, banned Church comment on the subject. Marshall launched his ineffectual, confrontational commission to address the problem and lied repeatedly about his early knowledge. Dupré gutted his Secret Archives. The week he arrived in Springfield in March 2004, McDonnell attacked in the press the first critical priest he encountered. It is not surprising that Springfield was the last diocese in Massachusetts to share the identities of accused priests with district attorneys.

Springfield pastors wanted to offer apologies similar to those coming from pulpits across the country during the early 2000s. The diocese categorically forbade any such public show of contrition. Marshall refused to apologize to one victim, writing, "If I understand the meaning of the word 'apology' correctly, it is an expression of sorrow, for which the speaker takes blame. Father Lavigne could do this; I could not." In an attempt to further absolve the diocese, he resorted to a brazen untruth: "neither the bishops nor the priests of the Diocese had any idea of the misconduct of Father Lavigne." Sandra Tessier experienced the abysmal lack of Church concern: "Not one Church official has ever said, 'We are sorry for what has happened.'"[9]

That everyone, from high-ranking bishop to low-level Church staffer, was unaware of abuse simply cannot be argued given the abundant contradictory proof. The most dedicated denier, Weldon, discussed the issue hundreds of times. A letter discovered in 2002 confirmed he discussed the crisis as early as 1963, when a Fall River pastor spoke to him half a dozen times about a serial abuser. It is fact Weldon was told about Lavigne by Griffin at St. Catherine's, who was warned by house-keeper Annie Sullivan, curates including Father Leo O'Neil, and parishioners. Griffin reportedly witnessed one assault and was so disgusted by Lavigne that he locked Lavigne out multiple times, recognizing "something wrong, and upset with his bedroom comings and goings." He told Carl as much, as did O'Neil. After Lavigne's transfer, O'Neil warned Griffin and Griffin's friend Maurice DeMontigny he did not want to follow Lavigne to St. Catherine's because of the damage left in his wake. O'Neil reiterated, "You won't see any coming into *my* room." Coincidentally, Lavigne once told DeMontigny that Griffin had warned him about entertaining boys. "He laughed and thought it was funny," DeMontigny recalled.[10]

DeMontigny, a founding parishioner at St. Catherine's, was among Weldon's closest confidantes, served on diocesan boards, and did free weekend accounting work for the diocese. Shortly after the Griffin-O'Neil-DeMontigny chat, Griffin approached DeMontigny. Griffin was visibly upset, breathing hard. He said a parishioner accused Lavigne of "abusing his sons and they could not press charges." Griffin wanted DeMontigny to know "how widespread the problem was and who and how many in the parish were involved." A friend at the courthouse—whose son was a Lavigne victim—fed DeMontigny details from the grand jury proceedings, which were passed on to Griffin. Griffin said he would pass them up to Weldon. DeMontigny had no doubt "diocesan officials confirmed, as of the late 1960s, that Lavigne was a child molester." DeMontigny also informed Weldon's successor Marshall about Lavigne, and he wrote Marshall, "I told you of the admonitions made by Lavigne's pastor relative to the boys being in his room."[11] Two of DeMontigny's nephews were Lavigne victims.

It is farcical to think Weldon heard nothing from Griffin, O'Neil or DeMontigny, or heard nothing of Carl's stories of abuse and murder allegations. O'Neil's suspicious $700 donation, which clearly appeared to be a bribe, reinforces that notion. Several priests witnessed Lavigne's abuse, including Father Armando Annunziato twice and later Father Robert Thrasher, as did non-priests, like a St. Mary's victim, later a Chicopee policeman, who walked in on Lavigne molesting a friend. Two St. Mary's curates and the pastor—whose brother became the bishop of Worcester and was himself accused of abuse—knew and informed Weldon.[12]

Weldon received regular briefings on the murder investigation, in daily contact with investigators almost from the moment Danny's body was discovered. Ryan's man Fitzgibbon met with diocesan officials dozens of times. His partner, Det. James Mitchell, recalled the "obligation to show our cards. Fitzy had a sit-down with them. Everything we knew, we told them." They told Weldon, who already knew, Lavigne molested the Croteau boys.[13]

Even so, as late as the 2010s, the diocese still maintained it was in the dark about Lavigne until 1986, when he was forced to undergo a mental health examination (he was deemed "not a threat to re-offend and could, with counseling, continue his duties"). The diocese doubled down, maintaining "adamantly they knew nothing" about Lavigne until his arrest in 1991.[14] Every utterance from the diocese over the course of four decades was false.

In 2002, Dupré inadvertently outed the whole crowd when he said, "It wasn't [just] the Church that knew it. Everybody knew it. The district attorney knew it, police knew it. Everybody knew there were rumors about it. But nobody took action." He excused himself, though, claiming, "I only went into the Chancery in '77 ... so I don't know what went on. All I know is the rumors I heard." Shortly after, Dupré wrote a piece for the *Catholic Observer* describing his personal offense taken when "in my first parish, I learned an older priest whom I respected a great deal had been accused of molesting a thirteen-year-old boy ... emotions welled up in me, including disbelief, anger, disappointment, a feeling of being let down."[15] Those emotions were different while he was abusing, apparently.

It is important to recognize Lavigne was one priest. Weldon was aware of hundreds. Father Thomas Doyle, a canonical law expert who researched thousands of abuse claims, reviewed Elliot Street's history of handling abusers. His findings were, as expected, unflattering.

- Officials realized the extent of clergy abuse prior to 1971.
- Lack of response and maintenance of absolute secrecy placed children at direct, serious risk prior to 1971.
- Law enforcement was never notified about abuse allegations received before or after 1971.
- The diocese did not conduct even cursory investigations prior to 1971.

- The diocese failed to adequately supervise priests known to have abused.[16]

Put simply, everyone at Elliot Street knew. They always knew. The decades-long obstinacy is astonishing, given that the diocese paid three million dollars during the 1990s, $7,700,000 in 2004, another $4,500,000 in 2008. As late as 2016, settlements were still being negotiated. Final costs are expected to top $35,000,000. The financial hit forced the diocese to completely reorganize, sell hundreds of valuable real estate parcels, and shutter or substantially alter half its parishes. McDonnell blamed the parishes, saying that "parish debt" had caused the shortfall. Tens of thousands of area Catholics left the Church.[17]

Elliot Street entrenchment was partly due to abuser priests holding positions of power. Edward Kennedy was a canon lawyer who ran the large Spanish Apostolate and controlled, politically and spiritually, its thousands of members. He headed the powerful marriage tribunal that approved annulments. E. Karl Huller was diocesan superintendent of schools and chief financial vicar. Frannie Lavelle was assistant to bishops Weldon and Maguire. Ronald Wamsher was a canon lawyer and a member of the marriage tribunal. David Welch was editor of the diocesan newspaper for more than three decades and executor of Weldon's estate. For years, Richard Meehan was director of vocations and oversaw the archives and the damning secret files.[18]

Beyond settlements, insincerity, and failed promises, the diocese treated victims with ambivalence verging on spite. A 1991 memorandum from Dupré summarizing his meeting with a victim's hospitalized father began, "Met with Mr. So and So at Mercy Hospital." The policy of administrative and legal foot-dragging and the deplorable delay tactics led U.S. Conference of Bishops' auditors to cite Springfield's commission as an example of a completely failed process. Every victim has a story. Andrew Nicastro had no intention of suing when he first approached the diocese about Lavigne's best friend Graves. Only after Nicastro waded through its labyrinthian processes, met with officials, spoke with victim advocates, and was grilled by in-house investigators did the diocese agree to pay for therapy. But just one of the twice-weekly sessions recommended by his therapist. So a disgusted Nicastro sued. During one of 30 suits in Vermont courts in 2007, a Church lawyer grilled a victim so aggressively the judge declared a mistrial. The excruciating process still today being forced upon victims was described by a lawyer: "The legalistic hair-splitting and the reluctance displayed by Church officials in settling accounts ... is a long, sad story."[19]

Elliot Street continues to confound. Robert Thrasher did nothing after allegedly interrupting Lavigne molesting boys twice, and he later claimed he did not know if Lavigne entertained overnight guests because he went to bed early. In 2017, he was a marriage tribunal member and diocesan vice-chancellor. Father John J. Bonzagni was accused in 2003 of abusing a 16-year-old girl and, though the diocese cleared him, it paid her as part of the $7,500,000 deal. In 2015, Bonzagni was named diocesan co-vicar.[20]

There has always been plenty of blame to go around, and Dupré may not have been the only Springfield bishop hiding from his past. In 2005, Texas inmate William Burnett claimed his uncle, Father Raymond Page, molested him and then handed him off to five other priests from 1950 through 1959. Most startling, Burnett said one abused him three dozen times at St. Michael's Cathedral between the ages of 10 and 16. Weldon. Burnett was admittedly a flawed accuser; the high school math teacher was imprisoned for robbing seven banks, and after his 1989 parole, knifed a 61-year-old man to death in a Houston motel. Some of his own relatives discounted his claims, but Burnett passed two polygraph examinations supporting his accusation of Weldon.[21]

Aftershocks hit Danny's school, Our Lady of the Sacred Heart. On July 3, 2011, 42-year-old Father Paul Archambault put a gun to his head in a closet in the rectory. He was a part-time priest at St. Mary's in Hampden and championed the pro-life movement, frequently seen picketing Planned Parenthood offices. A eulogist told 500 mourners the suicide resulted from lifelong battles with depression caused by bullying. Archambault faced more pressing demons. Two weeks earlier, a teenage boy confronted him about 50 incidents, the last in a series of accusations that began before his ordination in 2005. In 2007, a commission member parked at Our Lady of Epheses, a shrine in Jamaica, Vermont, and saw Archambault massaging a boy in an adjacent car. Archambault appeared before the commission with a lawyer and a certificate citing massage training therapy to explain away rubbing the teen. The board found nothing "actionable" and excused his "poor judgment in maintaining proper boundaries [due to] immaturity issues." When the boy sued in 2013, spokesman Mark Dupont offered an interesting mea culpa: "It now appears after being confronted with these allegations.... Rev. Archambault took his own life. In light of this, the Diocese now recognizes this victim's allegation as credible." *Now recognizes.*[22]

Despite everything, perhaps the clearest evidence of ongoing delusion in the diocese can be found at St. Michael's Cathedral. Inside the bishop's primary church is a large, richly decorated and paneled meeting room, the Father Karl Huller Meeting Room. Huller faced multiple abuse accusations and was affiliated with the Springfield ring.

Elliot Street's sex problems evidently still exist. In the early 2010s, a computer system linking far-flung rectories with downtown was implemented. A technician doing installations found one priest's computer bursting with "all kinds of male pornography ... thousands of files and images" downloaded from all manner of pornographic websites. She guessed "he must have spent two or three hours every single day at these websites."[23] The priest was in charge of diocesan vocations.

The legacy of Matty Ryan's 32-year reign—the longest in state history—was marred by the bungled investigation into Danny's murder, rumors of a deal with Weldon, and Ryan's own mob relationships. Not indicting Lavigne may have been legally reasonable, but he could never outrun the fallout and was dogged to the end by his mafia ties, particularly during a violent mob war in Springfield in the mid–1980s. Public and staff displeasure with his combative style also deepened. His finally lost his grip on the job in 1989 after one of his investigators tried to kill an assistant D.A. inside the courthouse. Ryan stonewalled, refusing to aggressively go after his cop. Then he was accused of pressuring a judge to go easy on a mob bookmaker at the behest of a state representative friend whose son worked for Ryan. Forced to retire in 1990, Ryan was a relic of a bygone era with a long-untenable style; a writer said he simply "accumulated too much baggage and ill will." The public would no longer ignore weekly racquetball matches with mob bosses at the YMCA. Ryan joined prominent Springfield law firm Doherty, Wallace, Pillsbury & Murphy, and he died in 2009. The man described as "bombastic and beloved" remained an enigma. When Ryan was asked about his nephews, Brian and Michael McMahon, who were victims of Lavigne, he brusquely replied, "They're not my kids. They're my sister's kids."[24]

During a 20-year career, William Bennett oversaw three failed investigations of Danny's murder, each one raising questions about his dedication to actually solving the mystery. In 2008, his retired investigator Edward Harrington reconfirmed Bennett's stubbornly-held belief: "We consider the Croteau case solved but never adjudicated." He retired in 2011 and joined the same firm as Ryan.

Many investigators who worked Danny's murder in 1972 are no longer living. Most never lost the bitter taste of an investigation they believed was derailed by the D.A. and the Church and remained close to people inside the case. One Chicopee detective played golf with a Lavigne victim's father every week. Ryan's lead investigator John Fitzgibbon remained close to the Croteaus and became obsessed with the case. Discussing it with Carl at the Keg Room in downtown Springfield years later, Fitzgibbon became infuriated and slammed his first on the table so hard that plates and glasses rattled loudly. He seethed, "Damn it, Carl, my hands are tied! If Lavigne was an average factory worker, he'd be gone." Fitzgibbon died in 1982 at 58. Friends said the case killed him.[25]

In 2005, investigator R.C. Stevens contacted 15 Springfield priests— most rumored or confirmed abusers—he believed knew of ring activities and abusers in contact with Danny. The letters, appropriately mailed on Easter Sunday, were sent to Mark Steltzer, Eugene Honan, Thomas Shea, William J. Hamilton, John J. Varley, Francis Walsh, Robert Thrasher, Ronald Wamsher, Charles J. Gonet, Timothy Murphy, Jeddie P. Brooks, J. Donald Lapointe, Edward Kennedy, Joseph Marchese, and Regis J. Giroux. All were offered anonymity. Just two bothered to respond. Both refused to speak. Stevens did receive another response, from diocesan law firm Egan, Flanagan & Cohen: a cease and desist letter. James Egan met with Stevens "as a courtesy," not, he said, as a diocesan attorney, but to help "troubled and/or confused clergy."[26]

Many clerics attached to Danny's death are also dead. Hobbled by heart ailments after his resignation in 1977, Weldon died in Springfield in 1982. To that day, he never once publicly, and rarely privately, discussed the murder. Maguire, who led the diocese for 15 years after Weldon and faced allegations of covering up abuse, died in 2014. Marshall, who buried accusations against Edward Paquette and created the ineffectual

Misconduct Commission, died in 1994. Father Leo O'Neil, who stuffed $700 into Carl's hand two weeks after the murder, was named the auxiliary bishop of Springfield in 1980 and then Manchester, New Hampshire, in 1990. He died in 1997. The enigmatic friar Father Barnabas Keck died in New Paltz, New York, in 2013.

The disgraced but still technically "Most Reverend" Thomas Dupré was the first U.S. Catholic bishop to be indicted for sex crimes. He was defrocked in 2006. Elliot Street said he "voluntarily retired." During a pre-trial hearing for a civil case involving child rape charges shortly after his departure from Springfield, he gave his name and date of birth, then invoked his Fifth Amendment right and refused to answer questions. This is almost never done in civil trials, because the refusal can be disclosed to a jury and can be potentially damaging. During a three-hour deposition in 2010, he refused to answer a single one of 150 questions. He remained at St. Luke until his death in 2016.[27]

James Scahill, a linchpin of Dupré's downfall, was particularly close to cousins David and Peter Bessone, two severely damaged victims of Lavigne. David committed suicide in 1985, and for 30 years, Scahill helped Peter battle addictions and then cancer. Peter was distraught as Christmas 2002 approached because his small disability pension left nothing to buy presents for his three children. Scahill learned a charity failed to delivered promised gifts, and when Peter returned to his tiny Springfield apartment on Christmas Eve, found a message from Scahill instructing him to come to the rectory. Peter took the bus to East Longmeadow. Under the doormat was an envelope containing $500. As he walked to a grocery store to wire the money to his children in Florida, he wept. Scahill left the priesthood and lives with another ex-priest near the Rhode Island shore.[28]

Bruce Teague, who blew the whistle on Lavigne at St. Brigid's, was run out of the priesthood, beginning when Dupré refused to reappoint him pastor in 2002. For many years, Teague worked in hospital pastoral care around Boston. In 2013, he joined the steering committee of Catholic Whistleblowers, a group dedicated to encouraging victims to come forward and forcing the Church to address the issue honestly. While wandering around a cemetery looking for a friend's headstone in 1993, Teague tripped over the grave marker of the priest who abused him when he was a child. Free of Church binds, he spends his time "trying to see the beauty of life."[29]

Charles Shattuck, founder of the Holy Trinity Lay Community, faced a relentless, Church-influenced smear campaign during Elliot Street's defense of Lavigne. He was denounced as a cult leader and his abused sons were branded liars until a Springfield priest took out a full-page newspaper ad defending the family. Trinity remains in Heath, now with more than 40 families.

Almost all the old guard and Springfield ring members eventually faced sanctions after being accused in the 1990s and 2000s. A few faced none, Church or otherwise.

Timothy Leary was the rector at St. Michael's Cathedral, consultant to two bishops, diocesan director of cemeteries, and vicar general.[30] He died in 1991 at 81. The diocese settled the first suit against him in 2008.

Karl Huller worked at dozens of parishes over 43 years and was diocesan superintendent of schools, Westover Air Force Base chaplain, and vicar of finance. He served on half a dozen diocesan commissions and outside boards, he died in 1997 at age 72. Multiple suits filed in 2002–2003 were settled in 2004.[31]

David Welch ran the local Catholic newspaper and as executor of Weldon's estate, supervised the destruction of Weldon's papers. He also allegedly ensured Weldon's directive that all abuse files be expunged. Welch retired to Deerfield Beach, Florida, owned several businesses, and was active in community projects. He died in 1982 and was accused in 2004 of abuse at St. Michael's High School in Northampton (since closed). In 2008, the diocese settled with William V. Derian, a successful Florida businessman appointed to an administrative position by President Ronald Reagan.[32]

Leo Landry was perhaps Springfield's most prolific abuser from his ordination in 1958 to the time he left the priesthood in 1970. He was defrocked in 1972, and then reportedly married a woman with three children. In 1974, he was fired as chairman of the department of foreign languages at Spaulding (New Hampshire) High School for abuse. He employed the method he used as a priest—teaching masturbation. In 2002, he was accused of abuse at Manchester parishes in the 1960s. Springfield settled three other claims. In 2004, he pled guilty to criminal sexual abuse charges in Boston and was sentenced to lifetime probation. He was last reported living in Colorado.

The Holy 13 part-timers all faced multiple allegations and church sanctions. Donald Dube was transferred among numerous parishes and was campus minister at North Adams State College and dean of Northern Berkshire Deanery. He was removed from the ministry in 1994, and his privileges were revoked in 2002. He died a year later at his Sturbridge home reportedly the site of ring gatherings. The diocese settled with one victim and another sued his estate in 2004.

Michael Devlin served in Greenfield, Springfield, and North Adams through the 1970s, then St. Thomas in West Springfield and St. Patrick's in Williamstown (where he was pastor) into the mid–1980s. After being accused of abusing a boy he was counseling at St. Thomas, Devlin was banished to a Baystate Medical Center chaplaincy. He lived in the rectory at All Souls in Ware and he said weekend Masses and abused altar boys. When he was suspended in 2004 after the St. Thomas and All Souls accusations came to light, nine parishioners created the "Michael H. Devlin Irrevocable Trust" to raise money so Devlin could "live a normal life [because] his pride, dignity, ability to care for people and his good name have been taken." Permanently suspended in December 2004, he retreated to a family home in Florida. Two months later, Springfield paid for a notice in the Miami diocesan newsletter: "FOR YOUR INFORMATION—The Reverend Michael H. Devlin (Diocese of Springfield) does not enjoy the faculties of the Archdiocese of Miami. Please contact Msgr. Souckar should he present himself to serve in your parish." A canonical trial was requested but never took place, and the diocese settled a suit in 2008. He kept up appearances as a priest, signing a comment about a May 26, 2010, newspaper story about abuse "Fr. Michael Devlin, Oakland Park, FL."[33]

Clarence Forand was accused by former altar boy Gary Singley in 1992 of a thousand incidents over nine years. Forand said Singley made everything up because "I think he maybe missed me when I left." The diocese refused to publicly name Forand and allowed him to work without restrictions in Palmer, Chicopee, and Monson.[34] In 1993, the commission found the accusations credible, but simply let Forand retire, still unrestricted. The Vatican's 2002 Dallas Norms—strict rules for handling abusers—forced the diocese to finally tether Forand. He died in 2005, and his funeral was at the Lavigne family church, St. Rose de Lima. The diocese settled with his accuser in 2008.

Richard Meehan was the rector at St. Michael's from 1984 to 1991, and he held powerful diocesan positions, among them director of vocations. He was removed from St. John the Evangelist in Agawam after an accusation in 1992, and Dupré sent him for counseling and banished him (with Kennedy) to Providence Place a Church-run retirement home in Holyoke. Dupré then tapped him to manage diocesan archives, which he did for ten years. Giving an accused abuser access to the Secret Archives seems somewhat ill advised. After additional accusations in 2002, Meehan was removed per the Dallas Norms and defrocked in 2006. He was, though, honored as Heritage Society member by alumni benefactors of the Pink Palace, St. Mary's, who arranged bequests and "value our past and are committed to our present and future."[35]

David Farland was accused in the early 1990s, prohibited from access to children, and listed on "medical leave, in limited ministry." He remained chaplain of the Springfield Fire Department. The fire department was not informed of the accusation. It first learned of Farland's past when he was removed in 2002 along with ring priests Kennedy, Meehan, Graves, Dube, Koonz and Wamsher. Dupré refused to identify his close friend Farland, saying, "I would rather make a mistake on the side of a person's right to privacy."[36] The diocese only confirmed Farland's ouster four years later when the *Republican* named him. He was indicted on child rape charges but not tried due to statute of limitations issues. Dupré's feeble commission found the complaints credible and ordered Farland to live "a life of prayer and penance." Farland's closest priest friend was Weldon's top aide, Father Hugh Crean, who hosted a support group for half a dozen priests including several ring veterans. They met weekly to "talk about work, life, needs, hopes, health, successes. We all depend upon family." Farland was last reported living near the beach in Rhode Island.

Most of the Holy 13 faced more severe sanctions. In addition to Lavigne, five were eventually defrocked: Alfred Graves, Frannie Lavelle, Edward Kennedy, John Koonz, and David Farland.

Alfred Graves, Lavigne's closest friend and roommate, was recognized by OLSH kids as an abuser and they tried to avoid him. Shortly after his arrival in 1970, he reached his hands down the pants of a 14-year-old and fondled him in the church. He climbed into bed with and tried to molest another 14-year-old and the parents of a 15-year-old informed pastor Father C. Leo Shea that Graves was molesting their son. Shea did nothing. Bishop Maguire actually assured one victim that Graves' groping was "I'm sure … just horseplay." Graves was then transferred to Greenfield and Williamstown, including postings where he was the only priest there. In 1977, he was abruptly appointed chaplain at Farren Memorial Hospital in Turners Falls. Maguire surprisingly gave him a church in Greenfield and appointed him Franklin Country catechism director from 1978 to 1981, responsible for overseeing all children's programs.

Graves resigned abruptly in 1992, took a two-year leave, and vanished from directories. He was barred from parish work after suits including a rape allegation when he was at OLSH were filed in 2002. The attack occurred when Danny was there. The diocese settled with one victim in 2004, Graves was defrocked in 2006, and more allegations arose in a 2009 suit that also named Maguire, Dupré, and Richard Sniezyk.[37] In 2017, Graves was living in a converted mill in Rutland, Vermont. He remained shockingly cavalier about his history. Elliot Street ordered him to respond to a letter outlining Andrew Nicastro's allegations. Graves circled the lengthy list in red marker and wrote "YES."[38]

George Paulin, another close friend of Lavigne's, spent his career shuttled throughout northern Vermont until he was removed in 2002 after he and five other priests were accused of abuse in the 1970s. Paul Babeu, shared by Lavigne with Paulin, was lied to by Springfield and Burlington when he accused the two in 1987. Burlington was particularly deceitful. Bishop John Marshall (later bishop of Springfield) summarily dismissed Babeu's complaint, claiming, "I have never heard any rumor, innuendo or complaint that would indicate [Paulin] possessed pedophilic tendencies." When ordered to provide Paulin's personnel files, Marshall included nothing from 1971 to 1997, repeatedly claiming what he had turned over "was all the diocese had." The files magically reappeared two years later, allegedly found in an old desk. A newspaper disdainfully noted, "Miracles do happen." Burlington paid several Paulin victims $300,000 and other suits were settled in 2007–2008. Paulin moved back to northern Vermont, complaining, "This has been such a torment."[39]

Ronald Wamsher was at St. Francis of Assisi in Belchertown in 2002 when Dupré's commission received its first complaint about him. He was exiled to canon law school, and three years later, was placed on the diocesan annulment tribune alongside Edward Kennedy. Wansher was outed in the 2003 Greenfield 6 suit that first mentioned an abuser ring. He was not removed until 2004, when he was placed on leave and tossed from the annulment tribunal. It took another year for the accusations to be deemed credible, for his privileges to be revoked, and a canonical trial to be requested. In 2017, he was living in an apartment in Springfield.[40]

Frannie Lavelle was a secretary to Weldon and Maguire and the rector at St. Michael's Cathedral during the 1980s. In 1999, he was shuffled to the Newman Center at the University of Massachusetts in Amherst, and in October 2001, he was named pastor at St. Mary's in Longmeadow. Six months later, he became the first priest relieved of duties since 1994. He was replaced by fellow ring member Michael Devlin. When Lavelle was named in the Greenfield 6 suit, he was permanently removed from the ministry. More allegations arose in another suit targeting ring friends Koonz and Devlin and old guarders Leary and Landry. The Vatican refused to defrock Lavelle. During the initial uproar in 2002, a childhood friend who owned a public relations firm offered to coordinate publicity and work with the press to burnish Lavelle's reputation. He said, "I have to ask, Frannie, if any of it is true." Lavelle abruptly hung up. He never spoke to his friend again. He has lived on Cape Cod since his expulsion.[41]

J. Roy Jenness served at a dozen western and central Massachusetts parishes from the 1970s to the 2000s. At his last posting, St. Bartholomew in Bondsville, Jenness hosted Dupré's 1977 clandestine conclave. In addition to being included in the 2003 Greenfield 6 suit, he was accused of bringing boys to a house in Sturbridge where they were abused by a group of priests. The suit was immediately settled. He died in 1988.[42]

Edward Kennedy abused countless Spanish Apostolate boys and shared them with friends. He had been the pastor at Blessed Sacrament in Northampton for a decade when he was first accused in 1991 and banished to St. Luke. He pronounced himself cured: "I'm very happy I had the opportunity to take part, to grow deeper in my values as a Christian and priest, and I'm grateful to the bishop and the diocese for providing that for me." He was then, like Wamsher, secreted at canon law school. Barred from the ministry, he was appointed assistant judicial vicar on the marriage tribunal alongside Wamsher and yet another accused canon lawyer, John J. Bonzagni. Kennedy faced multiple suits. He had counseled one victim after the death of the boy's father. Kennedy's best friend John Koonz made the introduction. The boy later became a priest and, coincidentally, ran Kennedy's old apostolate. The Vatican defrocked Kennedy in 2006. The diocese settled with his accuser and placed

Kennedy—and Meehan—as chaplains at Providence Place retirement home. In 2017, Kennedy was still there.[43]

John Koonz held many important diocesan positions, including vicar forane and the priests' senate. In response to public ire about abuse in the 1990s, he had railed during sermons the accusations were "all untrue!" At the time, he was abusing groups of Spanish apostolate boys Kennedy delivered to his farm. His exit in 2002 after 22 years as pastor at St. Agnes in Dalton was blamed on an unidentified "physical disability." Dupré was forced to suspend Koonz but had to "walk a fine line … conscious of the fact every priest is a human being who has his human and civil rights, which must be respected." Dupré reluctantly removed Koonz in 2004 after he was named in four suits. Koonz never accepted defeat. He founded a non–Church-affiliated ministry, Missionaries of Our Lady of La Salette, and in 2013 "celebrated the 50th anniversary of his ordination." Shortly after the party, he died at the West Springfield house he shared with his sister.[44]

Thomas O'Connor abused throughout his posting at St. Patrick's in Monson 1950s and 1960s and was among the Greenfield 6 group abusing through the 1980s. He was named in multiple suits, all settled in 2008. He died in 1999.

Donald Desilets was at St. Thomas Aquinas in Springfield when Danny died, and he was transferred half a dozen times after that. He was at St. Aloysius of Gonzaga in Indian Orchard when allegations were made against him in 1993. After two months at the Institute of Living and forced retirement, he requested a transfer to the Sulpician Fathers, a Canadian order responsible for pre-seminary training. He died in Montreal in 2001. The diocese settled with his accuser in 2008.[45]

Gerald Spafford—the "Movie Star Priest" of the tailored suits and new Porsches—was forced into a leave in 1991. He moved to New York City, and in 2005, relocated to Provincetown, Massachusetts, where he volunteered at an AIDS support group before dying in 2015.[46]

Richard J. Ahern was a member of the abuse-riddled Stigmatine order. When the dust settled, there were fewer than 300 priests worldwide and their elegant Waltham headquarters were sold to the Massachusetts Horticultural Society. Ahern's career was marked by transfers up and down the Eastern seaboard. During the 1990s, he faced multiple accusations in three states and was banished to the Church's House of Affirmation in Whitinsville, Massachusetts. He often shared victims with best friend and fellow Stigmatine Joseph Flood. The Church settled multiple suits, and Ahern died in 2001.[47]

Joseph Flood was trailed by complaints from the 1940s to the 1970s and shuttled even more often and farther afield than Ahern. He spent a dozen years "volunteering" in Thailand, the hub of the global child sex trade, before returning to run the Stigmatine retreat house in Waltham. He retired in 1993 and died in 1996. According to his obituary, he was "always faithful to his duties and showed himself an optimist and serene person, ready to give a hand to anybody."[48] The Church settled half a dozen suits.

The trail of abuse left by Springfield's ring priests left devastating wounds on the diocese's reputation and the public's perception of priests. At the height of the crisis, Maguire described the priesthood as a "noble profession" that for generations attracted "the best and brightest of the neighborhood heroes." He succinctly described the Springfield abusers' legacy when he added, "I'm afraid it doesn't carry the same prestige or social weight anymore."[49]

Anti-priest groupthink was not universal. Edward Paquette abused at a dozen parishes from Indiana to Vermont and was not removed until police found him in a parked car with a teen boy in 2008. When defrocked in 2009, he was the subject of 19 suits and cost Burlington more than $12,000,000. He lived into his 80s in a ranch house on Belleview Drive in Westfield built by his parents, sporting his Roman collar whenever venturing outside. His retirement was funded by a bequest from a former parishioner of Our Lady of the Blessed Sacrament in Westfield.[50]

Mitchell and Blanche Tenerowicz lived out their lives amidst the trappings of wealth and status. After Danny's murder, they built an impressive faux Tudor on a large wooded property at 52 Westview Terrace in Easthampton. Their medical practice evolved during the 1980s into Easthampton Health Center, a large office employing half a dozen doctors and nurses. He was director of the Massachusetts Academy of Family Practice and on the staff of Cooley Dickinson Hospital for 38 years, where he was a trustee and chief of staff from 1979 to 1982. He was also president of the Hampshire County Medical Society and a trustee of Easthampton Savings Bank. After he died in 1996, Blanche ran the practice until she moved to a retirement community where she died in 2006. The Goshen lake house frequented by Lavigne and his victims was later sold to actress Sandra Denny. It burned to the ground in the late 1980s.

Tenerowicz's son reportedly accused him of abuse and Tenerowicz's daughter Elizabeth was abused by Lavigne for almost a decade beginning when she was eight. The abuse, including everything from forced fellatio to rape, took place during "counseling sessions" at Sacred Heart in Easthampton, Precious Blood in Holyoke, St. Catherine's, and St. Mary's. The diocese settled her 2003 suit.

The Boy Scout officials involved with Lavigne and Danny did not fare as well as some of their priest friends. Escaping unscathed after brushes with the law in the 1960s–1970s, Ed Veroneau ran a home security business with his friend Dick Brown. After his release from prison following his 1979 child rape conviction, he returned to the cluttered Stapleton Street house he inherited from his parents, his used police car in the driveway. Carl described him as a "packrat ... [with] so much junk crammed into his van there was barely enough room for him to drive."[51] Veroneau committed suicide on January 20, 1984.

After Veroneau's suicide, Brown took over his home security business. At the time of this writing, he was reportedly living in Springfield.

Woronoco ranger Roger Norton was in and out of jail for child sex crimes from the 1970s to the 1990s, beginning with the two-year sentence he received just after Danny's death. He was sentenced to 16–20 years in 1991 for child rape and to another four years in 1993 on similar charges. The 1991 conviction was overturned in 2005 because prosecutors withheld evidence that indicated an alleged victim may have fabricated his original story.[52] After his release, Norton was registered as a Level 3 Offender in Florida in 2009, in 2012 in New York, but not in Massachusetts, for some reason. In 2014, he was living in Lehigh Acres, Florida.

Bruce Mooney, the Greenfield Scoutmaster accused of assisting five ring priests abusing children, was a longtime teacher. He retired in the 1990s.

A victim's mother said, "Lavigne murdered my son's soul." That could be said for most of his victims. Dupré foil Scahill described abuse as "a slaying of the spirit."[53] For victims, decades of keeping secrets was a costly enterprise. Bruce Teague said, "It's the secrets that kill. It leads people to alcoholism, drug abuse, and broken relationships, loss of jobs, unemployment, and violent behaviors."[54] Victim Raymond Chelte, Jr., never spoke about his abuse to anyone. When his brother, another victim, asked him, "Did he molest you, too?" Raymond said simply, "No, why?"[55] His father learned of it during morning coffee with a friend reading a *Republican* story about the initial lawsuits. He asked Chelte, "Do you have a son named Ray? He's in an article."

André Tessier never spoke of abuse to his parents until he came upon his mother Sandra reading a story about a Lavigne victim whose life disintegrated. He watched her in silence until she finished, then said, "That was my story, too." Flabbergasted, she asked, "What are you talking about?" Without looking at her, he quietly replied, "I can't talk about it now but I could have told the same story."[56]

Abuse altered the trajectories of countless lives. A victim of Donald Desilets described the result: "You can't touch. You can't love. You can't give a guy a handshake. You can't allow women to touch you, even clothed. You don't allow anybody to get into your personal space." Joseph Croteau echoed the reality: "I can instantly recognize an abuse victim just watching them walk past. Victims are always moving, always listening, constantly checking things out."[57]

Thousands of victims spent years straining to right personal ships while burying reminders of lost childhoods. Countless psyches were destroyed by isolation, shame, fear of relationships, fear of sex, fear of everything. Lives were littered with bad relationships, failed marriages, lost jobs, school problems, and every manner of addiction. The effects were heightened by double victimization. "First, the priest molests them," said a victim lawyer. "Then, they are victimized by an institution that covered up the abuse and has not dealt with them fairly." James Scahill called it "killing themselves by inches." A Lavigne victim described the process as "suicide on the installment plan." Too many Lavigne victims traveled that tragic road.[58]

Ray Chelte, Jr., an alcoholic and addict since his junior high Circle days, led a frenetic life. He moved all over the country after being expelled from the Navy for using drugs. Married and divorced twice, he found it impossible to forge stable relationships because he "could never get close to people." He was 37 when he received his settlement in 1993, but within a year he blew the money on drugs and alcohol. On

March 28, 1998, after a night of cocaine and heroin, he sat at his kitchen table and reached for a cigarette. He died, mid-reach. His father said, "It was a suicide. Lavigne ruined his life. He just hated himself." He was found with the cigarette in his hand.[59]

The psychological abuse Lavigne heaped on Shawn Dobbert was ultimately more damaging than the physical. His lawyer described Dobbert as his most "tortured Lavigne client," the result of ten years of Lavigne telling him he was too stupid, too fat, friendless, an utter failure, and threatening him with death if he spoke. Dobbert managed to earn a culinary degree from Newberry College in Boston, cooked at a local café, and was an aide for disabled children. By 2001, his fragile health finally left him unable to work. On August 10, 2004, the 36-year-old signed settlement papers guaranteeing him at least $80,000. He returned to his tiny North Adams apartment, sat in a chair, and simply died. His death was ruled an accidental overdose, but nobody who knew him believed drugs had much to do with it. A friend and fellow victim said, "I don't care what the medical examiner's report says, Shawn killed himself."[60] His mother refused to let the Catholic Church bury her son. She gave him an Episcopal service.

David Bessone and his best friend and cousin Peter spent their adult lives anesthetized by alcohol and drugs. David buried everything during Army service, studies at the University of Florida, and as a teacher in rural Florida. Peter bounced from job to job and prayed "to God every day 'Don't take me until I see this man defrocked.'" They spoke about the abuse between themselves, but never to anyone else. Peter said David kept silent because "he was too ashamed ... [and] didn't want to jeopardize his job." Battling his own addictions, Peter tried to help David off drugs and called him just after Christmas 1985 to again suggest he get clean. David hung up, lit a Hibachi grill inside his apartment, laid on a couch, and let the fumes from the grill kill him. He was only 23. It took Peter decades to get sober himself. Cancer killed him in 2003.[61]

Many Circle members were victims of Lavigne and others. Some managed to carve out successful lives, but most did not. One was discharged from the Marines for hitting an officer in the mouth with a hammer. They battled mental illness, some further damaged by post-traumatic stress from their experiences in Vietnam. Some simply died from "hard living." The trail of death began even before Danny died. In

James Coleman's book *The Circle*, the character Frank Archie was based on the real-life Francis Archidiacono and drowned in a local pond, but Archidiacono actually suffered a more violent death. In 1968, he was shot during a camping trip to Sturbridge. The shooting was ruled accidental, but considering the ring abusers' tendency to gather in that remote town, Circle members' historical silence, and Ed Veroneau's habit of taking victims into secluded woods to play with guns, questions linger. In 1971, a 20-year-old Circle member died in a motorcycle accident, another was a suicide in 1982, and still another, driving drunk, died in 1997.[62]

Michael Cavanaugh was the basis for Coleman's lead character and the wildest of the Circle. He spent his mid-teens in the Westfield juvenile jail for stabbing another boy. In his early 20s, he earned ten years in the Massachusetts Correctional Institution near Boston for robbing the same Gasland service station twice in four days to feed a heroin habit. Shortly after his release in 1983, he got into an argument with a doctor reducing his methadone prescription, which led to assault and battery and armed robbery charges. He was returned to prison. A few months later, he hung himself with a sheet. He was only 28. Ray Chelte, Jr., died in 1998. Another former Circle member died of a heroin overdose in 2000, and still another killed himself in 2003.

They are still dying. Glenn Cubin, the younger brother of a Circle member, had a string of drug-related arrests spanning most of his life. On April 23, 2017, the 52-year-old walked off the Madison, Connecticut, train station platform and stood in front of a train.[63]

The park where the Circle hung out is gone. The berms were leveled and the benches removed from around the oak tree in the back lawn of the library. The gang survived barely six months longer than Danny. In late 1972, the Circle and the Motleys merged with the Clan, Hood Street Boys, and the Pine Point and Boston Road gangs. That iteration lasted 15 years. Surviving Circle members remain closely bonded to one another and to the group's memory, though, even after 40-plus years. In 2013, they gathered beneath the tree to celebrate the life of founding member Phil Chechile, who died that spring at 62. They all were older and grayer, and fighting had long since given way to memories and tears.[64]

James Coleman's book was mostly unknown outside of Springfield, but other books of his were very successful. *Relativity for the Layman:*

A Simplified Account of the History, Theory, and Proofs of Relativity was first published in 1954. It was reprinted five times, sold more than a million copies, and earned Coleman a congratulatory letter from Albert Einstein. The Circle had an uneven reaction to *The Circle*—many members were angered by the negative portrayal of their parents—and shunned its author. Coleman continued working with kids, taught wrestling and boxing at YMCAs and the Springfield Wrestling Club, was the director at YMCA camps, and a volunteer chess coach at Cathedral and two middle schools. He had been married 59 years when he died in 2006.[65]

All Lavigne victims struggled on some level with the ruination of their childhoods, but some forged successful careers and built families. The McMahon brothers became successful. One became a television and movie director and the other the owner of a large insurance agency. Joseph Croteau had a long career with the largest insurance company in Massachusetts before opening his own agency. His brother Carl has worked in corporate purchasing for more than 30 years.

Lavigne victims battled contradiction. They hated him, but some asked him to perform their weddings or baptize their children. It was a kind of revenge. In the year after Raymond Gouin came forward in 1992, his marriage fell apart and he spent a month in two psychiatric hospitals. He had asked Lavigne to preside over his wedding because he wanted to "show him I turned out all right. I have a wife, I have a baby, you didn't ruin me." He described the deeply-rooted confusion when he said a "part of me still kind of respected him. The good part of Father Lavigne is very, very good." Kevin Sousa, ordained in 1982, signed the 1991 Amici Brief supporting Lavigne, even though he had been abused. He put Lavigne completely out of his mind until television coverage of Lavigne's arrest triggered a flood of repressed memories that left him increasingly withdrawn and ultimately led him to leave the priesthood.[66]

Paul Babeu's convoluted life is perhaps the clearest example of Lavigne's impact. Paul and his brother Francis were alleged victims. Both joined the Marines and did tours of duty in Iraq. Francis became the father of four. Paul succeeded in several arenas. He was elected to the North Adams City Council at 18 and became a Berkshire County commissioner later. He was headmaster of DeSisto School in Stockbridge, a private, "therapeutic boarding school" for troubled teens where tuition was $71,000 a year. In 2002, he moved to Arizona and became a police officer in the Phoenix suburb of Chandler. In 2008, he became the first Republican in history elected sheriff of Pinal County. The huge jurisdiction straddles the Mexican border, and Babeu became the face of national border security concerns after multiple national news appearances. He advocated the end of illegal—and most legal—immigration, and he aggressively sparred with Barack Obama on gun control during a nationally televised town hall. He maintained close friendships with U.S. senator John McCain and controversial Arizona sheriff Joe Arpaio, coincidentally, also from Springfield.[67]

But controversy stalked Babeu. DeSisto School came under scrutiny of the Cult Awareness Network after being described as "a notorious behavior modification gulag school" accused of employing abusive disciplinary methods. Students were beaten, restrained, prohibited from contact with family, not allowed to make eye contact for days, and forced to labor on punishing work details. Roger Kahn, in his bestseller *The Boys of Summer,* claimed the school's "tough love led to at least one death, a boy put off campus in mid-winter who froze to death on an icy Berkshire hill." DeSisto was shut down by the state in 2004.[68]

During Babeu's 2012 Congressional run at the end of his first term as sheriff, his arch-conservative voting base was shocked when he was outed as a homosexual. His Mexican-national ex-boyfriend claimed Babeu and his attorney threatened deportation if he exposed the four-year relationship. The lovers' spat erupted after Babeu cheated on him and was a massive political and professional embarrassment. Babeu was derisively nicknamed "Sheriff Underpants" when his sexually explicit text messages and underwear selfies surfaced. He had to resign as co-chairman of Mitt Romney's presidential campaign in Arizona and end his own run for Washington. Doubt was then cast on his allegations against Lavigne. After Babeau appeared on Fox News in March 2011 to discuss Lavigne, a friend of his sister contacted ABC News and claimed his accusations were fiction. A Fox website post, attributed to his sister, described a scandal-wracked family and claimed he had lied: "Paul as usual is lying about when he got abused … [Francis] was raped by the priest … and could have put him behind bars if it wasn't for you. Paul has been threatening me his sister to keep quiet about all the rape and molestation and incest in the family." She accused Babeu of liking "younger boys" and wrote, "Coming out with sexual abuse is a big step. But please come out with the whole story. No more secrets Paul."[69]

———————————

Lavigne could not abuse as successfully today, as mores have changed and priests do not receive the deference they once did. He would face hundreds of serious charges rather than half a dozen relatively minor ones. In the Shelburne Falls case alone, he would face scores of local felony counts, federal charges relating to transporting children across state lines, and charges in other states. He would not be offered a cushy plea bargain and he would not face a judge as willing to excuse him as Judge Volterra had been in Newburyport. Had Lavigne been accused today, his prospect would be life in prison.

His ten-year probation ended without incident, but probation officials were repeatedly stymied by the Church and St. Luke. Probation officials wanted to update the original order ensure that Lavigne participated in the aftercare program, so, in 1993, they requested a release to discuss his records. Michael Brenneis, director of St. Luke's program, was ordered by his bosses not to even *talk* to probation officials.[70]

Lavigne is included on dozens of sex offender databases and websites that have his photo, history, and a photo of his home at 86 Haven Street in Chicopee. It is barely five miles from Ferncliff. He is classified a Level 3 Offender, meaning he is most likely to re-offend. Seventy-four at this writing, he is the same athletic 170-pounder with piercing blue eyes he was when Danny died. He still closely resembles Claus von Bulow. Lavigne's coverage in the news has, over the years, led other jurisdictions to look at him as a possible perpetrator of crimes in their areas. Ithaca, New York, police considered him after the murder of a 12-year-old altar boy from Pittsfield, not far from Shelburne Falls. Granby, Massachusetts, detectives looked into his possible involvement in the death of a seven-year-old boy found drowned in 1965.[71]

Lavigne and Danny are resurrected with each newspaper story, though articles are more infrequent. Stories about Lavigne are universally unflattering, like one op-ed describing him as "a devil and/or fully possessed by the devil … smart, cunning, and devious." Opinions about him remain at odds. Some friends—and he still has many among priests—excuse his troubles with comments like "Dick is a misunderstood, moody artist, an enigma." Most, though, recognize him for what he was and remains, troubled. A friend said, "There has always been a dark cloud around Dick. He is a brilliant priest but a sometimes-difficult man." Among his supporters, according to a friend, are "a laundry list of old lady parishioners who take him to lunch three or four times a week."[72]

He has rarely spoken publicly, once saying, "Silence has been my salvation." In an interview, he told *Boston Globe* writer Kevin Cullen he considered communicating with the Croteaus over the years, but he never did. He didn't think he could talk to Carl because "he's so bitter." Lavigne still paints. For years, one of his canvases hung in the lobby of Mercy Hospital in Springfield. A St. Catherine's victim claimed

Lavigne's 2005 photograph on the Massachusetts Sex Offender Registry (Massachusetts State Sex Offender Registry).

Lavigne was a longtime regular at a gay club in downtown Springfield and a regular in the private S&M room in the club's basement.[73]

The contradiction that has always been Dickie Lavigne endures. In the 1970s, he did a drawing of the Last Supper for the parents of a St. Mary's altar boy. It hung in their kitchen for more than 30 years. It remained there even after their son accused Lavigne of molesting him.[74]

The lasting effects of Danny's murder on the Croteau family are not surprising. Their lives were altered in myriad ways, small and large, that April weekend in 1972. Before then, the family looked forward to their annual week-long vacation to Cape Cod. From a rented beach house, they explored the Cape, played in the sand and waves, fished, went crabbing, and enjoyed the local seafood. Those carefree times ended when Danny died. Carl and Bunny never returned. The impact, though, went much deeper than cancelled vacations. Almost immediately, the spark that so infused everyone in the fun-loving family was snuffed out. It was never reignited.

One of the many painful realities that haunted Carl and Bunny was not being able to say goodbye to Danny. Allowing Lavigne to convince them to keep the casket closed robbed them of the opportunity to see him one last time. "That was one of the toughest things," said Carl. "All we had was a picture of him on top of the casket." That picture graces the cover of this book. All her life, Bunny thought she saw Danny; she would "see someone in the street or in a store who looked like Danny. I'd stare at him, and then I'd tell myself, 'It just can't be.'"[75]

The scars left on all the boys by Danny's death were compounded by Lavigne's abuse; all were tortured with guilt for not stopping Lavigne. As if they could have. Carl once said they "blame themselves for Danny's death. It haunts them. It haunts us."[76] The abuse he and Bunny learned about days after the murder was never spoken of.[77] For whatever reason the conversation could never be had. That doubtless worsened already terrible struggles.

Carl Jr. was able to come to terms with the consequences of Lavigne's abuse and forged a successful 40-year career in business. He and his family live near Springfield.

Gregory was said to be the smartest Croteau child, a brilliant mathematician who earned straight As without studying. He was the only family member who distrusted Lavigne, never felt the infatuation everyone else did. "I just had a bad feeling about the guy," he said, "He never seemed priestly to me." Though he rebuffed Lavigne's early attempt to ply him with vodka at a motel in Vermont, he eventually became a victim. Through his teens, he developed an explosive, hair-trigger temper that took him "from zero to sixty in the blink of an eye" and sent him into rages that worsened after Danny's death. He once attacked Lavigne during a Confirmation practice. Friends and family alike were afraid of him, and his anger frequently got him in trouble.[78] For years, he obsessed about killing Lavigne, thoughts that eventually overwhelmed him.

One of the rowdier members of the Circle into his 20s, Gregory managed to graduate from Springfield Technical Community College and held jobs even while battling drugs and doing "really insane things." In a later interview, his simple explanation was "I've done some bad things, but I'm not a bad person. I'm grateful I'm not spending my life in jail." He bounced around the Midwest for several years before settling in St. Petersburg, Florida, in his 30s. He married, fathered two daughters, and ran a successful auto wholesale business. He became obsessed with body building and competed in events throughout the East Coast and the Midwest, all the while ingesting steroids to increase size and strength. A psychologist who studied his history said steroids and body building are common over-reactions to having been abused. Often, she said, victims make themselves as big and strong as they can to "prevent anyone from hurting them again."[79]

He got clean in the late 1990s, but years of drugs and steroids had taken their toll. He returned to Massachusetts in his late 40s in failing health. He had a brain tumor and suffered from AIDS. He settled in Montague, a remote mountain village near Greenfield, but after being confined to a wheelchair, spent his last decade in a nursing home. On October 1, 2015, he died in his sleep at ago 60. Besides his daughters, he left five grandchildren.[80] He was buried next to Danny.

Joseph, like Carl Jr., was stronger than his memories of Lavigne. Just before Joseph's suit against Lavigne and the diocese came to trial, Lavigne went into hiding so he could not be served a subpoena compelling him to appear. The suit was settled.[81] Joseph, his wife, children, and grandchildren live near Springfield. Before opening an insurance agency, he spent many years as a senior claims manager in the health care division at MassMutual, a large Springfield insurance company. In that role, he approved claims against the diocese.

Michael was said to have been as smart as Gregory, a gifted linguist who picked up languages without studying. He was as overtaken by his past as Gregory, though, retreating into himself after Danny died. He joined the Army at 17 and spent four years in Germany, but his life afterward was a solitary, nomadic existence, as he worked on railroads across the U.S. and Canada before returning to Springfield in his 30s. He was a hard worker, serving as a security guard at a local Milton Bradley plant for many years and selling magazine subscriptions or household products door to door. Outwardly carefree, he dulled inner pain with alcohol, which lead to a diagnosis of liver cancer in the late 1990s. The first thing he did after receiving the news was go back to college, but on May 22, 2009, he died at UMass Hospital in Holyoke at age 51. He left a son in Canada, a daughter in Kentucky, and a fiancée.[82] He was buried alongside Gregory and Danny.

Jacqueline and Catherine live with their families in the Springfield area.

Most difficult for Carl and Bunny was 40 years of interminable waiting. For answers, justice, maybe *some* small measure of peace. Instead they suffered Church disregard and justice system failure. Through it all, they somehow retained small shreds of hope, despite so many saying that "nothing would ever be done." In his later years, Carl sighed, "Justice will prevail. I just wish it would hurry up." His suffering was maybe the worst. He said in 1994, "I've found myself getting moodier, more depressed, and I cry more than I used to. It's like the pressure keeps mounting. I get my hopes up and it's more waiting."[83]

They spent the decades juggling regret, anger, faith, and forgiveness. Regret was a near constant. Anger came in waves as Danny's story reappeared or Lavigne's legal problems were covered in newspapers. Carl defied his faith, never forgiving Lavigne. Over the years, they had two chance encounters. The first was at the Holyoke Mall north of Springfield. Lavigne studiously ignored Carl as they passed. The second was as Carl and a friend strolled a downtown sidewalk. Despite having a lung removed recently and painful arthritis in his back, Carl had to be restrained and only calmed down when his friend said, "It isn't worth

Carl and Bunny, ca. 2005, in front of the painting of Danny that hung in the living room for 30 years (author's collection).

it, Carl." Lavigne scurried away wordlessly. Carl and Bunny followed every uptick in interest and read thousands of pages of police and court documents. The never looked at the autopsy records, though.[84]

After Danny died, Carl—and, for a time, Bunny—worked at the American Bosch plant in Springfield before he joined the Springfield Housing Authority in 1975. He became the chief housing specialist for the Hampden County Housing Court and a beloved figure at the courthouse. He was known for his scrupulous honesty. Not long after Carl took the job, Joseph came home to find a five-foot tall fruit basket on the front steps. Clipped to it was an envelope containing $5,000, an immense sum in 1975. He called his father, who told him, "Don't touch it, I'll be right home." Carl turned the money over to his boss, the top judge in the system, who infuriated the wealthy real estate developer who sent the "gift" by donating the money to a Shriners hospital. Carl would become the judge's right-hand man, once convincing him to leave the bench during a hearing to visit a home he considered unsafe.[85]

For years, Springfield politicos and city employees illegally manipulated Section 8 affordable housing rolls to poach low-rent apartments for friends and constituents. For years, though, someone secretly altered the politically-motivated grants, ensuring deserving families got the coveted apartments instead of connected pols. After a legitimate applicant received a rejection letter, an anonymous telephone caller informed him there was a mistake, that they actually had an apartment. Try as they might, frustrated higher-ups never identified the caller known as "The Angel of Mercy." It was Carl. After he retired in 2006, he and Bunny bought a concession truck and spent mornings visiting construction sites.

Carl never got over his Korean War experiences. If they were ever mentioned, he turned and walked away. He suffered from then-unrecognized post-traumatic stress disorder, often waking drenched in sweat, screaming, fists clenched. He only discussed those years with a small group of fellow veterans who gathered in the garage behind Ferncliff. The boys, even as adults, knew never to enter. The men often left the sit-downs with red-rimmed eyes.[86]

Their faith wavered over the years but was never lost. In 2005 Bunny said, "They can't take God away from us. That's one thing they can't have." Carl's reasons were more visceral. In 2002 he said, "Give up my faith for Lavigne? For the good-old-boy network that protects people like him? No." He was a Eucharistic minister at St. Catherine's for years and a member of the Holy Name Society and the Knights of Columbus. He and Bunny eventually returned to daily Mass, and Carl did the Stations of the Cross a couple of times a week, alone in the darkened church. Despite his bad back, he knelt on the cold floor, praying beneath each of a dozen plaques memorializing Jesus' crucifixion.[87]

He was a doting grandfather to 17 grandchildren—one named Danielle Dominique in honor of an uncle she never knew—and 21 great-grandchildren. He wondered about the man and uncle Danny would have been, once saying, "He'd be teaching them how to fish, that's for sure."[88] When he made that wistful comment in 2003, Carl looked little different than he did when police arrived in his driveway Easter Saturday, 1972. He ran ten miles almost every day into his 60s, remaining rail-thin, sporting the same pencil-thin moustache, and appearing decades younger. His health declined in the mid–2000s, and he was weakened by a brain tumor and suffered a heart attack in his kitchen in early November 2010. On November 11, surrounded by his whole family, he died at Mercy Medical Center at age 79. His wake was moved from

The Croteau family plot at Hillcrest Park Cemetery (author's collection).

a funeral home to St. Catherine's, the first time a wake was ever held there. Mourners filled the aisle five-wide for hours, waiting patiently to pay their respects, and included hundreds he never met. Some were among the anonymous souls he helped at the Housing Court. An elderly man approached one of Carl's boys and, shaking his hand, said quietly, "Everyone knew about 'the Angel of Mercy.' Nobody knew who he was. I just attended his wake." He walked out, head down, worn cap crumpled in his hands.

Carl talked to Danny daily. Whenever he drove over the Governor Robinson Bridge, he asked Danny to point people to his killer. He visited Danny's grave weekly, often gazing at the plot to Danny's left and saying, "Bun and I will be next to him."[89] He was buried there, next to his three boys.

Bunny remained at Ferncliff, as lively late in life as she was the day Danny helped roll out a rug and walked off into the darkness. The telephone number was the same as it was in 1953. She worked as an Avon representative, drove for handicapped students, and was at St. Catherine's daily. She was a greeter and sold raffle tickets at Wednesday bingo and was on every volunteer committee and the Women's Guild. At home she devoured mystery books, listened to Tom Jones, and doted on the grandchildren and great-grandchildren, making them countless needlepoint pillows, knitted scarves, and crocheted blankets. She was a jack-of-all-trades around the house, too, making repairs herself into her 70s.[90]

Like Carl, she mused about the life Danny would have led. She

Carl Sr.'s marker at Hillcrest Park Cemetery (author's collection).

wondered if he might have become a priest, a profession he often discussed. She was sure, though, that "if Danny was here, he would be spoiling the grandkids." Remembering him was no less difficult later in life than in 1972. "April is the toughest month, the cruelest month," she said. "It all comes back with a vengeance. It feels like it happened yesterday. Time heals some, but it doesn't heal all. The pain doesn't go away."[91]

She often listened to the recording of Danny proudly boasting of his medal and the then-beloved priest he would give it to. She was plagued by nightmares, often startled awake in a cold sweat, crying out for Danny. In most, she said, "Danny is yelling for help, and I can't get to him. I see him screaming, calling for help. It's horrible because you can't get to him." Sometimes, Lavigne appeared in her dreams. Of one she said, "I was swinging at him, hitting him with everything I had. But then I woke up, and there was nothing there. I was crying. I was calling out for Danny. And there was nothing there. Nothing."[92] Bunny's health declined in 2015, and she died November 10, 2016, at 80. Her wake was at the church and, like Carl's, packed with mourners. She was buried next to Carl and the boys.

Danny will forever be a freckle-faced, 13-year-old Huck Finn with a mischievous grin and tousled strawberry blond hair. Bunny made a lamp in the shape of the character that so reminded her of him. It sat

Bunny's marker, alongside Gregory's (author's collection).

on a living room table for more than 30 years. A painting of Danny in his OLSH uniform hung above it for 40 years, next to one of her needlepoints with the message "When somebody you love becomes a memory, the memory becomes a treasure." Danny's murder is listed on the "Unsolved Homicides" page of the Hampden County District Attorney's website, the convoluted case described simply: "April 15, 1972, thirteen-year-old Daniel Croteau's body was discovered in the Chicopee River in the area under Governor Robinson Bridge in Chicopee. Please call State Police Detective Unit (413) 505–5993 with information."[93]

Occasionally through the years, Carl and Bunny received crank calls and letters from misguided zealots excusing the behavior that so damaged their Church. Bunny once said, "If justice was served, if we knew, it wouldn't hurt as much."[94] Sadly, it didn't come to pass during their lifetimes. Hopefully, the telling of Danny's story might offer at least a little peace.

Chapter Notes

Chapter 1

1. Daniel Herrara is a pseudonym.
2. "Patch" from "Our Plural History: Irish Immigrants in Holyoke," from stcc.edu. "Hungry Hill" from *Republican, The Irish Legacy: A History of the Irish in Western Massachusetts,* Springfield, Massachusetts, Pediment Group, 2012. "French-Canadians" from *Republican, Building a Better Life: The French-Canadian Experience in Western Massachusetts,* Springfield, Massachusetts, Pediment Group, 2012. "shifts" from O'Connor, John, "Family Tree: Hungry Hill Neighborhood Long Home to Springfield's Irish," masslive.com.
3. "Fitton" from Cruickshank, Ginger, *Images of America: Springfield, Volume 1,* Charleston, South Carolina, Arcadia Publishing, 1999. "strength" from "Our Plural History: Irish Immigrants in Holyoke," from stcc.edu. "160" from McCoy, J.J., et al., *History of the Catholic Church in New England States,* Boston, Massachusetts, The Hurd & Everts Co., 1899, 588–658, and Fitton, Rev. James, *Sketches of the Establishment of the Catholic Church in New England,* Boston, Massachusetts, Patrick Donahue, 1872, 288–322.
4. "quarries" from Federal Census, 1920. "Walsh" from Commonwealth of Massachusetts, Massachusetts Vital Records, Index to Marriages, 1921–1925. "mills" from Federal Census, 1930. "Allendale" from Federal Census, 1930. "Elton" from Commonwealth, Massachusetts Vital Records, Index to Births, 1931–1935. "quarries" from Huntley, Heather Ewell, ed., *East Longmeadow Massachusetts: 1894–1994: Centennial Edition,* State College, Pennsylvania, Jostens Printing & Publishing Division, 1994.

5. "girls" from U.S. Federal Census, 1930. "Massasoit" from Directory, Springfield, 1948.
6. "downtown" from Directory, Springfield, 1951, and Croteau, Joseph.
7. "Fannie" from Federal Census, 1900. "studios" from Directory, Hartford, 1899–1900, Directory, Norwalk, 1903–1907, and Directory, Bridgeport, 1901–1915. "girls" from Federal Census, 1920. Everett children: Emma (b. 1899), Ester (1904), Robert (1907), Margaret (1911), and Viola (1916).
8. "Jenness" from Directory, Springfield, 1925–1927. "Westinghouse" from Directory, Springfield, 1924, 1925. "Jehovah's" from Croteau, J. "Indian" from Federal Census, 1920. "scattered" from Directory, Springfield, 1933–1937.
9. "married" from Commonwealth, Massachusetts Vital Records, Index to Marriages, 1926–1930. "Hood" from Directory, Springfield, 1934–1936. "Beatrice" from Commonwealth, Massachusetts Vital Records, Index to Births, Vol. 136, 1936–1940. "Atwood" from Directory, Springfield, 1942–1944. "Seuss" from "Maple Hill/Ridgewood," choosespringfield. com.
10. "2nd Indianhead Division," from 2ida. org. "first American unit" from "From D+1 to 105: The Story of the 2nd Infantry Division," "*The 2nd Infantry Division's Story: Second to None,*" lonesentry.com. "strategy" from Mossman, Billy C., *United States Army in the Korean War: Ebb and Flow, November, 1950– July, 1951,* U.S. Army Center of Military History, United States Army, Washington, D.C., 1990, Korean War Project, National Archives and Records Administration, College Park, Maryland.
11. "cooks" from 38th Infantry Regiment, *Command Report—September-October 1950,*

2nd Infantry Division, Korean War Project Record: USA-126, National Archives and Records Administration, College Park, Maryland, Record Group: RG-407. "musicians" from D+1 to 105. "clerks" from 38th Infantry Regiment, *Command Report—July–August 1950*, 2nd Infantry Division, Korean War Project Record: USA-126, National Archives and Records Administration, College Park, Maryland, Record Group: RG-407. "Americans" from Mossman.

12. "frostbite" from Personnel Periodic Report No 12, 16 Dec 50, 38th Infantry Regiment, *Miscellaneous Records—Awards—December 1950*, 2nd Infantry Division, Korean War Project Record: USA-127, National Archives and Records Administration, College Park, Maryland, Record Group: RG-407. "3,206" from D+1 to 105. "wounded" from Korean War Casualty File, 2/13/1950–12/31/1953; Records on Korean War Dead and Wounded Army Casualties, 1950–1970; Records of the Adjutant General's Office, National Archives and Records Administration, College Park, Maryland, and 38th, Sept.–Oct., *Regiment-Record Losses 1950*, 2nd Infantry Division, Korean War Project Record: USA-126, National Archives and Records Administration, College Park, Maryland, Record Group: RG-407. "600" from Mossman and 38th Infantry Regiment, *Command Report—November 1950*, Korean War Project Record: USA-126, National Archives and Records Administration, College Park, Maryland, Record Group: RG-407, and 38th Infantry Regiment, *Command Report—December 1950*, 2nd Infantry Division, Korean War Project Record: USA-125, National Archives and Records Administration, College Park, Maryland, Record Group: RG-407.

13. "Bernice's" from Directory, Springfield, 1952.

14. "hopeless" from Croteau, Bernice to EJF.

15. "cards" from Shea, Tom, "Parents Dream of Son, Long for Justice: 19 Years Later Croteau Boy's Death Unsolved," *Republican*, October 27, 1991. "spoon" from Croteau, J. "toilet" from Croteau, B. "parties" from Fitzgerald, Brian, "Hell's Acres," *The Danny Croteau Murder*, III, hellsacres.blogspot.com.

16. "Cheerios" from Shea, "Parents Dream."

17. "trouble" from Croteau, J.

18. The *Springfield Union-News* became the *Republican* around 2001.

19. "Guadalcanal" from "Bishop C.J. Weldon of Massachusetts," *New York Times*, March 20, 1982. "micromanager" from Zajac, Bill, "Priest Says Files Destroyed: Bishop Denies Making Statement," *Republican*, September 17, 2003. "me" from Weldon, Christopher J., Bishop of Springfield, to EJF, III (author's father). "water" from Crean, Fr. Hugh to EJF.

20. "withdrew" from O'Brien, Darby to EJF.

21. "society" from Ederly, Sabrina Rubin, "The Church's Secret Sex-Crime Files: How a Scandal in Philadelphia Exposed Documents That Reveal a High-Level Conspiracy to Cover Up Decades of Sexual Abuse," *Rolling Stone*, September 6, 2011. "authority" from Berry, Jason, "The Tragedy of Gilbert Gauthé, I," *The Times of Acadiana*, May 23, 1985, reprinted in the *National Catholic Reporter*.

22. "parents" from Zajac, "4 Brothers File Priest Abuse Suit," *Republican*, December 13, 2003.

23. "mentally" from Chicopee Police Department, Complaint Sheet 19–221A. "Hoss" from Croteau, J. "ox" from Fitzgerald, Brian, "Hell's Acres," *The Circle Gang*, V, hellsacres.blogspot.com.

24. "Coleman": More than three dozen of his students won high school championships, state and New England titles. "Pacific" from "Obituary, Coleman, James A.," *Republican*, October 22, 2006. "orphanage" from Mazzarino, Carole to EJF. "likeable" from Commonwealth, In the matter of Richard R. Lavigne, September 29, 1993. "type" from Maharaj, Jai, *The Daniel Croteau Murder*, V, croteaumurderblogspot.com.

25. "anybody" from CPD, 19–221A, April 24, 1972. "well-liked" from Statement of Thomas J. Daly, Affidavit in Support of Application for Search Warrant, September 2, 1993. "wanted" from Cullen, Kevin, "Danny's Story: Death of an Altar Boy, a Priest, a Boy, a Mystery," *Boston Globe*, December 14, 2003. "loved" from Croteau, B. "Bunny" from CPD, 19–221A.

26. "best" from Croteau, J. "play" from Lavigne, September 29, 1993, 13. "lost" from Croteau, J.

27. "goodies" from CPD, 19–221A, April 15, 1972. "dirty" from CPD, 19–221A, April 16, 1972. "three" from Maharaj, Jai, *The Daniel Croteau Murder*, X, from croteaumurderblogspot.com.

28. "Razorbacks" from Fitzgerald, Brian to EJF. "oak" from Daly, Warrant. "The Motleys" from Croteau, J.
29. "cool" from Fitzgerald, Brian, Circle, V. "power" from Croteau, J.
30. "Mush" from Mazzarino and Fitzgerald, Brian, Circle, V. "roughed" from Croteau, J. "babysitting" from Shea, "Stories of Alleged Victims: Years of Silence Ends Living with Betrayal," *Republican*, January 29, 1993. "Bud" from Hell's Acres, *The Circle Gang*, IV, hellsacres.blogspot.com.
31. "windows" from Maharaj, Jai, *The Daniel Croteau Murder*, I, croteaumurderblogspot.com. "blocks" from Croteau, J. "headstone" from Fitzgerald, B.
32. "guerrilla" from Croteau, J.
33. "skulls" from Hell's Acres, *The Circle Gang*, II, hellsacres.blogspot.com. "guardrail," etc., from Hell's Acres, *The Circle Gang*, I, hellsacres.blogspot.com. "Jerks" and "drove" from Hell's Fitzgerald, Brian, Circle, V, Comments. "Western New England College": Now Western New England University.
34. "lottery" from Shea, "Croteau Told Bishop About Lavigne in '88: Slain Boy's Father Was Obsessed with Killing Priest," *Republican*, March 23, 1993. "took" from Croteau, J.
35. "rights" from Fitzgerald, Brian, Circle, II. "disciplinarian" from Mazzarino. "trouble" from Maharaj, I.
36. "*The Circle*": Coleman, James A., *The Circle*, Pro Litho, Ludlow, MA, 1970, iUniverse, 2000. "liked" from Maharaj, I. "group" from Statement of James A. Coleman Affidavit, May 13, 1993. "shotgun" from Fitzgerald, Brian, Circle, II. "hopeless lot": Notes here from Coleman, 98–101.
37. "Fr. Ravine" from Coleman Affidavit, May 13, 1993.
38. "jolted" and Ryan comments from "Book Sparks Controversy in Sixteen Acres," *Republican*, August 3, 1970. "threats" from Fitzgerald, Brian, Circle, IV. "bail" from Ibid.
39. "hellion" from Devine, Tom, *Baystate Objectivist Archives*, May 30, 2009, tommydevine.blogspot.com. "fifteen" from Coleman, 98. "smuggled" from CPD 19–221A, April 17, 1972. "best" from Lavigne, September 29, 1993, 12. "outside" from Statement of Croteau, Carl, December 12, 2003, Exhibit A. "candles" from CPD 19–221A, April 22, 1972.

40. "hitchhiked" from CPD, April 15, 1972.
41. "cousins" from CPD, April 18, 1972.

Chapter 2

1. "Marcellin" from "Aldenville Traces Roots to Plymouth Colony," *Republican*, April 13, 2011. "Clerina": Variously spelled "Clerina," "Clorina," and "Clarina" in immigration and census files. "Clerina" is the most frequent spelling and utilized herein. "1906" from Province of Quebec, Vital and Church Records (Drouin Collection), 1906, Notre-Dame-de-Ham, Registries. "1870" from Canada, Census, Arthabaska, St. Valère de Bulstrode, 1871. "Chicopee" from United States Department of Labor, Immigration Service, Examination Certificate, Medical Record, Clerina Lavigne, April 23, 1923. "rejected" from United States Department of Labor, Immigration Service, List of Manifest of Alien Passengers Applying for Admission from Foreign Contiguous Territory, St. Albans, Vermont, June 1923. Sons: Alfred (1899), Wilfred (1907), Ovila (1909), Joseph (1911), Edmund (1912), and Girard (1914).
2. "$300" from United States Department of Labor, Immigration Service, Examination Record, Medical Certificate, April 18, 1923. "898 Granby Road" from Directory, Springfield Suburban, 1928–1931. "hip" from United States Department of Labor, Immigration Service, Primary Inspection Memorandum, November 30, 1922. "carpentry" from Federal Census, 1930. "1933" from Commonwealth, Department of Health, Registry of Vital Statistics, Massachusetts Vital Records, Index to Deaths, Vol. 91, 1931–1935. "88" from Federal Census, 1940.
3. "1896" from United States Department of Labor, Naturalization Service, Declaration of Intention, Petition for Naturalization, Joseph Phidime Cote, July 29, 1918. "married" from State of Maine, Marriage Records, Record of a Marriage Joseph Cote & Albertine Aucliare, June 2, 1902. "Westbrook" from Directory, Westbrook, 1916. "720 Main Street" from Registration Card/Registrar's Report, State of Maine, Cumberland County, Local Board for Division No. 2, Cote, Joseph Phidime, September 12, 1918 (World War I draft registration form).
4. "seven" from United States Department of Labor, Naturalization Service, Dec-

laration of Intention, Petition for Naturalization, Joseph Phidime Cote, July 29, 1918. "lost" from Federal Census, 1910. Children: Rene Louis (b. 1907), Florence Agnes (1909), Joseph Sylvio (1911), Marie Carmel (1912), Blanch Annette (1915), Marcel Joseph (1917), and Marie Jainette (1918). "died" from Commonwealth, Department of Health, Registry of Vital Statistics, Massachusetts Vital Records, Index to Deaths, Vol. 82, 1926–1930, 359. "butter" from Chicopee, 1940. "Carmel" from Commonwealth, Department of Health, Registry of Vital Statistics, Massachusetts Vital Records, Index to Births, Vol. 155, 1946–1950. "50" from Directory, Chicopee, 1950–1993.

5. "wasn't" from Shea, "Friends, Foes of Lavigne Call Priest Complex Man: Controversy No Stranger to Suspect in Molestations," *Republican*, December 15, 1991.

6. "bikinis" from Zajac and Mason, Warren, *The Six-Percent Solution*, unpublished manuscript, 2008. "hand" from Stevens, R.C. to EJF.

7. "cymbals" from Mason to EJF.

8. "laughed": Incidents here from Statement of Witness, November 1, 1991, Lavigne, September 29, 1993, 214.

9. "Assumptionists" from Henshaw, Fr. Robert, *The Spirit of the Order: What Is the Spirit of the Assumption Order?*, assumptionist.org.uk. The Assumption Preparatory School closed in 1970 and now houses Quinsigamond Community College.

10. "children": Letter of Termination, Richard R. Lavigne, Chicopee Parks & Recreation Department, August 4, 1968, summarized in Lavigne, September 29, 1993, 216–17.

11. "Latin": Curriculum from Transcript: LAVIGNE, Richard Roger, Office of the Registrar, Assumption College, Worcester, Massachusetts, June 9, 1962. Lavigne's results: Freshman, 2.83 (out of 4.00); Sophomore, 2.82; Junior, 2.87; and Senior, 2.90.

12. "recommendation" from Letter of Acceptance, Seminary of Our Lady of the Angeles, William J. Gormley, Office of the Rector to Msgr. John Harrington, Chancellor, Springfield Diocese, July 11, 1962. Our Lady closed in 1972 due to a shortage of candidates. "Cathechetics" from Report of Scholastic Standing, Richard R. Lavigne, Seminary of Our Lady of Angels, Spring 1963–Spring 1964. "D" from Lavigne, 1963–1964.

13. "humble" from letter, Richard R. Lav-

igne, Petition for Minor Orders, William J. Gormley, Office of the Rector, Seminary of Our Lady of Angels to Msgr. John Harrington, Chancellor, Springfield Diocese, February 15, 1964. "Nassau" from Pastoral Report, Richard R. Lavigne, Seminary of Our Lady of Angels, Eugene E. Guérin, September 5, 1964. "December" from Pastoral Report, Richard R. Lavigne, Seminary of Our Lady of Angels, Eugene E. Guérin, September 3, 1965.

14. "communicate" from Report of Scholastic Standing, Richard R. Lavigne, Seminary of Our Lady of Angels, Spring 1965–Spring 1966. "troubles" from letter, Recommendation of Ordination to Priesthood, Richard R. Lavigne, William J. Gormley, Office of the Rector, Seminary of Our Lady of Angels, to Msgr. Roger Viau, Springfield Diocese, May 2, 1966.

15. "reception" from Shea, "Friends, Foes."

16. "patron" from letter, Richard R. Lavigne to Fr. Roger Viau, Vicar, Springfield Diocese, undated, ca. 1969–1970. "obligation" from letter, Christopher J. Weldon, Bishop, Springfield Diocese, to Fr. Richard R. Lavigne, February 12, 1973.

17. "blue-collar" from Federal Census, 1930, 1940. "1943" from United States, Department of War, World War II Army Enlistment Records, 1938–1946. "Eighth" from "Obituary, Tenerowicz, Mitchell J.," *Republican*, September 26, 1996.

18. "physician" from Directory, Easthampton, 1956–1959. "advisor" from Directory, Easthampton, 1960. "Examiner" from Commonwealth, *A Manual for the Use of the General Court*, Boston, Massachusetts, 1983, p. 439.

19. "overseeing" from "Diocese Plans Education Boards to Direct Schools," *North Adams Transcript*, February 1, 1972. "Goshen": From Barrus, Hirum, *History of the Town of Goshen, Hampshire Country, Massachusetts, from Its First Settlement in 1761 to 1881, With Family Sketches*, Boston, 1881. and Lepore, Jill, *The Name of the War: King Phillip's War and the Origins of American Identity*, New York, Alfred A. Knopf, 1998. "cemetery" from Croteau, J. "stays" from Stevens, "Thursday, March 31, 2005, Update, Briefing Republican Co."

20. "easy" from Garvey, Dick, "Bishop's Investigation of Homicide Suspicion Is Recalled," *Republican*, October 29, 1991. "older"

from Maharaj, Jai, *The Daniel Croteau Murder*, III, from croteaumurderblogspot.com.
　21. "storm" from Statement of Witness, November 11, 1991, from Daly, Warrant. "sails" from Statement, November 1, 1991, Lavigne, September 29, 1993. "dynamic," etc., from Daly, Warrant. "outstanding" from Cullen, "Danny's Story." "stare" from Statement of Witness, November 21, 1991, Lavigne, September 29, 1993.
　22. "stained-glass" from Coleman, 99. "rhetoric" from Barry, Stephanie, "Priest's Letters Offer Clues to His Psyche," *Republican*, April 14, 2002. "midnight" from Croteau, J.
　23. "discounts" from Shea, "Croteau Told." "radical" from Shea and Goonan, Peter, "Diocese Denies Cover-up: Bishop Knew Priest Was Suspect in '72," *Republican*, October 24, 1991. "disenfranchised" from Shea, "Friends, Foes."
　24. "traditions" from Blow, Charles M., "Rise of the Religious Left," *New York Times*, July 2, 2010. "veteran" from Shea, "Parents Dream." "peacemaker" from Garvey, "Bishop's Investigation." "withdrawal" from Shea and Goonan, "Diocese Denies."
　25. "theories" from Garvey, "Bishop's Investigation."
　26. "priest" from Maharaj, I.
　27. "beer" from Zajac, "A Question of Faith: Mother Asks Church for Answers," *Republican*, March 21, 2004. "playboy" from Lavigne, September 29, 1993, 12. "serious" from Barry, Stephanie, "Court Documents Reveal Altar Boy's Ordeal," *The Republican*, February 8, 2008. "sons" from Croteau, C., Affidavit. "race" from Fitzgerald, B.
　28. "recruiting" from AR to EJF. "horror" from Shea, "Lavigne Backer Levels Charge: Teen Says Priest Molested Him," *Republican*, April 19, 1993.
　29. "stereo" from Shea, "Lavigne Backer." "Putney" from Statement of Witness, November 15, 1991, from Daly, Warrant. "snowmobiling" from *Lawrence P. Opitz v. Richard R. Lavigne, and Roman Catholic Springfield Diocese, a Corporation Sole*. "expeditions" from Shea, "Croteau Told." "junkman" from Simison, Cynthia, "72 Murder Case Linked to Priest, Reopened by DA," *Republican*, October 23, 1991. "ornaments" from Shea, "Friends, Foes." "chased" from Kelly, Ray, and Shea, "Lavigne Faces New Allegations: Ex-pastor Freed from MD Center," *Republican*,

January 29, 1993, and Zajac, "Abuse Seen as Cause of Suicides," *Republican*, June 12, 2005.
　30. "outside" from Statement, November 15, 1991, Lavigne, September 29, 1993.
　31. "iconoclast" from Melley, Brian, "Father Lavigne Pleads Guilty: Priest Avoids Jail Term," *Republican*, June 26, 1992. "neutral" from Shea, "Friends, Foes." "everything" from Shea, "Lavigne Backer." "irrational" from Statement of J. Shattuck, *Commonwealth v. Richard R. Lavigne*, no. 92 032, February 14, 1992.
　32. "missal" Shea, "Friends, Foes." "mouth" from Croteau, J. "name-calling" from Shea, "Friends, Foes." "pushed" from Lavigne, September 29, 1993, 13–14, and Maharaj, Jai, *The Daniel Croteau Murder*, II, croteaumurderblogspot.com. "tickle" from Statement of Witness, November 24, 1991, Lavigne, September 29, 1993. "knocked" from Lavigne, September 29, 1993, 13–15, and Shea, "Lab Tests Blood from Croteau Site: DA Wants Sample from Rev. Lavigne," *Republican*, January 30, 1993.
　33. "shoes" from Shea, "Parents Dream." "laid" from Cullen, "Danny's Story." "surgery" from Croteau, B., and Sullivan, Jack, "Priest Reportedly Was Suspect in Slaying," *Boston Globe*, October 22, 1991.
　34. "Chicopee" from Statement of Carl and Bernice Croteau, May 27, 1993. "unworried" from Zajac, "Lavigne's Words Drew Suspicion," *Springfield Sunday Republican*, November 18, 1998. "complained" from Shea, "Parents Dream." "woods" from Shea, "Croteau Told." "pals" from Croteau, J.
　35. "reprimanded" from Croteau, J.
　36. "meet" from Maharaj, II. "three" from Statement of Daly, Warrant, 21. "overnight" from Zajac, "Croteau Papers Chilling, Inconclusive," *Republican*, August 8, 2004.
　37. "conflicts" from Croteau, C., Affidavit. "gay" from Daly, Warrant.

Chapter 3

　1. "love" from Cullen, "Danny's Story."
　2. "Peeping" from Fitzgerald, B. "bathroom" from Croteau, J.
　3. "blue" from Garvey, "Bishop's Investigation." "albums" from Zajac, "Lavigne Haunts Past of a Priest," *Republican*, April 21, 2002.
　4. "modern" and "hymn" from Zajac, "Lavigne Haunts."

5. "Ashfield" from Croteau, C. to EJF, and Shea, "Parents Dream."

6. "primped" from Zajac, "Lavigne's Words." "someplace" from Barry, "Court Documents." "Herringbone" from Lavigne, September 29, 1993, 5. "called" from Zajac, "Lavigne's Words." "stay" from Lavigne, September 29, 1993, January 12, 1993, 6. "vomited" from Barry, "Court Documents," and Statement of Bernice Croteau, Chicopee Police Department, August 7, 1972.

7. "camping" from CPD, April 15, 1972. "wait" from Shea, "Parents Dream."

8. "College": from Stevens, "Croteau Timeline, Friday, April 14, 1972." "Sure" from Maharaj, Jai, *The Danny Croteau Murder*, VI, June 6, 2009, croteaumurderblogspot.com.

9. "kickball" from Maharaj, VI. "pocket" from Shea, "Parents Dream." "party" from Stevens. "paperboy" from Maharaj, Jai, *The Daniel Croteau Murder*, IV, croteaumurderblogspot.com.

10. "A&P" from CPD, April 15, 1972.

11. "see" from Croteau, B., Chicopee Police Department interview, August 7, 1992.

12. "kid" from Shea, "Parents Dream." "2:11" from Maharaj, VI.

13. "cluttered" from Croteau, J.

14. "stained" from Commonwealth, LAB No. 38039, Examination of Materials in Connection with the Fatal Beating at Chicopee on April 15, 1972. Victim: Daniel Croteau, 106 Ferncliff, Springfield.

15. "few" from Sullivan, Jack, "Rain Washed Away Clue in '72 Slaying: Sources Say Springfield DA Believed Priest Killed Boy," *Boston Globe*, October 24, 1991. "murdered" from Daly, Warrant.

16. "development" Stevens, R.C., "Case Status Notes as of April, 2006."

17. "pitched" from Stevens to EJF.

18. "edge" from Sullivan, "Rain Washed." "fifteen" from Fitzgerald, Brian, "Hell's Acres," *The Danny Croteau Murder*, I, hellsacres.blogspot.com. "washed" from Lavigne, September 29, 1993, 15. "speed" from CPD, April 15, 1972 and Lavigne, September 29, 1993, September 23, 1993, 1.

19. "sand" from Soule, Rolland L., "Reproduction of Foot and Tire Tracks by Plaster of Paris Casting," *Journal of Criminal Law and Criminology* 50, Issue 2, Chicago, Illinois, Northwestern School of Law Scholarly Commons, July–August 1959, 198–202. "useless"

from Sullivan, "Rain Washed." "¾" from Commonwealth, 38039.

20. "piece" from Lavigne, September 29, 1993, 1. Also CPD, 19–221A, April 15, 1972.

21. "search" from Croteau, B. to EJF, and Stevens Timeline. "his car" from Shea, "Parents Dream." "worse" from Croteau, C., Sr., to EJF. "dead" from Croteau, J.

22. "see" from Croteau, B.

23. "found": Notes here from Autopsy Report, Case A–72–49, Pathological Diagnosis on the Body of Daniel Croteau, 106 Ferncliff Street, Springfield, Massachusetts, April 15, 1972.

24. "night" from Zajac, "Probe Points to Prospective Ring," *Republican*, May 2, 2005.

25. ".18%" from Supplementary Report: Daniel Croteau, #38039, May 2, 1972. A subsequent Supplementary Report dated May 15, 1972, indicated a bile alcohol level of .20 percent.

26. "killer" from Daly, Warrant, 22, and Zajac, "Lavigne's Words."

27. "differently" from Stevens.

28. "paper" from "Obituary, Croteau, Daniel T.," *Republican*, April 16, 1972. "misplaced" from Statement of Mary Bobek, December 1, 1992.

29. "lost" from CPD, 19–221A, April 18, 1972. "Lavigne's" from CPD, 19–221A, April 17, 1972. "brief": Lavigne claimed Danny called the rectory (which would explain his question "Is Father Lavigne there?") and then Aldenville. Source: CPD, 19–221A, April 16, 1972.

30. "bless" from Fitzgerald, Brian, Croteau, I. "station" from Lavigne, September 29, 1993, January 1, 1995, 3, and CPD, 19–221A, April 17, 1972.

31. "night": One report noted 538 McKinstry Avenue, owned by a different Richard Lavigne. "brothers" from Lavigne, September 29, 1993, 295–97.

32. "errands" from Shea, "Friends, Foes." "Charleston" from Stevens. "Elks" from Stevens Timeline.

33. "SCAN" from Smith, Nicky, "Reading Between the Lines: An Evaluation of the Scientific Content Analysis Technique (SCAN)," Police Research Series, Paper 135, Home Office, Policing and Reducing Crime Unit, Research, Development and Statistics Directorate, Clive House, Petty France, London, 2001.

34. "thrown" from Lavigne, September 29, 1993, 5–6. "refused" from Melley, Brian, "Lavigne's Words Drew Suspicion," *Republican*, March 31, 1996.

35. "answered" from Daly, Warrant. "face" from Lavigne, September 29, 1993, 7, 10. In 1993, Carl Jr. suggested the call was made just after the funeral on April 18, but Carl Sr. maintained it took place the day of the wake. From Daly Search Warrant. "associate" from Daly, Warrant.

36. "wept" from Cullen, "Danny's Story." "hearted" from Croteau, C., Affidavit, and Carl and Bernice.

37. "file" from CPD, 19–221A, April 18, 1972.

38. "lights" from Fitzgerald, Brian, "Hell's Acres," *The Danny Croteau Murder*, II, hellsacres.blogspot.com.

39. "Appeal" from *Republican*, April 17, 1972. "Public" from *Republican*, April 18, 1972.

40. "hypnosis" from Barry, "Court Documents." "convenience": Not in the interview materials discussed in CPD Complaint, but provided to the Catholic Diocese in Springfield. "Queer" from CPD, 19–221A, April 21, 1972.

41. "oddball" from *Daniel Croteau Murder*, X and Coleman Affidavit, May 13,1993. "weird" from Croteau, J.

42. "aggresively" from Croteau, J.

43. "goodies" from CPD, 19–221A, April 15, 1972. "Marijuana" from CPD, 19–221A, April 19, 1972.

44. "fixated" from Joseph, F. Michael to EJF. "abusing" from Croteau, C., Affidavit.

45. "1951" from "Obituary, Keck, Barnabas, Father, O.F.M., Cap.," *The Daily Freeman*, August 14, 2013.

46. "speaking" from Lavigne, September 29, 1993.

47. "interested" from Affidavit of Croteau, C., and Maharaj, Jai, *The Daniel Croteau Murder*, III, croteaumurderblogspot.com. "friend" from Ibid.

48. "knocked," etc., from Tessier, Sandra to EJF.

49. "Pancakes," etc., from Ibid.

50. "breakdown" from Barry, "Court Documents."

51. "rectory" from Fitzgibbon, James, to Croteau, C. "regretted" from Maharaj, X and Coleman Affidavit, May 13, 1993.

52. "threshold" from Zajac, "Croteau Papers." "away" from Shea and Goonan, "Diocese Denies."

53. "one" from Carl and Bernice and Fitzgerald, Brian, Croteau, II. "member" from Blixt, Peter and Greig, June, "Priest Linked to 1972 Slaying: Pleads Innocent to Rape of Child," *Republican*, October 22, 1991. "nail" from Fitzgerald, Brian, Croteau, II. "complaint" from Croteau, C., Affidavit. "Joe." from Shea, "Lavigne Faced with Abuse Suit: Brother of Croteau Charges Molestation," *Republican*, December 9, 1993. "again" from Tessier.

54. "polygraph" from Shea, "Test Clears Priest in '72 Death, Lawyer Says," *Republican*, December 18, 1991.

55. "measurement": Notes here from National Research Council of the National Academies, *The Polygraph and Lie Detection: Committee to Review the Scientific Evidence on the Polygraph*, Washington, D.C., The National Academies Press, 2003.

56. "Ryan" from Shea, "Test Clears."

57. "truthfulness" from letter, John E. Reid and Associates, Chicago, Illinois, to William C. Flanagan, Springfield, Massachusetts, May 15,1972. "homosexual" from Shea, "Friends, Foes" and Shea, "Test Clears." "Technique" from Company History, John E. Reid & Associates, reid.com. "disturbances" from Reid, May 15, 1972, summarized in Zajac, "Croteau Papers."

58. "sheet" from Croteau, C., Affidavit. "told" from Zajac, "Altar Boy's Father Tells of Offers," *Republican*, January 11, 2004.

59. "trip" from Zajac, "Altar Boy's Father." "$700" from Shea, "Croteau Told." "sister" from Croteau, C., Affidavit, and Zajac, "Family of Late Bishop Responds," *Republican*, January 18, 2004. "money" from Shea, "Croteau Told."

60. "Egan" from Croteau, C., Affidavit. "wanted" from Zajac, "Altar Boy's Father." "know" from Croteau, C., Affidavit.

61. "saying" from Maharaj, III. "tornado" from Cullen, "Danny's Story."

62. "squeal" from Maharaj, II. "unusual" from Daly, Warrant.

63. "withheld" from Croteau, C. "ballistic" from Fitzgerald, Brian, Croteau, III.

64. "evidence" from Shea and Goonan, "Diocese Denies." "Bosch" from Zajac, "Croteau Papers."

65. "upset" from Zajac, "Croteau Papers."

"nail" from Croteau, B. and Croteau, C., Affidavit. "inactive" from Commonwealth, In re Richard Lavigne, Petitioner, Petitioner's Memorandum of Law in Support of His Motion for Return of His Blood Sample.

Chapter 4

1. "exploration" from Pfieffer, Sascha, "Geoghan Preferred Preying on Poorer Children, to Therapist, Priest Cited Sexual Revolution," *Boston Globe*, January 7, 2002. "2010" from Terry, Karen J., Smith, Margaret Leland, Schutt, Katarina, O.S.F., Kelly, James R., Vollman, Brenda, and Massey, Christina, *The Causes and Context of Sexual Abuse of Minors by Catholic Priests in the United States: A Report Presented to the Unites States Conference of Catholic Bishops by the John Jay College Research Team*, John Jay College of Criminal Justice, the City University of New York, United States Conference of Catholic Bishops, Washington, D.C., February 2011.

2. "allegations" from Reese, Thomas J., "Facts, Myths, and Questions," *America: The National Catholic Review*, March 22, 2004.

3. "indifference" from Allen, John L., Jr., "Fr. Tom Doyle on 'Crimen Sollicitationis," *National Catholic Reporter*, October 13, 2006.

4. "Egyptian," etc., from Podles, Leon J., *Sacrilege: Sexual Abuse in the Catholic Church*, Baltimore, Maryland, Crossland Press, 2008, 17–18. "schools" from Podles, 19.

5. 7. "deposed" from Peters, Edward, trans., *The 1917 or Pio-Benedictine Code of Canon Law: An English Translation with Extensive Scholarly Apparatus*, San Francisco, Ignatius Press, 2001. "confidential" from *Instruction on the Manner of Proceeding in Cases of Solicitation*, Vatican Press, 1922. "versions" from Allen, John L., Jr., "Fr. Tom Doyle on 'Crimen Sollicitationis," *National Catholic Reporter*, October 13, 2006.

6. "repository" from Deposition of Fr. Daniel Liston, *John Doe v. Richard R. Lavigne, et al.*, CA# 02385, April 9, 2003, transcript 43–49. "patterns" from Ederly. "Manchester, New Hampshire" from Hansberry, Thomas S., Internal Memorandum, "Osgood," Fr. Donald Osgood Files, March 3, 1965.

7. "superior" from Affidavit of Father Thomas Doyle, August 12, 2003. "oath" from Attestation, Fr. Maurice J. Dingman and Ralph A. Hayes, Bishop of Davenport (Iowa), October 3, 1938.

8. "position" from DeMontigny. "Crucify" from *Paul R. Babeu v. Richard R. Lavigne, Joseph F. Maguire, Robert W. Thrasher, Thomas L. Dupré, and Roman Catholic Springfield Diocese, a Corporation Sole*. "narcotic" from Wilson, Charles M., and Dunnigan, R. Michael, "The Narcotic of Secrecy: Canon Lawyer Charles Wilson on the Bishops," May 1, 2002, christifidelis.com.

9. "vacate" and "Laws" from Connolly, Fr. James L., Bishop of Fall River, to Paquette, Fr. Edward O., January 18, 1963. "quickly" from springfielddiocese.blogspot.com/2009/04/chapter-eleven-five-bishops.

10. "blow" from Diocese of Manchester, New Hampshire, Internal Memorandum, R.E.M., Fr. Donald Osgood File, undated. "leave" from Hansberry, Thomas S., "Report of Conferences with D.M. Osgood," January 29, 1968. "obstructionism," "public," and "coerce" from Doyle, August 12, 2003. "immunity" from Berry, Jason, *Lead Us Not Into Temptation: Catholic Priests and the Sexual Abuse of Children*, New York, Doubleday, 1992, 290, from Wilson, Charles M.

11. "advancement": Notes here from letter, Fr. Joseph P. Gausch to Fr. Charles L.G. Knapp, May 25, 1948.

12. "cure" from "Timeline of a Crisis," *National Catholic Reporter*, July 3–16, 2015. "Degollado": Details here from "Legionaries of Christ Denounce Founder, Marcial Maciel Degollado," *New York Times*, February 6, 2014, and Berry, Jason, "Father Marcial Maciel and the Popes He Stained," *Newsweek*, March 11, 2013.

13. "stonewalled" from Allen, John, "Will Ratzinger's Past Trump Benedict's Present?" *National Catholic Reporter*, March 17, 2010. "repented" from Lawrence, Fr. Robert, to Ratzinger, Fr. Joseph, January 12, 1998. "grave" from Pope John Paul II, *Sacramentorum sanctitatis tutela*, April 30, 2001. "footnoted" from Shaw, Kathleen A., "Vatican Papers Spark Debate," *Worcester Telegram & Gazette*, August 28, 2005.

14. "pure" from Grand Jury, No. 03–00–239. "seek" from *Ibid.*

15. "distance" from Doyle, August 12, 2003. "concern" from Convey, Eric, "California Parish Rips Hub's Silence on Priest's Past," *Boston Herald*, April 9, 2002. "informed"

from Wilson and Dunnigan. "problem" from Convey, "California Parish."

16. "shop" from Primeau, Fr. Ernest J., Bishop of Manchester, Internal Memorandum, "Memo from Bishop Primeau to Msgr. Hansberry," undated. "recommendations" from Primeau, Fr. Ernest J., Bishop of Manchester, to Gilbert, Fr. Leo P., January 11, 1967.

17. "years" from Carless, William, "South America Has Become a Safe Haven for the Catholic Church's Alleged Child Molesters. The Vatican Has No Comment," from pri.4org. "that country" from Nadeau, Barbie Latza, "Torture the Little Children? The Catholic Church Says It's Not Responsible," May 6, 2014, dailybeast.com.

18. "barred" from Careful Selection and Training of Candidates for the States of Perfection and Sacred Orders, Congregation for Religious, February 2, 1961, and Doyle, Thomas P., Sipe, A.W.R., and Wall, Patrick J., Sex, Priests and Secret Codes: The Catholic Church's 2000-Year Paper Trail of Sexual Abuse, Los Angeles, Volt Press, 2005. "allergy" from Diocese of Manchester, New Hampshire to Brown, S. George, M.D., March 23, 1964.

19. "unsettling" from letter, Fr. Gerald Fitzgerald, Servant General, Order of the Paraclete, Jemez Springs, New Mexico, to Fr. Matthew F. Brady, Bishop of Manchester, September 26, 1957. "fault," etc., from Marshall, John A., Bishop of Springfield, to all parishes, December 12, 1992.

20. "trouble" from Report of the Grand Jury, No. 03–00–239, Re: Joseph P. Gausch, September 17, 2003, Lynne Abraham, District Attorney, 119. "fault" from Nicastro. "psychiatrist" from Berry, I.

21. "seduced" from Ederly. "genitals" from Grand Jury, No. 03–00–239. "foreplay" from Spencer, Buffy, "Andrew Nicastro Testifies That Sexual Abuse by Former Priest Alfred Graves Made Him Angry, Emotionally Distant," Republican, July 25, 2012.

22. "fallout" from The Report of the Archdiocesan Commission of Enquiry into the Sexual Abuse of Children by Members of the Clergy, Archdiocese of St. Johns, 1990.

23. "covered": Notes here from Berry, I. "entered" from Moore, Evan, "Judge's Intervention for Pedophile Raising Questions: Ex-Priest Benefits from Free Legal Help, Special Treatment in Prison," Houston Chronicle, November 1, 1998.

24. "expression" from Berry, I. "believe" from Moore, "Judge's Intervention."

25. "career" from Berry, Jason, Lead Us Not Into Temptation: Catholic Priests and the Sexual Abuse of Children, Urbana, University of Illinois Press, 2000, 40. "Affirmation": The House of Affirmation was run by the Rev. Thomas Kane, who falsely claimed to have a doctorate in psychology, plundered millions in donations to purchase real estate, and was himself accused of abuse at the facility and participating in an abuse ring with a group of Massachusetts priests including the notorious John Geoghan. "confess": Notes here from Berry, I. "activities" from New Orleans Times-Picayune/States, October 20, 1985.

26. "prison": Gauthé spent nine years in prison but due to connection to a federal judge did not serve hard time and molested dozens of young inmates. Released in 1995, he pled in 1996 no contest to a charge of molesting a three-year-old and was sentenced to seven years' probation. He spent 1997–1999 in the Lafayette Parish Jail awaiting trial on a 20-year-old rape charge that was dropped. He spent 2008–2001 in a Texas jail for failing to register as a sex offender. At the time of this writing, he was living in the fishing community of San Leon, Texas. "young": In 1997, Kos' victims were awarded $120,000,000. "favors" from Podles, 211.

27. "Palace" from Rose, Michael S., Goodbye! Good Men: How Catholic Seminaries Turned Away Two Generations of Vocations, Los Angeles, California, Hope of St. Monica, 2002, 146.

28. "pool" from Delgado, Luz, "Two Defend Coverage of Ex-priest," Boston Globe, May 25, 1992. "baseball" from Fitzpatrick, Frank L., Isolation and Silence: A Male Survivor Speaks Out About Clergy Abuse from movingforward.org, from Podles. "dinner" from Ellement, John, "Victims Oppose Release of Porter," Boston Globe, April 6, 2004. "Twins" from Matchan, Linda, "Ex-priest Accused in Minnesota," Boston Globe, July 14, 1992.

29. "walked" from Kong, Dolores, "6 More Allege Priest Abused Them in the 60's," Boston Globe, May 9, 1992. "upstairs" from Bass, Allison, "30 More Allege Sex Abuse in 1960's by Priest," Boston Globe, May 12, 1992. Annunziato later claimed he heard about the allegations "after the fact." He died in 1993.

"during" from Matchan, "Ex-priest Accused." "release" from Podles, 122.

30. "God" from Podles, 123. *"Globe"* from Marantz, Steve, "Law Raps Ex-priest Coverage," *Boston Globe*, May 24, 1992.

Chapter 5

1. "drunk" from Statement of Witness, December 9, 1991, Lavigne, September 29, 1993. "communion" from Shea, "Lavigne Pleads Guilty: Supporters Surprised by Plea," *Republican*, June 26, 1992. "consciousness" from Blixt and Greig, "Priest Linked." "wonders" from Shea, "Friends, Foes."

2. "artist" from Statement, November 15, 1991, Lavigne, September 29, 1993.

3. "retirement" from Claffey, Kevin, "Bishop Maguire to Step Down: Marshall Will Lead Diocese," *Republican*, December 28, 1991. "vitriolic" from Shea, "Friends, Foes." "negative" from Simison, "'72 Murder Case." "fled" from letter, Mr. & Mrs. Rene Crete to Joseph F. Maguire, Bishop of Springfield, June 28, 1988.

4. "Bible" from Shea, "Father Forgives Priest: Sect Leader Raps Diocese," *Republican*, June 28, 1992. "1983" from Shea, "Lay Group's Founder Seeks Understanding: Lavigne Case Ends Years of Turmoil," *Republican*, July 22, 1992. "Apostolate" from Shea, "Father Forgives." "betrayal" from Shea, "Lay Group's Founder."

5. "$30,000" from "Test Clears." "feuds" from letter re The Shattuck Group in Heath, Massachusetts, Fr. Richard Lavigne to Bishop John F. Maguire, Bishop, Springfield Diocese, April 3, 1991. "Jones" from Shea, "Lay Group's Founder."

6. "thanked" from Shea, "Father Forgives." "income" from Ibid. "maligned" from letter, Fr. Richard R. Lavigne to Fr. Joseph F. Maguire, Bishop, Springfield Diocese, May 15, 1987.

7. "ceased" from Shea, "Father Forgives." "enough" from Shea, "Test Clears." "from us" from Lavigne, April 3, 1991. "blow" from Lavigne, April 3, 1991.

8. "unnamed" from Simison, "'72 Murder Case." "bigot" from Police Report, October 18, 1991, from *Commonwealth v. Richard R. Lavigne*, no. 92 031, February 14, 1992, 204, and Statement of Officer, October 14, 1991, from Daly, Warrant. "lawyer" from Statement of Officer, October 14, 1991, Daly, Warrant.

"$10,000" from Sullivan, Jack, "Catholic Pastor in Shelburne Falls Charged with Assaults on 2 Boys," *Boston Globe*, October 21, 1991. "offered" from Simison, "'72 Murder Case."

9. "mentor" from Loven, Charles, "Accusation Against Priest Upsets St. Joseph's Parish," *Republican*, October 21, 1991. "mind" from Simison, "'72 Murder Case." "beautiful" from Loven, "Accusation."

10. "President" from Blixt and Greig, "Priest Linked." "disaster" from "Priest Due in Court on Rape Counts," *Republican*, October 20, 1991. "good" from Heaney, Joe, "Report Says Priest Indicted for Child Rape," *Boston Herald*, February 20, 1992. "killer" from Loven, "Accusation." "conspiracy" from Shea, "Friends, Foes."

11. "Stations" from Shea, "No One Comes Between Croteaus and Their God," *Republican*, April 14, 2002.

12. "25" from Sullivan, "Priest Reportedly." "difficult" from Simison, "'72 Murder Case." "themes" from Downing, Jack to EJF.

13. "Maguire" from Statement, Bishop John F., Maguire, Bishop, Springfield Diocese, October 27, 1991, and Loven, Charles, "A 'Healing Prayer' Said for St. Joseph's," *Republican*, October 28, 1991.

14. "IOL" from Shea, "Lavigne Retains Top-Gun Lawyer," *Republican*, November 8, 1991. "apprehensive" from Simison, "'72 Murder Case." "wounded" from Shea, "Friends, Foes."

15. "prime" from WGGB-TV (Ch. 40), Springfield, October 21, 1991, and Blixt and Greig, "Priest Linked." "absence" from Sullivan, Jack, "Priest Reportedly." "convict" from Sullivan, "Priest Reportedly," and Ryan, Matthew to EJF, III. "prosecuted" from Simison, "'72 Murder Case."

16. "boxing," etc., from Sullivan, "Priest Reportedly." "Kennedy" from Barry, Stephanie and McCauliffe, Michael, "Matthew Ryan, Jr., Former Hamden County District Attorney, Dead at 92," *Republican*, August 24, 2009.

17. "camps" from Brault, Michael, "Matty Ryan Cast a Long Shadow," *Republican*, August 26, 2009. "buckled" from Barry and McCauliffe, "Matthew Ryan, Jr." "Mafia": Notes here from Barry, Stephanie, "Organized Crime in Springfield Evolved Through Death and Money," *Republican*, December 11, 2011, updated April 25, 2013. "Skiball" from "DA Accused of Being Soft on Mob," Associated

Press, June 3, 1981. "Bruno" from Brault, "Matty Ryan." "return" from DF to EJF. "Wops" from Fitzgerald, Joseph to EJF.

18. "good" from Shea and Goonan, "Diocese Denies."

19. "targeted" from Garvey, "Bishop's Investigation." "discussed" from Crean.

20. "masturbate" from Downing. "listen" from Downing, and O'Brien, D.

21. "comment" from Springfield Diocese, Statement of the Rev. Joseph Maguire, Bishop of Springfield, October 25, 1991, "Bishop's Statement," *Republican*, October 26, 1991, and Shea, "Bishop Cites Aid, Support for Priest-Maguire Orders Silence on '72 Slaying," *Republican*, October 26, 1991.

22. "judicial" from Shea, "Bishop Cites Aid."

23. "games" from Greig, June, "Old Charge Surfaces Against Priest," *Republican*, October 27, 1991.

24. "fondled" from Statement of Witness, November 5, 1991, Lavigne, September 29, 1993, 216–17, and Zajac, "Autopsy Revealed Alcohol, but No Sign of Sexual Abuse," *Republican*, July 28, 2004. "parents" from Zajac, "Autopsy Revealed." "undesirable" from City of Chicopee, Termination Notice, August 4, 1958, Richard Lavigne, and Lavigne, Termination, summarized in Lavigne, September 29, 1993, 216–17. "looking" from Lavigne, August 4, 1958, and Greig, "Old Charge."

25. "platform" from letter, Glynn, Eleanor, "Stories Show 'Anti-Catholicism," *Republican*, November 7, 1991. "lynched" from letter, Caron, Carol A., "We All Live in Glass Houses," *Republican*, November 15, 1991. "garbage" from letter, Sexton, John W., in McDermott, Larry, "Coverage of Church Crisis Draws Strong Response," *Republican*, April 7, 2002.

26. "answering" from Shea, "Parents Dream." "forgotten" from Blixt and Greig, "Priest Linked." "pray" from Mallia, Joseph, "I Just Want This Resolved: Slain Boy's Parents Seek the Truth," *Boston Herald*, November 8, 1993. "between" from Shea, "Parents Dream."

27. "cousin" from Kelly and Shea, "Lavigne Faces." "father's" from statements of witnesses, Commonwealth, no. 92 031, 206–16. "eighteen" from Lavigne, September 29, 1993, 8. "families" from name redacted to Mark Dupont, Springfield Diocese, April 29, 2002. "concerned" from Statement of Paul

Babeu, originally Statement of Witness, Anonymous, to Massachusetts State Police Barracks, Northampton, October 25, 1991, from Lavigne, September 29, 1993, and *Commonwealth v. Richard R. Lavigne*, Indictment Nos. 92–028 through 92–032, Change of Plea, June 25, 1992, and *Commonwealth v. Richard R. Lavigne*, No. 93–080, October 5, 1994, and Lavigne, September 29, 1993, 8–9, 195–96.

28. "refused" from Zajac and Goldberg, Marla A., "Unsealed Records Shed Light on Lavigne," *Republican*, November 3, 2002. "Springfield's" from Harrington Affidavit and Affidavit of First Assistant District Attorney David A. Angier and Assistant District Attorney Ariana D. Vuono, *Commonwealth v. Richard R. Lavigne*, Indictment No. 93–080. "1991" from *Commonwealth v. Richard R. Lavigne*, No. 03–080, 4, and Harrington Affidavit. "Disneyland" from Croteau, C., Affidavit.

29. "strategist" from Shea, "Lavigne Retains." "representative" from Shea, "Test Clears." "wasn't" from Shea, "Test Clears." "denied" from Sweet, William, "Parishioners Express Surprise at Bishop Maguire's Retirement," *Republican*, December 29, 1991.

30. "blue" from "Events in Lavigne Case," *Republican*, June 26, 1992. "tag" from Shea, "Lavigne Backer." "Friend" from Shea, "Lavigne Establishes Legal Defense Fund," *Republican*, January 12, 1992.

31. "visitors" from Shea, "Lavigne Backer." "belong" from Shea, "Lavigne Sex Abuse Trial to Open Today: Case Moved to Coastal Town," *Republican*, June 22, 1992. "trouble" from Shea, "Lavigne Backer."

Chapter 6

1. "J.S." from Transcripts, Commonwealth, Grand Jury, Franklin County, February 14, 1992.

2. "fourteen": Charges from *Commonwealth v. Richard R. Lavigne*, Indictments no. 92–028, no. 92–029, no. 92–030, no. 92–031, no. 92–032, all dated February 14, 1992.

3. "sentences" from Bourie, Richard, "Lavigne Denies New Charges of Assault," *Republican*, February 26, 1992. "far-away" from Zajac and Goldberg, "Unsealed Records."

4. "Parenthood" from Claffey, "Bishop Maguire."

5. "vindicated" from "Events in Lavigne

Case," *Republican*, June 26, 1992. "witch": Stern comments from Bourie, "Lavigne Denies."

6. "brothers": J.S. recollections from Statement of J. Shattuck, October 1991, from Lavigne, no. 92 032.

7. "McCarthy" from Zajac and Goldberg, "Unsealed Records." "squeeze" from Shattuck, October 1991, in Daly, Warrant.

8. "touching" from Shattuck, Daly, and Zajac, "4 New Suits Filed Against Lavigne," *Republican*, July 12, 2002.

9. "footsteps" from Shattuck, Daly. "appointments" from Statement of Witness, October 14, 1991, Lavigne, September 29, 1993. "buy" from *Ibid.* "trips" from Zajac and Goldberg, "Unsealed Records."

10. "threatened" from Shea, "Knife Threats Alleged," *Republican*, February 20, 1993, and from Statement of Witness, Lavigne, September 29, 1993, 134.

11. "shaking" from Statement of J. Shattuck's Sister, October 11, 1991, Lavigne, September 29, 1993, 201.

12. "single" from *Commonwealth v. Richard Lavigne*, Motion to Leave to File Memorandum as Amici Curiae on Behalf of Michael J. Slowinski, Bea Cevasco, Peter Dolan, Margaret J. Carlson, and 487 Other Named Individuals, April 20, 1992. "others" from Fosher, William, "Petition Seeks 5 Separate Trials: Supporters of Lavigne File Brief," *Republican*, April 22, 1992. "choir" et al. from Amici.

13. "Yankee" et al. from Commonwealth Motion, April 20, 1992.

14. "two" from Shea, "Friends, Foes."

15. "Newburyport" from Shea, "Lavigne Sex Abuse Trial."

16. "Ashfield" from *Commonwealth v. Richard R. Lavigne*, Indictments Nos. 92–028 through 92–032, Change of Plea, June 25, 1992, 10. "two" from Melley, Brian, "Priest Breaks Silence: Lavigne Faces Potential Jurors," *Republican*, June 23, 1992. "ramrod" from Melley, Brian, "Lavigne Trial to Begin Today," *Republican*, June 25, 1992. "face" from Melley, "Priest Breaks Silence."

17. "knocking" from Shea, "Lavigne Pleads Guilty."

18. "facility" from Commonwealth, 92–028–92–032, Change of Plea, June 25, 1992, 17–25. "worth" from Stern comments, Commonwealth, 92–028–92–032, 24–27. "trip" from Shea, "Lavigne Pleads Guilty."

19. "destroyed": Unless noted, Volterra comments from Commonwealth, 92–028–92–032, 28–34. "overblown" from McDermott, Larry, "Flogging Messenger Time," *Republican*, July 5, 1992.

20. "abusing" from Melley, "Father Lavigne Pleads Guilty." "draconian," etc., from Commonwealth, 92–028–92–032, Change of Plea, June 25, 1992, 34. "Fee" from *Commonwealth vs. Richard R. Lavigne*, Motion to Consider Modification of the Conditions of Probation, November 19, 1993. "10 years" from Commonwealth, 92–028–92–032, Change of Plea, June 25, 1992, 12.

21. "over" from Melley, "Father Lavigne Pleads Guilty." "behind" from Melley, Ibid.

22. "surprised" from Shea, "Lavigne Pleads Guilty." "ride" and "club" from Shea, "Lavigne Pleads Guilty."

23. "L.A." from Shea, "Families to Speak Out on Lavigne Plea," *Republican*, June 27, 1992. "admitted" from Melley, "Father Lavigne Pleads Guilty."

24. "trusting" from Fitzgerald, Brian, Croteau, IV.

25. "Christian" from Shea, "Diocese Foots Part of Bill for Lavigne," *Republican*, July 2, 1992. "troubled" from Springfield Diocese Press Release: Statement of John A. Marshall, Bishop, Springfield Diocese, June 26, 1992, and Melley, "Father Lavigne Pleads Guilty."

26. "12596" from Authorization to Obtain Records, Richard R. Lavigne, St. Luke's Institute, Inc., December 9, 1993. "Private": Details here from Moriarty, Jo-ann, "Where Abusing Priests Go," *Republican*, March 4, 2004. "dietary" from Moriarty, Jo-ann, "Lavigne Bound for Monitoring, Therapy, at Facility for Religious," *Republican*, June 26, 1992.

27. "aftercare" Frank E. Siano, Chief Probation Officer, Commonwealth to Francis X. Spina, Associate Justice, Berkshire Superior Court, Re: Richard Lavigne, FCS# 92–030 & 92–028, December 13, 1993. "cured" from Moriarty, "Lavigne Bound."

28. "camping" from Shea, "Lavigne Backer." "persecution" etc., from Barry, "Priest's Letters."

29. "same" from Barry, "Priest's Letter."

30. "certainty" from Dupré, Fr. Thomas L., Bishop of Springfield, to Liston, Rev. Daniel, September 16, 1992.

31. "violations" from Turner, Ford, "Marshall Criticizes Media Focus," *Republican*, December 15, 1992.

32. "recall" from Shea, "Bishop Cited Aid."
33. "Phonies" from Ryan, John B., Springfield, to *Republican*, February 8, 1993.
34. "100" from News broadcast, WBZ-TV (Ch. 4), Boston, Massachusetts, May 7, 1992. "New Mexico to Texas" from Matchan, Linda, "Town Secret," *Boston Globe*, August 29, 1993. "18" from Franklin, James L., "Porter's Plea Aids Victims Little, Church Paper Says," *Boston Globe*, October 8, 1993. Before Porter was released in 2004, the state moved to have him classified sexually dangerous and incarcerated indefinitely. He died in prison from cancer on February 11, 2005.
35. "intent" from Matchan, Linda, "Two Sides Spar on Clergy Abuse," *Boston Globe*, October 11, 1992. "exception" from Longscope, Kay, "Sexual Abuse by Priests Is a 'Betrayal,' 'Rare,' Law Says," *Boston Globe*, April 14, 1992.

Chapter 7

1. "co-chancellor" from Affidavit of Thomas L. Dupré, Bishop of Springfield, April 30, 2003. "destruction" from Zajac, "Suit: Dupre Said Files Destroyed," *Republican*, August 3, 2004 and Mason. "relieved" from *John Doe v. Roman Catholic Springfield Diocese*, July 29, 2004, and Zajac, "Suit." "guys" from Zajac, "For Dupre, the Pressure Was Too Much," *Republican*, March 28, 2004, and Zajac, "Files Destroyed."
2. "destroyed" from Deposition of Fr. James J. Scahill, Susan F. Morris v. Richard Lavigne, Joseph Maguire, Robert Thrasher and Roman Catholic Springfield Diocese, No. 03–241. "advise" and "glee" from Zajac, "Suit." "vaguely" from Statement of Dupré, Thomas L., Bishop, "The Diocese Will Seek Fair and Just Settlements of Abuse Cases," September 29, 2003.
3. "lied" from Zajac, "Affidavit Contradicts Church on Abuse," *Republican*, September 8, 2003. "Fr. Richard Meehan" from Cullen, "Prelate's Alleged Victim to Aid Probe: Will Help Prosecutors Investigating Dupre," *Boston Globe*, February 26, 2004.
4. "imprudent": Notes re letter from T.L.D. to Maguire, Thomas, Bishop of Springfield, July 14, 1987. "ends" from Dupré, Fr. Thomas, to Fr. Lavigne, Richard, July 11, 1988.
5. "St. Catherine's" from Kelly and Shea, "Lavigne Faecs." "confidante" from Zajac, "Lavigne Abuse Ignored by Church," *Repub-*

lican, September 29, 2003." "after" from Shea, "Lab Tests."
6. "grave" and "whispers" from Ibid.
7. "way" from Shea, "Marshall Bans Lavigne from Priest Duties," *Republican*, March 20, 1993. "repair" from "Text of Bishop's Letter on Priest," *Republican*, March 21, 1993.
8. "Gregory" from Shea, "2 More Men Claim Abuse by Lavigne," *Republican*, April 15, 1993. "harm" from Shea, "Croteau Told." "Carl" from Shea, "Croteau: Church Officials Knew Lavigne Was Suspect," *Republican*, March 25, 1993. "two" from Shea, "2 More Men." "believe" from Shea, "Marshall Bans," and Shea, "Alleged Sexual Abuse Takes Toll 26 Years Later," *Republican*, February 15, 1993.
9. "key" from Sullivan, October 24, 1991. "mistakes" from Zajac, "Croteau Papers." "forensics" from Sullivan, October 24, 1991
10. "portion" from Melley, Brian, "Lavigne Papers Released: Little Revealed in Documents," *Republican*, October 22, 1993. "inconclusive" from Melley, Brian, "Fate of Lavigne Rests with Expert: Slaying Case Hinges on DNA Test," *Republican*, January 15, 1995.
11. "warrant" from Trial Court of Massachusetts, Massachusetts Superior Court, Hampden Division, John H. Moriarty, September 2, 1993. "gallon" from Shea and Melley, Brian, "Court to Rule on Lavigne Blood Test: State Seeks Evidence in Altar Boy's Death," *Republican*, September 10, 1993.
12. "indicted" from Shea, "New Charge of Rape Leveled at Lavigne," *Republican*, November 16, 1993, and Shea, "Lavigne Faces New Rape Count," *Republican*, December 2, 1993. "1985" from Shea, "Lavigne Denies Child Rape Count," *Republican*, December 4, 1993. "Limitations" from Melley, Brian, "Judge Dismisses Last Lavigne Count," *Republican*, December 16, 1993, and Melley, Brian, "Croteau Suit Loses 2 Assault Charges," *Republican*, July 1, 1994.
13. "stone-faced" from Shea, "Abuse Victims Visit Bishop Marshall," *Republican*, February 11, 1994.
14. "$50,000" from Shea, "Sex Abuse Charge Settled by Priest," *Republican*, May 10, 1994. "torture" from Shea, "Family Hoping for Lavigne Link Answers," *Republican*, October 14, 1994.
15. "indict" from Melley, Brian, "Lavigne Agrees to DNA Test: Priest Offers Blood in Slaying Probe," *Republican*, November 23, 1994.

16. "order" from Melley, Brian, "Blood Tests Fail to Clear Lavigne: Sources; DA Has Results, But Has Not Dropped Case," *Republican*, June 13, 1995. "fear" from Melley, "Lavigne Agrees." "suspect" from Mallia, "I Just Want."

17. "Liberty," etc., from "Faneuil Hall Marketplace: History," faneuilhallmarketplace.com. "banners," etc., from Melley, Brian, "Lavigne's New Calling Found at Faneuil Hall," *Republican*, December 28, 1994.

18. "Chapel" from Melley, Brian, "Lavigne Aids Chapel Work Site," *Republican*, July 9, 1995.

19. "eliminate," etc., from Melley, "Fate of Lavigne." "moderately" from Melley, "Blood Tests." "lots" from Shea, "Probe of Altar Boy's Slaying Closed," *Republican*, October 26, 1995.

20. "accurate" from Melley, "Blood Tests." "prayed" from Melley, "Court to Rule."

21. "match" from Sullivan, Jack, "DA Drops Effort to Link Priest to Boy's Slaying: Blood Test Proved to Be Inconclusive," *Boston Globe*, October 26, 1995. "characteristics" from Shea, "Probe." "Lavigne was at the scene" from Melley, "Lavigne Papers Released." "conviction" from Zajac, "DNA Tests Underway in Croteau Case," *Republican*, March 23, 2003.

22. "uncertainty" from Shea, "Probe." "solved" from Ibid.

23. "Bishop" from Dupré, April 30, 2003. "staged" from Zajac and Mason. "assignments" from Cullen, "Priest Cites Cost of Speaking Out: Tells of Springfield Diocese Reprimand," *Boston Globe*, March 23, 2002.

24. "surprising" from Melley, Brian, "Lavigne Data in Question: Opposing Attorneys Unite to Keep Probe Reports Secret," *Republican*, January 23, 1996. "stopped" from Melley, Brian, "Gag Fought in Probe of Lavigne," *Republican*, February 28, 1996. "only" from Daly, Warrant, and Melley, "Lavigne's Words." "censored" from Melley, Brian, "Papers Outline Officials' Case Against Lavigne," *Republican*, March 28, 1996.

25. "scene" from Melley, "Lavigne's Words."

26. "testify" from Claffey, Kevin, "Lavigne Settles Suit, Avoids Trial," *Republican*, September 17, 1996. "2000" from "Obituary, Lavigne, Ovila R.," *Republican*, December 15, 2000.

27. "1929" from Zajac, "He Remembers,

Tries to Forgive," *Republican*, September 14, 2003.

28. "returned" from Cullen, "Priest Cites." "terminally" from Cullen, "Springfield Diocese Denies Retaliation Claim," *Boston Globe*, March 25, 2002. "forced" from Hamel, Chris, "Bishop Calls Punishment Claim False," *Republican*, March 24, 2002. "disgrace" from Cullen, "Priest Cites." "protect" from Ibid.

29. "anniversary" from Shea, "Mother Waits for Clue to Solve Son's Murder," *Republican*, April 15, 1997.

30. "playbook" from springfielddiocese.blogspot.com/2009/04/chapter-ten-confidentiality-concerns.

31. "relatively" from Cullen, "Priest Cites." "relatively" from Dupré, September 29, 2003. "trained" from MacQuarrie, Brian, "Bishop Places Priest on Leave: Springfield Prelate Acts in Abuse Probe," *Boston Globe*, April 16, 2004.

"forty" from Zajac, "Diocese Panel Handling More Sex Complaints," *Republican*, November 8, 2002.

32. "Vidnansky" details from Barry, Stephanie, "Ex-Nun Names in Sex-Abuse Suit," *Republican*, December 30, 2004. "five" from "Five Priests Barred from Parish Work," *Associated Press*, carried in the *Daily Hampshire Gazette*, July 31, 2002.

33. "decades" from Finer, Jonathan, "Mass. Bishop Charged with Rape: No Trial Planned," *Washington Post*, September 28, 2004.

34. "weighty" from Paulson, Michael, "Resignation Has Not Ended Law's Role in Church," *Boston Globe*, June 21, 2003. "glowing" from Kurkjian, Stephen, "Law Recommended Fired Dean for College Teaching Position," *Boston Globe*, May 15, 2002. "seventy" from Robinson, Walter V., "Scores of Priests Involved in Sex Abuse Cases," *Boston Globe*, January 31, 2002. "Paquin" from Kurkjian, Stephen, "Records Show Cardinal Law Reassigned Paquin After Settlements," *Boston Globe*, May 30, 2002. "150" from Rezendes, Michael, "Church Allowed Abuse by Priest for Years," *Boston Globe*, January 6, 2002. "stomped" from Farragher, Thomas, "In Death, Geoghan Triggers Another Crisis," *Boston Globe*, November 30, 2003, and Butterfield, Fox, "Long Planning Is Cited in Death of Farmer Priest," *New York Times*, August 26, 2003.

35. "serial" from Cullen, and Rezendes, Michael, "A Grand Jury Is Said to Weigh Case

Against Law: Grand Jury Mulls Charles Vs. Law," *Boston Globe*, June 19, 2002. "finalize" from Sennott, Charles M., "Rare Speed Displayed by Rome," *Boston Globe*, December 14, 2002.
    36. "Satan's" from Mason, "Diocese in Denial," from religiousnewsonline, provided by Mason.
    37. "failed" from Zajac, "Catholic Appeal Falls Short," *Republican*, June 1, 2002.
    38. "vindications": Dupré musings here from letter, Thomas L. Dupré, Bishop of Springfield to EJF, September 2, 2002.
    39. "ended" from Zajac, and Goldberg, Marla A., "Probation Over for Lavigne," *Republican*, June 29, 2002. "targeted" from Zajac, "Priest's Probation Ends Amid New Scandals," *Republican*, June 16, 2002.
    40. "documents" from Zajac and Goldberg, "Unsealed Records." "named" from Zajac, "Rev. Lavigne Faces 3 More Suits," *Republican*, September 24, 2002.

Chapter 8

    1. "dime" from Zajac and Mason.
    2. "nothing" from Finer, Jonathan, "Mass. Priest Urges Diocese's Reform," *Washington Post*, March 20, 2004. "threatened" from Zajac, "Priest, Bishop at Odds," *Republican*, October 29, 2003.
    3. "something" from Zajac and Mason.
    4. "sainthood" from Finer, March 20, 2004.
    5. "regrettable": Comments here from Finer, March 20, 2004.
    6. "wrong" from Mason, and Finer, March 20, 2004.
    7. "deep" from Finer, March 20, 2004. "staying" from CBS News, *60 Minutes*, "Murder Most Foul," May 2005. "anything" from Ederly. "unbalanced" from Zajac to EJF. "refused" from Mason. "problems" from Zajac, "Bishop Quits After Abuse Query: Dupre Abruptly Resigns," *Republican*, February 12, 2004.
    8. "daughter" from Germond.
    9. "scene" from Lavigne, September 29, 1993, Affidavit of Trooper Thomas J. Daly, October 18, 1993.
    10. "ill-perceived" from Affidavit of Lt. Edward E. Harrington, Massachusetts State Police Bureau of Investigative Services, Hampshire County CPAC, January 9, 1994.

    11. "copy": Bennett/Stevens relationship notes from Stevens.
    12. "never" from Barry, Stephanie, and Spencer, Buffy, "Judge: Open Altar Boy Murder File," *Republican*, January 13, 2006.
    13. "again" from Maharaj, VI.
    14. "threatened," from Zajac, "Priest, Bishop." "fifty" from Moriarty, Jo-ann, and Zajac, "Church Abuse Report Slated," *Republican*, November 12, 2003. "20" from Zajac, "Judge Combines Clergy Abuse Suits," *Republican*, December 20, 2003. "settling" from Zajac, "Diocese Considers Settling All Claims," *Republican*, October 15, 2003 "perspective" from Mellen, Kathleen, "Bishop Supports 'Just' Settlement in Abuse Cases," *Republican*, October 2, 2003.
    15. "intrinsically" from Zajac, "Diocese Says Constitution Protects It in Abuse Suit," *Republican*, April 19, 2003. "then-24" from Zajac, "Springfield Diocese Seeks Immunity," *Republican*, June 24, 2003. "immunity" from Zajac, "Judge Considers Ruling on Liability of Church," *Republican*, September 25, 2003.
    16. "Doherty" from Zajac, "Bishop Dupre Seeks to Testify Under Oath," *Republican*, September 19, 2003. "invited" from Zajac, "Bishop Never Comfortable in Spotlight," *Republican*, February 15, 2004. "oversimplification" from Cullen, "Ruined Files Spark Allegation," *Boston Globe*, September 17, 2003.
    17. "destruction" from Zajac, "Bishop, Priest Clash on Facts: Dupre Denies Saying Official Destroyed Sensitive Records," *Republican*, September 30, 2003. "never" from Pomerleau, Fr. Bill, "Bishop's Deposition Tops Two Weeks of Controversy," *The Catholic Observer*, October 5, 2003.
    18. "Hitler" from Zajac, "Priest, Bishop." "don't" from Mason, and Finer, Jonathan, "Priest Urges Diocese's Reform, *Washington Post*, March 20, 2004. "threaten" from Zajac, "Priest, Bishop."
    19. "ouster" from Zajac, "Protesters Want Bishop to Resign," *Republican*, December 9, 2003. "$85,000,000" from Zajac, "Diocese Considers." "indignation" from Moriarty and Zajac, "Church Abuse." "lanced" from Belkin, Douglas "Priest Castigates Springfield Diocese for Abuse Dealings," *Boston Globe*, February 17, 2003.
    20. "Check" from Zajac. "13" from Zajac, "Bishop Quits." "Precious" from Obituary,

Deshaises, Helen Teresa, *Republican*, October 10, 2011, and Zajac. "share" from Zajac.

21. "reasons" from Zajac, "Bishop Quits." "eighth-grader" from Cullen, "Bishop Resigns Following Claims: Springfield Prelate Had Faced Abuse Allegations," *Boston Globe*, February 12, 2004. "particularly" from Zajac, "Bishop Quits." "firefighter father" from Zajac.

22. "mention" from Mason. "unknown" from Cullen, "Prelate's Alleged Victim."

23. "Cote" from Zajac, "State Official Seeks Croteau Files," *Republican*, November 10, 2003. "rising public condemnation" from "Croteau File Ruling Victory for Disclosure," op-ed, *Republican*, November 10, 2003. "*Herald*" from Zajac, "Slaying Files," *Republican*, February 11, 2004. "Supreme" from Zajac, "Appeal Seeks to Unseal Files in Croteau Slaying," *Republican*, December 19, 2003, and Zajac, "Sealed," *Republican*, November 11, 2003.

24. "Satan's" from Mason, "Diocese in Denial," religiousnewsonline. "jeered" from Zajac, "A Question."

25. "translated" from Zajac, "Catholic Church Defrocks Lavigne," *Republican*, January 21, 2004. "indigent" and "removed" from Cullen, "Approval Given to Defrock Priest," *Boston Globe*, January 21, 2004.

26. "achieved" from Cullen, "Approval Given." "1986" from Zajac, "Family." "comfort" from Zajac, "Altar Boy's Father," and Zajac, "Family."

27. "prayed" from Cullen, "Approval Given." "$100,000" from Zajac, "Catholic Church Defrocks Lavigne." "felons" from Zajac, "Bishop Never Comfortable."

28. "forward" from Zajac. "friends" from Dewberry, Beatrice O'Quinn, "Dupre Accusers Tell Lurid Tale: Allege Ex-bishop Introduced Them to Gay Sex, Porn," *Republican*, February 20, 2004.

29. "telling" from Zajac.

30. "marriage" from Cullen, "Prelate's Alleged Victim." "vitriolic" from Zajac, "DA: 'Probable Cause': Bishop Allegations Go to Grand Jury," *Republican*, March 5, 2004. "infuriated" from Cullen, "Prelate's Alleged Victim."

31. "cognac" from Cullen, "Prelate's Alleged Victim." "sleeping" from Mason. "briefcase" and "together" from Dewberry, "Dupré Accusers."

32. "promiscuous" from Dewberry, "Dupré Accusers." "come" from Zajac, "Bishop Quits." "dating" from Dewberry, "Dupré Accusers." "sleeping" from Mason. "discuss" from Cullen, "Prelate's Alleged Victim," and Dewberry, "Dupré Accusers."

33. "scared" from Zajac. "dire" from Grossman, Cathy Lynn, "One Church Topples a Bishop," *USA Today*, March 11, 2004.

34. "history" from Mason. "questions" from Zajac, "For Dupré." "nothing": Timeline for the *Republican*/Dupré back and forth from Zajac, and Zajac, "For Dupré."

35. "votes" from Zajac, "For Dupré." "agitated" from Zajac, "For Dupré."

36. "nothing" from Zajac, "Bishop Quits."

37. "life-threatening" from Ibid. "issues" from Zajac. "letter" from Zajac, "Bishop Never Comfortable." "fair" from Zajac, "Bishop Quits."

38. "shocked" from Zajac.

39. "hours" from Cullen, "Bishop Resigns." "Lavigne" from Moriarty, "Where Abusing Priests Go."

40. "request" from Zajac, "For Dupré." "mind" from Zajac. "emeritus" from Zajac, "Ex-Bishop Case Shrouded in Mystery a Year Later," *Republican*, February 6, 2005. "honest" from Zajac, "Bishop Quits." "ashen-faced" from McAuliffe, Michael, "Wound Stings the Faithful: Dupre Abuse Allegation Is Mass Topic," *Republican*, February 15, 2004.

41. "network" from Zajac, "Bishop Never Comfortable." "minutes" from McAuliffe, "Wound Stings." "OK" from McElhenny, John, "Monsignor Says Harm of Abuse Wasn't Recognized," *Boston Globe*, February 23, 2004.

42. "sad" from McAuliffe, "Wound Stings." "some of the resistance" from Finer, "Priest Urges."

43. "lame" from "Diocese of Springfield," eurekaencyclopedia.com. "urgency" from Zajac, "A Time for Rebirth': Diocese Welcomes Bishop," *Republican*, March 10, 2004. "10,000" from Zajac, "Ex-priest's Home Raided by Police," *Republican*, April 9, 2004.

44. "investigators" from Zajac, "Alleged Victims Support DA in Bishop Probe," *Republican*, February 26, 2004. "photographs" from Zajac, "DA: Probable Cause." "cards" from Rosenwald, Michael S., and Cullen, "2nd Man Agrees to Aid Case Against Bishop," *Boston Globe*, February 27, 2004. "receipts" from Cullen, "Prelate's Alleged Vic-

tim." "charges" from Zajac, "DA: Probable Cause." "Statute" from Barry, Stephanie, "Charges Against Clergy Elusive," *Republican*, April 19, 2004.

45. "exorcism" from Zajac, "DA: Probable Cause." "fraction" from Cullen, "Diocese's Report on Sex Abuse Questioned," *Boston Globe*, February 21, 2004.

46. "humor" from Zajac, "A Time for Rebirth." "rebel" from Grossman, "One Church." "voices" from Mason. "single" from Cullen, "Alleged Victim's Lawyer to File Suit Against Dupre," *Boston Globe*, March 11, 2004. "word" from Ibid.

47. "lackey" from Zajac, "Rebel Priest, Bishop Clash," *Republican*, May 12, 2004. "damage" from Zajac, "Report of Remark Prompts Outrage," *Republican*, May 13, 2004, and "Springfield Bishop Apologizes for Remark: He Had Compared Critic, Pedophile," Associated Press, May 14, 2014.

48. "depended" from Zajac, "Ex-priest's Home."

49. "end" from Zajac, "Church Cuts Ties to Lavigne: Financial Aid to Ex-priest to End," *Republican,* May 28, 2004.

50. "$585,000" from "Priest Sex Abuse Settlement Reached: The Springfield, Mass., Diocese Will Pay 45 Alleged Victims More Than $7 Million," *Los Angeles Times*, August 6, 2004. "Western Massachusetts" from Zajac, "Sales New Diocese $2.7M: Priest Wants More Properties Sold," *Republican*, May 26, 2004.

51. "know" from Maharaj, I. "homosexual" from Statement of Witness, October 9, 1991, Lavigne, September 29, 1993, from Daly, Warrant. "forced" from Coleman, 100.

52. "suspect" from Fitzgerald, Brian, Croteau, J.

53. "bodybuilding" from Croteau, C., Affidavit. "chastised" from Cullen, "Danny's Story." "face" from Croteau, B, October 22, 2007. "confession" from Carl and Bernice.

54. "meet" from Maharaj, II. "three" from Daly, Warrant, 12. "uncle," etc., from Lavigne, September 29, 1993, 12, 134.

Chapter 9

1. "Chernobyl" from "As I Recall: Why I Wrote About the 8.5 Million Dollar Settlement," springfielddiocese.blogspot.com. "myself" from Shattuck, Daly.

2. "textbook" from Campbell, Linda, PhD, to EJF. "exploitive" from Campbell, and Seltzer, Leon F., PhD, "6 Signs of Narcissism You May Not Know About, *Psychology Today*, November 7, 2013. "originated" from Campbell.

3. "provocative" from Zajac and Mason, interviews with childhood friends of Richard Lavigne.

4. "links" from West, D.J., *Homosexuality: Its Nature and Causes*, London, Aldine Transactions, 2008, 208, and Miccio-Fonseca, L.C., "Reasons Why We Can't Profile Sex Offenders," from ccoso.org. "bald" from Fitzgerald, B. "bathroom" from Croteau, J. "1973" from Fitzgerald, B.

5. "unmistakable" from Haden, Sara C., and Scarpa, Angela, "Childhood Animal Cruelty: A Review of Research, Assessment, and Therapeutic Issues," *The Forensic Examiner* 14 (2005), 23–33, and Felthous, Ian R., M.D., "Aggression Against Cats, Dogs, and People," *Child Psychology and Human Development* 10 (1980), 169–77. "manifests" from Phillips, Ally, J.D., "Understanding the Links Between Violence to Animals and People: A Guidebook to Criminal Justice Professionals," National District Attorneys Association, Alexandria, Virginia, 2014. "disorders" from Gleyzer, Roman, and Felthous, Alan R., "Animal Cruelty and Psychiatric Disorders, *Journal of the American Academy of Psychiatry Law* 30, no. 65 (2002). "trauma" from Tapia, F., "Children Who Are Cruel to Animals," *Journal of Operational Psychiatry* 2 (1971), 70–77.

6. "arrested" from McDonald, Susan, "Childhood Animal Abuse and Violent Criminal Behavior: A Brief Review of the Literature," Commonwealth, Office of Strategic Planning, October 2011. "battery" from Degenhardt, B., "Statistical Summary of Offenders Charged with Crimes Against Companion Animals July 2001–July 2005," "cases" from Walton-Moss, B. J., Manganello, J., Frye, V., and Campbell, J. C., "Risk factors for intimate partner violence and associated injury among urban women," *Journal of Community Health* 30, no. 5 (2005), 377–84. "pets" from DeViney, E., Dickert, J., and Lockwood, R., "The care of pets within child abusing families," *International Journal for the Study of Animal Problems* 4 (1983), 3321–3329, and Deviney, Elizabeth et al., "The Care of Pets

Within Child Abusing Families," *International Journal for the Study of Animal Problems* 4 (1983), 321–29.

7. "torturing" from McDonald, and Goleman, Daniel, "Experts See Parallels Between Dahmer, Previous Serial Killers," *New York Times News Service*, August 11, 1991. "DeSalvo" from Vance, Andrea, "10-Year-Old Luke Kicked a Lamb to Death Like a Football," *News of the World*, January 23, 2005. "Dahmer" from Goleman, Aaniel, "Experts See Parallels Between Dahmer, Previous Serial Killers," *New York Times News Service*, August 11, 1991. "Rader" from Potter, Tim, "BTK Describes His Own Crimes," *The Wichita Eagle*, July 16, 2005." "Malvo" from Bradley, Paul, and Krishnamurthy, Kiran, "Right and Wrong 'An Illusion': Psychologist Who Met with Malvo Said Teen's Disorder Limited His Moral Judgment," *Richmond Times Dispatch*, December 9, 2003, and from peta.org. "Columbine" from Zuckoff, Michael, "Loners Drew Little Notice," *Boston Globe*, April 22, 1999.

8. "50%" from McDonald. "Australian" from "Animal Cruelty; Common in Many Killers," *Sunbury/Macedon Ranges Leader*, April 26, 2005. "down" from Mason.

9. "raped": Diagnostics here from Campbell. "attended" from Shaw, Kathleen A., "Sex Abuse Case Filed Against Augustinians," *Worcester Telegram & Gazette*, September 7, 2002.

10. "model" from Confoy, Maryanne, *Religious Life and Priesthood: Perfectaie Caritatis, Optatam Totius, Presbyterian Odinis*, Mahway, New Jersey, Paulist Press, 2008, 81. "benefitted" from *Ibid.*

11. "brainwashing" from Ederly. "shit" from New Hampshire State Police, Kimball, Kathleen M., Detective, "Transcript: Leo Landry Interview," September 4, 2002.

12. "1948": Weisberger study notes from Coville, Walter, D'Arcy, Paul, McCarthy, Thomas, and Rooney, John, *Assessment of Candidates for the Religious Life: Basic Psychological Issues and Problems*, Washington, D.C., Center for Applied Research in the Apostolate, 1968, from Podles, 93. "deviant" from Coville et al. from Podles, 93.

13. "age" from Kennedy, Eugene and Heckler, Victor J., *The Catholic Priest in the United States: Psychological Investigations*, Washington, D.C., United States Catholic Conference, 1972, from Podles, 94. "sin": Doyle, Thomas P., O.P., J.C.D., quoted in Shaw, Kathleen A., "Vatican Papers Spark Debate," *Worcester Telegram & Gazette*, August 28, 2005. "13-year-old" from Pfeiffer, Sacha, and Kurkjian, Stephen, "Priest Says He, Too, Molested Boys," *Boston Globe*, January 26, 2002. "families" from Guindon, André, *The Sexual Language: An Essay in Moral Theology*, Ottawa, University of Ottawa Press, 1977, 374, from Podles.

14. "princes" from Zajac and Mason.

15. "classmates": Michael Santillo left the priesthood in 1992. In 1997, he was accused of molesting at least three altar boys in Perth Amboy, New Jersey, in 1987, and he was sentenced in 1999 to ten years in prison. He died there in 2000.

16. "communicate" from Report of Scholastic Standing, Richard R. Lavigne, Seminary of Our Lady of Angels, Spring 1965–Spring 1966. "troubles" from letter, Recommendation of Ordination to Priesthood, Richard R. Lavigne, William J. Gormley, Office of the Rector, Seminary of Our Lady of Angels, to Msgr. Roger Viau, Springfield Diocese, May 2, 1966.

17. "Angels" from Psychological Profile, Richard Lavigne, Seminary of Our Lady of Angels, June, 1963. "anti-social" from Campbell.

18. "priest" from letter, Richard R. Lavigne, Petition for First Tonsure, William J. Gormley, Office of the Rector, Seminary of Our Lady of Angels to Msgr. John Harrington, Chancellor, Springfield Diocese, February 28, 1963.

19. "preferential," from Daly, Warrant, 15–16. "hunt" from Campbell.

20. "family" from Kelly and Shea, "Lavigne Faces." "set-up" from Gausch to Knapp.

21. "friend" from Zajac, "4 Brothers." "forced" from Shattuck, October 11, 1991, from Lavigne, September 29, 1993. "nude" from Statement of Witness, November 9, 1991, from Daly, Warrant. "drove" from Statement of Witness, October 16, 1991, Victim Statement #3.

22. "tickling" from Berry, I. "girls" from *Susan Morris, v. Richard Lavigne, Joseph F. Maguire, Robert W. Thrasher, and Roman Catholic Springfield Diocese, a Corporation Sole*, No. 03–241. "cute" from Croteau, C. "friends" from Croteau, B., and Shea and Goonan, "Diocese Denies." "targeting" from

Pfieffer, January 7, 2002. "board" from Statement, October 16, 1991, Lavigne, September
29, 1993. "special" from Kelly and Shea, "Lavigne Faces." "key" from Campbell. "chosen"
from Spencer, July 24, 2012.
   23. "friends" from Lavigne, September 29,
1993, 13.
   24. "monster" from Maharaj, V. "voodoo"
from Shea, "Alleged Sexual Abuse." "adults"
from Statement, October 24, 1991, taken by
Trooper Michael Habel, Franklin CPAC
Statement, October 24, 1991, from Daly, Warrant. "locker" from Shattuck, October 1991,
in Statement of Daly Search Warrant, in Lavigne, September 29, 1993.
   25. "cassocks" from Lavigne, September
29, 1993, 12.
   26. "Ray-Ray" from Shea, "Alleged Sexual
Abuse." "classical" from Zajac, "Lavigne
Haunts." "beaches" from Statement, November 21, 1991, Lavigne, September 29, 1993.
   27. "homework" from Shattuck, Daly.
   28. "feeding" from *Babeu v. Richard R.
Lavigne.* "law" from Shattuck, Daly. "teetotaler" from Commonwealth, Massachusetts
State Police, Bureau of Investigative Services,
Hampshire Country CPAC, Addendum to
Alleged Sexual Assaults in Franklin County,
CS#91–017–1199–0193. "encouraged" from
Lavigne, September 29, 1993, 12. "gum" from
Barry, "Court Documents." "Danny" from
Lavigne, September 29, 1993, 12.
   29. "dared" from Croteau, J. "cold" from
Statement, November 11, 1991, Lavigne, Sep-
tember 29, 1993, 161. "fully-stocked" from
Statement, November 15, 1991, Lavigne, Sep-
tember 29, 1993. "vodka" from Shea, "Croteau
Told." "martini" from Statement of Witness,
Lavigne, September 29, 1993, 207.
   30. "unconditionally" from Zajac, "Abuse
Seen." "with her" from Shattuck, Search Warrant.
   31. "arm" from Shattuck, Daly. "loosen"
from Statement, October 16, 1991, Lavigne,
September 29, 1993. "embracing" from Shattuck, February 14, 1992. "truly" from Shattuck,
Daly.
   32. "honor" from Statement, October 24,
1991. "permission" from Statement, March 24,
1992, Lavigne, September 29, 1993. "excuses"
from Shea, "Alleged Sexual Abuse," and Zajac,
"A Question." "bother" from Statement, October 16, 1991, Lavigne, September 29, 1993.
"started" from Statement, November 15,

1991, Lavigne, September 29, 1993, from
Daly, Warrant, in Lavigne, September 29,
1993. "clock" from Shattuck, October, 1991, in
Ibid.
   33. "help" from Statement, October 24,
1991, from Daly, Warrant. "quarters" from
Shea, "Alleged Abuse." "cold" from Shattuck,
October 11, 1991, from Lavigne, September
29, 1993. "shirts" from Hernandez, Patrick L.,
to Maguire, Fr. Joseph F., Bishop of Springfield, November 6, 1991. "unsanitary" from
Statement, November 11, 1991, Lavigne, September 29, 1993. "nightshirt" from Statement
of Witness, February 1, 1992, Lavigne, September 29, 1993, and Daly, Warrant.
   34. "five" from Statement, February 1,
1992, Lavigne, September 29, 1993. "sitting"
from Statement, December 24, 1991, Lavigne,
September 29, 1993. "nothing" from Shea,
"Alleged Abuse." "French" from Zajac, "Lavigne Haunts." "OK" from Statement, October
24, 1991, taken by Trooper Michael Habel,
Franklin CPAC, from Daly, Warrant. "turn"
from Statement, October 28, 1991, Lavigne,
September 29, 1993.
   35. "naked" from *Shawn M. Dobbert
v. Richard R. Lavigne, Joseph F. Maguire,
Robert W. Thrasher, and Roman Catholic
Springfield Diocese, a Corporation Sole,*
No. 02–728. Shattuck, October 1991, in
Lavigne, September 29, 1993. "thighs" from
Lavigne, September 29, 1993, 122–23, 134–
35, and Zajac, "Croteau Papers." "restless"
from *Babeu v. Richard R. Lavigne.* "avoid"
from Statement, November 8, 1991, Lavigne,
September 29, 1993. "stuck" from Statement,
November 15, 1991, from Daly, Warrant,
in Lavigne, September 29, 1993. "squeeze"
from Shattuck, Lavigne, 196. "imbalance"
from Statement of Babeu October 25,
1991, Lavigne, September 29, 1993, and Commonwealth, No. 93–080, 3 and Lavigne, September 29, 1993, 196.
   36. "tickle" from Statement of Michael
McMahon, December 31, 1991, Lavigne, September 29, 1993. "others" from Dobbert No.
02–728. "suits" from Statement, October 9,
1991, Lavigne, September 29, 1993, 158. "relax"
from Dobbert, No. 02–728.
   37. "fishing" from Zajac, "Croteau Papers."
"dirty" from Zajac, "A Question." "dried"
from Shattuck, October, 1991, from Lavigne,
no. 92 032. "toilet" from Shattuck, Daly.
"hand" Statement, October 11, 1991, Lavigne,

September 29, 1993, 158. "sack" from Shattuck, Daly.

38. "watched" from Statement, November 21, 1991, Lavigne, September 29, 1993. "wipe" from Statement, October 9, 1991, Lavigne, September 29, 1993, 158. "vanity" from Shattuck, Daly.

39. "refused" from Ovitz v Lavigne. "drive" from Shattuck, Daly, in Lavigne, September 29, 1993.

40. "U.S." from Zajac and Goldberg, "Unsealed Records."

41. "OK" from Shattuck, October 11, 1991, from Lavigne, September 29, 1993, 201. "hurt" from *Commonwealth, Stephen J. Block and Thomas M. Martin v. Richard R. Lavigne, Robert T. Thrasher, and Roman Catholic Springfield Diocese, a Corporation Sole*, Factual Allegations. "children" from Shattuck, Daly, in Lavigne, September 29, 1993. "fault" from Commonwealth, 92–028–92–032, Change of Plea, June 25, 1992, 21. "forgiveness" from Zajac, "4 New Lawsuits."

42. "polygraph" from Carroll, Matt, "Diocese Releases Priest's Files," *Boston Globe*, September 4, 2002. "walked" from Shattuck, October 1991, from Lavigne, September 29, 1993, and *Andre P. Tessier v. Richard R. Lavigne, Robert W. Thrasher, and Roman Catholic Springfield Diocese, a Corporation Sole*, No. 02–727, and Zajac, "4 New Lawuits." "exposed" from *Block, Martin v. Lavigne*, Factual Allegations. Other Thrasher notes from Massachusetts State Police, Bureau of Investigative Services, Hampshire Country CPAC, Addendum to Alleged Sexual Assaults in Franklin County, CS#91–017–1199–0193. "ignored" from Affidavit of Maurice E. DeMontigny, August 15, 1993.

43. "zipped" from Shattuck, October 1991, from Lavigne, September 29, 1993, and Francis Babeu v. Richard Lavigne, Joseph F. Maguire, Robert W. Thrasher, and Roman Catholic Springfield Diocese, a Corporation Sole, No. 02–726, and Zajac, "4 New Lawuits." "around" from Statement, October 24, 1991, from Daly, Warrant, in Lavigne, September 29, 1993. "cousin" from Kelly and Shea, "Lavigne Faces." Kenneth Chevalier, Lavigne's cousin, accused Lavigne of molesting him numerous times. "cousin's" from Statement, November 15, 1991, Lavigne, September 29, 1993.

44. "expensive" from Shea, "Lavigne

Backer." "both" from Commonwealth, 92–028–92–032, Change of Plea, June 25, 1992, 10. "exposed," from Morris et al., No. 03–241. "birthday" from *Elizabeth A. Germond v. Roman Catholic Springfield Diocese, a Corporation Sole*, John F. Harrington, Richard R. Lavigne, Robert W. Thrasher, March 5, 2003.

45. "hide" from in Daly, Warrant, in Lavigne, September 29, 1993. "view" from Statement, November 15, 1991, Lavigne, September 29, 1993. "down" from Statement, November 15, 1991, Lavigne, September 29, 1993. "woods" from Zajac, "Abuse Seen." "locked" from Shattuck, Daly, in Lavigne, September 29, 1993. "flashed" from Statement of Gouin, Raymond, Jr., October 28, 1991, from Lavigne, September 29, 1993, pgs. 210–11, and Kelly and Shea, "Lavigne Faces." "bricks" from Statement, October 28, 1991, Lavigne, September 29, 1993. "money" from Statement, October 28, 1991, Lavigne, September 29, 1993.

46. "retired" from Commonwealth, CS#91–017–1199–0193. "punish" from Shattuck, Daly, in Lavigne, September 29, 1993. "blinds" from Shattuck, Daly, in Lavigne, September 29, 1993.

47. "deal" from Zajac, April 21, 2002. "taunting" from Lavigne, September 29, 1993, 13–14.

48. "showers" from Shattuck, Daly, in Lavigne, September 29, 1993. "cruel" from Shattuck, Daly, in Lavigne, September 29, 1993. "bald" from Shea, "Lavigne Backer." "fat" from Zajac, "4 New Lawsuits." "weight" from Dobbert No. 02–728.

49. "begged" from Dobbert No. 02–728. "keep" from Shattuck, October 1991, from Lavigne, September 29, 1993, 196.

50. "ejaculated" from *David A. Galeziowski v. Richard R. Lavigne, Joseph F. Maguire, Robert W. Thrasher, and Roman Catholic Springfield Diocese, a Corporation Sole*, No. 02–991. "hurt" from Shattuck, Daly, in Lavigne, September 29, 1993. "bites" from Statement, McMahon, December 31, 1991, Lavigne, September 29, 1993, and Statement, November 24, 1991, Lavigne, September 29, 1993. "done" from JS to EJF. "suffered" from *Block, Martin v. Lavigne*, Factual Allegations, and "Murder Most Foul," *60 Minutes*, CBS-TV, May 24, 2005.

51. "grammar" from Zajac, "Lavigne Haunts." "fired" from Shattuck, Daly, in Lavigne, September 29, 1993. "taken" from Dob-

bert No. 02–728. "ashamed" from Statement, November 15, 1991, from Daly, Warrant, in Lavigne, September 29, 1993. "Barnabas" from Statement, November 15, 1991, Lavigne, September 29, 1993. "pool" from Kelly and Shea, "Lavigne Faces." "closed" from Dobbert No. 02–728.

52. "prominent" from Zajac, "Abuse Seen." "ashamed" from Zajac, "4 New Lawuits." "colored" from Grand Jury, No. 03–00–239.

53. "wouldn't" from Zajac and Goldberg, "Unsealed Records." "denied" from Shea, "Alleged Sexual Abuse." "move" and "life" from Zajac, "Past Still Haunts Accused Priest," *Republican*, February 27, 2005.

54. "clothes" from Cullen, "Asked to Help, Priest Allegedly Abused," *Boston Globe*, June 5, 2002. "Teague" from Zajac, "He Remembers."

55. "aggravated" from Statement, McMahon, Lavigne, September 29, 1993. "stolen" Statement, December 24, 1991, Lavigne, September 29, 1993, 162. "knife" from Statement, December 9, 1991, Lavigne, September 29, 1993, 162. "scared" from Shattuck, Daly, in Lavigne, September 29, 1993. "violently" from Shattuck, Daly, in Lavigne, September 29, 1993. "temper" from Statement, October 29, 1991, Lavigne, September 29, 1993.

56. "police" from Mazzarino. "alcohol" from Kelly and Shea, "Lavigne Faces," and, Lavigne, September 29, 1993, 133–36. "illegally" from Shattuck, Daly, in Lavigne, September 29, 1993. "hell" from Kelly and Shea, "Lavigne Faces."

57. "suicide" from Shattuck, October 11, 1991, from Lavigne, September 29, 1993, 201. "Accidents" from *John Doe v. Richard R. Lavigne, Joseph F. Maguire, Robert W. Thrasher, and Roman Catholic Springfield Diocese, a Corporation Sole*, No. 02–993, and Zajac, "3 More Lawuits." "site" from Zajac, "Lavigne Haunts." "else" from Finer, "Priest Urges." "wrenching" from *Block, Martin v. Lavigne*, Factual Allegations.

58. "parents" from Shea, "Knife Threats," and from Statement, Lavigne, September 29, 1993, 134. "again" from Zajac, "4 New Lawuits."

Chapter 10

1. "murdered" from Tessier.

2. "murderer" from Melley, Brian, "Priest Avoids Jail Term," *Republican*, June 26, 1992.

3. "time" from Lavigne, September 29, 1993, 5. "April 7" from Lavigne, September 29, 1993, 4–5.

4. "confessions" from Cullen, "Priest Cites."

5. "lied" from Lavigne, September 29, 1993, 126, and Daly, Warrant. "erratic" from Reid, May 15,1972.

6. "anything" from DeMontigny, August 15, 2003.

7. "withdrawn" from Croteau, J.

8. "find" from "Murder Most Foul." "molested" from Lavigne, September 29, 1993, 14.

9. "murdered" from Lavigne, September 29, 1993, 14.

10. "crying" from "Murder Most Foul." "*Republican*" from Zajac.

11. "squeal" from Maharaj, II. "blackmailing" from Mallia, "I Just Want."

12. "rectory" from Heaney, "Report Says."

13. "poker" from Stevens.

14. "well" from Croteau, J., and Interview with Joseph Croteau, from Daly, Warrant, 20–21. "size" from Supplementary Report: Daniel Croteau, #38039, May 2, 1972. "smell" from Daly, Warrant, 4.

15. "replaced" from Fitzgerald, B.

16. "investigated" from Stern, Max D., Stern and Garin, Patricia, to Media Outlets, "Press Release: Daniel Croteau Murder Investigation," August 5, 2004.

17. "process" from "Grand Jury," Cornell University School of Law, Legal Information Institute." "sandwich" from Wolfe, Tom, *The Bonfire of the Vanities*, New York, New York, Bantam Books, 1988, 269.

18. "involved": Notes here from "Rule 6. The Grand Jury," Cornell University Law School, Legal Information Institute.

19. "conviction": Notes here from American Bar Association, Criminal Justice Section, Part 1—Standards, No. 2–1.2, No. 3–3.4, No. 3–3.4, No. 3–3.4, No. 3–3.9, No. 3–3.9.

20. "darndest" from Ford, Beverly, and Ranalli, Ralph, "Slain Altar Boy Allegedly Spent Final Night in Rectory," *Boston Herald*, October 25, 1991.

21. "wild" from Fitzgerald, Brian, Croteau, III.

22. "reasonable" from Croteau, B., and Croteau, C., Affidavit. "twelve"; Ryan, M. to EJF, III. "hinder" from Croteau, C., Affidavit.

23. "expect" from Mallia, "I Just Want." "reality" from Zajac. "accusation" from Croteau, B., and Croteau, C., Affidavit.

24. "know" from Sullivan, "Catholic Pastor." "evidence" from Sullivan, "Catholic Pastor."
25. "smell" from Ballou, Brian R., "Victim's Family to Address Findings," *Boston Globe*, January 14, 2008.
26. "troopers" from Downing.
27. "stumbling" from Stevens, "Thursday, November 18, 2004, Briefing Republican Co." "rejected" from Stevens, "Thursday, October 14, 2004, Briefing Republican Co."
28. "tested" from Stevens, "Thursday, July 14, 2005, Briefing Republican Co." "integrity" from Stevens, "Thursday, October 14, 2004, Briefing Republican Co." "clothes" from Stevens, "Case Status Notes as of April, 2006." "unaware" from Zajac. "upstairs" from Stevens.
29. "riddled" from *The Republican Company, Petitioner, v. Massachusetts Appeals Court, Clerk of the Hampden Superior Court, Richard M. Lavigne, the District Attorney for the Hampden District, and John Doe, Respondents.*

Chapter 11

1. "know" from Cullen, "Danny's Story," and Croteau, C.
2. "ox" from Fitzgerald, Brian, Circle, V, "Comment section." "three" and "get him going" from Croteau, J.
3. "Moses" from Jendrysik, Stephen, "Friends of Horace Moses Reservation Rally to Save Scout Camp," *Republican*, June 13, 2012. "Lake Hazard" is now "Russell Pond."
4. "Pedophiles" from Boyle, Patrick, "Scouts Honor," *Washington Times*, 1991, and Boyle, Patrick, *Scout's Honor: Sexual Abuse in America's Most Trusted Institution*, Prima Publishing, 2013. "2,919" from "Boy Scout Perversion Files," boyscoutsexualabuse.com. "Shakespearean" from Christensen, Kim, and Felch, Jim, "Boy Scouts Helped Alleged Molesters Cover Tracks, Files Show," *Los Angeles Times*, September 16, 2012 and "Locals Helped Boy Scouts Cover Up Pedophilia," *Charleston Gazette-Mail*, October 19, 2012.
5. "duck," from Fitzgerald, J. "electronics" from "Troy Police Cooperation Noted in Youth Program," *Troy Record*, September 1, 1970.
6. "Academy" from Sherry, Frank, "Counselor Project Lacks Funds," *Troy Record*, December 12, 1970. "National Law Enforcement Academy": Miami, Florida. "saved" and "rapport" from Sherry, "Counselor Project."
7. "priesthood" from "Church's Role in Troy's Needs to Be Discussed," *Troy Record*, October 25, 1969. "Center": Details here from Sherry, "Counselor Project."
8. "alarm" from "Summer Program Gives Hand to Youngsters," *Berkshire Eagle*, July 25, 1969. "radio" from "Troy Police Cooperation Noted in Youth Program," *Troy Record*, September 1, 1970. "camping" from "Summer Program Gives Hand to Youngsters," *Berkshire Eagle*, July 25, 1969. "455" from Swantek, John, "Deputies Make Quick Arrest," *Troy Record*, February 3, 1970.
9. "sporting" from Swantek, "Deputies." "impersonating" from "Grand Jury Hears Several Charges," *Troy Record*, March 18, 1970. "surprisingly" from Dolan, Gerry, "Grand Jury Names 8 in Indictments," *Troy Record*, April 8, 1971.
10. "VCR" from Fitzgerald, Brian, Croteau, III.
11. "kill" from Ibid.
12. "strange," etc., Croteau, J. "athletic" from Fitzgerald, B.
13. "Masters" from Norton, Roger B., Confidential Record Sheet, Registration and Membership, Registration Division, Boy Scouts of America, November 29, 1973. "lookouts," from Croteau, J.
14. "hippie" from CPD 19–221A, April 15–24, 1972.
15. "child under 16" from Stevens, "Thursday, November 11, 2005, Republican Co. Briefing."
16. "fifty-five" from "Ex-camp Head Denies Guilt in Sex Cases," *Springfield Daily News*, November 26, 1973, and "Norton Pleads Innocent," *Republican*, November 27, 1973. Other details from Separation Notice, Roger B. Norton, Pioneer Valley Council, Boy Scouts of America, West Springfield, Massachusetts, October 29, 1973, and Norton, Roger B., Confidential Record Sheet, Separation Notice, Registration Division, Boy Scouts of America, November 26, 1973. "don't ever come back" from LG to EJF. "cabal" from Barry, Stephanie, "Roman Catholic Diocese of Springfield Pay $4.5 Million to 59 Clergy Abuse Victims," *Republican*, December 2, 2008. "escaped" from Johnson, Patrick, "Inside the Boy Scouts 'Perversion Files' Is Roger

Norton, a Convicted Child Molester with Western Massachusetts Ties," *Republican*, October 20, 2012.

17. "stocky" from Tessier.

18. "Phelps" from Stevens, November 11, 2005.

19. "Galaxie" from Maharaj, Croteau, X. "tan car" from Daly, Warrant.

20. "kids" from CPD 19–221A, April 15–24, 1972.

21. "Holy Cross" from "Obituary, Leary, Timothy J., Fr.," *Republican*, October 11, 1991. "school" from *The History of Cathedral High School: 1883–2012*, from cathedralhigh.org.

22. "admission" from Zajac, "Diocese Receives Abuse Complaints," *Republican*, January 8, 2005 and Zajac, "Priests Accused in Suits," *Republican*, January 7, 2005. "passing" from Zajac, "Diocese Receives." "badly" from Zajac, "Accused in Suits."

23. "campaigns" from "Obituary, Huller, E. Karl, Fr.," *Republican*, November 20, 1997, and Zajac, "Dead Priest in Abuse Suit Defended," *Republican*, March 24, 2003.

24. "newspaper" from Cullen, "Diocese's Report." "ride" from Zajac, "Bishop's Records at Issue Again," *Republican*, February 9, 2004.

25. "Stigmata" from Kimball, September 4, 2002. "prey," etc., from Carroll, Matt, "Abuse Alleged at Wellesley Seminary," *Boston Globe*, August 10, 2002.

26. "Manchester" from Stigmatine Fathers and Brothers, Office of the Provincial, Leo P. Landry, Chronology and Curriculum Vitae, November 14, 2002. "collections" from Memorandum of Interview, Attorney General's Office, Manchester, New Hampshire, re Leo Landry, October 4, 2002. "camps" from Kimball, September 4, 2002. "driving" from Landry, October 4, 2002. "single" from Kimball, September 4, 2002. "confessional" from Diocese of Manchester, New Hampshire, Brodeur, Paul E., Inv., Internal Memorandum, Complaints re Priest, April 24, 2002. "confess" from Meersman, Nancy, "Two More NH Suits vs. Priests," *Manchester Union Leader*, April 24, 2002. "aware" from Vos, Sarah C., "Priests, Diocese Accused: One Cleric Is on List of 14; Other Left Church," *Manchester Monitor*, April 24, 2002.

27. "apology" from Kimball, September 4, 2002. "rear-ends" etc., from Rochester (NH) Police Department, Incident Report, Narrative for Sergeant Paul G. Callahan, September

18, 1998. "stupid" from Rochester (NH) Police Department, Incident Report, Narrative for Patrolman Derek M. Davis, June 5, 1998.

28. "organized" from Olkovikas, A.W., "Notes for File on Worcester Priest's Report on a Group of Abusers, Including Genest [sic], in Strictissima," September 3, 1958.

29. "Greenfield": Notes here from "Five Priests Barred from Parish Work," *Associated Press*, carried in the *Daily Hampshire Gazette*, July 31, 2002. "per se" from Pomerleau, "Priest Removed from Ministry: New Suits Filed Before Legal Deadline," *The Catholic Observer*, January 7, 2005.

30. "passed" from *Babeu v. Richard R. Lavigne*, and Zajac, "Lavigne Criminal File Targeted," *Republican/Union-News*, June 11, 2002.

31. "Sturbridge" from Contrada, Fred, "Vatican Defrocks 2 Area Priests," *Republican*, December 2, 2006.

32. "swapping" from Barry, Stephanie, "Ex-Nun." "nest" from Olkovikas, "Notes." "pass-around" from Contrada, "Vatican Defrocks," and Contrada, "For Priest's Accusers, Pain Is Lasting Legacy," *The Republican*, December 10, 2006. Summary details from Nicastro. "family" from Broncaccio, Diane, "Lawyer John Stobierski Has Unique Perspective on Child Abuse by Catholic Priests Portrayed in 'Spotlight,'" *Daily Hampshire Gazette*, November 25, 2015.

33. "rid" from Zajac, "Probe Points."

34. "always" from Hemingway, Sam, "Suit Settlement Fails to Bring Peace to Priest-Molestation Victim," *The Burlington Free Press*, August 5, 2007. "broken" from Statement of Paul Babeu.

35. "moved" from Pomerleau, "Priest Removed." "careless" from Downing.

36. "decades" from Olkovikas, "Notes," and Diocese of Manchester, New Hampshire, Fr. Donald Osgood File, and "Category: Church Responsibility, Boston Ring," eurekaencyclopedia.com. "problems" etc., from Podles, Leo, *The Rev. Donald Osgood of New Hampshire: A Shallow, Likeable Guy With a Taste for Young Men* (unpublished essay), and Podles, Leon J., *Case Study: Donald Matthew Osgood (1927–)*, Baltimore, Maryland, Crossland Foundation, 2008.

37. "whiskey" from Zajac, "4 Brothers." "Sturbridge" from Contrada, "For Priest's Accusers."

38. "pretentious" from O'Brien, D. "built" from Zajac, "4 Brothers." "Hawaii" from Zajac, "Priest Plans to Take Year's Leave," *Republican*, October 15, 2005. "restaurant" from Contrada, "For Priest's Accusers." "Mooney" from Pomerleau, "Priest Removed."

39. "country" from Zajac, "Priest Plans."

40. "abused" from O'Quinn, Beatrice, "Allegations Lead to Priest's Retirement," *Republican*, December 23, 1993.

41. "movie" from O'Brien, D. "customers" from Daly, D., Asst. Mgr., A.O. White to EJF. "angst" from Shea, "Friends, Foes."

42. "Carmel" from "Waltham Priest Allegedly Hid Abuse," *Newton Daily News Tribune*, August 6, 2003.

43. "Ahern" from Memorandum and Order on Defendants' Motion for Summary Judgement, Thayer Fremont-Smith, Justice of the Superior Court, *Michael Moe et al. vs. The Trustees of the Stigmatine Fathers, Inc. aka Congregation of the Sacred Stigmata et al*, #05–0059, June 4, 2008.

44. "1,000" from Zajac, "Diocese Inaction Faulted," *Republican*, July 6, 2004. "penance" from Dupont, Mark, "Standards and Procedures," August 30, 2011.

45. "contact" from Barry, "Abuse Victims."

46. "keel" from Nicastro.

Chapter 12

1. "unbridled" from *Harold F. and Sheila Francis, Parents of James Francis, [Redacted] v. The Roman Catholic Archbishop of Boston, a Corporation Sole and Ronald Paquin*, Complaint and Jury Trial Demand, April 10, 2002. "gratified" from Cappadona, Bryanna, "The Story Behind the Most Disturbing Conversation in 'Spotlight,'" November 9, 2015, boston.com. "cabin" from Kurkjian, Stephen, and Robinson, Walter V., "Suit Ties Boy's Death to Abuse by Priest," *Boston Globe*, April 11, 2002. "Francis" from Anderson, Travis, and Ellement, John R., "Ex-priest Jailed in Abuse Scandal Has Been Released," *Boston Globe*, October 2, 2015, and Kurkjian and Robinson, "Suit Ties." "$80,000" from Pfeiffer, Sacha, "Priest Pleads Guilty to Raping Altar Boy," *Boston Globe*, January 1, 2003. "Erickson" from Stohlberg, Doug, "Double Murder Is Now 10 Years Old," *Hudson Star-Observer*, February 5, 2012.

2. "Pell": Details from Gelineau, Kristen,

"Australian Police Charge Cardinal with Sex Offenses," Associated Press, June 29, 2017.

3. "orgy" from "Vatican Police Break Up 'Drug-fueled Gay Orgy' at Home of One of Pope Francis' Key Advisor," July 5, 2017, dailymail.uk.com.

4. "acts" from Zenet News Service, December 3, 2002, from Dodecki, Paul R., *The Clergy Sex Abuse Crisis: Reform and Renewal in the Catholic Community*, Washington, D.C., Georgetown University Press, 2004. "Holocaust" from Cullen, "Piercing the Papal Shroud," *Boston Globe*, April 13, 2010. "conceivable" from Humm, Andy, "Vatican Gay Scapegoating Official," gaycitynews.com.

5. "rewards" from Nadeau, Barbie Latza, "Speak No Evil: Vatican Refuses to Talk About Sex Abuse," *The Daily Beast*, February 6, 2016, thedailybeast.com. "root" from Latkovic, Mark S., "Using Modern Science to Treat Homosexuality," *Crisis Magazine*, November 27, 2015. "family" from Moran, Rich, "New Vatican Guidelines for Bishops Make Reporting Abuse to Police Optional," *American Thinker*, February 11, 2016. "neighbors" from Kirchgaessner, Stephinia, "New Bishops Told Abuse Reporting 'Not Necessarily' Their Duty," *Irish Times*, February 10, 2016, irishtimes.com.

6. "stupid" from Gelineau. "allergy" from Wilson and Dunnigan. "bury" from Cullen, "Piercing." "10%" from Pew Research Center, "America's Changing Religious Landscape: Declining Number of Catholics, May 11, 2015. "losing" from Pew Research Center, "Faith in Flux," April 27, 2009. "41%" from Miller, Patricia, "The Catholic Church's American Downfall: Why Its Demographic Crisis Is Great News for the Country," *Salon Magazine*, May 21, 2015.

7. "billion" from "Sexual Abuse by U.S. Catholic Clergy: Settlements and Monetary Awards in Civil Suits," bishopaccountability.org, and "The Financial Cost," *Boston Globe*, October 26, 2015. "2002 alone" from Cooperman, Alan, and Sun, Lena H., "Hundreds of Priests Removed Since '60s," *Washington Post*, June 9, 2002. "Belleville" from Cooperman, Alan, and Sun, Lena H., "Hundreds of Priests Removed Since '60s," *Washington Post*, June 9, 2002. "accused" from "2014 Annual Report," United States Conference of Bishops, Secretariat of Child and Youth Protection, National Review Board, Report on

the Implementation of the Charter for the Protection of Children and Young People, March, 2014.

8. "Institute": Notes here from Lothstein, L.M., Ph.D., *Treating Clergy Who Sexually Abuse Minors: A 16-Year Experience in the Professionals and Clergy Program at the IOL.* "demanded" from Lothstein, L.M., *The Keepers, Ep. 3—The Revelation.*

9. "forbade" from Crean. "sorry" from Zajac, "Springfield Diocese Still Mum," *Republican*, July 24, 2003. "could": Notes here from Marshall, John A., Fr., Bishop of Springfield, to Babeu, Paul, February 23, 1994.

10. "serial-abuser" from O'Connor, Fr. Timothy F., to Gerard, James J., November 6, 1963. "Annie" from Carl and Bernice and Zajac, "Altar Boy's Father." "wrong" from Zajac, "Lavigne Abuse Ignored by Church," *Republican*, September 29, 2003. "Carl" from Croteau, C., Affidavit and Zajac, "Altar Boy's Father." "locked" from Zajac, "Lavigne Files, Letters Released," *Republican*, September 4, 2002. "won't" from Affidavit of Maurice E. DeMontigny, August 15, 2003. "laughed" from Zajac, "Lavigne Files."

11. "charges" from DeMontigny, August 15, 2003. "upset" from Zajac, "Lavigne Files." "boys" from Zajac, "Affidavit Contradicts." "molester" from Zajac, September 29, 2003. "upset" from Zajac, "Lavigne Files."

12. "policeman" from Shea, "Friends, Foes." "weekly" from Lavigne, September 29, 1993, 11.

13. "officials" from Zajac, "Ex-officers: Church Knew About Lavigne," *Republican*, November 17, 2002. "five" from Cullen, "Danny's Story."

14. "duties" from Zajac, "4 New Lawsuits." "adamantly" from Pomerleau, "Bishop's Depositions."

15. "knew" from Zajac, "Ex-officers." "disbelief" from "In Touch with His Feelings," February 15, 2004 from catholicculture.org.

16. "supervise" from Affidavit of Father Thomas Doyle, August 12, 2003.

17. "2016" from Barry, Stephanie, "Roman Catholic Diocese of Springfield Reaches Settlement, Adds Another Name to Its List of Priests Accused of Sexual Abuse," *Republican*, March 29, 2016. "debt" from Kelly, March 2010.

18. "rising" from Barry, Stephanie, "Accused Clergy Had Influential Posts," *Republican*, March 1, 2004.

19. "disgusted" from Nicastro. "mistrial" from Hemingway, "Lawsuit Settlement." "long" from Kelly, Robert M., "The True Cost of the Settlements," Western Massachusetts Catholics, March 2010, westernmassachusettscatholics.com. "So and So" from Dupré, Fr. Thomas F., to Files, Inter-Office Memo, Subject: Father Richard Lavigne, November 5, 1991.

20. "Chancellor" from Diocesan Directory, 2015.

21. "Weldon" from Zajac, "Murderer Alleges Clergy Sex Abuse," *Republican*, March 31, 2005. "relatives" from Roulier, Sharon, and Pomerleau, "Inmate Files Suit Against Two Dioceses," *The Catholic Observer*, March 31, 2005. "release" from Zajac, "Murderer Alleges."

22. "quarters" from DeForge, Jeanette, "Springfield Priest Found Dead in Rectory at Our Lady of the Sacred Heart Parish," *Republican*, July 4, 2011, and "Catholic Priest's Death Ruled a Suicide," *Boston Globe*, July 6, 2011. "fifty" from Dunn, Bob, "Chesterfield Man Alleges Sexual Abuse by Priest, Sues Catholic Diocese of Springfield," *Daily Hampshire Gazette*, July 11, 2013. "shrine" from Contrada, Fred, "Paul Archambault, Northampton Priest Who Committed Suicide, Named as Sex Abuser in Suit," *Republican*, July 11, 2013. "immaturity" from Barry, Stephanie, "New Details Emerge About Abusive Priest's History with Springfield Catholic Diocese," *Republican*, March 29, 2016. "filings" from Barry, Ibid.

23. "websites" from Downing.

24. "baggage" from Brault, "Matty Ryan." "influence" from Barry, Stephanie, and McCauliffe, "Matthew Ryan, Jr., former Hampden County District Attorney, dead at 92," *Republican*, August 29, 2009. "bombastic" from *Ibid.*

25. "tied" from Croteau, C. and Fitzgerald, Brian, Croteau, II. "1982" from "Obituary, Fitzgibbon, James J.," *Republican*, April 4, 2013.

26. "resolve" from Stevens, Director of Investigative Operations, PSII, Inc., March 27, 2005, to Frs. Mark Steltzer et al. "confused" from Pomerleau, "Private Investigator Sends Unusual Letter to Diocesan Clergy," *The Catholic Observer*, May 13, 2005.

27. "name" from Garver, Ben, "Former Springfield Bishop Thomas Dupré Dead at

83," *Berkshire Eagle*, January 3, 2017. "200" from Barry, Stephanie, "Judge Denies Former Springfield Bishop Thomas Dupré Motion to Keep Video Testimony from Public," *Republican*, July 15, 2010, and Johnson, Patrick, "Dupré, on Video, Refuses to Answer," *Republican*, October 3, 2010. "December" from "Correction: Bishop Thomas Dupré Stories," *Washington Post*, January 4, 2017.

28. "$500" from Shea, "Abuse Victim Tells the Story of a 'Great' Priest," *Republican*, September 14, 2003.

29. "stumbled" from Zajac, "He Remembers."

30. "Board" from "Obituary, Leary, Timothy J., Fr.," *Republican*, October 11, 1991.

31. "served" from "Obituary, Huller, E. Karl, Fr.," *Republican*, November 20, 1997.

32. "directive" from Zajac, "Bishop's Records."

33. "counseling" from Zajac, "Priests Accused in Suits," and "Ex-Williamstown Priest Accused of Molesting Teen," *The Berkshire Eagle*, December 31, 2004. "removed" from Pomerleau, "Priest Removed." "expenses" from Zajac, "Priest's Backers Soliciting Donations," *Republican*, July 15, 2005.

34. "missed" and "St. Patrick's" from Zajac, "Diocese Inaction Faulted."

35. "accused" from "New Suit Targets Priest Who Served at Lee Church," *Associated Press*, September 24, 2003. "archives": Notes here from Barry, "Accused Clergy." "several" from "Five Priests Barred from Parish Work," *Daily Hampshire Gazette*, July 31, 2002. "bequest" from *Class Notes: News and Information for Alumni of St. Charles College, St. Mary's Seminary College and St. Mary's Seminary*, Spring 2015.

36. "forced" from Zajac, "Removed Priest's Name Released," *Republican*, March 10, 2006.

37. "Wamsher" from Zajac, "Defrocked Priest Denied Pension," *Republican*, June 29, 2006. "only" from "Five Priests." "climbed" from Spencer, July 24, 2012. "horseplay" from Spencer July 25, 2012 and Pomerleau, Fr. Bill, "Lawyer Claims Bishop Maguire Knew of Abuse in 1976," *The Catholic Observer*, September 25, 2009. "returned" from DePasquale, Ron, "Catholics Protest Near Law's Residence, Demand Resignation," *Associated Press*, February 17, 2002. "barred" from "Five Priests." "Our Lady of Sacred Heart" from

Barry, "Ex-Nun" and Spencer, "Andrew Nicastro Testifies." "laicized" from "Vatican Defrocks Two Springfield Diocese Priests," *Associated Press via Worcester Telegram & Gazette*, December 1, 2006.

38. "YES" from Nicastro.

39. "five" from "Ludlow Priest Put on Leave," BC Cycle, June 2, 2002. "indication" from Barry, Stephanie, "6 Vt. Priests Removed From Their Parishes," *The Republican*, June 14, 2002. "Burlington" from Babeu v. Richard R. Lavigne. "denied" from Barry, "6 VT Priests." "diocese" from Hemingway, "Church Admits Finding Documents in Priest Abuse Case Thought to Be Missing," *The Burlington Free Press*, August 28, 2006. "Miracles" from Hemingway, "Missing Priest Files Found," *The Burlington Free Press*, August 28, 2006. "torment" from Hemingway, "Lawsuit Settlement."

40. "rules" from MacQuarrie, "Bishop Places."

41. "1994" from Zajac, "Accused Priest Departs," *Republican*, July 18, 2002.

42. "members" from Zajac, "4 Brothers." "Sturbridge" from Contrada, "Vatican Defrocks."

43. "Apostolate" from Zajac, "Year's Leave" and Contrada, "Vatican Defrocks." "excellent" from DePasquale, "Catholics Protest." "Springfield-Greenfield" from "Five Priests."

44. "untrue!" from Downing. "Southern Berkshire Deanery" from "Obituary, Koonz, John A., Fr.," *Republican*, November 29, 2013. "disability" from "Koonz, John A, Fr.," *Republican*, November 29, 2013. "suspension" from Greenberger, Scott S., "Parish Is Told of Abuse Probe," *Boston Globe*, September 16, 2002. "50th" from "Obituary, Koonz, John A, Fr.," *Republican*, November 29, 2013.

45. "contact" from O'Quinn, "Allegations Lead."

46. "facility" from "Obituary, Spafford, Gerald F.," *Cape Cod Times*, November 6, 2015.

47. "multiple" from "Waltham Priest Allegedly Hid Abuse," *Newton Daily News Tribune*, August 6, 2003.

48. "community" from Congregation of Sacred Stigmata, "Joseph E. Flood, Confratelli Stimmatini, After October 31, 1996," confrades.com.

49. "prestige" from Zajac, "Removed Priest's."

50. "Paquette" from "As I Recall: Why I Wrote About the 8.5 Million Dollar Settlement," springfielddiocese.blogspot.com.
51. "offender" from Stevens, November 11, 2005. "drive" from Maharaj, X.
52. "charges" from Johnson October 20, 2012, massline.com. "overturned" from Norton, Roger, The National Registry of Exonerations, University of Michigan, November 27, 2012.
53. "soul" from Tessier. "spirit" from Zajac, "Abuse Seen."
54. "secrets" from Zajac, "He Remembers."
55. "why?" from Zajac, "Abuse Seen."
56. "story" from Zajac, "A Question."
57. "space" from Oliva, Russ, "Healing Takes Time for Victims of Abuse," *The Woonsocket Call*, February 10, 2002. "always moving" from Croteau, J.
58. "institution" and "installment" from Zajac, "Abuse Seen." "inches" from Cullen, "Danny's Story."
59. "close" from Shea, "Silence Ends Living."
60. "tortured" from Norris, Patricia, "Lawyer Speaks of Client's Death," *Republican*, August 13, 2004. "health" from "Obituary, Dobbert, Shawn M.," *Republican*, August 12, 2004. "killed" from Zajac, "Abuse Seen."
61. "prayed" from Cullen, "Approval Given." "University" from "Obituary, Bessone, David John," *The Gainesville Sun*, January 1, 1986. "ashamed" from Zajac, "Abuse Seen."
62. "hammer" from Fitzgerald, Brian, Circle, V, Comments. "hard" from Fitzgerald, Brian, Circle, II. "camping" from Fitzgerald, B. "crash" from Maharaj, I.
63. "platform" from Ceneviva, Alex, "Amtrak Identifies Man Struck and Killed by Train in Madison," tnh.com, April 23, 2017.
64. "15" from Fitzgerald, Brian, Circle, V, Comments, former member.
65. "Einstein" from Mazzarino. "YMCA" from "Obituary, Coleman, James A.," *Republican*, October 22, 2006.
66. "hospitals" from Zajac, April 21, 2002. "good" from Shea, "26 Years." "brief" from *Commonwealth v. Richard Lavigne*, Motion to Leave to File Memorandum as Amici Curiae on Behalf of Michael J. Slowinski, Bea Cevasco, Peter Dolan, Margaret J. Carlson, and 487 Other Named Individuals, April 20, 1992. "withdrawn" from Zajac and Mason.

67. "Commissioner" from Alonzo, Monica, "Paul Babeu's Mexican Ex-lover Says Sheriff's Attorney Threatened Him with Deportation," *Phoenix New Times*, February 26, 2012. "immigration" from Montini, E.J., "Montini: Sheriff Underpants in Congress? Thank You," *The Arizona Republic*, October 5, 2015. "Obama" from Fabian, Jordon, "Obama Debates Controversial Arizona Sheriff on Guns," *The Hill*, January 7, 2016, thehill.com.
68. "gulag" from Gibson, J.G., "Disgraced Sheriff Paul Babeu Ran Massachusetts Boarding School with History of Physical Abuse," February 26, 2012, dailykos.com. "icy" from Kahn, Roger, *Into My Own: The Remarkable People and Events That Shaped a Life*, New York, Diversion Books, 2012, 272.
69. "outed" from Christie, Bob, "Paul Babeu Says He's Gay After Misconduct Claims," *Huffington Post*, April 20, 2012. "attorney" from Alonzo, "Paul Babeu's Mexican Ex-lover." "four-year" from Collom, Lindsey, and Hansen, Ronald J., "Paul Babeu's Ex-boyfriend Seeks $1 Million in Damages," *The Republic*, March 6, 2012. "Underpants" from Montini, "Montini." "Washington" from Stern, Ray, "Republican Sheriff Paul Babeu, Outed as Gay by Ex-lover, Running Again for Congress," *Phoenix New Times*, October 5, 2015.
70. "records" from Siano, Frank E., Chief Probation Officer, Commonwealth of Massachusetts, Probation Department, to Francis X. Spina, Associate Judge, Berkshire Superior Court, December 13, 1993. "aftercare" from Siano, Frank E., Chief Probation Officer, Commonwealth of Massachusetts, Probation Department, to Francis X. Spina, Associate Judge, Berkshire Superior Court, December 13, 1993. "ensure" from Siano, Frank E., Chief Probation Officer, Commonwealth of Massachusetts, Probation Department, to Francis X. Spina, Associate Judge, Berkshire Superior Court, December 17, 1993. "talk" from Transcript of Proceedings, *Commonwealth vs. Richard R. Lavigne*, Docket No. 92028, Telephone Lobby Conference, Berkshire Superior Court, December 7, 1993. "went" from *Commonwealth v. Richard R. Lavigne*, Motion Requesting Modification of the Conditions of Probation, November 19, 1993. "12/7/93" from Zajac and Goldberg, "Unsealed Records."
71. "databases" from State of Massachusetts,

Public Safety Division, State of Massachusetts Sex Offender Registry Board from mass.gov, and City of Chicopee Sex Offender Registry, Sex Offender Flyer from chicopeema.gov. "possibility" from Heaney, "Report Says." "drowned" from *The Republican Company v. Massachusetts Appeals Court, Clerk of the Hampden Superior Court, Richard R. Lavigne, the District Attorney for the Hampden District, and John Doe, Respondents*, December 18, 2003, Document Description, Privilege Claimed, Hampshire Country CPAD Reports—1991.

72. "devious" from DeMontigny, Maurice E., Letter to the Editor, *The Catholic Observer*, November 13, 2003. "enigma" from Shea, "Friends, Foes."

73. "salvation" from Cullen, "Danny's Story." "Mercy" from Melley, "Lavigne's New Calling."

74. "Supper" from Zajac, April 21, 2002.

75. "casket" from Fitzgerald, Brian, Croteau, III.

76. "haunts" from Cullen, "Danny's Story."

77. "died" from Carl and Bernice, May 27, 1993.

78. "priestly" from Shea, "Croteau Told." "overwhelmed" from Croteau, J.

79. "jail" Shea, "Croteau Told." "hurting" from Campbell.

80. "daughters" from "Obituary, Croteau, Gregory," *Republican*, October 2, 2015.

81. "behind" from Claffey, November 11, 1998, and Croteau, J.

82. "fiancée" from "Obituary, Croteau, Michael F.," *Republican*, May 22, 2009.

83. "hurry" from Shea, "Lavigne Link."

84. "worth" from Maharaj, VI, "uttering" from Shea, "Parents Dream."

85. "unsafe" from Bourie, Richard to EJF, May 26, 2005.

86. "disappear" from Croteau, J.

87. "take" from Croteau, B., "Murder Most Foul." "Stations" from Shea, "No One."

88. "sure" from Cullen, "Danny's Story."

89. "next" from *Ibid.*

90. "jack" from "Obituary, Croteau, Bernice," *Republican*, November 13, 2016.

91. "spoiling" from Shea, "Parents Dream." "cruelest" from Shea, "Mother Waits."

92. "yelling" from Cullen, "Danny's Story." "screaming" from Caywood, Thomas, "Mom Hopes New Probe Reveals Son's Killer," *Boston Herald*, August 6, 2004. "nothing" from Cullen, "Danny's Story."

93. "reminded" from Cullen, "Danny's Story."

94. "cruelest" from Shea, "2 More Men."

Bibliography

Books and Published Works

American Bar Association, Criminal Justice Section, Prosecution Function, Part 1—Standards, No. 2–1.2, The Function of the Prosecutor, Standards, No. 3–1.3, Conflicts of Interest, Standards, No. 3–2.8, Relationship with Police, Standards, No. 3–3.4, Decision to Charge, Standards, No. 3–3.9, Discretion in the Charging Decision.

Barrus, Hirum, *History of the Town of Goshen, Hampshire Country, Massachusetts, From its First Settlement in 1761 to 1881, With Family Sketches*, Boston, Hirum Barrus, 1881.

Berry, Jason, *Lead Us Not Into Temptation: Catholic Priests and the Sexual Abuse of Children*, Urbana, University of Illinois Press, 2002.

_____, *Render Unto Rome: The Secret Life of Money in the Catholic Church*, New York, Broadway Paperbacks, 2011.

Boyle, Patrick, *Scout's Honor: Sexual Abuse in America's Most Trusted Institution*, Prima Publishing, 2013.

Building a Better Life: The French Canadian Experience in Western Massachusetts, Springfield, Massachusetts, Pediment Group, 2012.

Burkett, Elinor, and Bruni, Frank, *A Gospel of Shame*, New York, Viking Press, 1994.

Careful Selection and Training of Candidates for the States of Perfection and Sacred Orders, Congregation for Religious, February 2, 1961.

Class Notes: News and Information for Alumni of St. Charles College, St. Mary's Seminary College and St. Mary's Seminary, Spring 2015.

Coleman, James A., *The Circle*, Ludlow, MA, Pro Litho, 1970, iUniverse, 2000.

Commission of Investigation, Report into the Catholic Archdiocese of Dublin, July 2009, and *Supplementary Report*, December 2010.

Confoy, Maryanne, *Religious Life and Priesthood: Perfectaie Caritatis, Optatam Totius, Presbyterian Odinis*, Mahway, New Jersey, Paulist Press, 2008.

Coville, Walter, D'Arcy, Paul, McCarthy, Thomas, and Rooney, John, *Assessment of Candidates for the Religious Life: Basic Psychological Issues and Problems*, Washington, D.C., Center for Applied Research in the Apostolate, 1968.

Cruickshank, Ginger, *Images of America: Springfield, Volume 1*, Charleston, South Carolina, Arcadia Publishing, 1999.

D'Antonio, Michael, *Mortal Sins: Sex, Crime, and the Era of Catholic Scandal*, New York, St. Martin's Press, 2013.

Deviney, Elizabeth, Dickert, J., Lockwood, R., et al., "The Care of Pets Within Child Abusing Families," *International Journal for the Study of Animal Problems* 4 (1983).

Diagnostic and Statistical Manual of Mental Disorders, 5th ed., Washington, D.C., American Psychiatric Association, 1952, 2015.

Dodecki, Paul R., *The Clergy Sex Abuse Crisis: Reform and Renewal in the Catholic Community*, Washington, D.C., Georgetown University Press, 2004.

Doyle, Thomas P., O.P., J.C.D., *The 1922 Instruction and the 1962 Instruction "Crimen Solicitationis,"* Promulgated by the Vatican, October 3, 2008.

Doyle, Thomas P., O.P., J.C.D., Sipe, A.W.R., and Wall, Patrick J., *Sex, Priests and Secret Codes: The Catholic Church's 2000-Year Paper Trail of Sexual Abuse*, Los Angeles, Volt Press, 2005.

Felthous, Ian R., M.D., "Aggression Against Cats, Dogs, and People," *Child Psychology and Human Development* 10 (1980).

Fitton, James, Rev., *Sketches of the Establishment of the Catholic Church in New England*, Boston, Massachusetts, Patrick Donahue, 1872.

Gleyzer, Roman, and Felthous, Alan R., "Animal Cruelty and Psychiatric Disorders," *Journal of the American Academy of Psychiatry Law* 30, no. 65 (2002).

"Grand Jury," Cornell University School of Law, Legal Information Institute.

Guindon, André, *The Sexual Language: An Essay in Moral Theology*, Ottawa, University of Ottawa Press, 1977.

Huntley, Heather Ewell, ed., *East Longmeadow Massachusetts: 1894–1994: Centennial Edition*, State College, Pennsylvania, Jostens Printing & Publishing Division, 1994.

The Irish Legacy: A History of the Irish in Western Massachusetts, Springfield, Massachusetts, Pediment Group, 2012.

Jenkins, P., *Pedophiles and Priests: Anatomy of a Contemporary Crisis*, New York, Oxford University Press, 1996.

John Paul II, Pope, *Sacramentorum sanctitatis tutela*, April 30, 2001.

Kahn, Roger, *Into My Own: The Remarkable People and Events That Shaped a Life*, New York, Diversion Books, 2012.

Kennedy, Eugene, and Heckler, Victor J., *The Catholic Priest in the United States: Psychological Investigations*, Washington, D.C., United States Catholic Conference, 1972.

Keystone Folklore Quarterly XII.I (1963).

Lanning, Kenneth, *Child Molesters: A Behavioral Analysis, for Law Enforcement Officers Investigating Cases of Child Abuse*, National Center for Missing and Exploited Children, 2010.

Latourette, Kenneth Scott, *Christianity in a Revolutionary Age: A History of Christianity in the Nineteenth and Twentieth Centuries*, New York, Harper & Brothers, 1958–62; reprint, Westport, Connecticut, Greenwood Press, 1973.

Lothstein, L.M., Ph.D., *Treating Clergy Who Sexually Abuse Minors: A 16-Year Experience in the Professionals and Clergy Program at the IOL*.

McCoy, J.J., et al., *History of the Catholic Church in New England States, Vol. 2*, Boston, Massachusetts, The Hurd & Everts Co., 1899.

Miccio-Fonseca, L.C., "Reasons Why We Can't Profile Sex Offenders," ccoso.org.

National Research Council of the National Academies, *The Polygraph and Lie Detection: Committee to Review the Scientific Evidence on the Polygraph*, Washington, D.C., The National Academies Press, American Psychiatric Association, 2003.

Newberger, Eli, M.D., *Abuse of Children by Priests in the Boston Archdiocese: Violations of Applicable Standards of Care*, March 3, 2003.

Norton, Roger, The National Registry of Exonerations, University of Michigan, November 27, 2012.

The Official Catholic Directory, New York, P.J. Kenedy & Sons, 1960, 1985, 1999, 2013.

Peters, Edward, trans., *The 1917 or Pio-Benedictine Code of Canon Law: An English Translation with Extensive Scholarly Apparatus*, San Francisco, Ignatius Press, 2001.

Phillips, Ally, J.D., *Understanding the Links Between Violence to Animals and People: A Guidebook to Criminal Justice Professionals*, Arlington, Virginia, National District Attorneys Association, 2014.

Podles, Leon J., *Case Study: Donald Matthew Osgood (1927–)*, Baltimore, Maryland, Crossland Foundation, 2008.

_____, *Sacrilege: Sexual Abuse in the Catholic Church*, Baltimore, Maryland, Crossland Press, 2008.

Poulet, Charles, and Raemers, Sidney A., *A History of the Catholic Church*, St. Louis, Missouri, B. Herder Book Co., 1934.

The Report of the Archdiocesan Commission of Enquiry into the Sexual Abuse of Children by Members of the Clergy, Archdiocese of St. Johns, 1990.

Robinson, Geoffrey, *Confronting Power and Sex in the Catholic Church*, Mulgrave, Victoria, Australia, John Garrett Publishing, 2007.

Rose, Michael S., *Goodbye! Good Men: How Catholic Seminaries Turned Away Two Generations of Vocations*, Los Angeles, California, Hope of St. Monica, 2002.

Sipe, R., *Sexuality and the Search for Celibacy*, New York, Brunner Mazel, 1990.

Smith, Nicky, "Reading Between the Lines: An Evaluation of the Scientific Content Analysis Technique (SCAN)," Police Research Series, Paper 135, Home Office, Policing and Reducing Crime Unit, Research, Development and Statistics Directorate, Clive House, Petty France, London, 2001.

Soule, Rolland L., "Reproduction of Foot and Tire Tracks by Plaster of Paris Casting," *Journal of Criminal Law and Criminology* 50, Issue 2, Chicago, Illinois, Northwestern School of Law Scholarly Commons, July–August 1959.

Studies in Psychology and Psychiatry 7, no. 3, April 1948.

Tapia, F., "Children Who Are Cruel to Animals," *Journal of Operational Psychiatry* 2 (1971).

Tapsell, Kieran, *Potiphar's Wife: The Vatican's Secret and Child Sex Abuse*, Hindmarsh, SA, Australia, ATF Press/ATF, 2014.

Terry, Karen J., Smith, Margaret Leland, Schutt, Katarina, O.S.F., Kelly, James R., Vollman, Brenda, Massey, Christina, *The Causes and Context of Sexual Abuse of Minors By Catholic Priests in the United States: A Report Presented to the United States Conference of Catholic Bishops by the John Jay College Research Team*, John Jay College of Criminal Justice, The City University of New York, United States Conference of Catholic Bishops, Washington, D.C., February 2011.

"2014 Annual Report," United States Conference of Bishops, Secretariat of Child and Youth Protection, National Review Board, Report on the Implementation of the Charter for the Protection of Children and Young People, March 2014.

Walton-Moss, B. J., Manganello, J., Frye, V., Campbell, J. C., "Risk Factors for Intimate Partner Violence and Associated Injury Among Urban Women." *Journal of Community Health* 30, no. 5 (2005).

West, D.J., *Homosexuality: Its Nature and Causes*, London, Aldine Transactions, 2008.

Wolfe, Tom, *The Bonfire of the Vanities*, New York, Bantam Books, 1988.

Census, City Directories, Immigration, Military, Birth and Death Records

Canada, Census, Arthabaska, St. Valère de Bulstrode, 1871.

Commonwealth of Massachusetts, Department of Health, Registry of Vital Statistics,

Massachusetts Vital Records, Index to Deaths, Vol. 82, 1926–1930, Vol. 89, 1931–1935, Vol. 91, 1931–1935.

_____, Index to Births, 1931–1935, 1936–1940.

_____, Index to Marriages, 1901–1955, 1921–1925, 1926–1930.

Directory, City of Bridgeport, Connecticut, 1901–1915.

_____, City of Chicopee, Massachusetts, 1931, 1964

_____, City of Easthampton, Massachusetts, 1956, 1960.

_____, City of Hartford, Connecticut, 1899–1900.

_____, City of Norwalk, Connecticut, 1903–1909.

_____, City of Springfield, Massachusetts, 1919–1951.

_____, City of Springfield, Massachusetts, Suburban Directory, 1928.

_____, City of Westbrook, Maine, 1916–1925.

Korean War Casualty File, 2/13/1950–12/31/1953; Records on Korean War Dead and Wounded Army Casualties, 1950–1970; Records of the Adjutant General's Office, Record Group 407; National Archives at College Park, College Park, Maryland.

Province of Quebec, Vital and Church Records (Drouin Collection), 1906, Notre-Dame-de-Ham, Registries.

Registration Card/Registrar's Report, State of Maine, Cumberland County, Local Board for Division No. 2, Cote, Joseph Phidime, September 12, 1918 (World War I draft registration form).

2nd Infantry Division, Korean War Project Record: USA-125, National Archives and Records Administration, College Park, Maryland, Record Group: RG-407.

State of Maine, Marriage Records, Record of a Marriage Joseph Cote & Albertine Auclaire, June 2, 1902.

38th Infantry Regiment, *Command and Unit Historical Report: 38th Infantry Regiment, for 1 September–30 October, 1950*, Korean War, 38th Infantry Regiment-Record Losses 1950, 2nd Infantry Division, Korean War Project Record: USA-126, National Archives and Records Administration, College Park, Maryland.

_____, *Command Report—December 1950, July–August 1950, September–October 1950, November 1950*, 2nd Infantry Division, Korean War Project Record: USA-126, National

Archives and Records Administration, College Park, Maryland, Record Group: RG-407.

_____, Miscellaneous Records—Awards—December 1950, 2nd Infantry Division, Korean War Project Record: USA-127, National Archives and Records Administration, College Park, Maryland, Record Group: RG-407.

United States, Department of War, World War II Army Enlistment Records, 1938–1946.

_____, Immigration Service, Examination Certificate, Medical Record, Clerina Lavigne, April 23, 1923.

_____, Immigration Service, Examination Record, Medical Certificate, April 18, 1923.

_____, Immigration Service, List of Manifest of Alien Passengers Applying for Admission from Foreign Contiguous Territory, St. Albans, Vermont, April 1923, June 1923.

_____, Immigration Service, Primary Inspection Memorandum, Newport, VT, Adlard [sic] Lavigne, November 30, 1922.

_____, Immigration Service, Primary Inspection Memorandum, November 30, 1922.

_____, Naturalization Service, Declaration of Intention, Petition for Naturalization, Joseph Phidime Cote, July 29, 1918.

United States Federal Census, 1900–1940.

Internet and Website Research

animalsandsoceity.org, Animals & Society Institute.

"As I Recall: Why I Wrote About the 8.5 Million Dollar Settlement," springfielddiocese.blogspot.com.

aspca.org, American Society for the Prevention of Cruelty to Animals.

avma.org, American Veterinary Medical Association.

"Boy Scout Perversion Files," boyscoutsexualabuse.com.

Carless, William, "South America Has Become a Safe Haven for the Catholic Church's Alleged Child Molesters. The Vatican Has No Comment," pri.org.

"Category: Church Responsibility, Boston Ring," eurekaencyclopedia.com.

"Catholic Bishops Who Helped Priests Rape Children," samesexprocreation.com.

Congregation of Sacred Stigmata, "Joseph E. Flood, Confratelli Stimmatini, After Oc-

tober 31, 1996," confrades.com/morti/mortifghijk/floodjosephinglese.

Devine, Tom, Baystate Objectivist Archives, May 30, 2009, 5 tommydevine.blogspot.com.

Duara, Nigel, "Boy Scouts 'Perversion' Files Show Locals Helped Cover Up Child Sex Abuse By Scoutmasters," Huffington Post, December 18, 2013, huffingtonpost.com.

"1st Cavalry Divison," koreanwar.org.

"1st Cavalry Division History: Korean War 1950–1951," first-team.us.com.

Fitzgerald, Brian, "Hell's Acres," The Danny Croteau Murder, Parts 1-6, The Circle Gang, Parts 1-6, The Gully, Parts 1-4, hellsacres.blogspot.com.

Fitzpatrick, Frank L., Isolation and Silence: A Male Survivor Speaks Out About Clergy Abuse, movingforward.org.

"From D+1 to 105: The Story of the 2nd Infantry Division," "The 2nd Infantry Division's Story: Second to None," lonesentry.com.

Henshaw, Fr. Robert, The Spirit of the Order: What is the Spirit of the Assumption Order?, http//:assumptionist.org.uk.

"History and Procedures for Handling of Misconduct Allegations," September 1, 2011, scidb.com.

"The History of Cathedral High School: 1883–2012," cathedralhigh.org, last visited March 1, 2016.

Humm, Andy, "Vatican Gay Scapegoating Official," gaycitynews.com.

ivfsa.org, International Veterinary Forensic Sciences Association.

Kelly, Robert M., "The True Cost of the Settlements," Western Massachusetts Catholics, March 2010, westernmassachusettscatholics.com.

Kirchgaessner, Stephinia, "New Bishops Told Abuse Reporting 'Not Necessarily' Their Duty," Irish Times, February 10, 2016, irishtimes.com.

Lavigne, Richard Roger, State of Massachusetts, Public Safety Division, State of Massachusetts Sex Offender Registry Board, mass.gov.

Maharaj, Jai, The Daniel Croteau Murder, Part 1–Part 6, Part 10, croteaumurderblogspot.com.

"Memo Outlines How Boy Scouts Responded to Abuse Allegations," ABC-10 News, San Diego, California, 10news.com.

Nadeau, Barbie Latza, "Torture the Little Chil-

dren? The Catholic Church Says It's Not Responsible," May 6, 2014, dailybeast.com.
ncadv.org, National Coalition Against Domestic Violence.
O'Connor, John, "Family Tree: Hungry Hill Neighborhood Long Home to Springfield's Irish," masslive.com.
O'Leary, Naomi, "Sex Abuse: The Scandal the Catholic Church Can't Shake," March 7, 2013, reuters.com.
"Our Plural History: French-Canadian Immigrants in Holyoke," stcc.edu.
"Our Plural History: Irish Immigrants in Holyoke," stcc.edu.
"2nd Indianhead Division," 2ida.org.
Sex Offender Flyer, Richard Roger Lavigne, City of Chicopee Sex Offender Registry, chicopeema.gov.
"Sexual Abuse by U.S. Catholic Clergy: Settlements and Monetary Awards in Civil Suits," bishopaccountability.com.
springfielddiocese.blogspot.com/2009/04 (Chapters 1–21).
"U.S. Army Second Infantry Division/ROK-US Combined Division: History," 2id. korea.army.com.
Wilson, Charles M., and Dunnigan, R. Michael, "The Narcotic of Secrecy: Canon Lawyer Charles Wilson on the Bishops," May 1, 2002, christifidelis.com.

Interviews

Bourie, Richard
Campbell, Linda, PhD
Childhood friends, Richard Lavigne, with Zajac, Bill and Mason, Warren.
Crean, Fr. Hugh
Croteau, Bernice (Bunny) Croteau
Croteau, Carl Croteau, Sr.
Croteau, Joseph
Downing, Jack
Frigo, Dino
Gelinas, Luke
Mason, Warren
Mazzarino, Carol
Nicastro, Drew
O'Brien, Darby
Rezendes, Michael
Ryan, Ann
Stevens, R.C.
Tessier, Sandra
Wirzbicki, Alan
Zajac, Bill

Legal, Church and Court Documents

Affidavit of Carl Croteau, December 12, 2003, Exhibit A.
Affidavit of Fr. Thomas Doyle, August 12, 2003.
Affidavit of First Assistant District Attorney David A. Angier and Assistant District Attorney Ariana D. Vuono, *Commonwealth of Massachusetts v. Richard R. Lavigne*, Indictment No. 93–080.
Affidavit of Lt. Edward E. Harrington, Massachusetts State Police Bureau of Investigative Services, Hampshire County CPAC, January 9, 1994.
Affidavit of Maurice E. DeMontigny, August 15, 2003.
Affidavit of Paul R. Babeu, *John Doe v. Clerk of the Franklin Superior Court, Richard R. Lavigne, and District Attorney for the Northwestern District*, June 4, 2002.
Affidavit of Thomas L. Dupré, Bishop of Springfield, April 30, 2003.
Andre P. Tessier v. Richard R. Lavigne, Robert W. Thrasher, and Roman Catholic Diocese of Springfield, a Corporation Sole, No. 02-727.
Attestation, Fr. Maurice J. Dingman and Ralph A. Hayes, Bishop of Davenport (Iowa), October 3, 1938.
Authorization to Obtain Records, Richard R. Lavigne, St. Luke's Institute, Inc., December 9, 1993.
Autopsy Report, Case A–72–49, Pathological Diagnosis on the Body of Daniel Croteau, 106 Ferncliff Street, Springfield, Massachusetts, April 15, 1972.
Chicopee Police Department, Complaint Sheet 19–221A, April 15–24, 1972.
City of Chicopee, Chicopee Parks & Recreation Department, Letter of Termination, Richard R. Lavigne, August 4, 1968.
Commonwealth of Massachusetts, *André Tessier v. Richard R. Lavigne.*
_____, *David A. Galeziowski v. Richard R. Lavigne, Joseph F. Maguire, Robert W. Thrasher, and Roman Catholic Diocese of Springfield, a Corporation Sole*, No. 02-991.
_____, *Elizabeth A. Germond v. Roman Catholic Diocese of Springfield, a Corporation Sole, John F. Harrington, Richard R. Lavigne, Robert W. Thrasher*, March 5, 2003.

_____, Harold F. and Shiela Francis, Parents of James Francis, [Redacted] v. The Roman Catholic Archbishop of Boston, a Corporation Sole and Ronald Paquin, Complaint and Jury Trial Demand, April 10, 2002.

_____, John Doe v. Richard R. Lavigne, Joseph F. Maguire, Robert W. Thrasher, and Roman Catholic Diocese of Springfield, a Corporation Sole, No. 02–993, Affidavit of Paul R. Babeu.

_____, John Doe v. Roman Catholic Diocese of Springfield, July 29, 2004.

_____, Paul R. Babeu v. Richard R. Lavigne, Joseph F. Maguire, Robert W. Thrasher, Thomas L. Dupré, and Roman Catholic Diocese of Springfield, a Corporation Sole.

_____, The Republican Company v. Massachusetts Appeals Court, Clerk of the Hampden Superior Court, Richard R. Lavigne, The District Attorney for the Hampden District, and John Doe, Respondents, December 18, 2003, Document Description, Privilege Claimed, Hampshire Country CPAD Reports–1991.

_____, The Republican Company, Petitioner, v. Massachusetts Appeals Court, Clerk of the Hampden Superior Court, Richard M. Lavigne, the District Attorney for the Hampden District, and John Doe, Respondents.

_____, Shawn M. Dobbert v. Richard R. Lavigne, Joseph F. Maguire, Robert W. Thrasher, and Roman Catholic Diocese of Springfield, a Corporation Sole, No. 02–728.

_____, Susan Morris, v. Richard Lavigne, Joseph F. Maguire, Robert W. Thrasher, and Roman Catholic Diocese of Springfield, a Corporation Sole, No. 03–241.

Commonwealth of Massachusetts, A Manual for the Use of the General Court, Boston, MA, 1983.

_____, Department of Civil Service, Authorization and Notification of Employment Form, Chicopee, Parks & Recreation, No. C8–7584, May 23, 1958.

_____, Department of Public Safety, LAB No. 38039, Examination of Materials in connection with the Fatal Beating at Chicopee on April 15, 1972. Victim Daniel Croteau, 106 Ferncliff, Springfield, and Supplementary Report: Daniel Croteau, #38039, May 2, 1972, May 15, 1972.

_____, In re Richard Lavigne, Petitioner, Petitioner's Memorandum of Law in Support of His Motion for Return of His Blood Sample.

_____, In the Matter of Richard R. Lavigne, September 29, 1993.

_____, In the Matter of Richard R. Lavigne, Affidavit of Trooper Thomas J. Daly, October 18, 1993.

_____, In the Matter of Richard R. Lavigne, 418 Mass. 831, May 3, 1994–November 16, 1994, Hampden County.

_____, Indictments Nos. 92–028 through 92–032, Change of Plea, June 25, 1992, Indictments No. 92–028, no. 92–029, no. 92–030, no. 92–031, no. 92–032, all dated February 14, 1992.

_____, Massachusetts State Police, Bureau of Investigative Services, Hampshire Country CPAC, Addendum to Alleged Sexual Assaults in Franklin County, CS#91–017–1199–0193.

_____, Motion Requesting Modification of the Conditions of Probation, November 19, 1993.

_____, Motion to Consider Modification of the Conditions of Probation, November 19, 1993.

_____, Motion to Leave to File Memorandum as Amici Curiae on Behalf of Michael J. Slowinski, Bea Cevasco, Peter Dolan, Margaret J. Carlson, and 487 Other Named Individuals, April 20, 1992.

_____, No. 93–080, October 5, 1994.

_____, Statement of Agreed Facts.

_____, Trial Court of Massachusetts, Massachusetts Superior Court, Hampden Division, John H. Moriarty, September 2, 1993.

Deposition of Fr. Bernard Flanagan, Bishop, Diocese of Worcester, Mark Barry v. Bishop of Worcester and Thomas Kane, Defendants, June 6, 1995.

Deposition of Fr. Daniel Liston, John Doe v. Richard R. Lavigne, et al., CA# 02385, April 9, 2003.

Deposition of Fr. James J. Scahill, Susan F. Morris v. Richard Lavigne, Joseph Maguire, Robert Thrasher and Roman Catholic Diocese of Springfield, No. 03–241.

Frank E. Siano, Chief Probation Officer, Commonwealth of Massachusetts to Francis X. Spina, Associate Justice, Berkshire Superior Court, Re: Richard Lavigne, FCS# 92–030 & 92–028, December 13, 1993.

Instruction on the Manner of Proceeding in Cases of Solicitation, The Vatican Press, 1922, 1962.

Interim Report of Number of Allegedly Abusive Priests in the United States, June 18, 2003, compiled by Survivors First, Inc.

Memorandum and Order on Defendants' Motion for Summary Judgement, Thayer Fremont-Smith, Justice of the Superior Court, *Michael Moe et al. v. The Trustees of the Stigmatine Fathers, Inc. aka Congregation of the Sacred Stigmata et al.*, #05–0059, June 4, 2008.

Memorandum of Interview, Attorney General's Office, Manchester, New Hampshire, re: Diocese of Manchester, Father Leo Landry, October 7, 2002, October 18, 2002.

_____, re: Leo Landry, October 4, 2002.

New Hampshire State Police, Fowler, Anthony, Investigator, "Transcript: [Redacted] Interview," October 15, 2002.

_____, "Transcript: [Redacted] Interview," October 18, 2002, October 23, 2002.

New Hampshire State Police, Kimball, Kathleen M., Detective, and Fowler, Anthony, Investigator, "Transcript: Leo Landry Interview," October 17, 2002, September 3, 2002, September 4, 2002.

Norton, Roger B., Confidential Record Sheet, Registration and Membership, Registration Division, Boy Scouts of America, November 29, 1973.

_____, Resignation Notice, Registration Division, Boy Scouts of America, November 29, 1973 (addendum).

_____, Separation Notice, Registration Division, Boy Scouts of America, August 8, 1973.

Pastoral Report, Richard R. Lavigne, Seminary of Our Lady of Angels, Eugene E. Guérin, September 3, 1965, September 5, 1964.

Psychological Profile, Richard Lavigne, Seminary of Our Lady of Angels, June 1963.

Report of Scholastic Standing, Richard R. Lavigne, Seminary of Our Lady of Angels, Spring 1963–Spring 1964, Spring 1965–Spring 1966.

Report of the Grand Jury, No. 03–00–239, Re: Joseph P. Gausch, September 17, 2003, Lynne Abraham, District Attorney.

Rochester (NH) Police Department, Incident Report, Narrative for Patrolman Derek M. Davis, June 5, 1998.

_____, Narrative for Sergeant Paul G. Callahan, September 18, 1998.

Separation Notice, Roger B. Norton, Pioneer Valley Council, Boy Scouts of America, West Springfield, Massachusetts, October 29, 1973.

Statement of Bernice Croteau, Chicopee Police Department, August 7, 1972.

Statement of Bishop John F. Maguire, Bishop, Springfield Diocese, October 27, 1991.

Statement of Carl and Bernice Croteau, May 27, 1993, from Commonwealth of Massachusetts, In the matter of Richard R. Lavigne, September 29, 1993.

Statement of Carl Croteau, from Statement of Thomas J. Daly, Affidavit in Support of Application for Search Warrant, September 2, 1993.

Statement of J. Shattuck, October 1991, from *Commonwealth v. Richard R. Lavigne*, No. 92 032, February 14, 1992.

Statement of J. Shattuck, September 18, 1991, and amended October 1991, in Statement of Thomas J. Daly, Affidavit in Support of Application for Search Warrant, September 2, 1993, in Commonwealth of Massachusetts, In the matter of Richard R. Lavigne, September 29, 1993.

Statement of J. Shattuck's Sister, October 11, 1991, from Commonwealth of Massachusetts, In the matter of Richard R. Lavigne, September 29, 1993.

Statement of James A. Coleman, May 13, 1993.

Statement of John A. Marshall, Bishop, Springfield Diocese, June 26, 1992

Statement of Mary Bobek, December 1, 1992.

Statement of Michael McMahon, December 31, 1991, Commonwealth of Massachusetts, In the matter of Richard R. Lavigne, September 29, 1993.

Statement of Officer, October 14, 1991, from Statement of Thomas J. Daly, Affidavit in Support of Application for Search Warrant, September 2, 1993.

Statement of Paul Babeu, originally Statement of Witness, Anonymous, to Massachusetts State Police Barracks, Northampton, October 25, 1991, from Commonwealth of Massachusetts, In the matter of Richard R. Lavigne, September 29, 1993.

Statement of Raymond Gouin, Jr., October 28, 1991, from Commonwealth of Massachusetts, In the matter of Richard R. Lavigne, September 29, 1993.

Statement of Thomas J. Daly, Affidavit in Support of Application for Search Warrant, September 2, 1993.

Statement of Thomas L. Dupré, Bishop, "The Diocese Will Seek Fair and Just Settlements of Abuse Cases," September 29, 2003.

Statement of Witness, December 9, 1991, from Statement of Thomas J. Daly, Affidavit in Support of Application for Search Warrant, September 2, 1993, in Commonwealth of Massachusetts, In the matter of Richard R. Lavigne, September 29, 1993.

Statement of Witness, December 24, 1991, from Statement of Thomas J. Daly, Affidavit in Support of Application for Search Warrant, September 2, 1993, in Commonwealth of Massachusetts, In the matter of Richard R. Lavigne, September 29, 1993, and Statement February 1, 1992, November 1, 1991, November 9, 1991, November 11, 1991, November 15, 1991, October 9, 1991, October 14, 1991, October 16, 1991, October 28, 1991, October 29, 1991, October 29, 1991, November 1, 1991, November 8, 1991, November 15, 1991, November 21, 1991, November 24, 1991, March 24, 1991.

Statement of Witness, October 24, 1991, taken by Trooper Michael Habel, Franklin CPAC, from Statement of Thomas J. Daly, Affidavit in Support of Application for Search Warrant, September 2, 1993, in Commonwealth of Massachusetts, *In the matter of Richard R. Lavigne*, September 29, 1993.

Statement of Witness, Victim Statement #3.

Transcript, Lavigne, Richard Roger, Office of the Registrar, Assumption College, Worcester, Massachusetts, June 9, 1962.

Transcript of Proceedings, *Commonwealth of Massachusetts vs. Richard R. Lavigne*, Docket No. 92028, Telephone Lobby Conference, Berkshire Superior Court, December 7, 1993.

Transcripts, Commonwealth of Massachusetts, Grand Jury, Franklin County, February 14, 1992.

Warren, Janet I., DSW, "Review of the Ineligible Volunteer (IV) Files of the Boy Scouts of America (BSA)," University of Virginia, August 25, 2011.

Letters, Inter-Office Memorandums, Press Releases and Correspondence

Babeu, Paul R., to Dupré, Fr. Thomas L., and Maguire, Fr. Joseph F., Bishop of Springfield, June 19, 2002.

Bertone, Fr. Tarcisio, to Weakland, Fr. Rembert, Bishop of Milwaukee, "Summary of May 30, 1998 Meeting Concerning the Case of the Rev. Lawrence Murphy," July 13, 1998.

Connolly, Fr. James L., Bishop of Fall River, to Paquette, Fr. Edward O., January 18, 1963.

Crete, Mr. & Mrs. Rene to Maguire, Fr. Joseph F., Bishop of Springfield, June 28, 1988.

DeMontigny, Maurice E., Letter to the Editor, *The Catholic Observer*, November 13, 2003.

Diocese of Manchester, New Hampshire, Blonigen, Brenda M., Sergeant, Internal Memorandum, Diocese of Manchester, September 17, 2002.

_____, Brodeur, Paul E., Inv., Internal Memorandum, Complaints re: Priest, April 19, 2002, April 24, 2009.

_____, Diocese of Manchester, New Hampshire, Brodeur, Paul E., Inv., Internal Memorandum, CRI–02–00103 Priests, April 22, 2002.

_____, Fr. Donald Osgood File.

_____, R.E.M. (author), Internal Memorandum, Fr. Donald Osgood File, undated.

Diocese of Manchester, New Hampshire, to Brown, S. George, M.D., March 23, 1964.

Diocese of Springfield, "Press Release," March 8, 2006.

_____, "Press Release," May 11, 2005.

_____, "Press Release: Statement of John A. Marshall, Bishop, Springfield Diocese," June 26, 1992

_____, "Press Release: Statement of Rev. Joseph Maguire, Bishop of Springfield," October 25, 1991.

Dupré, Fr. Thomas L., Bishop of Springfield (Massachusetts) to Edward J. Fleming, September 2, 2002.

_____, to Files, Inter-Office Memo, Subject: Father Richard Lavigne, November 5, 1991.

_____, to Lavigne, Fr. Richard, July 11, 1988.

_____, to Liston, Rev. Daniel, September 16, 1992.

Fitzgerald, Fr. Gerald, Servant General,

Order of the Paraclete, Jemez Springs, New Mexico, to Brady, Fr. Matthew F., Bishop of Manchester (New Hampshire), September 26, 1957.

Gausch, Fr. Joseph P., to Knapp, Fr. Charles L.G., May 25, 1948.

Gormley, William J., Office of the Rector, Seminary of Our Lady of Angels to John Harrington, Msgr., Chancellor, Springfield Diocese, re: Lavigne, Richard R. Lavigne, Petition for Minor Orders, February 15, 1964, February 28, 1963.

Hansberry, Thomas S., Internal Memorandum, "Osgood," Fr. Donald Osgood Files, March 3, 1965.

_____, Internal Memorandum, "Report of Conferences with D.M. Osgood," Fr. Donald Osgood Files, January 29, 1968.

Hernandez, Patrick L., to Maguire, Fr. Joseph F., Bishop of Springfield, November 6, 1991.

John E. Reid and Associates, Chicago, Illinois, to William C. Flanagan, Springfield, Massachusetts, May 15, 1972.

Lavigne, Fr. Richard, to Maguire, Fr. Joseph F., Bishop of Springfield, re: The Shattuck Group in Heath, Mass., April 3, 1991, May 15, 1987.

_____, to Viau, Fr. Roger, Vicar, Springfield Diocese, undated, ca. 1969–1970.

Lawrence, Fr. Robert, to Ratzinger, Fr. Joseph, January 12, 1998.

Letter of Acceptance, Seminary of Our Lady of the Angeles, William J. Gormley, Office of the Rector to Harrington, John, Msgr., Chancellor, Springfield Diocese, July 11, 1962.

Marshall, Fr. John A., Bishop of Springfield to all parishes, December 12, 1992.

Name redacted to Mark Dupont, Springfield Diocese, April 29, 2002.

O'Connor, Fr. Timothy F., to Gerard, James J., November 6, 1963.

Office of Stobierski & Stobierski, "Press Release. To Interested Media Outlets, re: Clergy Abuse Settlements," December 3, 2008.

Olkovikas, A.W., "Notes for File on Worcester Priest's Report on a Group of Abusers, Including Genest [sic], in Strictissima," September 3, 1958.

Primeau, Fr. Ernest J., Bishop of Manchester, Internal Memorandum, "Memo from Bishop Primeau to Msgr. Hansberry," undated.

_____, to Gilbert, Fr. Leo P., January 11, 1967.

Recommendation of Ordination to Priesthood, Richard R. Lavigne, William J. Gormley, Office of the Rector, Seminary of Our Lady of Angels, to Viau, Roger, Msgr., Springfield Diocese, May 2, 1966.

Ryan, John B., Springfield, to *Republican*, February 8, 1993.

Siano, Frank E., Chief Probation Officer, Commonwealth of Massachusetts, Probation Department, to Francis X. Spina, Associate Judge, Berkshire Superior Court, December 13, 1993, December 17, 1993.

Stern, Max D., and Garin, Patricia, to Media Outlets, "Press Release: Daniel Croteau Murder Investigation," August 5, 2004.

Stigmatine Fathers and Brothers, Office of the Provincial, Leo P. Landry, Chronology and Curriculum Vitae, November 14, 2002.

T.L.D. to Maguire, Fr. Thomas, Bishop, Springfield Diocese, July 14, 1987.

Weldon, Fr. Christopher J., Bishop, Springfield Diocese, to Fr. Richard R. Lavigne, February 12, 1973.

Newspapers and Periodicals— General Stories

Berkshire Eagle (Pittsfield, MA), December 31, 2004; August 18, 2004; March 29, 2004; May 20, 2010.

Boston Globe, November 21, 2003; February 21, 2004; April 14, 2004; April 16, 2004; May 19, 2004; June 11, 2004; August 10, 2002; March 23, 2002; November 21, 2003; May 12, 2004; April 25, 1992.

The Catholic Observer, January 7, 2005.

The Gazette (Gaithersburg, MD), July 9, 2008.

Houston Chronicle, November 1, 1998.

New Orleans Times-Picayune/States, October 20, 1985.

North Adams Transcript (North Adams, MA), September 18, 2009.

Providence Journal (Providence, RI), May 7, 2009.

Republican-American (Waterbury, CT), January 8, 2005.

Springfield Daily News/Springfield Unions News/Republican (Springfield, MA), April 15–30, 1972; December 14, 1992; December 23, 1993; February 25, 2002; March 28, 2002; June 7, 2002; June 17, 2002; March

24, 2003; Oct. 16, 2003; January 21, 2004; March 1, 2004; May 5, 2004; June 2, 2004; July 6, 2004; August 17, 2004; October 11, 2004; December 30, 2004; February 27, 2005; October 15, 2005; June 9, 2006; December 2, 2006; February 15, 2002; Jan.uary 8, 2005; March 10, 2006; June 29, 2006; July 22, 2006; April 9, 2008; May 15, 2008; December 2, 2008. NOTE: *Republican* is used for all citations referencing *Union-News, Springfield Daily News, Morning Union, Sunday Republican,* and *Republican.*

Newspapers and Periodicals— Specific Citations

"Accused Priest Will No Longer Play Church Organ," *The Barre Montpelier Times Argus,* September 16, 2004.
"Aldenville Traces Roots to Plymouth Colony," *Republican,* April 13, 2011.
Alderson, Iris, "Popular Priest Hugh Crean to Celebrate 50 Years of Priesthood at Mass on June 24," *Republican,* June 22, 2012.
Allen, John L., Jr., "Fr. Tom Doyle on 'Crimen Sollicitationis,'" *National Catholic Reporter,* October 13, 2006.
_____, "What New Catholic Bishops Are, and Aren't, Being Told on Sex Abuse Abuse," *Boston Globe,* February 7, 2016.
_____, "Will Ratzinger's Past Trump Benedict's Present?" *National Catholic Reporter,* March 17, 2010.
Alonzo, Monica, "Paul Babeu's Mexican Ex-lover Says Sheriff's Attorney Threatened Him with Deportation," *Phoenix New Times,* February 26, 2012.
"Anatomy of a Mob Murder: The Life, Death, and Legal Afterlife of Adolfo 'Big Al' Bruno," *Republican,* February 21, 2010.
Anderson, Travis, and Ellement, John R., "Ex-priest Jailed in Abuse Scandal Has Been Released," *Boston Globe,* October 2, 2015.
Anderson, Travis, and Finucane, Martin, "List of 1,200 Suspected Child Abusers Barred from Volunteering with Boy Scouts Includes 45 Mass. Men," *Boston Globe,* October 19, 2012.
"Animal Cruelty; Common in Many Killers," *Sunbury/Macedon Ranges Leader,* April 26, 2005.

Ballou, Brian R., "Victim's Family to Address Findings," *Boston Globe,* January 14, 2008.
Barry, Stephanie, "Bishop's Tape Sparks Dispute," *Republican,* July 15, 2010.
_____, "Court Documents Reveal Altar Boy's Ordeal," *Republican,* February 8, 2008.
_____, "Ex-Nun Named in Sex-Abuse Suit," *Republican,* December 30, 2004.
_____, "Judge Denies Former Springfield Bishop Thomas Dupré Motion to Keep Video Testimony from Public," *Republican,* July 15, 2010.
_____, "New Details Emerge About Abusive Priest's History with Springfield Catholic Diocese," *Republican,* March 29, 2016.
_____, "Organized Crime in Springfield Evolved Through Death and Money," *Republican,* December 11, 2011, updated April 25, 2013.
_____, "Priest's Letters Offer Clues to His Psyche," *Republican,* April 14, 2002.
_____, "Roman Catholic Diocese of Springfield Pay $4.5 Million to 59 Clergy Abuse Victims," *Republican,* December 2, 2008.
_____, "Roman Catholic Diocese of Springfield Reaches Settlement, Adds Another Name to Its List of Priests Accused of Sexual Abuse," *Republican,* March 29, 2016.
_____, "6 Priests Were Removed in 1990s: Last Action Taken in 1994," *Republican,* February 17, 2002.
_____, "6 Vt. Priests Removed from Their Parishes," *Republican,* June 14, 2002.
_____, and McCauliffe, Michael, "Matthew Ryan, Jr., Former Hamden County District Attorney, Dead at 92," *Republican,* August 24, 2009.
_____, and Spencer, Buffy, "Judge: Open Altar Boy Murder File," *Republican,* January 13, 2006.
Bass, Allison, "30 More Allege Sex Abuse in 1960's by Priest," *Boston Globe,* May 12, 1992.
Belkin, Douglas, "Priest Castigates Springfield Diocese for Abuse Dealings," *Boston Globe,* February 17, 2003.
Berry, Jason, "Father Marciel Maciel and the Popes He Stained," *Newsweek,* March 11, 2013.
_____, "The Tragedy of Gilbert Gauthe, Part 1," *The Times of Acadiana,* May 23, 1985, reprinted in the *National Catholic Reporter.*
_____, "The Tragedy of Gilbert Gauthe, Part 2," *The Times of Acadiana,* May 30, 1985,

reprinted in the *National Catholic Reporter*.

"Bishop's Statement," *Republican*, October 26, 1991.

Blixt, Peter, and Greig, June, "Priest Linked to 1972 Slaying: Pleads Innocent to Rape of Child," *Republican*, October 22, 1991.

Blow, Charles M., "Rise of the Religious Left," *New York Times*, July 2, 2010.

Bourie, Richard, "Lavigne Denies New Charges of Assault," *Republican*, February 26, 1992.

Boyle, Patrick, "Scouts Honor," *Washington Times*, 1991.

Bradley, Paul, and Krishnamurthy, Kiran, "Right and Wrong 'An Illusion': Psychologist Who Met with Malvo Said Teen's Disorder Limited His Moral Judgment," *Richmond Times Dispatch*, December 9, 2003.

Brault, Michael, "Matty Ryan Cast a Long Shadow," *Republican*, August 26, 2009.

Broncaccio, Diane, "Lawyer John Stobierski Has Unique Perspective on Child Abuse by Catholic Priests Portrayed in 'Spotlight,'" *Daily Hampshire Gazette*, November 25, 2015.

_____, "Putting His Faith in Justice: Greenfield Lawyer Represents Alleged Abuse Victims," *Greenfield Recorder*, January 31, 1992.

Butterfield, Fox, "Long Planning Is Cited in Death of Farmer Priest," *New York Times*, August 26, 2003.

Cappadona, Bryanna, "The Story Behind the Most Disturbing Conversation in 'Spotlight,'" boston.com, November 9, 2015.

Caron, Carol A., "We All Live in Glass Houses," *Republican*, November 15, 1991.

Carroll, Matt, "Abuse Alleged at Wellesley Seminary," *Boston Globe*, August 10, 2002.

_____, "Diocese Releases Priest's Files," *Boston Globe*, September 4, 2002.

"Catholic Priest's Death Ruled a Suicide," *Boston Globe*, July 6, 2011.

Caywood, Thomas, "Mom Hopes New Probe Reveals Son's Killer," *Boston Herald*, August 6, 2004.

Ceneviva, Alex, "Amtrak Identifies Man Struck and Killed by Train in Madison," tnh.com, April 23, 2017.

Chokshi, Nirah, "The Religious States of America," *Washington Post*, February 26, 2015.

Christensen, Kim, and Felch, Jim, "Boy Scouts Helped Alleged Molesters Cover Tracks, Files Show," *Los Angeles Times*, September 16, 2012.

Christie, Bob, "Paul Babeu Says He's Gay After Misconduct Claims," *Huffington Post*, April 20, 2012.

"Church's Role in Troy's Needs to Be Discussed," *Troy Record*, October 25, 1969.

Claffey, Kevin, "Bishop Maguire to Step Down: Marshall Will Lead Diocese," *Republican*, December 28, 1991.

_____, "Lavigne Settles Lawsuit, Avoids Trial," *Republican*, September 17, 1996.

_____, "Lavigne Settles Suit, Avoids Trial," *Republican* November 11, 1998.

"Clergy Abuse Scandal Turns to Rackets Law," *Worcester Voice*, May 4, 2004.

Collom, Lindsey, and Hansen, Ronald J., "Paul Babeu's Ex-boyfriend Seeks $1 Million in Damages," *The Republic*, March 6, 2012.

Contrada, Fred, "Chesterfield Man Files Sexual Assault Suit Against Springfield Roman Catholic Diocese," *Republican*, July 11, 2013.

_____, "For Priest's Accusers, Pain Is Lasting Legacy," *Republican*, December 10, 2006.

_____, "Paul Archambault, Northampton Priest Who Committed Suicide, Named as Sex Abuser in Suit," *Republican*, July 11, 2013.

_____, "Vatican Defrocks 2 Area Priests," *Republican*, December 2, 2006.

Convey, Eric, "California Parish Rips Hub's Silence on Priest's Past," *Boston Herald*, April 9, 2002.

_____, "Cover-up Charges Made in Alleged Abuse Case," *Boston Herald*, April 5, 2002.

_____, "Springfield Pedophile Booted Out of Priesthood," *Boston Herald*, January 21, 2004.

Cooperman, Alan, and Sun, Lena H., "Hundreds of Priests Removed Since '60s," *Washington Post*, June 9, 2002.

"Correction: Bishop Thomas Dupré Stories," *Washington Post*, January 4, 2017.

"Croteau File Ruling Victory for Disclosure," op-ed, *Republican*, November 10, 2003.

"Court Opens Slain Altar Boy Investigation Files," *Associated Press*, July 29, 2004.

Cullen, Kevin, "Alleged Victim's Lawyer to File Suit Against Dupré," *Boston Globe*, March 11, 2004.

_____, "Approval Given to Defrock Priest," *Boston Globe*, January 21, 2004.

_____, "Asked to Help, Priest Allegedly Abused," *Boston Globe*, June 5, 2002.

_____, "Bishop Resigns Following Claims: Springfield Prelate Had Faced Abuse Allegations," *Boston Globe*, February 12, 2004.

_____, "A Boy's Death Revisited," *Boston Globe*, January 17, 2008.

_____, "Danny's Story: Death of an Altar Boy, A Priest, a Boy, a Mystery," *Boston Globe*, December 14, 2003.

_____, "Diocese Releases Priest's Files," *Boston Globe*, September 4, 2002.

_____, "Diocese's Report on Sex Abuse Questioned," *Boston Globe*, February 21, 2004.

_____, "Files on Ex-priest Ordered Unsealed," *Boston Globe*, July 28, 2004.

_____, "Piercing a Papal Shroud," *Boston Globe*, April 13, 2010.

_____, "Prelate's Alleged Victim to Aid Probe: Will Help Prosecutors Investigating Dupré," *Boston Globe*, February 26, 2004.

_____, "Priest Cites Cost of Speaking Out: Tells of Springfield Diocese Reprimand," *Boston Globe*, March 23, 2002.

_____, "Rain Washed Away Clue in '72 Slaying: Sources Say Springfield DA Believed Priest Killed Boy," *Boston Globe*, October 24, 1991.

_____, "Ruined Files Spark Allegation," *Boston Globe*, September 17, 2003.

_____, "Springfield Bishop Denies Retaliation Claim," *Boston Globe*, March 25, 2002.

_____, "Threat Preceded Boy's Death, Police Told: 1993 Statement Unsealed in Case of Defrocked Priest," *Boston Globe*, August 5, 2004.

_____, "Victim's Family to Address Findings," *Boston Globe*, January 14, 2008.

"DA Accused of Being Soft on Mob," Associated Press, June 3, 1981.

DeForge, Jeanette, "Springfield Priest Found Dead in Rectory at Our Lady of the Sacred Heart Parish," *Republican*, July 4, 2011.

Delgado, Luz, "Two Defend Coverage of Ex-priest," *Boston Globe*, May 25, 1992.

DePasquale, Ron, "Catholics Protest Near Law's Residence, Demand Resignation," *Associated Press*, February 17, 2002.

Dewberry, Beatrice O'Quinn, "Dupré Accusers Tell Lurid Tale: Allege Ex-bishop Introduced Them to Gay Sex, Porn," *Republican*, February 20, 2004.

_____, "Dupré Himself Resigns Amid Charges of Molestation," *Republican*, February 12, 2004.

"Diocese Plans Education Boards to Direct Schools," *North Adams Transcript*, February 1, 1972.

Dolan, Gerry, "Grand Jury Names 8 in Indictments," *Troy Record*, April 8, 1971.

"Doubles Club to Hear Talk by Veroneau," *Troy Record*, February 7, 1970.

Drake, Rebecca, "Retired Priests, Religious Offer Prayers, Gratitude for ACA Support," *The Catholic Mirror*, February/March 2013.

Dreher, Rod, "Sins of the Fathers," *National Review*, February 11, 2002.

Dunn, Bob, "Chesterfield Man Alleges Sexual Abuse by Priest, Sues Catholic Diocese of Springfield," *Daily Hampshire Gazette*, July 11, 2013.

Ederly, Sabrina Rubin, "The Church's Secret Sex-Crime Files: How a Scandal in Philadelphia Exposed Documents That Reveal a High-Level Conspiracy to Cover Up Decades of Sexual Abuse," *Rolling Stone*, September 6, 2011.

Ellement, John, "Victims Oppose Release of Porter," *Boston Globe*, April 6, 2004.

"Events in Lavigne Case," *Republican*, June 26, 1992.

"Ex-camp Head Denies Guilt in Sex Cases," *Republican*, November 26, 1973.

"Ex-Scouter Faces Trial in Sex Case," *Republican*, December 26, 1973.

"Ex-Williamstown Priest Accused of Molesting Teen," *The Berkshire Eagle*, December 31, 2004.

Fabian, Jordon, "Obama Debates Controversial Arizona Sheriff on Guns," *The Hill*, January 7, 2016.

Farragher, Thomas, "In Death, Geoghan Triggers Another Crisis," *Boston Globe*, November 30, 2003.

"The Financial Cost," *Boston Globe*, October 26, 2015.

Finer, Jonathan, "Mass. Bishop Charged with Rape: No Trial Planned," *Washington Post*, September 28, 2004.

_____, "Priest Urges Diocese's Reform, *Washington Post*, March 20, 2004.

"First Aid Instructors End Course," *Troy Record*, October 16, 1970.

"Five Priests Barred from Parish Work," *Daily Hampshire Gazette*, July 31, 2002.

Foley, Megan, "New Abuse Claims Against Bishops," *The Berkshire Eagle*, May 20, 2010.

Ford, Beverly, and Ranalli, Ralph, "Slain Altar

Boy Allegedly Spent Final Night in Rectory," *Boston Herald*, October 25, 1991.

Fosher, William, "Petition Seeks 5 Separate Trials: Supporters of Lavigne File Brief," *Republican*, April 22, 1992.

Franklin, James L., "Porter's Plea Aids Victims Little, Church Paper Says," *Boston Globe*, October 8, 1993.

Garver, Ben, "Former Springfield Bishop Thomas Dupré Dead at 83," *Berkshire Eagle*, January 3, 2017.

Garvey, Dick, "Bishop's Investigation of Homicide Suspicion Is Recalled," *Republican*, October 29, 1991.

Gelineau, Kristen, "Australian Police Charge Cardinal with Sex Offenses," Associated Press, June 29, 2017.

Glynn, Eleanor, "Stories Show 'Anti-Catholicism,'" *Republican*, November 7, 1991.

Goleman, Daniel, "Experts See Parallels Between Dahmer, Previous Serial Killers," *New York Times News Service*, August 11, 1991.

Goodstein, Laurie, "Vatican Declined to Defrock U.S. Priest Who Abused Boys," *The New York Times*, March 24, 2010.

"Grand Jury Gets Morals Case," *Republican*, October 29, 1973.

"Grand Jury Hears Several Charges," *Troy Record*, March 18, 1971.

Gray, Mark M., ed., "What Was Behind the 1960s Vocation Boom? Not Your Parents Apparently...," Georgetown University, Center for Applied Research in the Apostolate, August 15, 2013.

Greenberger, Scott S., "Parish Is Told of Abuse Probe," *Boston Globe*, September 16, 2002.

Greig, June, "Old Charge Surfaces Against Priest," *Republican*, October 27, 1991.

Grossman, Cathy Lynn, "One Church Topples a Bishop: Quiet Rebels Take a Stand Against Abuse," *USA Today*, March 10, 2004.

Hamel, Chris, "Bishop Calls Punishment Claim False," *Republican*, March 24, 2002.

Heaney, Joe, "Report Says Priest Indicted for Child Rape," *Boston Herald*, February 20, 1992.

Heinen, Tom, "Bishops Back Weakland in Dispute Over Cathedral," *Milwaukee Journal-Sentinel*, July 4, 2001.

Hemingway, Sam, "Church Admits Finding Documents in Priest Abuse Case Thought to Be Missing," *The Burlington Free Press*, August 28, 2006.

_____, "Diocese Settles Priest Abuse Case for $965,000," *The Burlington Free Press*, April 20, 2006.

_____, "Lawsuit Settlement Fails to Bring Peace to Priest-Molestation Victim," *The Burlington Free Press*, August 5, 2007.

_____, "Missing Priest Files Found," *The Burlington Free Press*, August 28, 2006.

_____, "New Revelations in Priest-Abuse Case," *The Burlington Free Press*, July 6, 2008.

Hepp, Christopher K., "How Church Fights Back in Abuse Cases," *Philadelphia Inquirer*, March 22, 2002.

Jendrysik, Stephen, "Friends of Horace Moses Reservation Rally to Save Scout Camp," *Republican*, June 13, 2012.

Johnson, Patrick, "Dupré, on Video, Refuses to Answer," *Republican*, October 3, 2010.

_____, "Inside the Boy Scouts' 'Perversion Files' Is Roger Norton, a Convicted Child Molester with Western Massachusetts Ties," *Republican*, October 20, 2012, from mass line.com, last visited February 19, 2016.

_____, "7 Western Massachusetts Cases Included in Release of Boy Scouts of America's 14,000 Page 'Perversion Files,'" *Republican*, October 19, 2012.

Kelly, Michael, "The Systematic Corruption of the Catholic Church," *Washington Post*, March 20, 2002.

Kelly, Ray, and Shea, Tom, "Lab Tests Blood from Croteau Site: DA Wants Sample from Rev. Lavigne," *Republican*, January 30, 1993.

_____, "Lavigne Faces New Allegations: Expastor Freed from MD Center," *Republican*, January 29, 1993.

Keneally, Thomas, "Cold Sanctuary: How the Church Lost Its Mission," *New Yorker*, June 17, 2002.

Kong, Dolores, "6 More Allege Priest Abused Them in the 60's," *Boston Globe*, May 9, 1992.

Kurkjian, Stephen, "Law Recommended Fired Dean for College Teaching Position," *Boston Globe*, May 15, 2002.

_____, "Records Show Cardinal Law Reassigned Paquin After Settlements," *Boston Globe*, May 30, 2002.

_____, and Robinson, Walter V., "Suit Ties Boy's Death to Abuse by Priest," *Boston Globe*, April 11, 2002.

Latkovic, Mark S., "Using Modern Science to Treat Homosexuality," *Crisis Magazine*, November 27, 2015.

"Legionairies of Christ Denounce Founder, Marcial Maciel Degollado," *New York Times*, February 6, 2014.

Litman, Malia, "The Private Life of Paul Babeu," February 12, 2012, malialitman. com.

"Locals Helped Boy Scouts Cover Up Pedophilia," *Charleston Gazette-Mail*, October 19, 2012.

Longscope, Kay, "Sexual Abuse by Priests Is a 'Betrayal,' 'Rare,' Law Says," *Boston Globe*, April 14, 1992.

Loven, Charles, "Accusation Against Priest Upsets St. Joseph's Parish," *Republican*, October 21, 1991.

_____, "A 'Healing Prayer' Said for St. Joseph's," *Republican*, October 28, 1991.

"Ludlow Priest Put on Leave," BC Cycle, June 2, 2002.

MacQuarrie, Brian, "Bishop Places Priest on Leave: Springfield Prelate Acts in Abuse Probe," *Boston Globe*, April 16, 2004.

Mallia, Joseph, "'I Just Want This Resolved: Slain Boy's Parents Seek the Truth," *Boston Herald*, November 8, 1993.

_____, "Priest Eyed in Altar Boy's Slaying to Appeal for Return of Blood Sample," *Boston Herald*, November 3, 1993.

Martinez, Joel, "Former Springfield Bishop Thomas Dupré Has Died," January 2, 2017, wwlp.com, last visited January 4, 2017.

Mason, Warren, "Diocese in Denial," from religiousnewsonline, provided by Mason, Warren.

_____, "Law and the Timid Voice of the Faithful," *Providence Journal*, December 14, 2002.

Matchan, Linda, "Ex-priest Accused in Minnesota," *Boston Globe*, July 14, 1992.

_____, "Town Secret," *Boston Globe*, August 29, 1993.

_____, "Two Sides Spar on Clergy Abuse," *Boston Globe*, October 11, 1992.

McAuliffe, Michael, "Wound Stings the Faithful: Dupré Abuse Allegation Is Mass Topic," *Republican*, February 15, 2004.

McDermott, Larry A., "Abuse Case Requires Special Sensitivity," *Republican*, November 3, 1991.

_____, "Coverage of Church Crisis Draws Strong Response," letter of John W. Sexton, Sr., South Hadley, *Republican*, April 7, 2002.

_____, "Flogging Messenger Time," *Republican*, July 5, 1992.

McElhenny, John, "Monsignor Says Harm of Abuse Wasn't Recognized," *Boston Globe*, February 23, 2004.

Meersman, Nancy, "Two More NH Suits vs. Priests," *Manchester Union Leader*, April 24, 2002.

Mellen, Kathleen, "Bishop Supports 'Just' Settlement in Abuse Cases," *Republican*, October 2, 2003.

Melley, Brian, "Blood Tests Fail to Clear Lavigne; Sources: DA Has Results, But Has Not Dropped Case," *Republican*, June 13, 1995.

_____, "Croteau Suit Loses 2 Assault Charges," *Republican*, July 1, 1994.

_____, "Fate of Lavigne Rests with Expert: Slaying Case Hinges on DNA Test," *Republican*, January 15, 1995.

_____, "Father Lavigne Pleads Guilty: Priest Avoids Jail Term," *Republican*, June 26, 1992.

_____, "Gag Fought in Probe of Lavigne," *Republican*, February 28, 1996.

_____, "Judge Dismisses Last Lavigne Count," *Republican*, December 16, 1993.

_____, "Lavigne Agrees to DNA Test: Priest Offers Blood in Slaying Probe," *Republican*, November 23, 1994.

_____, "Lavigne Aids Chapel Work Site," *Republican*, July 9, 1995.

_____, "Lavigne Data in Question: Opposing Attorneys Unite to Keep Probe Reports Secret," *Republican*, January 23, 1996.

_____, "Lavigne Papers Released: Little Revealed in Documents," *Republican*, October 22, 1993.

_____, "Lavigne Trial to Begin Today," *Republican*, June 25, 1992.

_____, "Lavigne's New Calling Found at Faneuil Hall," *Republican*, December 28, 1994.

_____, "Lavigne's Words Drew Suspicion," *Republican*, March 31, 1996.

_____, "Papers Outline Officials' Case Against Lavigne," *Republican*, March 28, 1996.

_____, "Priest Avoids Jail Term," *Republican*, June 26, 1992

_____, "Priest Breaks Silence: Lavigne Faces Potential Jurors," *Republican*, June 23, 1992.

Merle, Renea, "Ex-diocesan Official Says Parents Share Blame for Sex Abuse," *Associated Press*, August 10, 1997.

Miller, Patricia, "The Catholic Church's American Downfall: Why Its Demographic Crisis Is Great News for the Country," *Salon Magazine*, May 21, 2015.

Mindner, Raphael, "In Granada, Spain, the Worst Sexual Abuse Scandal Pope Francis Faces," *New York Times*, February 17, 2015.

"Ministry Aiding Area Programs," *Troy Record*, July 10, 1970.

Montini, E.J., "Montini: Sheriff Underpants in Congress? Thank You," *The Arizona Republic*, October 5, 2015.

Moore, Evan, "Judge's Intervention for Pedophile Raising Questions: Ex-Priest Benefits from Free Legal Help, Special Treatment in Prison," *Houston Chronicle*, November 1, 1998.

Moran, Rich, "New Vatican Guidelines for Bishops Make Reporting Abuse to Police Optional," *American Thinker*, February 11, 2016.

Moriarty, Jo-ann, "Lavigne Bound for Monitoring, Therapy, at Facility for Religious," *Republican*, June 26, 1992.

_____, "Where Abusing Priests Go," *Republican*, March 4, 2004.

_____, and Zajac, Bill, "Church Abuse Report Slated," *Republican*, November 12, 2003.

Morin, Brad, "Former Altar Boy Suing Priest for Abuse in Dover," *Manchester Democrat*, May 4, 2002.

Nadeau, Barbie Latza, "Speak No Evil: Vatican Refuses to Talk About Sex Abuse," *The Daily Beast*, February 6, 2016, thedailybeast.com.

"New Lawsuit Targets Priest Who Served at Lee Church," *Associated Press*, September 24, 2003.

Norris, Patricia, "Lawyer Speaks of Client's Death," *Republican*, August 13, 2004.

"Norton Pleads Innocent," *Republican*, November 27, 1973.

"Obituary, Bessone, David John," *The Gainesville Sun*, January 1, 1986.

"Obituary, Coleman, James A.," *Republican*, October 22, 2006.

"Obituary, Croteau, Bernice B." *Republican*, November 13, 2016.

"Obituary, Croteau, Carl F.," *Republican*, November 12, 2011.

"Obituary, Croteau, Daniel T.," *Republican*, April 16, 1972.

"Obituary, Croteau, Gregory G.," *Republican*, October 2, 2015.

"Obituary, Croteau, Michael F.," *Republican*, May 22, 2009.

"Obituary, Deshaise, Helen Teresa, *Republican*, October 10, 2011.

"Obituary, Dobbert, Shawn M.," *Republican*, August 12, 2004.

"Obituary, Dube, Donald V., Rev.," *Republican*, December 18, 2003.

"Obituary, Fitzgibbon, James J.," *Republican*, April 4, 2013.

"Obituary, Huller, E. Karl, Fr.," *Republican*, November 20, 1997.

"Obituary, Keck, Barnabas, Father, O.F.M., Cap.," *The Daily Freeman*, August 14, 2013.

"Obituary, Koonz, John A, Fr.," *Republican*, November 29, 2013.

"Obituary, Lavigne, Ovila R.," *Republican*, December 15, 2000.

"Obituary, Leary, Timothy J., Fr.," *Republican*, October 11, 1991.

"Obituary, Spafford, Gerald F.," *Cape Cod Times*, November 6, 2015.

"Obituary, Tenerowicz, Blanche M.," *Republican*, May 7, 2006.

"Obituary, Tenerowicz, Mitchell J.," *Republican*, September 26, 1996.

O'Connor, Kevin, "Church Settles Latest Abuse Case," *Rutland Herald*, April 13, 2007.

Oliva, Russ, "Healing Takes Time for Victims of Abuse," *The Woonsocket Call*, February 10, 2002.

_____, "In Touch with His Feelings," February 15, 2004, catholicculture.org.

O'Quinn, Beatrice, "Allegations Lead to Priest's Retirement," *Republican*, December 23, 1993.

Paulsen, Michael, "Bishops Say Theologians May Teach Without OK," *Boston Globe*, November 16, 2000.

_____, "Resignation Has Not Ended Law's Role in Church," *Boston Globe*, June 21, 2003.

Pfieffer, Sascha, "Geoghan Preferred Preying on Poorer Children, to Therapist, Priest Cited Sexual Revolution," *Boston Globe*, January 7, 2002.

_____, "Priest Pleads Guilty to Raping Altar Boy," *Boston Globe*, January 1, 2003.

_____, and Kurkjian, Stephen, "Priest Says He, Too, Molested Boys," *Boston Globe*, January 26, 2002.

Pomerleau, Fr. Bill, "Bishop's Deposition Tops Two Weeks of Controversy," *The Catholic Observer*, October 5, 2003.

_____, "Lawyer Claims Bishop Maguire Knew of Abuse in 1976," *The Catholic Observer*, September 25, 2009.

_____, "Priest Removed from Ministry: New Lawsuits Filed Before Legal Deadline," *The Catholic Observer*, January 7, 2005.

_____, "Private Investigator Sends Unusual Letter to Diocesan Clergy," *The Catholic Observer*, May 13, 2005.

_____, "State Supreme Court Orders Release of Croteau Murder Documents," *The Catholic Observer*, July 28, 2004.

Potter, Tim, "BTK Describes His Own Crimes," *The Wichita Eagle*, July 16, 2005.

"Priest Due in Court on Rape Counts," *Republican*, October 20, 1991.

"Priest Sex Abuse Settlement Reached: The Springfield, Mass., Diocese Will Pay 45 Alleged Victims More Than $7 Million," *Los Angeles Times*, August 06, 2004.

Raskin, Laura, "Accused Ex-clergy Now an Organist," *Bennington Banner*, September 13, 2004.

Reese, Thomas J., "Facts, Myths, and Questions," *America: The National Catholic Review*, March 22, 2004.

"The Rev. Richard Lavigne Becomes Richard Lavigne," op-ed, *Republican*, December 18, 2002.

Rezendes, Michael, "Church Allowed Abuse by Priest for Years," *Boston Globe*, January 6, 2002.

Robinson, Walter V., "Scores of Priests Involved in Sex Abuse Cases," *Boston Globe*, January 31, 2002.

"Roman Catholic Diocese Unaware of Accused Priest Activities," *Associated Press*, September 14. 2004.

Rosenwald, Michael S., "2nd Man Agrees to Aid Case Against Bishop," *Boston Globe*, February 27, 2004.

Roulier, Sharon, and Pomerleau, Fr. Bill, "Inmate Files Lawsuit Against Two Dioceses," *The Catholic Observer*, March 31, 2005.

Seelye, Katherine Q., "In Philadelphia, a Changing of the Guard in the Shadow of Scandal," *New York Times*, July 19, 2011.

Seltzer, Leon F., PhD, "6 Signs of Narcissism You May Not Know About," *Psychology Today*, November 7, 2013.

Sennott, Charles M. "Rare Speed Displayed by Rome," *Boston Globe*, December 14, 2002.

Shaw, Kathleen A., "Sex Abuse Case Filed Against Augustinians," *Worcester Telegram & Gazette*, September 7, 2002.

_____, "Vatican Papers Spark Debate," *Worcester Telegram & Gazette*, August 28, 2005.

_____, "Women File Sex Abuse Lawsuits Against Priest," *Republican*, March 6, 2003.

Shea, Tom, "Abuse Victim Tells the Story of a 'Great' Priest," *Republican*, September 14, 2003.

_____, "Abuse Victims Visit Bishop Marshall," *Republican*, February 11, 1994.

_____, "Alleged Sexual Abuse Takes Toll 26 Years Later," *Republican*, February 15, 1993.

_____, "Bishop Cites Aid, Support for Priest-Maguire Orders Silence on '72 Slaying," *Republican*, October 26, 1991.

_____, "Croteau Told Bishop About Lavigne in '88: Slain Boy's Father Was Obsessed with Killing Priest," *Republican*, March 23, 1993.

_____, "Diocese Foots Part of Bill for Lavigne," *Republican*, July 2, 1992.

_____, "Families to Speak Out on Lavigne Plea," *Republican*, June 27, 1992.

_____, "Family Hoping for Lavigne Link Answers," *Republican*, October 14, 1994.

_____, "Father Forgives Priest: Sect Leader Raps Diocese," *Republican*, June 28, 1992.

_____, "Friends, Foes of Lavigne Call Priest Complex Man: Controversy No Stranger to Suspect in Molestations," *Republican*, December 15, 1991.

_____, "Knife Threats Alleged," *Republican*, February 20, 1993.

_____, "Lab Tests Blood from Croteau Site: DA Wants Sample from Rev. Lavigne," *Republican*, January 30, 1993.

_____, "Lavigne Backer Levels Charges: Teen Says Priest Molested Him," *Republican*, April 19, 1993.

_____, "Lavigne Denies Child Rape Count," *Republican*, December 4, 1993.

_____, "Lavigne Establishes Legal Defense Fund," *Republican*, January 12, 1992.

_____, "Lavigne Faced with Abuse Suit: Brother of Croteau Charges Molestation," *Republican*, December 9, 1993.

_____, "Lavigne Faces New Rape Count," *Republican*, December 2, 1993.

_____, "Lavigne Pleads Guilty: Supporters Surprised by Plea," *Republican*, June 26, 1992.

_____, "Lavigne Retains Top-Gun Lawyer," *Republican*, November 8, 1991.

_____, "Lavigne Sex Abuse Trial to Open Today: Case Moved to Coastal Town," *Republican*, June 22, 1992.

_____, "Lay Group's Founder Seeks Understanding: Lavigne Case Ends Years of Turmoil," *Republican*, July 22, 1992.

_____, "Marshall Bans Lavigne from Priest Duties," *Republican*, March 20, 1993.

_____, "Mother Waits for Clue to Solve Son's Murder," *Republican*, April 15, 1997.

_____, "New Charge of Rape Leveled at Lavigne," *Republican*, November 16, 1993.

_____, "No One Comes Between Croteaus and Their God," *Republican*, April 14, 2002.

_____, "Parents Dream of Son, Long for Justice: 19 Years Later Croteau Boy's Death Unsolved," *Republican*, October 27, 1991.

_____, "Probe of Altar Boy's Slaying Closed," *Republican*, October 26, 1995.

_____, "Sex Abuse Charge Settled by Priest," *Republican*, May 10, 1994.

_____, "Slain Boy's Family Waits for Justice: April Is a Terrible Month for Us," *Republican*, April 14, 1992.

_____, "Stories of Alleged Victims: Years of Silence Ends Living with Betrayal," *Republican*, January 29, 1993.

_____, "Test Clears Priest in '72 Death, Lawyer Says," *Republican*, December 18, 1991.

_____, "2 More Men Claim Abuse by Lavigne," *Republican*, April 15, 1993.

_____, and Goonan, Peter, "Diocese Denies Cover-up: Bishop Knew Priest Was Suspect in '72," *Republican*, October 24, 1991.

_____, and Melley, Brian, "Court to Rule on Lavigne Blood Test: State Seeks Evidence in Altar Boy's Death," *Republican* September 10, 1993.

Sherry, Frank, "Counselor Project Lacks Funds," *Troy Record*, December 12, 1970.

_____, "Decrease in Delinquency Spurs Action in 5th District," *Troy Record*, September 22, 1969.

Simison, Cynthia, "'72 Murder Case Linked to Priest, Reopened by DA," *Republican*, October 23, 1991.

Spencer, Buffy, "Andrew Nicastro Describes Alleged Sexual Abuse by Defrocked Priest Andrew Graves, Says 2 Former Bishops Should Have Prevented It," *Republican*, July 24, 2012.

_____, "Andrew Nicastro Testifies That Sexual Abuse by Former Priest Alfred Graves Made Him Angry, Emotionally Distant," *Republican*, July 25, 2012.

_____, "Bishops Face Suit in Sex Abuse Case," *Republican*, July 24, 2012.

_____, "Father of Alleged Clergy Sexual Abuse Victim Andrew Nicastro, Testifies of Implicit Trust in Priests," *Republican*, July 26, 2012.

_____, "Father Sought Church for Moral Direction," *Republican*, July 27, 2012.

_____, "Lawsuit Against Bishops in Court," *Republican*, July 25, 2012.

_____, "Lawyers Want Lawsuit Dropped Against Bishops," *Republican*, April 27, 2011.

_____, "Witness Testifies on Abuse Results," *Republican*, July 26, 2012.

"Springfield Bishop Apologizes for Remark: He Had Compared Critic, Pedophile," *Associated Press*, May 14, 2014.

Stern, Ray, "Republican Sheriff Paul Babeu, Outed as Gay by Ex-lover, Running Again for Congress," *Phoenix New Times*, October 5, 2015.

Stohlberg, Doug, "Double Murder Is Now 10 Years Old," *Hudson Star-Observer*, February 5, 2012.

Sullivan, Jack, "Catholic Pastor in Shelburne Falls Charged with Assaults on 2 Boys," *Boston Globe*, October 21, 1991.

_____, "DA Drops Effort to Link Priest to Boy's Slaying: Blood Test Proved to Be Inconclusive," *Boston Globe*, October 26, 1995.

_____, "Priest Reportedly Was Suspect in a Slaying: Priest Reportedly Was Suspect in '72 Slaying," *Boston Globe*, October 22, 1991.

_____, "Rain Washed Away Clue in '72 Slaying: Sources Say Springfield DA Believed Priest Killed Boy," *Boston Globe*, October 24, 1991.

"Summer Program Gives Hand to Youngsters," *Berkshire Eagle*, July 25, 1969.

Swantek, John, "Deputies Make Quick Arrest," *Troy Record*, February 3, 1971.

Sweet, William, "Parishioners Express Surprise at Bishop Maguire's Retirement," *Republican*, December 29, 1991.

Tantraphol, Roselyn, "Boy's Death Follows Priest: Alleged Abuse Victims Questioned About a 30-Year-Old Homicide," *Hartford Courant*, August 12, 2002.

"Text of Bishop's Letter on Priest," *Republican*, March 21, 1993.

"Timeline of a Crisis," *National Catholic Reporter*, July 3–16, 2015.

"Timeline of Sex-Abuse Fallout in the Catholic Church," *Seattle Times*, October 4, 2003.

Timmons, Annmarie, and McConnell, Amy, "Bishop John McCormack Files: Complaints Didn't Dim Bishops Faith in Priests, Papers Shed Light on McCormack's Role," *Concord Monitor*, June 6, 2002.

"Troy Police Cooperation Noted in Youth Program," *Troy Record*, September 1, 1970.

Turner, Ford, "Marshall Criticizes Media Focus," *Republican*, December 15, 1992.

Tynen, Trudy, "After Dupré Thrown Out, Lay Board Still Stonewalls Until New Bishop Comes in and Says 'Enough Already,' *Associated Press*, March 6, 2004.

_____, "Dupré Leaves and Spfld Wants to Settle," *Associated Press*, April 14, 2004.

_____, "Springfield Diocese Settles with Accusers of Clergy Sex Abuse: Each to Get at Least $80,000," *Associated Press*, July 23, 2004.

Vachon, Duane A., Ph. D., "Almost Forgotten Hero: First Lieutenant Frederick H. Henry, U.S. Army, Korean War, Medal of Honor (1919–1950)," *Hawaii Reporter*, November 17, 2012.

Vance, Andrea, "10-Year-Old Luke Kicked a Lamb to Death Like a Football," *News of the World*, January 23, 2005.

"Vatican Defends Decision Not to Defrock Priest Accused of Molesting Deaf Boys in Wisconsin," *Associated Press*, March 25, 2010.

"Vatican Defrocks Two Springfield Diocese Priests," *Associated Press* via *Worcester Telegram & Gazette*, December 1, 2006.

Vos, Sarah C., "Priests, Diocese Accused: One Cleric Is on List of 14; Other Left Church," *Manchester Monitor*, April 24, 2002.

"Waltham Priest Allegedly Hid Abuse," *Newton Daily News Tribune*, August 6, 2003.

Weber, David, "SJC: Release Records on Priest's Slay Probe," *Boston Herald*, July 28, 2004.

"Worker's Arrest Hits Priest Hard," *Times Union* (Albany, NY), August 23, 1997.

Zajac, Bill, "Abuse Seen as Cause of Suicides," *Republican*, June 12, 2005.

_____, "Accused Priest Departs," *Republican*, July 18, 2002.

_____, "Affidavit Contradicts Church on Abuse," *Republican*, September 8, 2003.

_____, "Alleged Victims Support DA in Bishop Probe," *Republican*, February 26, 2004.

_____, "Altar Boy's Father Tells of Offers," *Republican*, January 11, 2004.

_____, "Appeal Seeks to Unseal Files in Croteau Slaying," *Republican*, December 19, 2003.

_____, "Autopsy Revealed Alcohol, but No Sign of Sexual Abuse," *Republican*, July 28, 2004.

_____, "Battle of St. Michaels," *Republican*, November 13, 2003.

_____, "Bishop Dupre Seeks to Testify Under Oath," *Republican*, September 19, 2003.

_____, "Bishop Dupre Still in Treatment," *Republican*, July 22, 2006.

_____, "Bishop Never Comfortable in Spotlight," *Republican*, February 15, 2004.

_____, "Bishop Quits After Abuse Query: Dupre Abruptly Resigns," *Republican*, February 12, 2004.

_____, "Bishop, Priest Clash on Facts: Dupre Denies Saying Official Destroyed Sensitive Records," *Republican*, September 30, 2003.

_____, "Bishop's Records at Issue Again," *Republican*, February 9, 2004.

_____, "Catholic Appeal Falls Short," *Republican*, June 1, 2002.

_____, "Catholic Church Defrocks Lavigne," *Republican*, January 21, 2004.

_____, "Catholics: Faithful Want to Be Heard," *Republican*, September 5, 2002.

_____, "Church Cuts Ties to Lavigne: Financial Aid to Ex-priest to End," *Republican*, May 28, 2004.

_____, "Court May Act on '72 Slaying Files," *Republican*, February 11, 2004.

_____, "Croteau Files to Remain Sealed," *Republican*, November 11, 2003.

_____, "Croteau Papers Chilling, Inconclusive," *Republican*, August 8, 2004.

_____, "DA: 'Probably Cause': Bishop Allegations Go to Grand Jury," *Republican*, March 5, 2004.

_____, "Dead Priest in Abuse Suit Defended," *Republican*, March 24, 2003.

_____, "Defrocked Priest Denied Pension," *Republican*, June 29, 2006.

_____, "Diocese Considers Settling All Claims," *Republican*, October 15, 2003.

_____, "Diocese Inaction Faulted," *Republican*, July 6, 2004.

_____, "Diocese Panel Handling More Sex Complaints," *Republican*, November 8, 2002.

_____, "Diocese Receives Abuse Complaints," *Republican*, January 8, 2005.

_____, "Diocese Says Constitution Protects It in Abuse Lawsuit," *Republican*, April 19, 2003.

_____, "DNA Does Not Link Lavigne to Scene of Boy's '72 Slaying," *Republican*, July 29, 2005.

_____, "Dupre Said Files Destroyed," *Republican*, August 3, 2005.

_____, "Ex-Bishop's Case Shrouded in Mystery a Year Later," *Republican*, January 6, 2005.

_____, "Ex-Officers: Church Knew About Lavigne," *Republican*, November 17, 2002.

_____, "Ex-Priest's Home Raided by Police," *Republican*, April 9, 2004.

_____, "Family of Late Bishop Responds," *Republican*, January 18, 2004.

_____, "For Dupre, the Pressure Was Too Much," *Republican*, March 28, 2004.

_____, "4 Brothers File Priest Abuse Suit," *Republican*, December 13, 2003.

_____, "4 New Lawsuits Filed Against Lavigne," *Republican*, July 12, 2002.

_____, "He Remembers, Tries to Forgive," *Republican*, September 14, 2003

_____, "Judge Considers Ruling on Liability of Church," *Republican*, September 25, 2003.

_____, "Late Berkshire Priest's Estate Sued," *Republican*, May 5, 2004.

_____, "Lavigne Abuse Ignored by Church," *Republican*, September 29, 2003.

_____, "Lavigne Criminal File Targeted," *Republican*, June 11, 2002.

_____, "Lavigne Files, Letters Released," *Republican*, September 4, 2002.

_____, "Lavigne Haunts Past of a Priest," *Republican*, April 21, 2002.

_____, "Lavigne's Words Drew Suspicion," *Springfield Sunday Republican*, November 18, 1998.

_____, "Letters Detail Charges of Abuse by Priest," *Springfield Sunday Republican*, July 3, 2006.

_____, "Murderer Alleges Clergy Sex Abuse," *Republican*, March 31, 2005.

_____, "Past Still Haunts Accused Priest," *Republican*, February 27, 2005.

_____, "Priest, Bishop at Odds," *Republican*, October 29, 2003.

_____, "Priest Honored by Victims' Group," *Republican*, November 13, 2003.

_____, "Priest Plans to Take Year's Leave," *Republican*, October 15, 2005.

_____, "Priest Removed from Ministry: New Lawsuits Filed Before Legal Deadline," *Republican*, January 7, 2005.

_____, "Priest Says Files Destroyed: Bishop Denies Making Statement," *Republican*, September 17, 2003.

_____, "Priests Accused in Suits," *Republican*, January 7, 2005.

_____, "Priest's Backers Soliciting Donations," *Republican*, July 15, 2005.

_____, "Priest's Probation Ends Amid New Scandals," *Republican*, June 16, 2002.

_____, "Priest's Status Raises Questions," *Republican*, December 19, 2003.

_____, "Probe Points to Prospective Ring," *Republican*, May 2, 2005.

_____, "Protesters Want Bishop to Resign," *Republican*, December 9, 2003.

_____, "A Question of Faith: Mother Asks Church for Answers," *Republican*, March 21, 2004.

_____, "Questions Riddle Croteau Case," *Republican*, August 15, 2004.

_____, "Rebel Priest, Bishop Clash," *Republican*, May 12, 2004.

_____, "Removed Priest's Name Released," *Republican*, March 10, 2006.

_____, "Report of Remark Prompts Outrage," *Republican*, May 13, 2004.

_____, "Rev. Lavigne Faces 3 More Lawsuits," *Republican*, September 24, 2002.

_____, "Sales Net Diocese $2.7M: Priest Wants More Properties Sold," *Republican*, May 26, 2004.

_____, "Sex-abuse Scandal Divides Catholics, Priests: Catholics Divided Over Abuse Scandal," *Republican*, March 10, 2002.

_____, "Springfield Diocese Still Mum," *Republican*, July 24, 2003.

_____, "State Official Seeks Croteau Files," *Republican*, November 10, 2003

_____, "Suit: Dupré Said Files Destroyed," *Republican*, August 3, 2004.

_____, "2 Women Accuse Lavigne of Abuse," *Republican*, March 7, 2003.

_____, "Unsealed Records Shed Light on Lavigne," *Republican*, November 3, 2002.

_____, "Vatican Defrocks Lavigne: Springfield MA Priest," *Republican*, January 21, 2004.

_____, and Goldberg, Marla A., "Probation

Over for Lavigne," *Republican*, June 29, 2002.

_____, and _____, "Unsealed Records Shed Light on Lavigne," *Republican*, November 3, 2002.

Zuckoff, Michael, "Loners Drew Little Notice," *Boston Globe*, April 22, 1999.

Other Documents and Published Works

Arkow, P., "Form of Emotional Blackmail: Animal Abuse as a Risk Factor for Domestic Violence," *Do¬mestic Violence Report*, 2015.

Degenhardt, B, "Statistical Summary of Offenders Charged with Crimes against Companion Animals July 2001–July 2005," Chicago Police Department, 2006.

Directory, Springfield Diocese, 2008 (necrology).

Haden, Sara C., and Scarpa, Angela, "Childhood Animal Cruelty: A Review of Research, Assessment, and Therapeutic Issues," *The Forensic Examiner* 14 (2005).

Lanning, Kenneth, *Child Molesters: A Behavioral Analysis, For Law Enforcement Officers Investigating Cases of Child Abuse*, National Center for Missing and Exploited Children, 2010.

McDonald, Susan, "Childhood Animal Abuse and Violent Criminal Behavior: A Brief Review of the Literature," Commonwealth of Massachusetts, Office of Strategic Planning, October, 2011.

The Nature and Scope of Sexual Abuse of Minors by Catholic Priests and Deacons in the United States 1950–2002, John Jay College of Criminal Justice, The City University of New York, United States Conference of Catholic Bishops, Washington, D.C., February 2004.

Pew Research Center, "America's Changing Religious Landscape: Declining Number of Catholics," May 11, 2015.

_____, "America's Changing Religious Landscape: Geography," May 11, 2015.

_____, "Faith in Flux," April 27, 2009.

Television/Documentary/ Unpublished Works/ Miscellaneous

ABC News Special, *Bless Me Father For I Have Sinned: The Catholic Church in Crisis*, April 3, 2002.

CBS3-TV, December 9, 2008.

CBS-TV, "Murder Most Foul," *60 Minutes*, CBS-TV.

EWTN News, Medlin, Marianne, "Springfield Catholic Community Mourns Suicide of Local Priest," July 8, 2011.

Lessard, Fr. John, Eulogy for Fr. Paul Archambault, July 12, 2011.

NBC-TV, New York, *Timeline of Catholic Church Sexual Abuse Crisis in the U.S.*, September 27, 2015.

Podles, Leo, *The Rev. Donald Osgood of New Hampshire: A Shallow, Likeable Guy with a Taste for Young Men* (unpublished essay).

WGGB-TV (Ch. 40), Springfield, October 21, 1991.

Zenet News Service, December 3, 2002.

Unpublished Works and Investigative Files

Stevens, R.C., "Case Status Notes as of April, 2006."

_____, "Croteau Timeline, Friday, April 14, 1972."

_____, "Thursday, July 14, 2005, Briefing Republican Co."

_____, "Thursday, March 31, 2005, Update, Briefing Republican Co."

_____, "Thursday, November 11, 2005, Republican Co. Briefing"

_____, "Thursday, November 18, 2004, Republican Co. Briefing"

_____, "Thursday, October 14, 2004, Briefing Republican Co."

Zajac, Bill, and Mason, Warren, *The Six-Percent Solution*, unpublished manuscript, 2008.

Index

A & P Supermarket (Sixteen Acres, Massachusetts) 15, 22, 27, 47, 64, 184
ABC News 222
Acquired Immunodeficiency Syndrome (AIDS) 135, 215, 226
Adams, Samuel 115
Ahern, Fr. Richard J. 190, 193, 194, 215, 216
All Souls Church (Ware, Massachusetts) 211
American Bar Association (ABA) 170, 171, 172
American Graffiti (film) 25
Ames, Aldrich 68
Amherst Police Department (Amherst, Massachusetts) 119
Anatrella, Tony, Fr. 200
And to Think That I Saw It on Mulberry Street (book) 12
Anderson, John 105
Angier, David 128
Annunziato, Fr. Armando A. 83, 84, 203
Anthony, Susan B. 115
Antisocial Personality Disorder (ASPD, APD) 146, 148, 151, 165
The Apostolate Formation Center 86; Divine Intimacy of the Holy Seed rite 87, 98
Archambault, Fr. Paul J. 206, 207
Archidiancono, Francis 220
Arpaio, Joseph (Joe; sheriff, Pinal County, Arizona) 222
Assumption College (Worcester, Massachusetts) 32, 33
Assumption Preparatory School (Worcester, Massachusetts) 32, 33, 147
Augustinians of the Assumption (Assumptionists) 32, 147

Babeu, Francis 141, 221
Babeu, Paul 141, 163, 189, 191, 213, 221, 223; scandals 221, 222, 223
Balthazar, Paul F., Sgt. 48
Basilica di Santa Maria Maggiore (Rome) 200
Baystate Medical Center (Springfield, Massachusetts) 114, 116, 194, 211
Benedict XVI (Joseph A. Ratzinger) 77, 78, 82, 199
Bennett, William M. (district attorney, Hamp-

den County, Massachusetts 90, 101, 108, 112, 114, 115, 116, 117, 127, 128, 129, 132, 133, 139, 140, 141, 143, 164, 169, 173, 174, 175, 176, 177, 182, 183, 185, 189, 197, 208; court battle with Springfield Republican 113, 117, 129
Berkowitz, David 180
Berlin, Fred 171
Bernardin, Cardinal Joseph F. 201
Bernstein, Edward 170
Berrigan, Fr. Daniel 37
Berry, Jason 81
Berthold, Fr. George C. 121
Bessone, David 134, 209, 219
Bessone, Peter 134, 209, 219
Bevilacqua, Bishop Anthony J. (Philadelphia) 80
Bier, William 149, 150
Blake, Edward, M.D. 113, 116, 117, 143, 169
Blessed Sacrament Church (Greenfield, Massachusetts) 116
Blessed Sacrament Church (Northampton, Massachusetts) 214, 216
Block, Stephan (Steve) 22, 158, 161, 163
Blocker, Dan 21
Bobek, Mary 57, 58
Bonanza (television program) 21
The Bonfire of the Vanities (book) 170
Bonzagni, Fr. John J. 206, 214
The Book of Gomorrah (book) 74
Boston Bruins (National Hockey League) 187
The Boston Globe (newspaper) 3, 84, 131, 136, 138, 185, 198, 200, 224
Boston Herald (newspaper) 133
Boy Scouts of America: abusive volunteers 81, 120, 177–179, 182, 183, 188, 217; Camp Woronoco (Russell, Massachusetts) 177, 179, 181, 182, 183, 189, 217; campsites used for abuse 187, 189; connections with cleric abusers 177, 182, 183, 184, 188, 189, 196, 197; ineligible volunteer list 177; and murder of Daniel Croteau 177, 181, 182, 183, 184, 196, 197; similarity to Catholic Church re: abuse 177, 181; Troop 118 (Springfield, Massachusetts) 22, 47, 179, 183; Troop 132 (Chicopee, Massachusetts) 183

281

Index